JUSTICE FRAMED

Why are certain responses to past human rights violations considered instances of transitional justice while others are disregarded? This study interrogates the history of the discourse and practice of the field to answer that question. Zunino argues that a number of characteristics inherited as transitional justice emerged as a discourse in the 1980s and 1990s have shaped which practices of the present and the past are now regarded as valid responses to past human rights violations. He traces these influential characteristics from Argentina's transition to democracy in 1983, the end of communism in Eastern Europe, the development of international criminal justice and the South African truth commission of 1995. Through an analysis of the post-World War II period, the decolonisation process and the Cold War, he identifies a series of episodes and mechanisms omitted from the history of transitional justice because they did not conform to its accepted characteristics.

Marcos Zunino is Research Fellow in Judicial Independence and Constitutional Transitions at the British Institute of International and Comparative Law. He has previously worked for the United Nations, international non-governmental organisations and the Argentine judiciary. He served as a Legal Officer at the Extraordinary Chambers in the Courts of Cambodia. Marcos completed a PhD in Law at the University of Cambridge and was a Scholar in Residence at the Center for Human Rights and Global Justice of New York University.

Justice Framed

A GENEALOGY OF TRANSITIONAL JUSTICE

MARCOS ZUNINO
British Institute of International and Comparative Law

CAMBRIDGE
UNIVERSITY PRESS

CAMBRIDGE
UNIVERSITY PRESS

University Printing House, Cambridge CB2 8BS, United Kingdom

One Liberty Plaza, 20th Floor, New York, NY 10006, USA

477 Williamstown Road, Port Melbourne, VIC 3207, Australia

314–321, 3rd Floor, Plot 3, Splendor Forum, Jasola District Centre, New Delhi – 110025, India

79 Anson Road, #06–04/06, Singapore 079906

Cambridge University Press is part of the University of Cambridge.

It furthers the University's mission by disseminating knowledge in the pursuit of education, learning, and research at the highest international levels of excellence.

www.cambridge.org
Information on this title: www.cambridge.org/9781108475259
DOI: 10.1017/9781108693127

First published 2019

Printed and bound in Great Britain by Clays Ltd, Elcograf S.p.A.

A catalogue record for this publication is available from the British Library.

Library of Congress Cataloging-in-Publication Data
NAMES: Zunino, Marcos, 1978– author.
TITLE: Justice framed : a genealogy of transitional justice / Marcos Zunino, British Institute of International and Comparative Law
DESCRIPTION: Cambridge [UK] ; New York, NY : Cambridge University Press, 2018.
IDENTIFIERS: LCCN 2018045108 | ISBN 9781108475259 (hardback) | ISBN 9781108466011 (paperback)
SUBJECTS: LCSH: Transitional justice–History. | Human rights. | Reparation (Criminal justice) | BISAC: LAW / International.
CLASSIFICATION: LCC K5250 .Z86 2018 | DDC 340/.115–DC23
LC record available at https://lccn.loc.gov/2018045108

ISBN 978-1-108-47525-9 Hardback

This book is dedicated to Elena, with hope of a kinder world for her to grow up in.

Contents

Preface

This book is essentially about origins and the stories we tell about them. The genesis of this book, in a certain way, is rooted in my own origins. I was born in Argentina during the last dictatorship of 1976–1983. The day I was born, Argentina won the football World Cup while people were being tortured and disappeared. The children of those who disappeared, the same age as I was, were taken from them and given to people aligned with the regime. I grew up alongside the young democracy that replaced the dictatorship and that struggled to come to terms with a dark past, facing military uprising for trying to bring those responsible to justice. I studied law under the shadow of an impunity that seemed irreversible. I was working in the Argentine judiciary when the tide changed and prosecutions for the crimes of the dictatorship became the norm. Therefore, when I first heard of the term 'transitional justice' while I was in my master's program at the University of Queensland in 2008, I felt, paraphrasing Monsieur Jourdain in Molière's *Le Bourgeois Gentilhomme*, that I had been doing transitional justice all my life without knowing. From then on, I became interested in the systematic study of situations like that of my own country – which was trying to respond to its legacy of widespread violence – and eventually decided to carry out a doctoral project on transitional justice. This book is the ultimate result of that project that I undertook at the University of Cambridge and, in a way, the result of the larger personal project I have been embarked on since 1978. While this book is on the global discourse of transitional justice, I want to acknowledge here its genealogical roots in the history of my country and my personal relationship with it.

The history of transitional justice was initially meant to be merely a section of a chapter of my doctoral dissertation. As often happens, this part ended up swallowing the whole project. Early discussions with my supervisor convinced me that the history of the discourse of transitional justice was a topic that deserved a doctoral dissertation and possibly a book. The next few years were devoted to trying to bring that project to fruition.

I received help from more people than I can acknowledge here. First and foremost, I would like to thank my doctoral supervisor Dr Sarah Nouwen for her tireless advice, support and encouragement. Her insightful comments and suggestions certainly helped me to refine the project and strengthen the final product. She was able to see the book at the end of the tunnel when I was still grappling with the foundations. I am also indebted to my doctoral examiners Professor Eyal Benvenisti and Professor Kieran McEvoy for carefully reading my dissertation and providing excellent feedback that proved invaluable for turning it into a book. This book has also benefitted from the input of the participants in the different venues where I presented my work: the University of Cambridge, the University of Oxford, the University of Essex, the University of East London, New York University, the University of Glasgow and the International Studies Association.

This book would not have been possible without the generous support of the Cambridge Trust, whose funding enabled me to carry out my research. Thanks are due to the fellows and staff of the University of Cambridge, the Faculty of Law and Queens' College for the various important ways in which they helped me, allowing me to concentrate on my research. I am thankful for the year I spent as a scholar in residence at the Center for Human Rights and Global Justice of New York University's School of Law. The Center provided me with a stimulating environment where I benefitted from conversations with Pablo de Greiff, Philip Alston and other scholars. Discussions with many colleagues at the Extraordinary Chambers in the Courts of Cambodia also contributed to this book. I would like to thank Jaime Malamud Goti for kindly agreeing to be interviewed. I am indebted to Oxford University Press for permission to use parts of an article published in the International Journal of Transitional Justice. Thanks are due to Finola O'Sullivan and Tom Randall of Cambridge University Press for all their help during book production.

I would not have finished this book without my friends and family. Friends from Argentina and further afield were a constant source of support and encouragement, fortunately too many to be individually named. My family has been with me always. My siblings Inés, Hernán, Lucía and Paula always believed in me even more than I believed in myself. I am indebted to my parents Laura and Jorge for encouraging my curiosity and love of knowledge. I want to dedicate this book to my daughter Elena, who brightened the last stages of its writing. Lastly, my deepest debt of gratitude is to my wife Rose, who unfalteringly supported me in each step of the process.

Abbreviations

ANC	African National Congress
CONADEP	National Commission on the Disappearance of People (Spanish Acronym)
CSCE	Conference on the Security and Co-operation in Europe
CVSR	Centre for the Study of Violence and Reconciliation
ECCC	Extraordinary Chambers in the Courts of Cambodia
ECHR	European Court of Human Rights
FRELIMO	Mozambique Liberation Front (Portuguese Acronym)
IACtHR	Inter-American Court of Human Rights
ICC	International Criminal Court
ICJ	International Court of Justice
ICCPR	International Covenant on Civil and Political Rights
ICESCR	International Covenant on Economic, Social and Cultural Rights
ICTJ	International Center for Transitional Justice
ICTR	International Criminal Tribunal for Rwanda
ICTY	International Criminal Tribunal for the former Yugoslavia
IJTJ	International Journal of Transitional Justice
ILC	International Law Commission
IMT	International Military Tribunal
MFA	Armed Forces Movement (Portuguese Acronym)
NGO	non-governmental organisation
NMT	Nuremberg Military Tribunal
OHCHR	United Nations Office of the High Commissioner for Human Rights
PIDE	Portuguese Political Police (Portuguese Acronym)
SATRC	Truth and Reconciliation Commission of South Africa

UDHR	Universal Declaration of Human Rights
UN	United Nations
UNDP	United Nations Development Program
UNGA	United Nations General Assembly
UNHRC	United Nations Human Rights Council
UNMIK	United Nations Interim Administration Mission in Kosovo
UNSC	United Nations Security Council
UNSG	United Nations Secretary-General
UNTAET	United Nations Transitional Authority in East Timor
USIP	United States Institute of Peace

Table of Cases

INTERNATIONAL CASES

Permanent Court of International Justice

International Court of Justice

International Criminal Court

International Criminal Tribunal for the Former Yugoslavia

International Criminal Tribunal for the Former Yugoslavia

International Military Tribunal

Major War Criminals (Opinion and Judgment) Nazi Conspiracy and Aggression (Red Series) 1 October 1946 (IMT Judgment), 134, 139, 143–4, 147, 160.

International Military Tribunal for the Far East

Araki et al (Dissenting Opinion of the Member from France) in Neil Boister and Robert Cryer (eds), Documents on the Tokyo International Military Tribunal (Oxford University Press, 2008), 152.
Araki et al (Dissenting Opinion of the Member from India) in Neil Boister and Robert Cryer (eds), Documents on the Tokyo International Military Tribunal (Oxford University Press, 2008), 153.
Araki et al (Judgment of the International Military Tribunal for the Far East) 4 November 1948 in Neil Boister and Robert Cryer (eds), Documents on the Tokyo International Military Tribunal (Oxford University Press, 2008) (IMTFE Judgment), 134, 153.
Araki et al (Opinion of the Member from the Netherlands) in Neil Boister and Robert Cryer (eds), Documents on the Tokyo International Military Tribunal (Oxford University Press, 2008), 153.
Araki et al (Separate Opinion of the President) in Neil Boister and Robert Cryer (eds), Documents on the Tokyo International Military Tribunal (Oxford University Press, 2008), 152.

CASES BEFORE MIXED CRIMINAL TRIBUNALS

Special Tribunal for Lebanon

Ayyash, Badreddine, Oneissi and Sabra (Decision on the Defence Appeals against the Trial Chamber's 'Decision on the Defence Challenges to the Jurisdiction and Legality of the Tribunal') STL-11-01/PT/AC/AR90.1 (24 October 2012), 100.

Extraordinary Chambers in the Courts of Cambodia

Khieu, Nuon, Ieng and Ieng (Case 002/01 Appeal Judgement) Case 002-F36 (23 November 2016), 107, 143.
Khieu, Nuon, Ieng and Ieng (Case 002/01 Judgment) Case 002-E313 (7 August 2014), 198, 217.
Khieu, Nuon, Ieng and Ieng (Closing Submissions in Case 002/01) Case 002-E295/6/3 (26 September 2013) 198.
Khieu, Nuon, Ieng and Ieng (Decision on Ieng Sary's Rule 89 Preliminary Objections [*Ne bis* in *idem* and Amnesty and Pardon]) Case 002-E51/15 (3 November 2011), 221.
Khieu, Nuon, Ieng and Ieng (Decision on Immediate Appeal against Trial Chamber's Second Decision on Severance of Case 002) Case 002-E284/4/8 (25 November 2013), 42.

TRIALS UNDER CONTROL COUNCIL LAW NO. 10 AND OTHER TRIALS BY OCCUPYING POWERS

United States

United Kingdom

France

CASES BEFORE REGIONAL COURTS

European Commission of Human Rights

European Court of Human Rights

Inter-American Court of Human Rights

CASES BEFORE NATIONAL COURTS

Argentina

Bolivia

Cambodia

France

Germany

Israel

Poland

South Africa

United States

Table of Treaties, Peace Agreements, International Instruments, Legislation and Other Official Documents

INTERNATIONAL TREATIES

African Charter on Human and Peoples' Rights (adopted 27 June 1981, entered into force 21 October 1986) 1520 UNTS 217, 179.
Agreement between the State of Israel and the Federal Republic of Germany, Signed in Luxembourg on 10 September 1952 (adopted 10 September 1952, entered into force 27 March 1953) 345 UNTS 91, 164.
Agreement between the United Nations and the Government of Sierra Leone on the Establishment of a Special Court for Sierra Leone (adopted 16 January 2002, entered into force 12 April 2002) 2178 UNTS 138, 100, 110.
Agreement between the United Nations and the Royal Government of Cambodia concerning the prosecution under Cambodian Law of Crimes Committed during the Period of Democratic Kampuchea (adopted 6 June 2003, entered into force 29 April 2005) 2329 UNTS 117, 100, 198.
Agreement for the Prosecution and Punishment of the Major War Criminals of the European Axis (adopted and entered into force 8 August 1945) 82 UNTS 279 (London Agreement), 134, 142, 145.
American Convention on Human Rights (adopted 21 November 1969, entered into force 18 July 1978) 1144 UNTS 123, 109, 179.
Charter of the United Nations (adopted 26 June 1945, entered into force 24 October 1945) 1 UNTS XVI, 107, 138.
Convention against Torture and Other Cruel, Inhuman or Degrading Treatment or Punishment (adopted 10 December 1984 UNGA Resolution 39/46, entered into force 26 June 1987) 1465 UNTS 85, 75, 179.
Convention on the Elimination of All Forms of Discrimination against Women (adopted 18 December 1979 UNGA Resolution 34/180, entered into force 3 September 1981) 1249 UNTS 13, 75, 179.
Convention on the Rights of the Child (adopted 20 November 1989 UNGA Resolution 44/25, entered into force 2 September 1990) 1577 UNTS 3, 179.
Convention on the Prevention and Punishment of the Crime of Genocide (adopted 9 December 1948 UNGA Resolution 260 (III) A, entered into force 12 January 1951) 78 UNTS 277 (Genocide Convention), 107, 179.

PEACE AGREEMENTS

UN DOCUMENTS

Guidance Note of the Secretary-General: United Nations Approach to Rule of Law Assistance (30 April 2008), 52, 108.
Guidance Note of the Secretary-General: United Nations Approach to Transitional Justice (10 March 2010) (UN Approach to Transitional Justice), 3, 36, 39–40, 50, 52, 55, 58.
ILC 'Report of the International Law Commission on the Question of International Criminal Jurisdiction' (1950), UN Doc A/CN.4/20 (1950), reprinted in *Yearbook of the International Law Commission* 1950, vol II, 178.
ILC 'Report of the International Law Commission on the Work of its Forty-Sixth Session' (17 February 1995) UN Doc A/RES/49/51, 100.
OHCHR, *Rule-of-Law Tools for Post-Conflict States: Amnesties* (United Nations, 2009), 35, 41.
OHCHR, *Rule-of-Law Tools for Post-Conflict States: National Consultations on Transitional Justice* (United Nations, 2009), 44.
OHCHR, *Rule-of-Law Tools for Post-Conflict States: Prosecution Initiatives* (United Nations, 2006), 35, 41.
OHCHR, *Rule-of-Law Tools for Post-Conflict States: Reparation Programmes* (United Nations, 2008), 35, 41.
OHCHR, *Rule-of-Law Tools for Post-Conflict States: Truth Commissions* (United Nations, 2006), 35, 41.
OHCHR, *Rule-of-Law Tools for Post-Conflict States: Vetting* (United Nations, 2006), 35, 41.
Statute of the International Tribunal for the Prosecution of Persons Responsible for Serious Violations of International Humanitarian Law Committed in the Territory of the Former Yugoslavia since 1991, Annex to UNSC Resolution 827 (25 May 1993) UN Doc S/RES/827, 98.
Statute of the International Criminal Tribunal for Rwanda, Annex to UNSC Resolution 955 (8 November 1994) UN Doc S/RES/955, 98.
Statute of the Special Tribunal for Lebanon, Annex to UNSC Resolution 1757 (30 May 2007) UN Doc S/RES/1757 (2007), 110.
UNDP 'Complementarity and Transitional Justice: Synthesis of Key Emerging Issues for Development' (2012), 35.
UNDP 'Perceptions on Transitional Justice: Kosovo' (2012), 35.
UNGA 'Letter Dated 21 June 1997 from the First and Second Prime Ministers of Cambodia Addressed to the Secretary-General', Annex to the Identical Letters Dated 23 June 1997 from the Secretary-General Addressed to the President of the General Assembly and to the President of the Security Council, UN Docs A/51/930, S/1997/48, 104.
UNGA 'Report of the Special Rapporteur on the Promotion of Truth, Justice, Reparation and Guarantees of Non-Recurrence' (13 September 2012) UN Doc A/67/368, 52.
UNGA Resolution 95(1) 'Affirmation of the Principles of International Law Recognized by the Charter of the Nurnberg Tribunal' (11 December 1946) UN Doc A/RES/1/95, 178.

UNTAET Regulation No 2000/11 'On the Organization of Courts in East Timor' (6 March 2000) UN Doc UNTAET/REG/2000/11, 100.
Vienna Declaration and Programme of Action, World Conference on Human Rights (25 June 1993) UN Doc A/CONF.157/23, 49.

OTHER INTERNATIONAL DOCUMENTS

Allied Resolution on German War Crimes (12 January 1942) II Inter-Allied Review No 1 (1942), 169.
Assembly of States Parties ICC, Resolution ICC-ASP/16/Res.5 (14 December 2017), 144.
Charter of the International Military Tribunal, Annex to Agreement for the Prosecution and Punishment of the Major War Criminals of the European Axis (adopted and entered into force 8 August 1945) 82 UNTS 279 (Nuremberg Charter), 141, 143, 148.
Charter of the International Military Tribunal for the Far East, General Order 1, General Headquarters Supreme Commander of the Allied Forces (19 January 1946) 4 Bevans 20 (as amended 26 April 1946, 4 Bevans 27) (IMTFE Charter), 134, 152.
Conference on Security and Co-Operation in Europe Final Act, Helsinki (1 August 1975), 214.
Control Council Law No. 10 'Punishment of Persons Guilty of War Crimes, Crimes against Peace and against Humanity' (20 December 1945) 3 Official Gazette Control Council for Germany 50–55 (1946) (Control Council Law No. 10), 135.
Declaration of German Atrocities (1 November 1943) 3 Bevans 834 (Moscow Declaration), 142.
Elements of Crimes, Official Records of the Assembly of States Parties to the Rome Statute of the International Criminal Court (First Session, New York 3–10 September 2002), 110.
European Union 'The EU's Policy Framework on Support to Transitional Justice' (16 November 2015) Annex to Doc 13576/15, 35, 103.
Resolution on the Subject of Restitution, Annex to the Final Act of the Paris Conference on Reparation (21 December 1945) Miscellaneous No 1 (1946) Cmd 6721, 163.
ICC, 'President of Uganda Refers Situation Concerning the Lord's Resistance Army (LRA) to the ICC' (29 January 2004) Press Release ICC-20040129–44, 104.
ICC, 'Prosecutor Receives Referral Concerning Central African Republic' (7 January 2005) Press Release ICC-OTP-20050107–86, 104.
ICC, 'Prosecutor Receives Referral of the Situation in the Democratic Republic of Congo' (19 April 2004) Press Release ICC-OTP-20040419–50, 104.
Inter-Allied Declaration against Acts of Dispossession Committed in Territories Under Enemy Occupation or Control (5 January 1943) Miscellaneous No 1 (1943) Cmd 6418, 163.
Inter-American Commission on Human Rights 'Annual Report of the Inter-American Commission on Human Rights 1988–1989' (18 September 1989) OEA/Ser.L/V/II.76 Doc 10, 221.

Inter-American Commission on Human Rights 'Report on the Situation of Human Rights in the Republic of Nicaragua' (30 June 1981) OEA/Ser.L/V/II.53 Doc 25, 221.
Joint Declaration of the Governments of the Federal Republic of Germany and the German Democratic Republic on the Settlement of Open Property Questions (15 June 1990), 88.
Protocol of the Proceedings of the Berlin (Potsdam) Conference (1 August 1945) 3 Bevans 1207, 137, 157.
Rules of Procedure and Evidence, Official Records of the Assembly of States Parties to the Rome Statute of the International Criminal Court (First Session, New York 3–10 September 2002), 36.
United Nations Monetary and Financial Conference Final Act, Bretton Woods (22 July 1944) US Department of State Publication 2187 (1944), 163.

LEGISLATION

Argentina

Código de Procedimiento Penal (Criminal Procedure Code) Ley 2372 (4 October 1888), 64.
Delimita Alcances del Deber de Obediencia Debida (Precises Scope of Due Obedience Duty) Ley 23521 (9 June 1987), 65.
Desaparición de Personas (Enforced Disappearances) Ley 24411 (3 January 1995), 65.
Extinción de Acciones Penales a Fuerzas Armadas (Extinction of Prosecutions to Armed Forces) Ley 23492 (24 December 1986), 65.
Indemnizaciones (Compensation) Ley 24043 (2 January 1992), 65.
Decreto 157/83 (13 December 1983), 63.
Decreto 158/83 (13 December 1983), 63.
Decreto 187/83 (15 December 1983), 73.

Cambodia

Constitution du Kampuchea Democratique (Constitution of Democratic Kampuchea) (1975), 217.
People's Revolutionary Council of Kampuchea Decree Law No 1 Establishment of People's Revolutionary Tribunal at Phnom Penh to Try the Pol Pot-Ieng Sary Clique for the Crime of Genocide (15 July 1979), 220.
People's Revolutionary Council of Kampuchea Decree Law No 4 Appointment of Presiding Judge and Alternate (20 July 1979), 220.
People's Revolutionary Council of Kampuchea Decree Law No 25 Appointment of Members of the Tribunal (20 July 1979), 220.
Law on the Establishment of Extraordinary Chambers in the Courts of Cambodia for the Prosecution of Crimes Committed During the Period of Democratic Kampuchea (NS/RKM/1004/006) (Amended 27 October 2004), 100, 106, 110, 198.

Chile

Decreto Supremo N° 355 (25 April 1990), 37.

Colombia

Ley 975 de 2005 Justicia y Paz (Justice and Peace), 23.

France

Ordonnance No 120 du Commandant en Chef Français en Allemagne relative à la restitution des biens ayant fait l'objet d'actes de spoliation (Ordinance No 120 of the French Commander-in-Chief in Germany Concerning the Restitution of Assets Object of Acts of Spoliation) (1947) 119 *Journal Officiel du Commandement en Chef Français en Allemagne* 1219, 163.

Germany

Bundesgesetz zur Regelung der rückerstattungsrechlichen Geldverbindlichkeiten des Deutschen Reichs und gleichgestellter Rechtsträger (Bundesrückerstattungsgesetz – BrüG) (Federal Law on Restitution) 1957, 164.

Gesetz gegen Wettbewerbsbeschränkungen (Law against Restraints of Competition) 1957, 159.

Mozambique

Constituição da República de Moçambique (Constitution of the Republic of Mozambique) (1990), 224.

Lei da Organização Judiciária n° 12/78 (Law of Judicial Organisation) (2 December 1978), 223.

Nicaragua

Ley de Tribunales Populares Antisomocistas (Law of Anti-Somocist Popular Tribunals) Decreto N° 1233 (11 April 1983), 220.

Ley sobre el Mantenimiento del Orden y Seguridad Pública (Law on Public Order and Security) Decreto N° 1074 (6 July 1982), 226.

Peru

Decreto Supremo N° 065–2001-PCM (2 June 2001), 33.

Portugal

Lei 8/75 (25 July 1975), 186.
Decreto-lei 277/74 (25 June 1974), 186.
Decreto-lei 123/75 (11 March 1975), 186.

South Africa

Constitution of the Republic of South Africa (1993), 112.
Constitution of the Republic of South Africa (1996), 124.
Promotion of National Unity and Reconciliation Act (1995), 49, 113–16, 124, 233.
Restitution of Land Rights Act (1994), 212.

Spain

Ley 46/1977 de Amnistía (Amnesty) (15 October 1977), 188.

Union of Soviet Socialist Republics

Statute on Comrades' Courts, Edict of the Presidium of the Supreme Soviet of the RSFSR (3 July 1961), No 26, Item 371, 222.

United Kingdom

Prohibition of Excessive Concentration of German Economic Power (British Military Government Ordinance No 78) 1947, 158.
Regulations for the Trial of War Criminals (Royal Warrant 0160/2498 AO 81/1945), 136.
Restitution of Identifiable Property to Victims of Nazi Oppression (Military Government Law No 59) (1949), 163.

United States

Decentralization of Banks (US Military Government Law No 57 [Revised]) 1949, 158.
Prohibition of Excessive Concentration of German Economic Power (US Military Government Law No 56) 1947, 158.
Reorganization of German Coal and Iron and Steel Industries (US Military Government Law No 75) 1948, 158.
Restitution of Identifiable Property (US Military Government Law No 59) 1947, 163.

Uruguay

Funcionarios Militares y Policiales, Se Reconoce que ha Caducado el Ejercicio de la Pretensión Punitiva del Estado Respecto de los Delitos Cometidos hasta el 1 de Marzo de 1985 (Military and Police Officers, It Is Recognised That the Exercise of the Punitive Intention of the State Regarding the Crimes Committed until 1 March 1985 Has Lapsed) Ley 15848 (22 December 1986), 76.

OTHER OFFICIAL DOCUMENTS

Government Documents

Atrocities and War Crimes: Report from Robert H. Jackson to the President (7 June 1945) 12 Department of State Bulletin (No 311) 1071 (US), 159.
Federal Trade Commission 'Report of the Committee Appointed to Review the Decartelizaton Program in Germany' (Secretary of the Army 1949) 89 (US), 159.
John Simon, Lord Chancellor 'Major War Criminals Memorandum' (4 September 1944) (UK), 147, 169.
Ministry of Justice and Correctional Services 'Parole Decisions on Inmates Ferdi Barnard, Eugene Alexander De Kock and Clive Derby Lewis' (30 January 2015) Media Statement (South Africa), 111.
Presidential Directive/NSC-30 (17 February 1978) (US), 181.
Report of Robert H. Jackson, United States Representative to the International Conference on Military Trials (Department of State 1949) (US), 155.
Report of the Department of the Army Review of the Preliminary Investigations into the My Lai Incident' (14 March 1970) (US), 196.
Secretaría de Derechos Humanos 'Informe de Investigación sobre Víctimas de Desaparición Forzada y Asesinato, por el Accionar Represivo del Estado y Centros Clandestinos de Detención y otros Lugares de Reclusión Clandestina' (Investigative Report on Victims of Enforced Disappearance and Murder by the Repressive Behaviour of the State and Clandestine Detention Centres and Other Locations of Clandestine Reclusion) (November 2015) (Argentina), 63.

Reports of Truth Commissions

Comisión de la Verdad y Reconciliación (Truth and Reconciliation Commission) (Peru), 33.
Comisión Nacional sobre la Desaparición de Personas (National Commission on the Disappearance of People – CONADEP) (Argentina), 63, 73–4.
Comissão de Acolhimento, Verdade e Reconciliação (Commission for Reception, Truth and Reconciliation) (Timor Leste), 51.
Comisión de la Verdad para El Salvador (Commission on the Truth for El Salvador), 76, 195.

1

Introduction

Two men kneel on the dusty ground facing each other. A gourd filled with a brown liquid lies equidistant between them. They lean forward with ceremonial gravity and drink deeply from the vessel, keeping their hands neatly clasped behind their backs, the sides of their heads almost touching. They are surrounded by members of their clans who follow their actions with attention. The two groups have already exchanged sheep, which lie limp by a grass-roofed hut, their still-warm blood slowly thickening with the dust.

A woman wearing a long black robe with two white bands stands behind a long wooden table. She wears headphones and talks into a microphone. She is questioning a man sitting behind two computer screens on an individual table. He wears a suit, and his ears are also bracketed by headphones. A group of people sits at the table around the woman; another group sits at the other end of the room. Between the two groups, on a platform, three men in long black robes with scarlet trimmings listen to the questioning with attention. More people watch the scene from behind a glass screen. The room is decorated withaustere, pastel furnishings.

Five people sit at a long table: three men and two women, facing an audience. The man in the middle wears a clerical collar and a heavy crucifix. The long table is punctuated by plastic water bottles, one for each person. An enormous flag covers the wall behind them. Its blue and green halves are bisected diagonally by a yellow bar; five white stars twinkle on the blue field. The whole room listens while a man wearing an orange shirt recounts how he was beaten. Other people wait for their turn to speak to the assembly.

Behind an iron fence stands a solid white building. It has a portico with four columns and two rows of windows. The portico is ornamented with an oval-shaped coat of arms. Underneath it says in Spanish: 'Naval Mechanics School' in bold lettering. Between two of the cylindrical columns, a banner is suspended. The banner reads, also in Spanish: 'Space for memory and the promotion and defence of human rights.' A group of students walks up the steps and into the building.

These four scenes do not seem to have much in common: they take place in different countries (Uganda, the Netherlands, the Solomon Islands and Argentina); in different continents; they involve different actors taking part in diverse settings and practices; and they are enmeshed in distinct and separate cultures, histories and political trajectories. Yet, despite these glaring differences, there is a thread that gives this group of disparate scenes coherence: the discourse of transitional justice. That discourse examines, informs and unites these four examples of responses to past widespread or systematic violence: the *mato oput* ceremony of the Acholi in northern Uganda,[1] the trials at the International Criminal Tribunal for the former Yugoslavia (ICTY),[2] the proceedings of the Solomon Islands' Truth and Reconciliation Commission,[3] and the Naval Mechanics School human rights memorial in Argentina.[4] For the discourse, they are all instances of transitional justice.

Why are some responses to past widespread or systematic violence considered relevant for transitional justice while others are overlooked? This question has not been sufficiently explored. It remains unclear why the discourse of transitional justice recognises the previously described practices and not others. This book looks into the history of transitional justice to better understand the current contours of this discourse and what forms of dealing with past violence it acknowledges. It argues that the discourse of transitional justice has some characteristics at its core which have framed existing accounts of the history of transitional justice determining which responses are recognised as relevant and which are ignored.

Examining how a distinct discourse came into being and what circumstances influenced this process can help explain the characteristics that the discourse of transitional justice has today, which situations it examines and which mechanisms it privileges. Knowing how historical conditions influence current scholarly debate and policy choices can lead to questioning assumptions and moving beyond the most constraining aspects of some of the

[1] See, eg, Erin Baines, 'The Haunting of Alice: Local Approaches to Justice and Reconciliation in Northern Uganda' (2007) 1 *International Journal of Transitional Justice* 91.

[2] See, eg, Kirsten Campbell, 'The Gender of Transitional Justice: Law, Sexual Violence and the International Criminal Tribunal for the Former Yugoslavia' (2007) 1 *International Journal of Transitional Justice* 411.

[3] See, eg, ICTJ, *Transitional Justice Mechanisms in Solomon Islands* (2010) www.ictj.org/sites/default/files/ICTJ-SolomonIslands-Fact-Sheet-2011-English.pdf, accessed 30 July 2018.

[4] See, eg, Elizabeth Jelin, 'Public Memorialization in Perspective: Truth, Justice and Memory of Past Repression in the Southern Cone of South America' (2007) 1 *International Journal of Transitional Justice* 138.

characteristics of transitional justice. With that purpose, this book interrogates the established narrative of the history of transitional justice.

I TWO DIMENSIONS OF TRANSITIONAL JUSTICE

The term transitional justice can refer to two different dimensions: a set of practices and the discourse that originates from these practices.

Most definitions of transitional justice refer to the first dimension, designating a set of practices or processes.[5] The United Nations (UN) defines transitional justice as comprising 'the full range of processes and mechanisms associated with a society's attempts to come to terms with a legacy of large-scale past abuses, in order to ensure accountability, serve justice and achieve reconciliation'.[6] Since this is the most influential definition of transitional justice, it is a suitable starting point for this analysis.[7] The definition can be dissected in three parts: a range of mechanisms or processes, the situations where they are implemented and the goals they serve.

In this definition, transitional justice is associated with a set of mechanisms for responding to large-scale past abuses. The most widely discussed mechanisms are criminal trials, commissions to establish the truth of what happened, reparations for victims, vetting processes to purge people implicated in abuses and programmes of institutional reform. As some of the scenes described at the beginning of this book show, transitional justice is also linked to other initiatives such as community reconciliation practices[8] and memorials.[9]

The second part of the UN definition refers to which situations the mechanisms address: societies attempting to come to terms with large-scale past

5 Harvey M Weinstein and Laurel E Fletcher, 'Violence and Social Repair: Rethinking the Contribution of Justice to Reconciliation' (2002) 24 *Human Rights Quarterly* 573, 574; Jon Elster, *Closing the Books: Transitional Justice in Historical Perspective* (Cambridge University Press, 2004) 1; Naomi Roht-Arriaza, 'The New Landscape of Transitional Justice' in Naomi Roht-Arriaza and Javier Mariezcurrena (eds), *Transitional Justice in the Twenty-First Century: Beyond Truth versus Justice* (Cambridge University Press, 2006) 2; Paige Arthur, 'Introduction: Identities in Transition' in Paige Arthur (ed), *Identities in Transition: Challenges for Transitional Justice in Divided Societies* (Cambridge University Press, 2011) 1.

6 UNSC 'Report of the Secretary-General on the Rule of Law and Transitional Justice in Conflict and Post-Conflict Societies' (23 August 2004) UN Doc S/2004/616 (2004) (2004 UNSG Transitional Justice Report), para 8; 'Guidance Note of the Secretary-General: United Nations Approach to Transitional Justice' (10 March 2010) (UN Approach to Transitional Justice) 3.

7 Pádraig McAuliffe, 'From Molehills to Mountains (and Myths?): A Critical History of Transitional Justice Advocacy' (2011) 22 *Finnish Yearbook of International Law* 1, 2.

8 Baines, 'The Haunting of Alice' 91 (n 1).

9 Susanne Buckley-Zistel and Stefanie Schäfer, *Memorials in Times of Transition* (Intersentia, 2014).

abuses. Originally, these were limited to countries trying to transition – hence the name transitional justice – from an authoritarian and repressive past to a democratic future. However, transitional justice mechanisms and concepts are increasingly used in a variety of other settings, even in situations without a clear transition.[10] While the idea of transition that framed transitional justice has somewhat eroded, what remains constant is that the mechanisms and policies respond to 'large-scale past abuses'.[11]

The last part of the UN definition concerns the goals that transitional justice mechanisms pursue: ensuring accountability, serving justice and achieving reconciliation.[12] Transitional justice policies are thus meant to achieve a range of goals, from the narrower aim of combating impunity by punishing wrongdoers to the more ambitious attainment of societal reconciliation and positive peace.[13]

Once the deconstructed definition is reassembled, it shows that transitional justice broadly designates a set of practices used to respond to past widespread or systematic violence to pursue a set of goals. Other definitions of transitional justice replicate these elements.[14] For instance, according to Paige Arthur, transitional justice 'is a response to massive or systematic violations of human rights that aims to recognize victims and to prevent the recurrence of abuse. It is often associated with a set of measures that, taken together, work toward those two aims in ways that reinforce one another'.[15]

Other definitions narrow down the scope of transitional justice by referring to a limited number of mechanisms or requiring the existence of political transition.[16] For example, Jon Elster defines transitional justice as 'made up of the processes of trials, purges and reparations that take place after the transition from one political regime to another'.[17] However, transitional justice is currently widely understood to include a much broader array of responses

[10] See Chapter 2, 23–24.
[11] 2004 UNSG Transitional Justice Report, para 8 (n 6).
[12] For a critical approach, see Bronwyn Leebaw, 'The Irreconcilable Goals of Transitional Justice' (2008) 30 *Human Rights Quarterly* 95.
[13] See Dustin Sharp, 'Addressing Economic Violence in Times of Transition: Toward Positive-Peace Paradigm for Transitional Justice' (2012) 35 *Fordham International Law Journal* 780.
[14] Weinstein and Fletcher, 'Violence and Social Repair' 574 (n 5); Roht-Arriaza, *Transitional Justice in the Twenty-First Century* 2 (n 5); Arthur 1(n 5).
[15] Arthur 1 (n 5).
[16] Weinstein and Fletcher, 'Violence and Social Repair' 574 (n 5); Roht-Arriaza, *Transitional Justice in the Twenty-First Century* 2 (n 5); Christine Bell, Colm Campbell and Fionnuala Ní Aoláin, 'Justice Discourses in Transition' (2004) 13 *Social & Legal Studies* 305; Sharp, 'Addressing Economic Violence in Times of Transition' 780 (n 13).
[17] Elster, *Closing the Books* 1 (n 5).

than trials, purges and reparations and its mechanisms are applied in situations without a clear transition. Other scholars do not concentrate on the practices of transitional justice in their definitions and refer instead to the legal, political and moral dilemmas that arise when responding to widespread violence[18] or to the conception of justice associated with political transitions.[19] These definitions are primarily concerned with the second dimension of transitional justice that is examined in this section.

In this book, transitional justice practices are defined as responses to past widespread or systematic violence. Only this ample approach captures the whole range of mechanisms and situations that the discourse of transitional justice currently addresses. Since the object of this book is the whole discourse of transitional justice, this broad definition is capacious enough to suit its purposes. Referring to responses to violence rather than to human rights violations or abuses avoids restricting transitional justice to instances where an act of violence is in breach of an obligation under international human rights law. This is especially important when this book examines historical practices that took place before human rights obligations were incorporated into international law.

The definition adopted for this book limits the practices it includes to those that respond to past widespread or systematic violence. Characterising the violence as widespread or systematic excludes sporadic and isolated episodes of violence. Limiting the definition to past violence ensures that initiatives that target violence in the present or in the future, such as humanitarian interventions, are not included. These two limitations prevent the definition from becoming overbroad and therefore losing its descriptive power.

It is important to clarify that the definition does not limit the responses to past widespread or systematic violence to those conforming to human rights standards or promoting democracy, liberalism or any other expressly normative content. Most authors do not expressly ascribe normative value to transitional justice.[20] For instance, Brian Grodsky and Anja Mihr have explored the

[18] Sharp, Addressing Economic Violence in Times of Transition' 780 (n 13); Bell, Campbell and Ní Aolaín, 'Justice Discourses in Transition' 305 (n 16).

[19] Ruti Teitel, 'Transitional Justice Genealogy' (2003) 16 *Harvard Human Rights Journal* 69.

[20] This does not mean that their conception of transitional justice is entirely value-free but that they do not expressly acknowledge its normative content. As examined throughout the book, the discourse of transitional justice does indeed have a normative framework that influences which mechanisms and initiatives are regarded as instances of transitional justice. For a recent examination of the values inherent in evaluating transitional justice programmes, see Kirsten Ainley, 'Evaluating the Evaluators: Transitional Justice and the Contest of Values' (2017) 11 *International Journal of Transitional Justice* 421.

use of transitional justice by repressive and autocratic regimes.[21] Accordingly, most definitions of transitional justice do not restrict the practices they include to those subscribing to a particular set of values, ideology or political standpoint.[22] For example, for Dustin Sharp, transitional justice 'relates to a set of legal, political, and moral dilemmas about how to deal with past violence in societies undergoing some form of political transition'.[23] This definition concentrates on the dilemmas surrounding a political transition but does not prescribe the normative content of the responses to these dilemmas.

At the same time, those definitions that do include a normative element usually frame it around a set of goals that the responses to past widespread or systematic violence must pursue. However, these goals are broad enough to accommodate a wide range of normative viewpoints. Thus, in the definition proposed by Arthur, these goals are to recognise victims and to prevent the recurrence of abuse; and in the UN's definition, on which this book's definition is based, the goals are to ensure accountability, serve justice and achieve reconciliation.[24] The breadth of these goals is such that few, if any, responses to past widespread or systematic violence could not claim to pursue them in some way. Furthermore, given that the purpose of the definition of transitional justice practice in this book will be to assess whether a particular practice or mechanism constitutes an instance of transitional justice, adopting a relatively value-free definition would avoid excluding some responses for purely normative reasons. Hence, throughout this book, transitional justice practices are defined as responses to past widespread or systematic violence.

The second dimension of transitional justice refers to the discourse that has developed around the practices of transitional justice. The discourse of transitional justice encompasses all knowledge referring to that social practice. This is an enormous archive including books, journal articles, policy papers, judicial decisions, legislation establishing mechanisms and journalistic coverage referring to transitional justice practices. This massive collection of statements dealing with transitional justice practices constitutes the discourse. To give a sense of its extent, the bibliography of transitional justice compiled by Andrew

[21] Brian Grodsky, 'Justice without Transition: Truth Commissions in the Context of Repressive Rule' (2008) 9 *Human Rights Review* 281; Anja Mihr, 'Regime Consolidation through Transitional Justice in Europe: The Cases of Germany, Spain and Turkey' (2017) 11 *International Journal of Transitional Justice* 113.

[22] Weinstein and Fletcher, 'Violence and Social Repair' 574 (n 5); Elster, *Closing the Books* 1 (n 5); Roht-Arriaza 2 (n 5); Sharp, 'Addressing Economic Violence in Times of Transition' 780 (n 13); Bell, Campbell and Ní Aoláin, 'Justice Discourses in Transition' 305 (n 16).

[23] Sharp, 'Addressing Economic Violence in Times of Transition' 780 (n 13).

[24] 2004 UNSG Transitional Justice Report, para 8 (n 6); Arthur, 'Introduction' 1 (n 5).

Reiter in 2010 listed 2,497 entries.[25] This bibliography did not take into account the contributions from non-scholarly sources. The number of scholarly and non-scholarly statements referring to transitional justice has continued to grow steadily since then. For instance, while a search of the term 'transitional justice' on Google Scholar for the year 2010 yields 3,020 results, for 2017 there are 5,010 results.

Discourses are dynamic. Michel Foucault defined a discourse as a regularity in dispersion.[26] That is, discourses can harbour contradiction and change. Within a given discourse, many contradictory positions can be held; scholars and practitioners can argue over what transitional justice means and what purposes it should serve. Yet in that dispersion, there is some regularity. There are some characteristics that mark the core of the discourse and frame most discussions. At the same time, even these characteristics can change over time because discourses are not closed entities; their meanings are open to contestation and reconfiguration.[27]

The two dimensions differ in how they conceive the temporality of transitional justice. In its first dimension, transitional justice is a descriptive label that can be applied to any practice that fits the parameters of the definition. This label is timeless because it can be applied to a practice in the past. In contrast, in its second dimension, the discourse of transitional justice is historically situated in the sense that it reflects the context of the time. The discourse of transitional justice appeared at a specific point in time with a particular political and intellectual baggage tied to this historical juncture. The analogy of medicine can help to illustrate these two dimensions of transitional justice. Medicine refers to a set of practices and techniques used to heal the body. Any such technique, regardless of its antiquity, can be regarded as a medical practice. The label as such is ahistorical. At the same time, medicine also refers to the knowledge related to these practices as manifested in textbooks, medical journals, research institutes and academic institutions. This medical discourse is situated in time and has a specific history.[28]

[25] Andrew G Reiter, 'Transitional Justice Bibliography' (*Transitional Justice Data Base*, 2015) https://sites.google.com/site/transitionaljusticedatabase/transitional-justice-bibliography, accessed 13 March 2018.

[26] Michel Foucault, *L'Archéologie du Savoir* (Gallimard, 1969) 53.

[27] Ernesto Laclau and Chantal Mouffe, *Hegemony and Socialist Strategy: Towards a Radical Democratic Politics* (Verso, 1985) 105.

[28] See Michel Foucault, *Naissance de la Clinique: Une Archéologie du Regard Médical* (Presses Universitaires de France, 1963).

There are other ways of characterising the second dimension of transitional justice instead of as a discourse. One of them is as an academic discipline. Indeed, transitional justice can boast specialised academic journals, dedicated courses and research centres. However, the knowledge related to transitional justice is not limited to an academic pursuit; it includes the activity of policy-makers, judges and international organisations. Moreover, people from different disciplines participate in the transitional justice conversation which has led to its characterisation as a 'rendezvous discipline'.[29] As Phil Clark and Nicola Palmer note, transitional justice 'encompasses manifold disciplines: law, politics, international relations, sociology, development studies, history, philosophy, psychology, anthropology, criminology and area studies'.[30] Given this diversity, transitional justice lacks the agreed norms and methods that a discipline entails.

By far the most popular way to refer to the second dimension of transitional justice is as a field.[31] The concept of 'field' has the advantage of being broader and more fluid than the concept of 'discipline'. Scholars of many disciplines could contribute to the field of transitional justice. Moreover, the concept of field covers both scholarship and practice. Thus, unlike discipline, it does not exclude the practice of transitional justice. Accordingly, Louis Bickford characterises transitional justice as a 'field of activity and inquiry'.[32] Nevertheless, in an influential 2009 article, Christine Bell criticised the idea of transitional justice as a field for cloaking contradictions and tensions under the guise of a

[29] Kieran McEvoy, 'Beyond Legalism: Towards a Thicker Understanding of Transitional Justice' (2007) 34 *Journal of Law and Society* 411, 433.

[30] Phil Clark and Nicola Palmer, 'Challenging Transitional Justice' in Nicola Palmer, Phil Clark and Danielle Granville (eds), *Critical Perspectives in Transitional Justice* (Intersentia, 2012) 1.

[31] See, eg, Vasuki Nesiah, 'Discussion Lines on Gender and Transitional Justice' (2006) 15 *Columbia Journal of Gender and the Law* 799; IJTJ, 'Editorial Note' (2007) 1 *International Journal of Transitional Justice* 1; McEvoy, 'Beyond Legalism' (n 29); Erin Baines, 'Spirits and Social Reconstruction after Mass Violence: Rethinking Transitional Justice' (2010) 109 *African Affairs* 409; Kora Andrieu, 'Dealing with a "New" Grievance: Should Anticorruption Be Part of the Transitional Justice Agenda?' (2012) 11 *Journal of Human Rights* 537; Fionnuala Ni Aolain, 'Advancing Feminist Positioning in the Field of Transitional Justice' (2012) 6 *International Journal of Transitional Justice* 205; Par Engstrom, 'Transitional Justice and Ongoing Conflict' in Chandra Lekha Sriram and others (eds), *Transitional Justice and Peacebuilding on the Ground: Victims and Ex-Combatants* (Routledge, 2013); Nevin Aiken, *Identity, Reconciliation and Transitional Justice: Overcoming Intractability in Divided Societies* (Routledge, 2013); Dustin Sharp, 'Interrogating the Peripheries: The Preoccupations of Fourth Generation Transitional Justice' (2013) 26 *Harvard Human Rights Journal* 149; Lavinia Stan and Nadya Nedelsky, *Encyclopedia of Transitional Justice* (Cambridge University Press, 2013).

[32] Louis Bickford, *Transitional Justice* (Macmillan Reference, 2004) 1045.

coherent arena.[33] Despite the ripple of citations generated by that article, characterising transitional justice as a field has become, if anything, more popular since then.[34]

Approaching transitional justice as a discourse has a number of advantages. First, its broadness allows for including all facets of the practice and knowledge of transitional justice. Inasmuch as the discourse includes the statements produced by practitioners, transitional justice mechanisms and policymaking bodies, it effectively covers the scholarly and practical aspects of transitional justice. Second, calling transitional justice a discourse underscores the importance that language, concepts and tropes have in this phenomenon. Third, it countenances internal tensions and accommodates change. The meaning of the concepts and objects of a discourse is contested and open to change. It thus avoids the problem that some ascribe to the notion of 'field' of focusing on the reproductive aspects whilst neglecting its changeability.[35] Accordingly, this book examines transitional justice as a discourse.

II HISTORIES OF TRANSITIONAL JUSTICE

Every history has to begin somewhere. Narratives are temporally bound with a beginning and an end. Existing historical accounts of transitional justice can be sorted depending on their starting points. The choice of a particular point in time as the beginning of transitional justice's history reflects how transitional justice is conceived. There are three approaches to transitional justice history with diverging beginnings. Yet, in spite of these differences, one narrative has become established as the prevalent account of the origin and development of transitional justice. This dominant narrative accommodates elements of all three approaches, reconciling their differences.

For some, the origin of transitional justice lies in Ancient Greece. If transitional justice is approached exclusively as a timeless descriptive label, any historical practice fitting a modern definition of transitional justice can be considered an instance of transitional justice. Following this approach, Jon Elster traced transitional justice to the retributive policies implemented in ancient Greece in the aftermath of the collapse of oligarchic regimes in the fifth century BC.[36] This method is grounded on a comparative perspective

33 Christine Bell, 'Transitional Justice, Interdisciplinarity and the State of the "Field" or "Non-Field"' (2009) 3 *International Journal of Transitional Justice* 5.

34 As evidenced by the chronology of citations in note 31.

35 Patricia Thomson, 'Field' in Michael Grenfell (ed), *Pierre Bourdieu Key Concepts* (Acumen, 2008).

36 Elster, *Closing the Books* (n 5).

that aims at finding suitable lessons in the past. The dilemmas of transitional justice are thus assumed to be similar and comparable across time and space. Hence, for Elster, the 'Athenians faced problems and proposed solutions that are strikingly similar to those of recent transitions'.[37] Using the definition of transitional justice as a descriptive label, other authors have found episodes of transitional justice following the French Revolution,[38] the Napoleonic Wars,[39] and the American Civil War.[40]

While this approach has the advantage of unearthing past examples which might be of use today, it ignores the historicity of the modern discourse of transitional justice.[41] In conceiving of transitional justice as a timeless practice, this method fails to take into account historical differences. Whereas the Athenians might have confronted problems that, to a certain extent, can be compared with those besetting transitional societies today, the intervening 2,500 years pose some limits to the comparison. The historical context in which the Athenians grappled with the legacy of the oligarchs' rule was radically different from that of societies in the twenty-first century. Of course, the limits of commensurability apply to any comparative endeavour, but the more distant in time and context two examples are, the wider the gulf precluding meaningful comparisons. More importantly, the *discourse* of transitional justice certainly did not exist in classical Greece. Categories, concepts and ideas of the present cannot automatically be transposed to the past without taking into account the different historical context.[42] Thus while the contemporary concept of transitional justice can certainly be applied to the past, it has to be recognised that the concept did not exist at the time and the meaning of attending categories like justice, crime and rights might have been quite different. Failing to do it risks falling into what Quentin Skinner has called

[37] Ibid 21.

[38] Ronen Steinberg, 'Transitional Justice in the Age of the French Revolution' (2013) 7 *International Journal of Transitional Justice* 267.

[39] Gary Jonathan Bass, *Stay the Hand of Vengeance: The Politics of War Crimes Tribunals* (Princeton University Press, 2000).

[40] Robert Meister, 'Forgiving and Forgetting: Lincoln and the Politics of National Recovery' in Carla Alison Hesse and Robert Post (eds), *Human Rights in Political Transitions: Gettysburg to Bosnia* (Zone Books, 1999).

[41] For a similar argument about human rights, see Samuel Moyn, *The Last Utopia: Human Rights in History* (Belknap, 2010).

[42] See Paige Arthur, 'How "Transitions" Reshaped Human Rights: A Conceptual History of Transitional Justice' (2009) 31 *Human Rights Quarterly* 321, 328.

'the mythology of prolepsis' in which 'the episode has to await the future to learn its meaning'.[43]

For others, the origin of transitional justice is located at the end of World War II. From this perspective, transitional justice refers to a set of historically situated practices with their roots in twentieth century's international law and politics. Transitional justice's opening event for this historical account is the Nuremberg trial of Nazi leaders at the end of World War II. This trial is considered to have inaugurated international processes of criminal accountability for massive violations of human rights. The main proponent of this approach is Ruti Teitel who in 2003 authored an influential history of transitional justice.[44] She divides the history of modern transitional justice into three phases. The first begins in 1945 with the Nuremberg trial and encompasses the post-war policies that were characterised by individual criminal accountability based on international law. After the onset of the Cold War antagonism precluded significant development for this model of international criminal justice, transitional justice went into an impasse. The second phase covers the decline and fall of the Soviet Bloc and the wave of liberalisation that it kindled. According to Teitel, this period saw national responses to human rights violations that were nonetheless inspired and guided by international law. Post–Cold War transitional justice was marked by debates about whether political considerations should temper calls for justice and by an expansion towards nonjudicial mechanisms to respond to violence. The last phase of Teitel's history, beginning with the new millennium focuses on the normalisation of transitional justice with the creation of the International Criminal Court (ICC). For Teitel, in this phase transitional justice has become a permanent feature of international politics.[45]

Since this second approach to the origin of transitional justice conceives of it as a set of modern practices shaped by politics and social context, it is more appropriate for grasping the particularities that the discourse has today. Instead of concentrating on transitional justice as a timeless label, it seeks to understand its modern historical origins. Yet, while it gives an account of the modern history of the practice of transitional justice, it does not identify when transitional justice became an autonomous discourse. Therefore, this approach does not take into account the influence that the development of

[43] Quentin Skinner, *Visions of Politics* (Cambridge University Press, 2002) 74. For a similar point, Frederick Cooper, *Colonialism in Question: Theory, Knowledge, History* (University of California Press, 2005) 105.

[44] Teitel, Transitional Justice Genealogy' (n 19). See also Sharp, 'Interrogating the Peripheries' (n 31).

[45] Teitel, 'Transitional Justice Genealogy' 89 (n 19).

a specific discourse with certain characteristics had in how transitional justice practices were framed.

The last point of origin of transitional justice is traced to its appearance as a self-aware discourse. Scholars following this approach do not examine the history of certain practices of transitional justice but of transitional justice as an autonomous discourse or field that emerged in the last decades of the twentieth century. From this perspective, Paige Arthur wrote an insightful conceptual history of transitional justice in which she explored the influence of a series of conferences that took place between 1988 and 1994.[46] She argued that these international gatherings of scholars and practitioners shaped the understanding of transition as a movement toward democracy that structured the conceptual boundaries of the field and influenced which mechanisms it would include. In a similar vein, Pádraig McAuliffe situated the origin of transitional justice in the late 1980s and divided the history of its advocacy in four stages. The first stage covered the debates over whether calls for accountability for past human rights violations should be trumped by the need to ensure political stability (the peace versus justice debate). Whereas in the second stage the discussions were dominated by the question of whether truth commissions or prosecutions were better suited to respond to the violations, in the third there was a consensus that both should be implemented as part of a comprehensive approach. Finally, in the fourth stage as transitional justice became more established critical voices began to be heard.[47] Both Arthur's and McAuliffe's accounts approach transitional justice as a distinct and self-conscious field which began to emerge in the late 1980s.

Concentrating on the recent history of transitional justice as a distinct discourse has several advantages. It avoids the problem of anachronistically ascribing concepts and ideas to actors that did not exist or were different at the time. It also underscores the changes brought about by transitional justice's emergence and development as a specific discourse. However, this approach can fail to take into account some of the older roots of transitional justice.

Combining aspects of all three approaches, a dominant narrative of the history of transitional justice has emerged. From the timeless practice approach, the policies adopted in classical Athens are mentioned as an example of the perennial relevance of transitional justice's dilemmas.[48] The

46 Arthur, 'How "Transitions" Reshaped Human Rights' (n 42).

47 McAuliffe, 'From Molehills to Mountains (and Myths?)' (n 7).

48 Alexandra Barahona de Brito, Carmen González Enríquez and Paloma Aguilar Fernández, 'Introduction' in Alexandra Barahona de Brito, Carmen González Enríquez and Paloma Aguilar Fernández (eds), *The Politics of Memory: Transitional Justice in Democratizing Societies* (Oxford University Press, 2001) 2; Louis Bickford, 'Unofficial Truth Projects' (2007) 29

modern practices approach has added Nuremberg as the starting point of modern transitional justice, as well as a number of other historical milestones.[49] The third approach has contributed the acceptance that transitional justice emerged as a self-aware discourse only after the late 1980s.[50] As more transitional justice authors reiterate this narrative when they briefly introduce the history of transitional justice, this account has consolidated.[51]

According to the dominant narrative, modern transitional justice begins in Nuremberg in 1945 with the policies implemented to respond to the atrocities of World War II. The advent of the Cold War with its political stalemate brought to an end this initial period and precluded any significant development of transitional justice for the next 40 years.[52] The wave of transitions to democracy in Latin America, Eastern Europe and South Africa, which coincided with the end of the confrontation between East and West, sparked a debate on accountability for past human rights violations. At the same time, the creation of the ad hoc international criminal tribunals for the former Yugoslavia and Rwanda in the mid-1990s brought a new impetus to international criminal justice. From these two developments – the wave of democratic transitions and the reinvigoration of international criminal justice – a distinct

Human Rights Quarterly 994, 996; Mark Arenhovel, 'Democratization and Transitional Justice' (2008) 15 Democratization 570, 587; Leebaw, 'The Irreconcilable Goals of Transitional Justice' 98 (n 12); Patricia Lundy and Mark McGovern, 'Whose Justice? Rethinking Transitional Justice from the Bottom Up' (2008) 35 *Journal of Law and Society* 265, 268; Sharp, 'Addressing Economic Violence in Times of Transition' 780 (n 13).

49 de Brito, González Enríquez and Aguilar Fernández, 'Introduction' 2–11 (n 48); Kora Andrieu, 'Transitional Justice: A New Discipline in Human Rights' (2010) *Online Encyclopedia of Mass Violence* http://www.sciencespo.fr/mass-violence-war-massacre-resistance/fr/document/transitional-justice-new-discipline-human-rights-0, accessed 30 July 2018; Chandra Lekha Sriram, 'Liberal Peacebuilding and Transitional Justice: What Place for Socioeconomic Concerns?' in Dustin Sharp (ed), *Justice and Economic Violence in Transition* (Springer, 2014) 28–29.

50 See Catherine Turner, 'Deconstructing Transitional Justice' (2013) 24 Law and Critique 193; Engstrom, 'Transitional Justice and Ongoing Conflict' (n 31); Susanne Buckley-Zistel and others, 'Transitional Justice Theories: An Introduction' in Susanne Buckley-Zistel and others (eds), *Transitional Justice Theories* (Routledge, 2014); Thomas Obel Hansen, 'The Vertical and Horizontal Expansion of Transitional Justice: Explanations and Implications for a Contested Field' in Susanne Buckley-Zistel and others (eds), *Transitional Justice Theories* (Routledge, 2014); Dustin Sharp, 'Introduction: Addressing Economic Violence in Times of Transition' in Dustin Sharp (ed), *Justice and Economic Violence in Transition* (Springer, 2014); Simon Robins, 'Mapping a Future for Transitional Justice by Learning from Its Past' (2015) 9 *International Journal of Transitional Justice* 181.

51 For a recent and condensed version of the narrative, Nicola Henry, 'From Reconciliation to Transitional Justice: The Contours of Redress Politics in Established Democracies' (2015) 9 *International Journal of Transitional Justice* 199, 206.

52 Teitel, 'Transitional Justice Genealogy' 70 (n 19).

discourse or field of transitional justice emerged.[53] Transitional justice discourse then consolidated and expanded. It became institutionalised with the appearance of dedicated non-governmental organisations, research centres and publications. It also grew to cover more situations and mechanisms. A period of self-doubt and criticism followed when transitional justice's concepts, normative aims and effectiveness were brought under scrutiny.[54]

This established narrative highlights some historical experiences as formative to transitional justice. They are as follows:

> the Nuremberg and Tokyo trials after the Second World War, the transitions of South American countries from dictatorship to democracy, international criminal tribunals, such as the tribunals for the former Yugoslavia and Rwanda, [and] the Truth and Reconciliation Commission (TRC) in South Africa.[55]

III APPROACH AND ARGUMENT

This book interrogates the established narrative of the history of transitional justice. Its purpose is to show how the historical conditions amidst which the autonomous discourse of transitional justice emerged shaped which present and past practices the discourse considers relevant. It distinguishes the point in time when a distinct discourse appeared from previous historical practices. This distinction has the effect of dividing the established narrative in two. One part is the account of the emergence of an autonomous discourse of transitional justice around a number of experiences of political change and accountability for past abuses. These experiences shaped the discourse by contributing a series of key characteristics that continue to frame transitional justice to this day.

The other part of the established narrative covers the period of time before transitional justice became an autonomous discourse. These previous developments can be considered the prehistory of the discourse. Once the autonomous discourse emerged, the 'transitional justice label' was retroactively applied to some past events and not to others. This book interrogates both parts of the dominant narrative: the emergence of the autonomous discourse of transitional justice and the prehistory of older practices retrospectively

[53] For a summary, Bell, 'Transitional Justice' 7 (n 33).

[54] Ibid 13; McAuliffe, 'From Molehills to Mountains (and Myths?)' 70 (n 7); Sharp, 'Interrogating the Peripheries' (n 31).

[55] Buckley-Zistel and others, 'Transitional Justice Theories' 1 (n 50).

considered transitional justice. It also first examines the current form of the discourse of transitional justice to identify its characteristics.

Existing historical accounts of transitional justice as a discourse focus exclusively on its point of emergence[56] or on its progress since then.[57] By looking at both the emergence of the discourse and its prehistory, this book engages with the whole established narrative and reveals its blind spots and assumptions. Although some authors do distinguish between the moment in time when a self-conscious transitional justice discourse appeared and previous influential events,[58] the period predating the emergence has not been examined as a retrospective creation.[59] In contrast, this book identifies the influence that the emergence of an autonomous discourse had in the retrospective construction of the history of transitional justice.

The book covers the period from the end of World War II, which is the most widely accepted starting point of modern transitional justice, until the moment when the discourse of transitional justice became consolidated in the early 2000s. Earlier episodes, such as the purges in Ancient Greece and the trials after the French Revolution, are not examined because they are not presented in the discourse as part of a historical narrative of the development of transitional justice but as earlier isolated events. Since several excellent works have covered the progress of transitional justice after it consolidated as a discourse,[60] there is no need to do it here. The focus of this book is the dominant narrative of the origin and development of transitional justice, distinguishing between the emergence of the discourse and its retrospective prehistory.

Throughout the book, we make a distinction between the two dimensions of transitional justice referred to earlier: the *discourse* of transitional justice and the *practices* that can be considered transitional justice according to the descriptive definition adopted. The discourse of transitional justice appeared at a specific point in time. At the same time, responses to mass violence that predate the appearance of a distinct discourse can be designated as instances of transitional justice. We use the descriptive definition of responses to past widespread or systematic violence to identify practices that have not been included in the established narrative.

56 Arthur, 'How "Transitions" Reshaped Human Rights' (n 42).

57 McAuliffe, 'From Molehills to Mountains (and Myths?)' (n 7); Sharp, 'Interrogating the Peripheries' (n 31); Bell, 'Transitional Justice' (n 33).

58 Pádraig McAuliffe, 'From Molehills to Mountains (and Myths?)' (n 7); Sharp, 'Addressing Economic Violence in Times of Transition' (n 13).

59 Turner, 'Deconstructing Transitional Justice' 195 (n 50).

60 McAuliffe, 'From Molehills to Mountains (and Myths?)' (n 7); Bell, 'Transitional Justice' (n 33); Hansen, The Vertical and Horizontal Expansion of Transitional Justice' (n 50).

Conceiving transitional justice as a discourse means that we recognise the dispersion and variety of positions and understandings that transitional justice harbours. The discourse of transitional justice is full of contradictions. Its borders are fuzzy and overlap with other discourses like human rights law and international criminal law. We are careful not to anthropomorphise the discourse into a clear-cut entity with its own agency and ideas. When we write about the discourse of transitional justice doing – or, more often, not doing – something we are using shorthand for referring to the majority of scholars, practitioners and organisations working on issues of transitional justice.

As reflected in its title, this book follows a genealogical approach. Genealogy, as pioneered by Friedrich Nietzsche and developed by Michel Foucault, rejects gradual historical evolution and questions ingrained narratives.[61] Analysing the work of Nietzsche, Foucault distinguished between three historical notions in relation to genealogy: emergence, origin and descent.[62] Genealogy is concerned with the process of *emergence* of a discourse. The emergence is not the final term of a historical development but its moment of arising. This point of emergence is often contingent and the result of a particular interaction of forces.[63] While we tend to think that the *origin* is the moment of the greatest perfection of a phenomenon, genealogy seeks to show that historical origins are lowly.[64] It looks for the modest details and accidents that mark any beginning, dispelling its chimeras and myths.[65] Genealogy concentrates on the *descent* or pedigree of a phenomenon identifying 'the accidents, the minute deviations – or conversely, the complete reversals – the errors, the false appraisals, and the faulty calculations that gave birth to those things that continue to exist and have value for us'.[66] Therefore, genealogy stresses discontinuity and questions dominant narratives of historical evolution.[67]

This book challenges the linear evolution of transitional justice by emphasising the role of contingent factors that interrupt its apparent natural progress. By critically engaging with the dominant narrative of transitional justice, it is

[61] Michel Foucault, 'Nietzsche, Genealogy, History' in Paul Rabinow (ed), *The Foucault Reader* (Penguin, 1986). See also Michael Mahon, *Foucault's Nietzschean Genealogy: Truth, Power, and the Subject* (State University of New York Press, 1992); Rudi Visker, *Michel Foucault: Genealogy as Critique* (Verso, 1995); Colin Koopman, 'Foucault's Historiographical Expansion: Adding Genealogy to Archaeology' (2008) 2 *Journal of the Philosophy of History* 338.

[62] Foucault, 'Nietzsche, Genealogy, History' (n 61).

[63] Ibid 83.

[64] Ibid 79.

[65] Ibid 80.

[66] Ibid 81.

[67] Tyler Krupp, 'Genealogy as Critique?' (2008) 2 *Journal of the Philosophy of History* 315.

possible to unearth other practices and mechanisms that have not been given much attention.

Following a genealogical approach, this book shows that the *emergence* of transitional justice was contingent and not a necessary occurrence, that its *origins* were retrospectively chosen and that its *descent* was marked by forgotten episodes.[68] Indeed, the process of emergence influenced the retrospective choice and content of transitional justice discourse's origin and descent. The main argument put forward in this book is that the characteristics of the discourse of transitional justice have framed which practices the discourse recognises as relevant. This set of characteristics can be traced to the circumstances that shaped the emergence of transitional justice as an autonomous discourse.

IV STRUCTURE

The book is divided into two parts. The first engages with the history of the discourse of transitional justice, describing its current form and how it emerged. The second part looks into the prehistory of the origin and the descent of transitional justice before it became an autonomous discourse.

In Part I, Chapter 2 maps the contours of the discourse of transitional justice today. The first necessary step for engaging with the history of transitional justice is understanding its present. The chapter describes the objects transitional justice discourse refers to, the concepts it deploys and the actors that participate in it. While emphasising that the discourse is open to contestation and debate, the chapter identifies those characteristics that lie at the core of the contemporary discourse of transitional justice. These characteristics give structure to the discourse and frame most discussions on the subject. The rest of the book traces the sources of these characteristics and reveals their influence on the construction of the established narrative of the history of transitional justice.

Chapter 3 explores the process of the emergence of transitional justice discourse. It does so by looking into the influence of four events that are widely considered formative for transitional justice. These are the transition to democracy of Argentina in the mid-1980s, the collapse of the Soviet Bloc in the early 1990s, the growth of international criminal justice that started with

68 It has to be noted that Ruti Teitel called her influential history of transitional justice a genealogy. However, this endeavour did not challenge existing histories but actually ended up providing the backbone for the dominant narrative of transitional justice's history. In contrast, this book seeks to question and problematise that narrative using the genealogical method, Teitel, 'Transitional Justice Genealogy' (n 19).

the creation of the ad hoc tribunals in the mid-1990s and the establishment of the South African Truth and Reconciliation Commission (SATRC) in 1995. While these events are normally lumped together as important for the emergence of the discourse of transitional justice, this chapter looks at the specific contribution of each event and shows how the current characteristics of the discourse are traced to them.

Part II of the book turns to the portion of the established narrative predating the emergence of the discourse. Its purpose is to show how the characteristics inherited from the emergence of the discourse conditioned the account of the prehistory of transitional justice. Chapter 4 examines the Nuremberg trial as the origin of transitional justice. It describes the role that Nuremberg plays in the contemporary discourse, showing why it was retroactively chosen as a suitable starting point. The chapter also shows how other post-war practices that could be defined as instances of transitional justice, but did not adhere to the later discourse's characteristics, have not been included in the established narrative.

The subject of Chapter 5 is the Cold War period and the forgotten episodes that punctuate the descent of transitional justice. The chapter questions the common conception of this period as mostly barren of transitional justice practices. It critically engages with the established narrative, discussing the democratic transitions in Southern Europe in the mid-1970s and the development of human rights. The chapter also identifies mechanisms for responding to past widespread or systematic violence that were implemented during this period but have not been discussed as part of transitional justice's history. It argues that these practices have not been included in the dominant history of transitional justice because they did not conform to the key characteristics of the discourse of transitional justice today. These excluded practices comprise responses to past widespread or systematic violence taken in the context of the Cold War proxy wars, decolonisation and non-liberal transitions.

This book explains how the particular circumstances of the emergence of the discourse of transitional justice went on to shape both the current form of the discourse and the established narrative of its origin. The characteristics inherited from the birth of the discourse frame which situations transitional justice addresses and which mechanisms it considers as suitable responses to past widespread or systematic violence. More generally, it shows how the historically contingent appearance of a discourse with its own concepts and tropes can influence social practices.

PART I

History

2

The Discourse of Transitional Justice

Objects, Concepts, Actors and Characteristics

I INTRODUCTION

In January 2013, Cambridge University Press published the *Encyclopedia of Transitional Justice*. The appearance of this three-volume work is in itself a testament of the growth and autonomy of this discourse.[1] Moreover, as with other encyclopaedias, it serves as a reminder of the ordering function of discourse and how it can influence its subject matter. In his short story *Tlön, Uqbar and Orbis Tertius*, writer Jorge Luis Borges describes the discovery of an encyclopaedia from another planet – Tlön – which turns out to be apocryphal. The 40 volumes of the encyclopaedia describing every aspect of the history, geography, biology, languages, science and philosophy of the planet were the invention of a secret society.[2] Despite being fictional, humanity ends up embracing the knowledge contained in the *First Encyclopaedia of Tlön* because it offered a systematically ordered world.[3] The discursive, and fictional, space of the encyclopaedia influenced the 'real' world.

Like the *First Encyclopaedia of Tlön*, the discourse of transitional justice covers a distinctive space populated by objects, concepts and actors. This space also has certain characteristics that are central to the discourse, infusing it with a certain order. In the same way that the fictional extraterrestrial encyclopaedia influenced reality, the characteristics of the discourse of transitional justice shape which responses of past widespread or systematic violence are considered valid instances of transitional justice. The key characteristics of

[1] Lavinia Stan and Nadya Nedelsky, *Encyclopedia of Transitional Justice* (Cambridge University Press, 2013); Pablo de Greiff, 'Transitional Justice Gets Its Own Encyclopedia: Vitamins or Steroids for a Developing Field?' (2013) 7 *International Journal of Transitional Justice* 547, 550.

[2] Jorge Luis Borges, *Ficciones* (Emecé, 1971).

[3] Silvia G Dapía, '"This Is Not a Universe": An Approach to Borges's "Tlön, Uqbar, Orbis Tertius"' (1997) 26 *Chasqui* 94, 103.

the discourse of transitional justice are that it is comparative, technical, teleological, liberal, multilevel and state-centric. These characteristics are closely linked and sometimes overlap. Some of them have several dimensions.

The purpose of this chapter is to provide an image of the contemporary discourse of transitional justice. It first delineates the components of the discursive space: the objects transitional justice addresses, the concepts most frequently deployed and the main actors in the discourse. The second part of the chapter turns to the characteristics that frame the discourse of transitional justice.

II DISCURSIVE SPACE

The discourse of transitional justice comprises every statement referring to transitional justice practices, including academic publications, judicial decisions, policy reports, legislation and media coverage. This profuse and varied collection of statements is strewn over a discursive space, vast and boundless like the night sky. Within the discursive space, there are common objects to which the statements refer to, key concepts used in these statements and main actors participating in the discourse.

In order to identify these objects, concepts and actors, this section scans the current discursive space of transitional justice, looking for consensus and dissent, permanency and change, central tenets and outlying ideas. In this process, the views of scholars and practitioners are used to recognise trends and general understandings, as well as areas of contestation and debate. Since the *International Journal of Transitional Justice* is the main self-identified publication in transitional justice, it is a useful resource to feel the pulse of the discourse. Authors publishing in this journal consciously and expressly place themselves within the discourse of transitional justice. Therefore, in this chapter we often analyse the articles that appear in that publication to chart the discursive space of transitional justice.

1 *Objects*

The discourse of transitional justice refers to certain objects that form the matter the discourse deals with.[4] Transitional justice has three main objects: the situations it examines, the mechanisms applied to them and its self-referential engagement with transitional justice.

[4] For the role of objects in discourses, see Michel Foucault, *L'Archéologie du Savoir* (Gallimard, 1969) 46.

The discourse of transitional justice is concerned with certain situations. By situation, we mean the country, society or community under examination. The situation is characterised by its experience of violence. As was indicated in the introduction, the definition of transitional justice *practice* adopted in this book is restricted to responses to past widespread or systematic violence. However, the discourse has indeed addressed situations where the violence was not thus qualified. Since the purpose of this chapter is to chart the current extent of the discourse in full, these approaches that exceed the adopted definition are equally taken into account.

In addition to the 'paradigmatic transition' from authoritarianism to democracy,[5] the discourse of transitional justice has examined situations of ongoing violence, transitions to authoritarian regimes and established democracies.[6] Thus, transitional justice discourse has addressed the situations in Colombia,[7] Israel–Palestine[8] and Libya[9] where the widespread or systematic violence was not in the past. It has also referred to situations in which the

5 Colm Campbell and Fionnuala Ni Aolain, 'The Paradox of Transition in Conflicted Democracies' (2005) 27 *Human Rights Quarterly* 172, 173.

6 See UNHRC 'Report of the Special Rapporteur on the Promotion of Truth, Justice, Reparation and Guarantees of Non-Recurrence' (9 August 2012) UN Doc A/HRC/21/46; Pádraig McAuliffe, 'Transitional Justice's Expanding Empire: Reasserting the Value of the Paradigmatic Transition' (2011) 2 *Journal of Conflictology* 32; Thomas Obel Hansen, 'The Vertical and Horizontal Expansion of Transitional Justice: Explanations and Implications for a Contested Field' in Susanne Buckley-Zistel and others (eds), *Transitional Justice Theories* (Routledge, 2014); Dustin Sharp, 'Emancipating Transitional Justice from the Bonds of the Paradigmatic Transition' (2015) 9 *International Journal of Transitional Justice* 150. For transitional justice during ongoing conflict, see Par Engstrom, 'Transitional Justice and Ongoing Conflict' in Chandra Lekha Sriram and others (eds), *Transitional Justice and Peacebuilding on the Ground: Victims and Ex-Combatants* (Routledge, 2013).

7 Ley 975 de 2005 Justicia y Paz (Justice and Peace) (Colombia); Lisa J Laplante and Kimberly Theidon, 'Transitional Justice in Times of Conflict: Colombia's Ley de Justicia y Paz' (2006) 28 *Michigan Journal of International Law* 49; Donny Meertens and Margarita Zambrano, 'Citizenship Deferred: The Politics of Victimhood, Land Restitution and Gender Justice in the Colombian (Post?) Conflict' (2010) 4 *International Journal of Transitional Justice* 189.

8 Ariel Meyerstein, 'Transitional Justice and Post-Conflict Israel/Palestine: Assessing the Applicability of the Truth Commission Paradigm' (2006) 38 *Case Western Reserve Journal of International Law* 281; Ron Dudai, 'A Model for Dealing with the Past in the Israeli Palestinian Context' (2007) 1 *International Journal of Transitional Justice* 249; Ron Dudai and Hillel Cohen, 'Dealing with the Past When the Conflict Is Still Present: Civil Society Truth-Seeking Initiatives in the Israeli-Palestinian Conflict' in Rosalind Shaw, Lars Waldorf and Pierre Hazan (eds), *Localizing Transitional Justice: Interventions and Priorities after Mass Violence* (Stanford University Press, 2010).

9 Victor Peskin and Mieczyslaw P Boduszynski, 'The Rise and Fall of the ICC in Libya and the Politics of International Surrogate Enforcership' (2016) 10 *International Journal of Transitional Justice* 272.

regime change has not necessarily led to democracy such as in Rwanda,[10] Uzbekistan[11] and Ethiopia.[12] Finally, transitional justice discourse has also engaged with situations in countries that have not undergone a transition. These include the treatment of indigenous peoples and minorities in countries considered established democracies such as Canada,[13] New Zealand[14] and the United States.[15] The discourse of transitional justice has thus expanded the situations it addresses beyond transitions to democracy.

In this context of expansion, for the discourse of transitional justice the defining trait of the situation is its experience of violence. This experience places a country, region or community in the realm of possible objects of transitional justice. Hence, what constitutes violence for the discourse is a fundamental part of this object of transitional justice. The experience of violence is usually denoted by the legal term 'human rights violations' or with the more general terms of 'atrocity', 'abuses' or 'violence'. Despite their important semantic and legal differences, these terms are generally used interchangeably within the discourse with the common meaning of experience of widespread or systematic violence. When authors refer to violations of human rights, they do not necessarily spell out what particular legal obligations have been breached and what is their legal basis.

[10] See, eg, Philip Clark and Zachary D Kaufman, *After Genocide: Transitional Justice, Post-Conflict Reconstruction and Reconciliation in Rwanda and beyond* (C Hurst, 2008); Jennie E Burnet, '(In)Justice: Truth, Reconciliation, and Revenge in Rwanda's Gacaca' in Alexander Laban Hinton (ed), *Transitional Justice: Global Mechanisms and Local Realities after Genocide and Mass Violence* (Rutgers University Press, 2010).

[11] Brian Grodsky, 'Justice without Transition: Truth Commissions in the Context of Repressive Rule' (2008) 9 *Human Rights Review* 281.

[12] Priscilla Hayner, *Unspeakable Truths: Confronting State Terror and Atrocity* (Routledge, 2001) 20; Kjetil Tronvoll, Charles Schaefer and Girmachew Alemu Aneme, *The Ethiopian Red Terror Trials: Transitional Justice Challenged* (James Currey, 2009).

[13] Courtney Jung, 'Transitional Justice for Indigenous People in a Non-Transitional Society' (ICTJ, 2009) www.ictj.org/sites/default/files/ICTJ-Identities-NonTransitionalSocieties-ResearchBrief-2009-English.pdf, accessed 30 July 2018; Kim Stanton, 'Canada's Truth and Reconciliation Commission: Settling the Past?' (2011) 2 *International Indigenous Policy Journal* 2; Kirsten Anker, 'Symptoms of Sovereignty? Apologies, Indigenous Rights and Reconciliation in Australia and Canada' in Ruth Margaret Buchanan and Peer Zumbansen (eds), *Law in Transition: Human Rights, Development and Transitional Justice* (Hart, 2014).

[14] Stephen Winter, 'Towards a Unified Theory of Transitional Justice' (2013) 7 *International Journal of Transitional Justice* 224.

[15] David Androff, 'Can Civil Society Reclaim Truth? Results from a Community-Based Truth and Reconciliation Commission' (2012) 6 *International Journal of Transitional Justice* 296; Adrian Vermeule, 'Reparations as Rough Justice' in Melissa Williams, Rosemary Nagy and Jon Elster (eds), *Transitional Justice* (New York University Press, 2012).

Moreover, the violence is often qualified according to its extent or severity. Among the former, the object can be restricted to 'massive or systematic'[16] or 'large-scale' violence.[17] But in some cases, transitional justice mechanisms have been used to respond to individual events – for instance, the Special Tribunal for Lebanon that investigates the assassination of Lebanese Prime Minister Rafik Hariri.[18] In terms of severity, when in 2011 the United Nations (UN) Human Rights Council created a Special Rapporteur on the Promotion of Truth, Justice, Reparation and Guarantees of Non-Recurrence, it restricted the mandate to 'situations in which there have been gross violations of human rights and serious violations of international humanitarian law'.[19] Many authors use the term gross human rights violations to refer to the violence examined by transitional justice discourse.[20]

The mechanisms implemented to respond to violence are another object of the discourse of transitional justice. The 2004 UN Secretary-General's report 'The Rule of Law and Transitional Justice in Conflict and Post-Conflict Societies' (2004 UNSG Transitional Justice Report) lists those mechanisms most commonly associated with transitional justice as 'individual prosecutions, reparations, truth seeking, institutional reform, vetting and dismissals'.[21] The criminal trial and the truth commission are transitional justice's most iconic mechanisms to the point that they dominate the discourse.[22] For

16 Paige Arthur, 'Introduction: Identities in Transition' in Paige Arthur (ed), *Identities in Transition: Challenges for Transitional Justice in Divided Societies* (Cambridge University Press, 2011) 1.

17 UNSC 'Report of the Secretary-General on the Rule of Law and Transitional Justice in Conflict and Post-Conflict Societies' (23 August 2004) UN Doc S/2004/616 (2004) (2004 UNSG Transitional Justice Report), para 8.

18 Another example is the Greensboro Truth and Reconciliation Commission created to examine one particular massacre in North Carolina.

19 UN Human Rights Council (UNHRC) Resolution 18/7 'Special Rapporteur on the Promotion of Truth, Justice, Reparation and Guarantees of Non-Recurrence' (13 October 2011) UN Doc A/HRC/RES/18/7, preamble.

20 Harvey M Weinstein and Laurel E Fletcher, 'Violence and Social Repair: Rethinking the Contribution of Justice to Reconciliation' (2002) 24 *Human Rights Quarterly* 573; Miriam J Aukerman, 'Extraordinary Evil, Ordinary Crime: A Framework for Understanding Transitional Justice' (2002) 15 *Harvard Human Rights Journal* 39; Nicola Henry, 'Witness to Rape: The Limits and Potential of International War Crimes Trials for Victims of Wartime Sexual Violence' (2008) 3 *International Journal of Transitional Justice* 114; Kora Andrieu, 'Dealing with a "New" Grievance: Should Anticorruption Be Part of the Transitional Justice Agenda?' (2012) 11 *Journal of Human Rights* 537.

21 2004 UNSG Transitional Justice Report, para 17 (n 17).

22 Dustin Sharp, 'Bridging the Gap: The United Nations Peacebuilding Commission and the Challenges of Integrating DDR and Transitional Justice' in Chandra Lekha Sriram and others (eds), *Transitional Justice and Peacebuilding on the Ground: Victims and Ex-Combatants* (Routledge, 2013) 27. See also Lisa J Laplante, 'The Plural Justice Aims of Reparations' in Susanne Buckley-Zistel and others (eds), *Transitional Justice Theories* (Routledge, 2014) 66.

instance, 25.73 per cent of the articles published in the *International Journal of Transitional Justice* refer to trials, and 16.60 per cent to truth commissions.[23] This popularity is not restricted to academic debate: trials and truth commissions are the measures most often adopted in transitional situations, with the exception of amnesties.[24] The truth commission is probably the mechanism most readily associated with transitional justice. For example, the resolution that created the Special Rapporteur on the Promotion of Truth, Justice, Reparation and Guarantees of Non-Recurrence used the truth commission as the exemplary mechanism of transitional justice when it tasked the special rapporteur with gathering relevant information on 'national practices and experiences, such as truth and reconciliation commissions and other mechanisms'.[25]

Reparations for victims are another important mechanism of transitional justice whose current prominence is linked to an increasing preoccupation with victims within the discourse.[26] The fact that reparations are expressly included in the title of the special rapporteur that concentrates on transitional justice illustrates their importance in the discourse. Other significant mechanisms are vetting of public officials,[27] reform of state institutions[28] and amnesties.[29]

[23] IJTJ, '*International Journal of Transitional Justice*' (2018) http://ijtj.oxfordjournals.org/, accessed 30 July 2018. This takes into account the 241 full-length articles published between the creation of the journal and the July 2018 issue.

[24] Tricia Olsen, Leigh Payne and Andrew Reiter, 'Transitional Justice in the World, 1970–2007: Insights from a New Dataset' (2010) 47 *Journal of Peace Research* 803, 807. See also Transitional Justice Database Project, *Transitional Justice Database Project* (2016) www.tjdb project.com, accessed 30 July 2018.

[25] UNHRC 18/7 'Special Rapporteur on the Promotion of Truth, Justice, Reparation and Guarantees of Non-Recurrence', para 1 (n 19).

[26] Pablo De Greiff, *The Handbook of Reparations* (Oxford University Press, 2008); Gary Jonathan Bass, 'Reparations as a Noble Lie' in Melissa Williams, Rosemary Nagy and Jon Elster (eds), *Transitional Justice* (New York University Press, 2012); Amy Rothschild, 'Victims versus Veterans: Agency, Resistance and Legacies of Timor-Leste's Truth Commission' (2017) 11 *International Journal of Transitional Justice* 443.

[27] Pablo de Greiff and Alexander Mayer-Rieckh, *Justice as Prevention: Vetting Public Employees in Transitional Societies* (Social Science Research Council, 2007); Adam Czarnota, 'Lustration, Decommunisation and the Rule of Law' (2009) 1 *Hague Journal on the Rule of Law* 307.

[28] Mary O'Rawe, 'Security System Reform and Identity in Divided Societies: Lessons from Northern Ireland' in Paige Arthur (ed), *Identities in Transition: Challenges for Transitional Justice in Divided Societies* (Cambridge University Press, 2011); Marcos Zunino, 'Releasing Transitional Justice from the Technical Asylum: Judicial Reform in Guatemala Seen through Techne and Phronesis' (2011) 5 *International Journal of Transitional Justice* 99.

[29] Louise Mallinder, *Amnesty, Human Rights and Political Transitions: Bridging the Peace and Justice Divide*, vol 21 (Hart, 2008); Mark Freeman, *Necessary Evils: Amnesties and the Search for Justice* (Cambridge University Press, 2009).

In the same way that the discourse of transitional justice is increasingly engaging with situations that transcend its initial concern with transitions to democracy, it is also constantly incorporating new mechanisms into its remit. Among the more recent additions to the transitional justice toolbox, it is worthwhile to mention public memorialisations of violence,[30] ceremonies of reconciliation,[31] artistic expression[32] and education reform.[33] While these mechanisms are less readily identified with transitional justice than criminal trials and truth commissions, they are still considered part of the menu available for societies seeking to address past violence. The discourse of transitional justice examines all these responses to widespread or systematic violence.

The final object of the discourse of transitional justice is transitional justice itself. Transitional justice discourse often refers to itself in a reflexive manner. What is transitional justice? What are its goals? Where is it heading? Many articles and books are devoted to trying to answer these questions. For example, 13.27 per cent of all articles published in the *International Journal of Transitional Justice* do not refer to a specific situation or to a particular mechanism but are concerned with refining and elaborating what transitional justice means.[34] This self-referential engagement is a constant preoccupation

[30] Elizabeth Jelin, 'Silences, Visibility, and Agency: Ethnicity, Class and Gender in Public Memorialization' in Paige Arthur (ed), *Identities in Transition: Challenges for Transitional Justice in Divided Societies* (Cambridge University Press, 2011); Janine Natalya Clark, 'Reconciliation through Remembrance? War Memorials and the Victims of Vukovar' (2013) 7 *International Journal of Transitional Justice* 116; Susanne Buckley-Zistel and Stefanie Schäfer, *Memorials in Times of Transition* (Intersentia, 2014).

[31] Dionísio Babo-Soares, 'Nahe Biti: The Philosophy and Process of Grassroots Reconciliation (and Justice) in East Timor' (2004) 5 *The Asia Pacific Journal of Anthropology* 15; Amy Senier, 'Traditional Justice as Transitional Justice: A Comparative Case Study of Rwanda and East Timor' (2008) XXIII *PRAXIS The Fletcher Journal of Human Security* 67; Janine Ubink and Anna Rea, 'Community Justice or Ethnojustice? Engaging with Customary Mechanisms to Reintegrate Ex-Combatants in Somalia' (2017) 11 *International Journal of Transitional Justice* 276.

[32] Siona O'Connell, 'Injury, Illumination and Freedom: Thinking about the Afterlives of Apartheid through the Family Albums of District Six, Cape Town' (2015) 9 *International Journal of Transitional Justice* 297; Eliza Garnsey, 'Rewinding and Unwinding: Art and Justice in Times of Political Transition' (2016) 10 *International Journal of Transitional Justice* 471.

[33] Elizabeth Cole, 'Transitional Justice and the Reform of History Education' (2007) 1 *International Journal of Transitional Justice* 115; Briony Jones, 'Exploring the Politics of Reconciliation through Education Reform: The Case of Brcko District, Bosnia and Herzegovina' (2012) 6 *International Journal of Transitional Justice* 126; Clara Ramírez-Barat and Roger Duthie, 'Education and Transitional Justice: Opportunities and Challenges for Peacebuilding' (International Center for Transitional Justice, 2015) www.ictj.org/sites/default/files/ICTJ-UNICEF-Report-EducationTJ-2015.pdf, accessed 30 July 2018.

[34] IJTJ, '*International Journal of Transitional Justice*' (n 23).

of a discourse that, although already established, is still trying to refine its epistemological boundaries, theoretical content and methodological tools. In this sense, transitional justice discourse is an object of transitional justice discourse.[35]

The self-referential engagement seems to serve the purpose of ordering and systematising the other objects: the situations and mechanisms. As we have seen, the situations and mechanisms that transitional justice discusses tend to expand. New situations of widespread or systematic violence and mechanisms to responding to them are constantly included within transitional justice discourse. This expansion goes beyond situations and mechanisms strictly speaking as scholars include other objects of study within transitional justice discourse such as natural disasters[36] and the role of emotions.[37] This dispersion threatens the unity of the discourse. Pablo de Greiff calls these 'centrifugal forces' which require more theorisation 'to draw systematic links between diverse phenomena, and in this way to contribute to dispelling puzzlement'.[38] Thus, although there are many works already devoted to providing a framework to organise and systematise the discourse, it is repeatedly said that transitional justice is under-theorised.[39] The dispersion of the other objects always demands more theorisation to make sense of this seemingly disparate collection of objects. Therefore, the self-referential third object of transitional justice functions as an ordering mechanism that seeks to keep the other objects together in the face of the expansion of the discourse.

35 See, eg, Christine Bell, Colm Campbell and Fionnuala Ní Aoláin, 'Transitional Justice: (re) conceptualising the Field' (2007) 3 *International Journal of Law in Context* 81; Bronwyn Leebaw, 'The Irreconcilable Goals of Transitional Justice' (2008) 30 *Human Rights Quarterly* 95; Brian Grodsky, 'Re-Ordering Justice: Towards a New Methodological Approach to Studying Transitional Justice' (2009) 46 *Journal of Peace Research* 819; Pablo de Greiff, 'Theorizing Transitional Justice' in Melissa Williams, Rosemary Nagy and Elster (eds), *Transitional Justice* (New York University Press, 2012); Wendy Lambourne, 'Transformative Justice, Reconciliation and Peacebuilding' in Susanne Buckley-Zistel and others (eds), *Transitional Justice Theories* (Routledge, 2014).

36 Megan Bradley, 'More than Misfortune: Recognizing Natural Disasters as a Concern for Transitional Justice' (2017) 11 *International Journal of Transitional Justice* 400.

37 Mihaela Mihai, *Negative Emotions and Transitional Justice* (Columbia University Press, 2016).

38 Pablo de Greiff, 'A Normative Conception of Transitional Justice' (2010) 50 *Politorbis* 17, 29.

39 Phil Clark and Nicola Palmer, 'Challenging Transitional Justice' in Nicola Palmer, Phil Clark and Danielle Granville (eds), *Critical Perspectives in Transitional Justice* (Intersentia, 2012) 3; de Greiff, 'Theorizing Transitional Justice' 17 (n 35); Derk Venema, 'Transitions as States of Exception: Towards a More General Theory of Transitional Justice' in Nicola Frances Palmer, Philip Clark and Danielle Granville (eds), *Critical Perspectives in Transitional Justice* (Intersentia, 2012); Susanne Buckley-Zistel and others, 'Transitional Justice Theories: An Introduction' in Susanne Buckley-Zistel and others (eds), *Transitional Justice Theories* (Routledge, 2014) 1.

2 *Concepts*

In order to engage with these objects, a set of concepts is deployed in the discourse of transitional justice. These shared concepts provide a common lexicon to discuss the issues that the different objects – situations, mechanisms and transitional justice itself – raise. The main concepts used in transitional justice are 'transition', 'justice', 'truth' and 'reconciliation'.[40]

The concept of 'transition' is fundamental because it serves to demarcate transitional justice from justice in general. Transition refers to the circumstances in which transitional justice operates. Transition implies a period of change from one state to another. With the expansion of the discourse beyond 'the shift from a non-democratic regime type to a democratic one',[41] the concept of transition has become more flexible.[42] Still, the notion of transition embodies a temporal element. The transition is the period of change between the violent past and the hopefully peaceful future.[43] As Kimberly Theidon notes, the concept of transition 'performs temporalizing functions, serving to mark discontinuities, invoking a before-and-after narrative of change'.[44]

The concept of 'transition' also presupposes knowledge of the destination. The transition marks the passage from a predetermined stage to the next as

40 See, among many others, Rama Mani, *Beyond Retribution: Seeking Justice in the Shadows of War* (Polity, 2002); Eric A Posner and Adrian Vermeule, 'Transitional Justice as Ordinary Justice' (2004) 117 *Harvard Law Review* 761; Erin Daly, 'Truth Skepticism: An Inquiry into the Value of Truth in Times of Transition' (2008) 2 *International Journal of Transitional Justice* 23; Jon Elster, 'Justice, Truth, Peace' in Melissa Williams, Rosemary Nagy and Jon Elster (eds), *Transitional Justice* (New York University Press, 2012); Susanne Buckley-Zistel, 'Narrative Truths: On the Construction of the Past in Truth Commissions' in Susanne Buckley-Zistel and others (eds), *Transitional Justice Theories* (Routledge, 2014); Nevin Aiken, 'Rethinking Reconciliation in Divided Societies: A Social Learning Theory of Transitional Justice' in Susanne Buckley-Zistel and others (eds), *Transitional Justice Theories* (Routledge, 2014); Lambourne, 'Transformative Justice, Reconciliation and Peacebuilding' (n 35).

41 Alexandra Barahona de Brito, Carmen González Enríquez and Paloma Aguilar Fernández, 'Introduction' in Alexandra Barahona de Brito, Carmen González Enríquez and Paloma Aguilar Fernández (eds), *The Politics of Memory: Transitional Justice in Democratizing Societies* (Oxford University Press, 2001) 11.

42 Leebaw, 'The Irreconcilable Goals of Transitional Justice' 103 (n 35). See also Kimberly Theidon, 'Editorial Note' (2009) 3 *International Journal of Transitional Justice* 295; McAuliffe, 'Transitional Justice's Expanding Empire' (n 6).

43 Jennifer Balint, Julie Evans and Nesam McMillan, 'Rethinking Transitional Justice, Redressing Indigenous Harm: A New Conceptual Approach' (2014) 8 *International Journal of Transitional Justice* 194, 200–1.

44 Theidon, 'Editorial Note' 295 (n 42).

part of an evolutionary narrative.[45] The concept of transition is a source of constant debate in the discourse. Some authors have taken issue with the concept itself for its short-term focus[46] and echoing of the colonial idea of a predetermined path to development.[47] There have been calls for reorienting the concept of transition towards 'positive peace',[48] shedding it from its liberal assumptions,[49] replacing it with the broader concept of 'transformation',[50] and preserving it as a bulwark against the tendency of the discourse to overreach.[51] Contested and debated, the transition remains one of the key concepts of the discourse of transitional justice.

The twin concept of 'transition' is naturally 'justice'. The concepts are conjoined in the term that designates the discourse. From a purely semantic perspective, the discourse examines justice considerations within transitions. Since the mechanisms associated with transitional justice cover both judicial and nonjudicial initiatives, the concept of justice is not circumscribed to exclusively legal understanding or approaches. Accordingly, scholars and practitioners have mined extensively the veins of the concept of justice to enrich understandings of transitional justice.[52] For instance, according to Wendy Lambourne, transitional justice encompasses 'all aspects of justice, including legal, psychosocial, socioeconomic and political'.[53] This understanding goes well beyond legal approaches to justice. There is contention

45 Nicolas Guilhot, 'The Transition to the Human World of Democracy: Notes for a History of the Concept of Transition, from Early Marxism to 1989' (2002) 5 *European Journal of Social Theory* 219, 236.

46 Naomi Roht-Arriaza, 'The New Landscape of Transitional Justice' in Naomi Roht-Arriaza and Javier Mariezcurrena (eds), *Transitional Justice in the Twenty-First Century: Beyond Truth versus Justice* (Cambridge University Press, 2006); Cath Collins, 'The End of Impunity? "Late Justice" and Post-Transitional Prosecutions in Latin America' in Nicola Palmer, Phil Clark and Danielle Granville (eds), *Critical Perspectives in Transitional Justice* (Intersentia, 2012); Lambourne, 'Transformative Justice, Reconciliation and Peacebuilding' (n 35).

47 Abdullahi Ahmed An-Na'im, 'Editorial Note: From the Neocolonial "Transitional" to Indigenous Formations of Justice' (2013) 7 *International Journal of Transitional Justice* 197.

48 Sharp, 'Emancipating Transitional Justice from the Bonds of the Paradigmatic Transition' (n 6).

49 Nicola Henry, 'From Reconciliation to Transitional Justice: The Contours of Redress Politics in Established Democracies' (2015) 9 *International Journal of Transitional Justice* 199.

50 Lambourne, 'Transformative Justice, Reconciliation and Peacebuilding' (n 35).

51 McAuliffe, 'Transitional Justice's Expanding Empire' (n 6).

52 See, eg, Mani, *Beyond Retribution* (n 40); Ismael Muvingi, 'Sitting on Powder Kegs: Socioeconomic Rights in Transitional Societies' (2009) 3 *International Journal of Transitional Justice* 163; Aiken, 'Rethinking Reconciliation in Divided Societies' (n 40); Kora Andrieu, 'Political Liberalism after Mass Violence: John Rawls and a "Theory" of Transitional Justice' in Susanne Buckley-Zistel and others (eds), *Transitional Justice Theories* (Routledge, 2014).

53 Wendy Lambourne, 'Transitional Justice and Peacebuilding after Mass Violence' (2009) 3 *International Journal of Transitional Justice* 28, 46.

among scholars regarding whether transitional justice entails a special conception of justice. For Ruti Teitel, the transition necessitates a special type of justice that is qualitatively different from that operating during ordinary times.[54] Nevertheless, other authors consider that in the exceptional circumstances of a political transition, the conception of justice remains the same.[55]

'Truth' is another crucial concept in the discourse. The concern with truth in the discourse appeared alongside the need to establish what had happened in situations marked by secrecy, denial and enforced disappearances in Latin America. In this context, truth was considered the first step towards justice.[56] The concept grew in importance and scope as part of what Priscilla Hayner has called the 'turn toward truth' manifested in a proliferation of truth commissions throughout the world.[57] Although in the 20 years between 1974 and 1994, only 8 truth commissions were created, 19 truth commissions were established in the 10 years between 1995 and 2005.[58] As the truth commission became a paradigmatic mechanism of transitional justice, the concept of truth itself became closely associated with transitional justice. The title of the special rapporteur mandated by the UN Human Rights Council with focusing on transitional justice evidences the importance of the concept of truth in the discourse: Special Rapporteur on the Promotion of Truth, Justice, Reparation and Guarantees of Non-Recurrence.[59] The long-winded title aside, the fact that the first concept named is truth is telling of the primacy of this notion.

The concept of truth has been problematised within the discourse. Tasking a single institution, or even a comprehensive policy of transitional justice, with establishing truth is setting it for failure. The influential South African Truth and Reconciliation Commission (SATRC) recognised four kinds of truth: factual or forensic, personal or narrative, social or dialogical and healing or restorative truth.[60] In addition to seeking factual truth, the SATRC was thus

[54] Ruti Teitel, *Transitional Justice* (Oxford University Press, 2000) 6.

[55] De Greiff, 'Theorizing Transitional Justice' (n 35); Posner and Vermeule, 'Transitional Justice as Ordinary Justice' (n 40); Juan Méndez, 'Editorial Note' (2009) 3 *International Journal of Transitional Justice* 157.

[56] Roht-Arriaza, 'The New Landscape of Transitional Justice' 3 (n 46).

[57] Hayner, *Unspeakable Truths* 14 (n 12).

[58] United States Institute of Peace (USIP), 'Truth Commission Digital Collection' (2011) www.usip.org/publications/2011/03/truth-commission-digital-collection, accessed 30 July 2018.

[59] UNHRC 18/7 'Special Rapporteur on the Promotion of Truth, Justice, Reparation and Guarantees of Non-Recurrence' (n 19).

[60] Truth and Reconcliation Commission of South Africa, Truth and Reconciliation Commission of South Africa Report (Macmillan Reference, 1999), vol 1, 110 (SATRC Report).

concerned with the truth that emerges from victims and perpetrators narrating their experiences, the social truth that emerges from dialogue and the healing truth that contributes to repairing past damage and preventing future abuses.[61] However, this expansive approach to truth did not save the SATRC from being criticised for not fulfilling its multifarious truth-finding promises.[62] Scholars have also criticised the concept of truth in transitional justice due to its subjectivity and impossibility of achieving a definitive truth.[63]

The concept of 'reconciliation' is also pervasive in transitional justice discourse. While the meanings of transition, justice and truth have changed over time, no concept has experienced such a dramatic transformation as that of reconciliation. In the early days of the discourse, reconciliation was regarded as a euphemism for impunity, especially in Latin America.[64] According to an Argentine human rights activist, during the political transition from the military dictatorship to democracy in 1983, reconciliation stood for oblivion and the triumph of impunity.[65] The SATRC, created in 1995, helped to recast the concept of reconciliation as a desirable value for transitional justice. For the SATRC, the revelation of the truth would contribute to the reconciliation of the South African society.[66] Since then reconciliation has been presented as a goal of both theoretical models and actual mechanisms of

61 Ibid, vol 1, 114.

62 Fiona C Ross, 'An Acknowledged Failure: Women, Voice, Violence, and the South African Truth and Reconciliation Commission' in Rosalind Shaw, Lars Waldorf and Pierre Hazan (eds), *Localizing Transitional Justice: Interventions and Priorities after Mass Violence* (Stanford University Press, 2010); Madeleine Fullard and Nicky Rousseau, 'Truth Telling, Identities, and Power in South Africa and Guatemala' in Paige Arthur (ed), *Identities in Transition: Challenges for Transitional Justice in Divided Societies* (Cambridge University Press, 2011).

63 See, eg, Daly, 'Truth Skepticism' (n 40); Patricia Lundy and Mark McGovern, 'A Trojan Horse? Unionism, Trust and Truth-Telling in Northern Ireland' (2008) 2 *International Journal of Transitional Justice* 42; Sativa January, 'Tribunal Verité: Documenting Transitional Justice in Sierra Leone' (2009) 3 *International Journal of Transitional Justice* 207; Antonius CGM Robben, 'Testimonies, Truths, and Transitions of Justice in Argentina and Chile' in Alexander Laban Hinton (ed), *Transitional Justice: Global Mechanisms and Local Realities after Genocide and Mass Violence* (Rutgers University Press, 2010); Jaime Malamud Goti, 'Editorial Note: A Turbulent Past and the Problem with Memory' (2010) 4 *International Journal of Transitional Justice* 153.

64 For this early perspective, Jose Zalaquett, 'Balancing Ethical Imperatives and Political Constraints: The Dilemma of New Democracies Confronting Past Human Rights Violations' (1991) 43 *Hastings Law Journal* 1; Jamal Benomar, 'Justice after Transitions' (1993) 4 *Journal of Democracy* 3; David Pion-Berlin, 'To Prosecute or to Pardon? Human Rights Decisions in the Latin American Southern Cone' (1994) 16 *Human Rights Quarterly* 105.

65 Interview with Argentine human rights activist (Buenos Aires 17 September 2013).

66 Charles Villa-Vicencio, *Walk with Us and Listen: Political Reconciliation in Africa* (2009) 1. The causal link between truth and reconciliation has been questioned by Aiken, 'Rethinking Reconciliation in Divided Societies' (n 40).

transitional justice.[67] From this perspective, reconciliation has been hailed as 'the litmus test of a successful political transition and endeavour'.[68] Despite its popularity, the concept of reconciliation has been criticised for being imprecise,[69] for implying a return to a non-existent harmonious society[70] and for depriving victims of their moral choice of not forgiving.[71]

In sum, 'transition', 'justice', 'truth' and 'reconciliation' have been the main concepts of the discourse of transitional justice while being almost entirely open as to their meaning.[72] This openness has two implications. First, meanings can (and do) change over time. As mentioned in the previous paragraph, the meaning of reconciliation has changed, and not many people maintain

67 Regarding theory, see de Greiff, 'Theorizing Transitional Justice' (n 35); Nevin Aiken, *Identity, Reconciliation and Transitional Justice: Overcoming Intractability in Divided Societies* (Routledge, 2013); Aiken, 'Rethinking Reconciliation in Divided Societies' (n 40). For mechanisms, see, eg, Peace Agreement between the Government of Sierra Leone and the Revolutionary United Front of Sierra Leone, Annex to the Letter Dated 12 July 1999 from the Chargé d'affaires ad interim of the Permanent Mission of Togo to the United Nations Addressed to the President of the Security Council UN Doc S/1999/777 (Lomé Peace Agreement), art XXVI(1); Sierra Leone Truth and Reconciliation Commission, *Witness to Truth: Report of the Sierra Leone Truth and Reconciliation Commission* (Graphic Packaging, 2004), vol I, 5; Decreto Supremo N° 065–2001-PCM (2 June 2001) (Peru), art 1; Comisión de la Verdad y Reconciliación, *Informe Final* (CVR 2003) (Peru) 20.

68 Villa-Vicencio, *Walk with Us and Listen* 1 (n 66).

69 Harvey M Weinstein, 'Editorial Note: The Myth of Closure, the Illusion of Reconciliation: Final Thoughts on Five Years as Co-Editor-in-Chief' (2011) 5 *International Journal of Transitional Justice* 1, 6. Gibson also recognised the indeterminacy of the concept but tried to give it more precision, *Overcoming Apartheid: Can Truth Reconcile a Divided Nation?* (Russell Sage Foundation, 2004) 12.

70 Claire Moon, 'Prelapsarian State: Forgiveness and Reconciliation in Transitional Justice' (2004) 17 *International Journal for the Semiotics of Law* 185, 187.

71 Andrieu, 'Political Liberalism after Mass Violence' (n 52).

72 For the openness of the concept of reconciliation, see Judith Renner, 'A Discourse Theoretic Approach to Transitional Justice Ideals: Conceptualising "Reconciliation" as an Empty Universal in Times of Political Transition' in Nicola Frances Palmer, Philip Clark and Danielle Granville (eds), *Critical Perspectives in Transitional Justice* (Intersentia, 2012). In a similar vein, Hannah Franzki and María Carolina Olarte have argued that the concept of 'rule of law' acts as an empty signifier, 'Understanding the Political Economy of Transitional Justice: A Critical Theory Perspective' in Susanne Buckley-Zistel and others (eds), *Transitional Justice Theories* (Routledge, 2014). In turn, Siphiwe Dube has maintained that the concept of transition is open, albeit normally understood in a positive way, 'Transitional Justice beyond the Normative: Towards a Literary Theory of Political Transitions' (2011) 5 *International Journal of Transitional Justice* 177. Weinstein and Stover have called reconciliation: 'a murky concept with multiple meanings', 'Introduction: Conflict, Justice and Reclamation' in Eric Stover and Harvey M Weinstein (eds), *My Neighbor, My Enemy: Justice and Community in the Aftermath of Mass Atrocity* (Cambridge University Press, 2004): 5. Finally, Eric Stover has noted that reconciliation, justice and forgiveness are ambiguous terms, *The Witnesses: War Crimes and the Promise of Justice in The Hague* (University of Pennsylvania Press, 2005).

now that reconciliation always means impunity. Second, antagonistic positions over the meaning of a concept are held simultaneously within the discourse at any given time. For instance, there is debate over whether the conception of justice is different in transitional justice settings. As a result of these changes and contestation, the concepts of transitional justice do not form a perfectly coherent and uniform system. Transitional justice is an open-textured discourse 'subject to contest and reconceptualization'.[73]

3 *Actors*

Many actors participate in the discourse of transitional justice examining the objects and deploying the concepts. The main actors in transitional justice discourse are experts, institutions, donors, states and people from the situations examined.

Experts are the main drivers of conceptual change and discursive expansion in the discourse.[74] Academic research on transitional justice issues or professional experience in a mechanism or relevant organisation is often the source of their expertise from which they derive an authoritative voice. Based on their epistemic authority, experts design, implement and critique transitional justice policies. They often propose and discuss ideas that are later generalised within the discourse, such as victim-centred approaches and addressing socio-economic issues. Transitional justice experts form an epistemic community that has grown alongside the discourse.[75] Within this epistemic community of scholars and practitioners working on transitional justice, ideas are circulated, mechanisms are proposed and concepts are debated.

Experts often work within institutions. The main non-governmental organisation (NGO) in this area is the International Center for Transitional Justice

[73] Dustin Sharp, 'Introduction: Addressing Economic Violence in Times of Transition' in Dustin Sharp (ed), *Justice and Economic Violence in Transition* (Springer, 2014) 9.

[74] Leslie Vinjamuri and Jack Snyder, 'Advocacy and Scholarship in the Study of International War Crime Tribunals and Transitional Justice' (2004) 7 *Annual Review of Political Science* 345, 348–51; Theidon, 'Editorial Note' 296 (n 42); Pádraig McAuliffe, 'From Molehills to Mountains (and Myths?): A Critical History of Transitional Justice Advocacy' (2011) 22 *Finnish Yearbook of International Law* 14–15; Jelena Subotic, 'The Transformation of International Transitional Justice Advocacy' (2012) 6 *International Journal of Transitional Justice* 106; Jelena Obradovic-Wochnik, 'The "Silent Dilemma" of Transitional Justice: Silencing and Coming to Terms with the Past in Serbia' (2013) 7 *International Journal of Transitional Justice* 328, 37–38; Judith Renner, *Discourse, Normative Change and the Quest for Reconciliation in Global Politics* (Manchester University Press, 2013) 121.

[75] For the development of transitional justice expertise, see Vinjamuri and Snyder, 'Advocacy and Scholarship' (n 74); Subotic, 'The Transformation of International Transitional Justice Advocacy' (n 74).

(ICTJ) which has worked in more than 30 countries providing technical advice, engaging with civil society and producing research.[76] UN agencies, such as the Office of the High Commissioner for Human Rights (OHCHR) and the United Nations Development Programme (UNDP), also participate in the discourse, producing documents and advising states undergoing transitional processes.[77] Research centres focusing on transitional justice and specialised publications take part in the discourse: shaping discussions, organising events and disseminating ideas.[78] The activity of experts and institutions depends to a large extent on the support of donors which fund mechanisms, NGOs, conferences and research projects. States participate in the discourse as well. They implement national transitional justice policies and their courts issue relevant decisions for transitional justice. States also discuss international norms and standards in diplomatic forums.[79]

[76] ICTJ, 'About Us' (2018) http://ictj.org/about, accessed 30 July 2018.

[77] UNSC 'Report of the Secretary-General on the Rule of Law and Transitional Justice in Conflict and Post-Conflict Societies' (12 October 2011) UN Doc S/2011/634 (2011 UNSG Transitional Justice Report); UNHRC 'Annual Report of the United Nations High Commissioner for Human Rights and Reports of the Office of the High Commissioner and the Secretary-General: Analytical Study on Human Rights and Transitional Justice' (6 August 2009) UN Doc A/HRC/12/18; OHCHR, *Rule-of-Law Tools for Post-Conflict States: Truth Commissions* (United Nations, 2006); OHCHR, *Rule-of-Law Tools for Post-Conflict States: Prosecution Initiatives* (United Nations, 2006); OHCHR, *Rule-of-Law Tools for Post-Conflict States: Vetting* (United Nations, 2006); OHCHR, *Rule-of-Law Tools for Post-Conflict States: Reparation Programmes* (United Nations, 2008); OHCHR, *Rule-of-Law Tools for Post-Conflict States: Amnesties* (United Nations, 2009); UNDP, 'Perceptions on Transitional Justice: Kosovo' (2012); UNDP, 'Complementarity and Transitional Justice: Synthesis of Key Emerging Issues for Development' (2012); UNDP, *Supporting Transitional Justice* (2018) www.undp.org/content/undp/en/home/ourwork/democratic-governance-and-peacebuilding/rule-of-law–justice-and-security/transitional-justice/, accessed 30 July 2018.

[78] Transitional Justice Institute, 'About' (2018) www.ulster.ac.uk/research-and-innovation/research-institutes/transitional-justice-institute/about, accessed 30 July 2018; 'Centre for Transitional Justice and Post-Conflict Reconstruction' (2018) http://tjcentre.uwo.ca/index.html, accessed 30 July 2018; 'London Transitional Justice Network' (2016) www.londontjnetwork.org/, accessed 16 April 2016; 'Cambridge Transitional Justice Research Network' (2018) www.ctjrn.law.cam.ac.uk/, accessed 30 July 2018; 'Oxford Transitional Justice Research' (2018) www.law.ox.ac.uk/research-subject-groups/oxford-transitional-justice-research, accessed 30 July 2018; 'Transitional Justice Network New York Law School' (2018) www.nyls.edu/global_law_justice_and_policy/transitional-justice-network/, accessed 30 July 2018; 'African Transitional Justice Research Network' (2016) www.transitionaljustice.org.za/, accessed 17 April 2016; IJTJ, '*International Journal of Transitional Justice*' (n 23); 'Transitional Justice Review' (2018) http://ir.lib.uwo.ca/tjreview/, accessed 30 July 2018.

[79] The European Union also participates in transitional justice discourse, supporting and funding mechanisms and projects, see 'The EU's Policy Framework on Support to Transitional Justice' (16 November 2015) Annex to Doc 13576/15; Laura Davis, 'The European Union and Transitional Justice' (European Peacebuilding Liaison Office, 2014).

Finally, the people of the societies examined constitute another actor of transitional justice. In the discourse, their voices are not as loud as that of other actors. Transitional justice mechanisms often divide people affected by violence into victims and perpetrators, without leaving much scope for ambiguity and moral complexity. This is despite increasing calls for a more nuanced approach that takes into account the responsibility of people who benefitted from violent regimes and recognises the existence of a 'grey zone' where victims and perpetrators meet.[80]

The suffering of the victims sustains the moral call for justice and, accordingly, arguments for making transitional justice more oriented to victims' needs abound.[81] Indeed, one of the guiding principles of the UN's approach to transitional justice is to ensure the centrality of victims in the design and implementation of mechanisms.[82] Victims are so important for the discourse that an editorial of the *International Journal of Transitional Justice* claimed that 'without victims, transitional justice ceases to exist'.[83] However, the construction of the figure of victim can be problematic. Assigning the label of victim to some people affected by the violence means excluding others. For example, in the context of proceedings before the International Criminal Court (ICC), victims are 'natural persons who have suffered harm as a result of the commission of any crime within the jurisdiction of the Court'.[84]

80 See Ruben Carranza, 'Plunder and Pain: Should Transitional Justice Engage with Corruption and Economic Crimes?' (2008) 2 *International Journal of Transitional Justice* 310; Zinaida Miller, 'Effects of Invisibility: In Search of the "Economic" in Transitional Justice' (2008) 2 *International Journal of Transitional Justice* 266; Rosemary Nagy, 'Transitional Justice as Global Project: Critical Reflections' (2008) 29 *Third World Quarterly* 275; Elisabeth Porter, *Connecting Peace, Justice and Reconciliation* (Lynne Rienner Publishers, 2015). For the concept of grey zone, Primo Levi, *The Drowned and the Saved* (Abacus, 1989).

81 See, to name a few, Kirk Simpson, 'Voices Silenced, Voices Rediscovered: Victims of Violence and the Reclamation of Language in Transitional Societies' (2007) 3 *International Journal of Law in Context* 89; Simon Robins, 'Towards Victim-Centred Transitional Justice: Understanding the Needs of Families of the Disappeared in Postconflict Nepal' (2011) 5 *International Journal of Transitional Justice* 75; Wendy Lambourne, 'Outreach, Inreach and Civil Society Participation in Transitional Justice' in Nicola Palmer, Philip Clark and Danielle Granville (eds), *Critical Perspective in Transitional Justice* (Intersentia, 2012). For a critical view, see Susan F Hirsch, 'The Victim Deserving of Global Justice: Power, Caution, and Recovering Individuals' in Mark Goodale and Kamari Maxine Clarke (eds), *Mirrors of Justice: Law and Power in the Post-Cold War Era* (Cambridge University Press, 2010).

82 'Guidance Note of the Secretary-General: United Nations Approach to Transitional Justice' (10 March 2010) (UN Approach to Transitional Justice) 6.

83 IJTJ, 'Editorial Note' (2014) 8 *International Journal of Transitional Justice* 1, 3.

84 'Rules of Procedure and Evidence' Official Records of the Assembly of States Parties to the Rome Statute of the International Criminal Court (First session, New York, 3–10 September 2002), Rule 85(a).

Therefore, who receives the status of victim will depend on the scope of the court's jurisdiction and the individual crimes investigated. Similarly, the 1991 Chilean truth commission was mandated to investigate torture only when it resulted in death, thus excluding other victims of torture.[85] Even the label of victim itself is a subject of debate with many actors preferring the term survivor.[86]

Perpetrators play a more muted role in the discourse. Transitional justice policies tend to focus on victims as the main stakeholders, and many mechanisms do not engage with perpetrators. Often truth commissions do not name the perpetrators of violence, leaving them anonymous.[87] Reparations, institutional reform and memorialisation programmes are largely not concerned with perpetrators. Conversely, in criminal trials, perpetrators occupy the central stage. The purpose of the trial is to allocate personal responsibility. As Antonio Cassese expressed it, criminal trials 'establish individual responsibility over collective assignation of guilt, ie, they establish that not all Germans were responsible for the Holocaust'.[88] This individualisation of the crime on the person of the defendant makes the perpetrator the central figure. At the same time, as subject of study, perpetrators attract less interest than victims do.[89] For instance, a recent book on perpetrators of mass violence was advertised as focusing on a largely neglected topic of transitional justice.[90]

There is a certain relationship of forces among the actors of the discourse of transitional justice. All these actors (experts, NGOs, international organisations, research centres, states and people of the societies examines) take part in the discourse of transitional justice, but they do not do so equally. Due to their trajectory or their affiliation, some experts command more epistemic authority within the discourse. Similarly, because of their experience, size or resources available, some NGOs are more prominent than others. States and their institutions can also have different levels of influence depending on their international projection, history and relative power. Even groups of victims

85 Decreto Supremo N° 355 (25 April 1990), art 1.
86 See, for example, Lambourne, 'Transformative Justice, Reconciliation and Peacebuilding' (n 35).
87 Hayner, *Unspeakable Truths* 107 (n 12).
88 Antonio Cassese, 'Reflections on International Criminal Justice' (1998) 61 *Modern Law Review* 1, 6.
89 For a book concentrating on the actions and motivations of individual perpetrators, see Timothy Williams and Susanne Buckley-Zistel (eds), *Perpetrators and Perpetration of Mass Violence: Action, Motivations and Dynamics* (Routledge, 2018).
90 Susanne Buckley-Zistel, 'New Release "Perpetrators and Perpetration of Mass Violence"' (2018) 117 *TJnetwork Digest*.

who are well organised and from a high-profile situation would be more influential than others.

The relationship of forces between the actors of transitional justice is a key factor in the expansion of objects and redefinition of concepts within the discourse. If incorporating a new mechanism or changing the meaning of a concept has the support of actors with weight within the discourse, it is much more likely that the change would be accepted and a new consensus formed. Contrariwise, those views maintained and changes proposed by actors with less influence would take much more time and effort to be adopted.

In their different roles and according to their relationship of forces, these actors shape the discursive space of transitional justice; interacting with the objects and concepts, redefining and reformulating them. Alongside the expanding objects, open concepts and diverse actors, the discourse has some persistent characteristics.

III CHARACTERISTICS

Amidst the contestation and change of objects and concepts, the characteristics provide the discourse of transitional justice with some stability. They are constant features that constitute a gravitational centre in an otherwise dispersed discourse. The characteristics operate as a frame of reference to most discussions and condition which situations are addressed and which responses are considered valid. The discourse of transitional justice is comparative, technical, teleological, liberal, multilevel and state-centric. Some of these six characteristics have several dimensions. Whereas the work of some authors may not reflect or may even contest some of the characteristics, they remain constant features of the mainstream discourse of transitional justice today. These alternative approaches have not yet shifted the axis of the discourse of transitional justice from the gravitational pull of these characteristics. The characteristics described next provide regularity to the discourse of transitional justice, mark the centre of the discursive space and frame which responses to past widespread or systematic violence are considered valid.

1 *Comparative*

The comparative knowledge base of transitional justice is one of its distinctive characteristics.[91] The discourse of transitional justice relies on a comparative

[91] Paige Arthur, 'How "Transitions" Reshaped Human Rights: A Conceptual History of Transitional Justice' (2009) 31 *Human Rights Quarterly* 321; Teitel, *Transitional Justice* (n 54).

method that contrasts the responses to past widespread or systematic violence implemented in different situations. The main purpose of this comparative exercise is to distil lessons to be used in different contexts, thus transferring knowledge from one situation to the next. The comparative method is built on two assumptions: that the situations are commensurable and that the lessons derived from one situation would be useful to another. The comparative method does not necessarily entail assuming that mechanisms from one situation can be transplanted automatically to another one. The contemporary discourse of transitional justice is awash with cautions against 'one-size-fits-all' models.[92] But as long as lessons from one situation are considered useful to another, there is comparison.

The majority of the corpus of knowledge of transitional justice is developed through accumulating case studies from which insights for future situations can be gleaned.[93] Some studies compare different mechanisms applied in the same situation,[94] whereas others compare the performance of one mechanism in a variety of situations.[95] Even when a single situation is examined but general lessons are derived from it, the comparative method is at play.[96] This characteristic of comparing different responses to past widespread or systematic violence to build knowledge encourages the expansion of the discourse of transitional justice. Since the creation of knowledge is subject to finding new situations and mechanisms from which lessons can be learned, the comparative method is one of the drivers of the constant expansion of the discourse of transitional justice.

At the same time, the comparative method cements the existing characteristics of the discourse. The new situations and mechanisms have to be commensurate to other situations and mechanisms already well established within transitional justice to be able to draw meaningful comparisons or extract transferable lessons. If they were too disparate, the comparative method

92 See UN Approach to Transitional Justice 5 (n 82).

93 See, eg, Rosemary Nagy and Melissa Williams, 'Introduction' in Melissa Williams, Rosemary Nagy and Jon Elster (eds), *Transitional Justice* (New York University Press, 2012).

94 William A Schabas, 'The Relationship between Truth Commissions and International Courts: The Case of Sierra Leone' (2003) 25 *Human Rights Quarterly* 1035.

95 Priscilla Hayner, 'Fifteen Truth Commissions – 1974 to 1994: A Comparative Study' (1994) 16 *Human Rights Quarterly* 597; Hayner, *Unspeakable Truths* (n 12).

96 Transitional justice experts and institutions constantly rely on the comparative method. The ICTJ asserts that it provides expertise and knowledge 'of relevant comparative experiences in transitional justice from across the globe,' ICTJ, 'About Us' (n 76). For its part, the UN seeks to develop best practices and standards based on its experience of working in different countries, 2004 UNSG Transitional Justice Report, para 2 (n 17); UN Approach to Transitional Justice 3 (n 82).

would be stretched too thin. Therefore, by incorporating new cases that are analogous to situations and mechanisms already examined by transitional justice, the comparative method reinforces the prevailing characteristics of the discourse. In this manner, the comparative method simultaneously drives the expansion of the discourse and entrenches its existing characteristics.

2 *Technical*

A second characteristic of transitional justice discourse is that it is technical. The discourse of transitional justice uses technical vocabulary, it is ministered by technocratic experts and it proposes technical solutions. As Phil Clark and Nicola Palmer note, transitional justice emphasises 'technical institutional responses to past violations'.[97] As a technical discourse, transitional justice relies on a special type of knowledge that is specialised and transmissible.

According to philosopher Hans-Georg Gadamer, technical knowledge, acquired through experience, allows someone to choose the appropriate means to achieve a predetermined end.[98] For instance, a carpenter applies the knowledge acquired in his experience of carpentry to a set of materials to produce the desired chair. However, while technical knowledge is adept at selecting the best means, it does not seriously question the predetermined end.[99] Using the knowledge accumulated through the comparative method, transitional justice experts are able to prescribe what the right means (mechanisms) for responding to the particular circumstances of a given transition are. While the means themselves can be modified or rejected, the experts seldom question the ultimate goal of implementing a transitional justice response. Accordingly, the question 'is never whether to pursue accountability and justice, but rather when and how'.[100] The mechanisms can be adapted to the particular circumstances of the situation, in the same way as a carpenter may alter the design of the chair to adapt it to some special use. But the knowledge used remains technical if it chooses the best means to a predetermined end.

The rule-of-law tools produced by the OHCHR illustrate the technical approach. These documents are meant to 'provide practical guidance to field missions and transitional administrations in critical transitional justice and

97 Clark and Palmer, 'Challenging Transitional Justice' 6 (n 39).
98 Hans-Georg Gadamer, *Truth and Method* (William Glen-Doepel tr, Sheed and Ward, 1979).
99 Zunino, 'Releasing Transitional Justice from the Technical Asylum' (n 28).
100 UN Approach to Transitional Justice 4 (n 82).

rule of law-related areas'.[101] The areas include reparation programmes, prosecution initiatives, truth commissions, vetting, and amnesties.[102] The fact that they are called 'tools' reveals that they are perceived as equivalent to the carpenter's hammer and adze. The text reads that the 'principles used in this tool have been primarily garnered from previous experience'.[103] The experiential source of the technical knowledge and the use of the comparative method are readily apparent. However, there is also room for adaptation to different circumstances, because strategic and programmatic decisions need 'to be made in the field in the light of the particular circumstances within each post-conflict environment'.[104] Albeit with these necessary alterations, the technical knowledge embodied in the tools should provide advice on how to achieve the desired ends of transitional justice. Similarly, the ICTJ boasts of the technical base of its expertise and knowledge.[105] The technical characteristic of transitional justice discourse has three specific dimensions: being multidisciplinary, being legalistic and appearing apolitical.

a Multidisciplinary

The current discourse of transitional justice is markedly multidisciplinary. The technical characteristic of the discourse is manifested in a plurality of technical knowledges. For instance, the *International Journal of Transitional Justice* was created to be a journal 'where the perspectives, methods, and theories of diverse disciplines can come together in lively and readable interaction'.[106] Hence, the discourse of transitional justice receives contributions from philosophy, history, ethics, education, economics, cultural studies, anthropology, political science, theology, sociology, psychology and development studies, among others.[107] Transitional justice is multidisciplinary in that it contains different disciplinary approaches. Unlike interdisciplinarity, multidisciplinarity does not analyse, synthesise and harmonise 'links between

[101] OHCHR, *Rule-of-Law Tools for Post-Conflict States: Prosecution Initiatives* v (n 77).

[102] OHCHR, *Rule-of-Law Tools for Post-Conflict States: Vetting* (n 76); OHCHR, *Rule-of-Law Tools for Post-Conflict States: Truth Commissions* (n 77); OHCHR, *Rule-of-Law Tools for Post-Conflict States: Prosecution Initiatives* (n 77); OHCHR, *Rule-of-Law Tools for Post-Conflict States: Reparation Programmes* (n 77); OHCHR, *Rule-of-Law Tools for Post-Conflict States: Amnesties* (n 77).

[103] OHCHR, *Rule-of-Law Tools for Post-Conflict States: Prosecution Initiatives* v (n 77).

[104] Ibid.

[105] ICTJ, 'About Us' (n 76).

[106] IJTJ, 'Editorial Note' (2007) 1 *International Journal of Transitional Justice* 1, 2.

[107] Christine Bell, 'Transitional Justice, Interdisciplinarity and the State of the "Field" or "Non-Field"' (2009) 3 *International Journal of Transitional Justice* 5, 9.

disciplines into a coordinated and coherent whole'.[108] Undoubtedly, in transitional justice discourse, there is some dialogue between disciplines, but they have not been harmonised into a coordinated and coherent whole. The different disciplines bring their own methodologies and specific technical knowledges to the discourse of transitional justice.

b Legalistic

Despite being multidisciplinary, the discourse of transitional justice remains legalistic. The legal is the predominant technical language that the discourse employs. Judith Shklar defined legalism as 'the morality of rule following'.[109] Legalism regards law and trials as the ideal way of solving social conflict. While trials are the epitome of legalism, other institutions and mechanisms can also be legalistic to varying degrees. According to Shklar, there is a continuum of legalism with the court of law at one end and personal rule following at the other.[110] Moreover, legalism separates law from the rest of the social sphere. From the legalist perspective, law functions as a self-contained system with its own history, philosophy and values.[111] In this manner, law 'is sealed off from the world of conflict, lifted out of the sphere of social dispute'.[112]

As the professional group most closely concerned with law, lawyers are instrumental in preserving and promoting legalism as well as keeping the legal sphere separate from the rest of the social world.[113] The Supreme Court Chamber of the Extraordinary Chambers in the Courts of Cambodia (ECCC) expressed the separateness of the legal sphere with religious lexicon when it held that while 'judges are at all times certainly obligated to be mindful of the efficiency of proceedings, they must always act within the sacrum sphere of the law, the tenets of which cannot be overridden by the profanum of budgetary savings'.[114] In this manner, legal professionals are meant to operate in the insulated sphere of the law.

[108] Choi and Pak, cited in David Alvargonzález, 'Multidisciplinarity, Interdisciplinarity, Transdisciplinarity, and the Sciences' (2011) 25 *International Studies in the Philosophy of Science* 387, 388. See also Bell, 'Transitional Justice' 17 (n 107).
[109] Judith Shklar, *Legalism* (Harvard University Press, 1964) 87.
[110] Ibid 156.
[111] Ibid 105.
[112] Ibid.
[113] Shklar, *Legalism* (n 109).
[114] *Prosecutor* v. *Khieu Samphan, Nuon Chea, Ieng Sary and Ieng Thirith* (Decision on Immediate Appeal Against Trial Chamber's Second Decision on Severance of Case 002) Case 002-E284/4/7 (25 November 2013), para 75.

The pervasiveness of legalism in transitional justice discourse means that rather than the legal being another discipline in transitional justice discourse, it has a qualitatively different standing.[115] Legalism is apparent in the special role that law, lawyers and legal responses have in the discourse of transitional justice. Law, lawyers and legal responses are not on a par with other disciplines, professions and mechanisms. Even in the quintessentially interdisciplinary *International Journal of Transitional Justice*, 25.73 per cent of the articles published in that journal discuss criminal trials.[116] Equally, lawyers have contributed more articles than people from any other discipline (29.88 per cent).[117] However, a diachronic analysis evidences the impact of multidisciplinarity. In the first two years of the *International Journal of Transitional Justice* (2007–2008), pieces on criminal trials and contributions from legal scholars amounted to 20 per cent and 42.85 per cent, respectively, of all articles published. In contrast, in 2016–2017 they represented 28.26 per cent and 32.61 per cent, respectively.[118] This shows that while articles from lawyers dwindled with the participation of authors from other disciplines, the interest in trials, the epitome of legalism, has markedly increased.

c Apolitical Façade

The technical characteristic of the discourse entails presenting questions of transitional justice as if they were apolitical. How to respond to past widespread or systematic violence is eminently a political question. Transitional justice mechanisms do not concentrate on random violence but on abuses animated by political motives and justifications, whether in armed conflict or internal repression. However, the technical character of the discourse of transitional justice can suppress the political in three ways.

First, the technical character of transitional justice can interfere with the political debate in the societies involved. It is not controversial that the people affected should decide transitional justice policies through genuine political discussions. Most institutions and experts agree that carrying consultations

[115] For legalism in transitional justice, see Vinjamuri and Snyder, 'Advocacy and Scholarship' (n 74); Kieran McEvoy, 'Beyond Legalism: Towards a Thicker Understanding of Transitional Justice' (2007) 34 *Journal of Law and Society* 411; Susan Thomson and Rosemary Nagy, 'Law, Power and Justice: What Legalism Fails to Address in the Functioning of Rwanda's Gacaca Courts' (2011) 5 *International Journal of Transitional Justice* 11; Subotic, 'The Transformation of International Transitional Justice Advocacy' (n 74).

[116] IJTJ, '*International Journal of Transitional Justice*' (n 23).

[117] Ibid.

[118] Ibid.

with different stakeholders is crucial when deciding transitional justice policies.[119] However, in practice, since transitional justice relies on technical knowledge, the views of experts and specialised institutions carry a lot of weight and can shape the responses adopted in the societies in question. As the 2004 UNSG Transitional Justice Report conceded, too 'often, the emphasis has been on foreign experts, foreign models and foreign-conceived solutions'.[120]

Even when consultations are carried out, the technical character of transitional justice can serve to depoliticise the debate by predetermining the available options. In Tunisia, three months after President Ben Ali was ousted, and before the elections, the ICTJ, the Arab Institute for Human Rights, the Tunisian League for Human Rights and the OHCHR convened a conference on transitional justice held in April 2011. The conference had sessions on criminal accountability, security sector reform and vetting, truth seeking, gender justice, and reparations.[121] A year later, a public consultation on transitional justice was launched.[122] When a transitional justice law was eventually passed in December 2013, the ICTJ lauded it for addressing truth seeking, accountability, institutional reform, reparations and gender.[123] These are exactly the same areas that the pre-elections, pre-consultation conference focused on. Although a national consultation was carried out and the law was passed by parliament, the technical character of transitional justice, embodied in international experts and specialised institutions, had shaped the agenda of the political debate, narrowing the available options.

Second, the technical character suppresses the political in relation to the violence that transitional justice mechanisms address. The technical language, concepts and mechanisms of transitional justice can travel across contexts but are not necessarily well-suited for reflecting the political particularities and nuances of each situation. As a consequence, most mechanisms of transitional justice do not engage with the politics of the past violence. By relying on neutral legal categories of crimes, trials tend to gloss over the political

[119] 2004 UNSG Transitional Justice Report, para 20 (n 17); OHCHR, Rule-of-Law Tools for Post-Conflict States: National Consultations on Transitional Justice (United Nations, 2009); ICTJ, Pursuing Justice in Changing Times: Strategic Plan 2015–2018 (2015) 9.

[120] 2004 UNSG Transitional Justice Report, para 15 (n 17).

[121] ICTJ, 'Addressing the Past, Building the Future: Justice in Times of Transition Conference Report' (ICTJ, 2011).

[122] Christopher K Lamont and Héla Boujneh, 'Transitional Justice in Tunisia: Negotiating Justice during Transition' (2013) 49 *Croatian Political Science Review* 32, 43.

[123] ICTJ, 'ICTJ Welcomes Tunisia's Historic Transitional Justice Law' (17 December 2013) www.ictj.org/news/ictj-welcomes-tunisia's-historic-transitional-justice-law, accessed 30 July 2018.

dimension of the violence they examine. Reparation programmes often target general categories of victims without addressing their political activity. Truth commissions are more adept at elaborating on the political dimension of the violence in the historical narrative contained in their reports, but they often bundle the people involved in the violence in broad apolitical categories.

Transitional justice mechanisms present people who have suffered violence as victims of crimes or human rights violations without consideration of their political affiliation and present perpetrators as criminals regardless of their political motivation. For example, Peruvian peasants who fought against the guerrilla forces resented that the truth commission labelled them with the legal figure of 'victim of violation' because it denuded them of their political activity.[124] Likewise, members of liberation movements during apartheid South Africa felt aggrieved when the SATRC's amnesty process classified them as perpetrators on an equal footing with the regime's henchmen.[125] Transitional justice mechanisms apply broad apolitical labels on victims and perpetrators that effectively strip their acts and identity of their political meaning. This failure to capture the full gamut of the political motivations of agents involved in a conflict or situation of violence is partly the result of relying on technical legal categories that are universal and neutral rather than context specific and partly the result of the simplification of highly complex human situations caused by the pressure to process large numbers of people in a limited period of time. In any case, despite being presented as apolitical, 'transitional justice institutions continue to judge political violence and so are implicated in political judgments'.[126]

Third, legalism helps to suppress the political from the functioning of legal systems. Supporters of legalism tend to present law as apolitical. From this standpoint, law appears as separate and superior to politics.[127] As Kieran McEvoy has noted, this aspect of legalism has a special allure for transitional justice discourse. Since transitional justice practices operate in situations of political violence and fragile transitions, legalism can be a way of avoiding politics.[128] Using universal and neutral legal categories can thus be a strategy to

[124] Jemima García-Godos, 'Victim Reparations in the Peruvian Truth Commission and the Challenge of Historical Interpretation' (2008) 2 *International Journal of Transitional Justice* 63, 77.

[125] Fullard and Rousseau, 'Truth Telling, Identities, and Power in South Africa and Guatemala' 72 (n 62).

[126] Leebaw, 'The Irreconcilable Goals of Transitional Justice' 106 (n 35). See also Nagy, 'Transitional Justice as Global Project' (n 80).

[127] Shklar, *Legalism* 8 (n 109).

[128] McEvoy, 'Beyond Legalism' 417 (n 115).

escape the context-specific political pitfalls of a particular situation. Legalism thus allows experts to operate in a technical vacuum from where the potentially flammable gases of politics have been seemingly pumped off. In this way, legalistic approaches can obscure the politics inherent in transitional justice situations, thus contributing to making transitional justice discourse appear apolitical.

3 *Teleological*

A third characteristic of the discourse of transitional justice is that it is teleological because it relies on a framework of goals. While there might not be agreement on what the goals of transitional justice are, or should be, the fact that it should serve some ends is hardly disputed. Accordingly, 'transitional justice has a clear teleological nature'.[129]

The teleological characteristic of transitional justice is particularly manifested in the concept of transition.[130] As was discussed earlier, the concept has connotations of temporality and change, of passage to an ultimate stage. This process also presupposes an instrumental rationale. The transition is inscribed on a general teleological narrative where '"before" was worse, and "after" will lead to something better'.[131] Transitional justice mechanisms are the means to achieve the aims.[132]

The teleological characteristic of the discourse of transitional justice appears in the importance accorded to goals. The goals of transitional justice are frequently discussed within the discourse with different models being offered.[133] The UN definition of transitional justice includes responses implemented 'in order to ensure accountability, serve justice and achieve reconciliation'.[134] The fact that the goals of transitional justice are contested does not undermine the point made earlier that technical knowledge chooses the best means but does not question ends. When the suitability of some goals is being

[129] Andrieu, 'Political Liberalism after Mass Violence' 96 (n 52).
[130] Sharp, 'Emancipating Transitional Justice from the Bonds of the Paradigmatic Transition' 156 (n 6).
[131] Theidon 295 (n 42).
[132] Christine Bell and Catherine O'Rourke, 'Does Feminism Need a Theory of Transitional Justice? An Introductory Essay' (2007) 1 *International Journal of Transitional Justice* 23, 24.
[133] See, eg, 2004 UNSG Transitional Justice Report (n 17); David A Crocker, 'Reckoning with Past Wrongs: A Normative Framework' (1999) 13 *Ethics & International Affairs* 43; Mark Freeman, 'Transitional Justice: Fundamental Goals and Unavoidable Complications' (2000) 28 *Manitoba Law Journal* 113; Leebaw, 'The Irreconcilable Goals of Transitional Justice' (n 35); Pablo de Greiff, 'Theorizing Transitional Justice' (n 35); Elster, 'Justice, Truth, Peace' (n 40).
[134] 2004 UNSG Transitional Justice Report, para 8 (n 17).

discussed in transitional justice discourse, it is against the benchmark of other more ultimate ends which are not questioned, such as promoting reconciliation or achieving a transition to democracy. The success of particular mechanisms is also evaluated according to their attainment of some goals.[135] In recent years, there has been increasing interest in determining the impact of transitional justice policies to evaluate whether they have been successful. The impact is measured in relation to the achievement of certain goals.[136] Transitional justice discourse thus operates with an instrumental rationale geared towards attaining goals.

4 *Liberal*

A fourth characteristic of transitional justice discourse is its liberal imprint. Liberalism is a broad label attached to political ideology, political philosophy and political activity spanning hundreds of years.[137] The liberal tradition is mainly concerned with ensuring freedom, understood in a variety of ways.[138] While some modern liberal thinkers give equality a prominent place in their

[135] Coleen Duggan, '"Show Me Your Impact": Evaluating Transitional Justice in Contested Spaces' (2012) 35 *Evaluation and Program Planning* 199.

[136] Marek M Kaminski and Monika Nalepa, 'Judging Transitional Justice: A New Criterion for Evaluating Truth Revelation Procedures' (2006) 50 *The Journal of Conflict Resolution* 383; Phuong Pham and Patrick Vinck, 'Empirical Research and the Development and Assessment of Transitional Justice Mechanisms' (2007) 1 *International Journal of Transitional Justice* 231; Laurel E Fletcher, Harvey M Weinstein and Jamie Rowen, 'Context, Timing and the Dynamics of Transitional Justice: A Historical Perspective' (2009) 31 *Human Rights Quarterly* 163; Tricia D Olsen, Leigh A Payne and Andrew G Reiter, *Transitional Justice in Balance: Comparing Processes, Weighing Efficacy* (United States Institute of Peace, 2010); Geoff Dancy, 'Impact Assessment, Not Evaluation: Defining a Limited Role for Positivism in the Study of Transitional Justice' (2010) 4 *International Journal of Transitional Justice* 355; Oskar NT Thoms, James Ron and Roland Paris, 'State-Level Effects of Transitional Justice: What Do We Know?' (2010) 4 *International Journal of Transitional Justice* 329; Martien Schotsmans, '"But We Also Support Monitoring": INGO Monitoring and Donor Support to Gacaca Justice in Rwanda' (2011) 5 *International Journal of Transitional Justice* 390; Duggan, '"Show Me Your Impact"' (n 135); Diane F Orentlicher, 'From Viability to Impact: Evolving Metrics for Assessing the International Criminal Tribunal for the Former Yugoslavia' (2013) 7 *International Journal of Transitional Justice* 536. For a critical view of evaluations, see Kirsten Ainley, 'Evaluating the Evaluators: Transitional Justice and the Contest of Values' (2017) 11 *International Journal of Transitional Justice* 421.

[137] Steven Wall, 'Introduction' in Steven Wall (ed), *The Cambridge Companion to Liberalism* (Cambridge University Press, 2015) 1–2.

[138] Paul Kelly, *Liberalism* (Polity, 2005). For diverse liberal understandings of freedom, compare Friedrich von Hayek, *The Road to Serfdom* (G Routledge & Sons, 1944) with Jeremy Waldron, 'Theoretical Foundations of Liberalism', *Liberal Rights: Collected Papers, 1981–1991* (Cambridge University Press, 1993).

theoretical edifice, in traditional liberalism, equality has played second fiddle to freedom.[139] Liberalism also believes in limited government that is restrained to ensure individual autonomy.[140] Most liberals hold that institutions such as the market or constitutional democracy are integral components of this tradition.[141] Liberal ideology has animated politics for a long time. During the second half of the twentieth century, liberalism was the ideology supported by the United States and its allies against the Soviet Bloc's socialism.

The liberal imprint of transitional justice is apparent in its focus on the political sphere and in its reliance on institutions such as liberal democracy and the market.[142] Liberalism separates the political and economic spheres. Whereas the political sphere is subject to democratic participation and debate, the economic sphere is left to the self-regulated forces of the market. Within this liberal framework, transitional justice operates predominantly in the political sphere, while the economic realm is not examined.[143] Transitional justice's concentration on the political realm does not run counter to its being presented as apolitical. Although as a technical discourse transitional justice does not engage in political debate and contestation, it does focus on the political arena, understood as the site of democracy, government and the rule of law, in contrast with the economic realm of property, labour, production and distribution. The liberalism of the discourse of transitional justice is manifested in three dimensions – namely an emphasis on violations of civil and political rights and instances of physical violence, preference for liberal democracy and sympathy for capitalism.

139 John Rawls, *A Theory of Justice* (Belknap Press of Harvard University Press, 1971); Jeremy Waldron, *Liberal Rights: Collected Papers, 1981–1991* (Cambridge University Press, 1993); Ronald Dworkin, *Sovereign Virtue: The Theory and Practice of Equality* (Harvard University Press, 2000).

140 John Gray, *Liberalism* (Open University Press, 1995); Norberto Bobbio, *Liberalism and Democracy* (Verso, 2005).

141 Wall, 'Introduction' 3 (n 137).

142 For the liberal imprint of transitional justice, see Chandra Lekha Sriram, 'Justice as Peace? Liberal Peacebuilding and Strategies of Transitional Justice' (2007) 21 *Global Society* 579; Sharp, 'Emancipating Transitional Justice from the Bonds of the Paradigmatic Transition' (n 6); Henry, 'From Reconciliation to Transitional Justice' (n 49); Andrieu, 'Political Liberalism after Mass Violence' (n 52); Nagy, 'Transitional Justice as Global Project' (n 80); Simon Robins, 'Mapping a Future for Transitional Justice by Learning from Its Past' (2015) 9 *International Journal of Transitional Justice* 181;

143 Franzki and Olarte 208 (n 72). See also Emilios Christodoulidis and Scott Veitch, 'Reconciliation as Surrender: Configurations of Responsibility and Memory' in François Du Bois and Antje Du Bois-Pedain (eds), *Justice and Reconciliation in Post-Apartheid South Africa* (Cambridge University Press, 2008).

a Emphasis on Violations of Civil and Political Rights and Physical Violence

As part of its liberal imprint, the discourse of transitional justice concentrates on violations of civil and political rights and instances of physical violence to the detriment of violations of socio-economic rights and structural violence. Historically, civil and political rights developed within liberal ideology and political practice.[144] Although liberalism can also accommodate socio-economic rights,[145] within this tradition, civil and political rights have always been more prominent. For liberalism, civil and political rights provide individuals with their protected sphere of autonomy.[146] Within the liberal framework, severe instances of physical violence, such as murder and torture, constitute the most serious violations of civil and political rights.

Most mechanisms of transitional justice are set up to respond to violations of civil and political rights, primarily those involving physical violence. Instances of murder, enforced disappearances, torture, illegal detention and sexual violence are those more often examined. For instance, the mandate of the SATRC was limited to gross violations of human rights understood as 'killing, abduction, torture or severe ill-treatment of any person'.[147] In contrast, mechanisms associated with transitional justice often do not engage with violations of socio-economic rights or instances of structural violence.[148] Transitional justice scholars also traditionally concentrated almost exclusively on violations of civil and political rights to the detriment of economic and social rights.[149] This neglect occurs despite the widely recognised indivisibility of human rights.[150] The marginalisation of socio-economic rights in transitional justice was exposed in a 2006 speech by the then UN High

144 Bobbio, *Liberalism and Democracy* (n 140) 5–9.

145 See Jeremy Waldron, 'Liberal Rights: Two Sides of the Coin', *Liberal Rights: Collected Papers, 1981–1991* (Cambridge University Press, 1993); Louise Mallinder, Siobhán Wills and Thomas Hansen, *Economic Liberalism, Democracy, and Transitional Justice: Workshop Report* (Transitional Justice Institute, 2018).

146 Kelly, *Liberalism* 10 (n 138).

147 Promotion of National Unity and Reconciliation Act (1995) (South Africa), s 1.

148 For an excellent analysis of how socio-economic rights and social inequality grievances were excluded from the transitional justice process in Nepal, see Tafadzwa Pasipanodya, 'A Deeper Justice: Economic and Social Justice as Transitional Justice in Nepal' (2008) 2 *International Journal of Transitional Justice* 378.

149 Naomi Roht-Arriaza, 'Reparations and Development' in Ruth Margaret Buchanan and Peer Zumbansen (eds), *Law in Transition: Human Rights, Development and Transitional Justice* (Hart, 2014) 191.

150 See, eg, 'Vienna Declaration and Programme of Action' World Conference on Human Rights (25 June 1993) UN Doc A/CONF.157/23, para 5.

Commissioner for Human Rights, Louise Arbour, when she called for the inclusion of these rights in transitional justice mechanisms.[151] Many scholars followed suit, advocating for a broader transitional justice that tackles socio-economic rights and social justice.[152] In 2010, the UN adopted an approach to transitional justice that strives to 'take account of the root causes of conflict or repressive rule, and address the related violations of all rights, including economic, social, and cultural rights in a comprehensive and integrated manner'.[153] These calls for a transitional justice that goes beyond violations of civil and political rights and instances of physical violence illustrate how hitherto the emphasis has been on these areas.

Some transitional justice policies have indeed engaged with violations of socio-economic rights or patterns of structural violence.[154] Truth commissions have been at the forefront of that effort.[155] For instance, the 2014 Tunisian Truth and Dignity Commission was expressly mandated to examine financial corruption.[156] The engagement of truth commissions with violations of socio-economic rights and other social issues, however, has not resulted in any significant change. For example, the SATRC proposed several mechanisms to collect funds from businesses for reparations.[157] Even though they were all gradual and progressive taxes and levies rather than expropriations, they were not implemented and were replaced by a business

[151] Louise Arbour, 'Economic and Social Justice for Societies in Transition' (2007) 40 *New York University Journal of International Law and Politics* 1.

[152] Muvingi, 'Sitting on Powder Kegs' (n 52); Miller, 'Effects of Invisibility' (n 80); Pasipanodya, 'A Deeper Justice' (n 148); Gaby Oré Aguilar and Felipe Gómez Isa, *Rethinking Transitions: Equality and Social Justice in Societies Emerging from Conflict* (Intersentia, 2011); Dustin Sharp, 'Addressing Economic Violence in Times of Transition: Toward Positive-Peace Paradigm for Transitional Justice' (2012) 35 *Fordham International Law Journal* 780; Dustin Sharp, *Justice and Economic Violence in Transition* (Springer, 2014); Paul Gready and Simon Robins, 'From Transitional to Transformative Justice: A New Agenda for Practice' (2014) 8 *International Journal of Transitional Justice* 339; Sam Szoke-Burke, 'Not Only "Context": Why Transitional Justice Programs Can No Longer Ignore Violations of Economic and Social Rights' (2015) 50 *Texas International Law Journal* 465. This expansion towards socio-economic rights has also been criticised, see Lars Waldorf, 'Anticipating the Past: Transitional Justice and Socio-Economic Wrongs' (2012) 21 *Social & Legal Studies* 171.

[153] UN Approach to Transitional Justice 10 (n 82). See also UNHRC 'Annual Report' (n 77).

[154] It is important not to conflate socio-economic rights as legal entitlements and socio-economic issues more broadly, see Evelyne Schmid and Aoife Nolan, '"Do No Harm"? Exploring the Scope of Economic and Social Rights in Transitional Justice' (2014) 8 *International Journal of Transitional Justice* 362.

[155] The truth commissions of Guatemala, Peru, Kenya, Timor Leste and Sierra Leone have all dealt with socio-economic issues.

[156] Isabel Robinson, 'Truth Commissions and Anti-Corruption: Towards a Complementary Framework?' (2014) 9 *International Journal of Transitional Justice* 33, 45.

[157] SATRC Report, vol 6, 143 (n 60).

trust to which corporations could make voluntary contributions.[158] Similarly, although the Timor Leste truth commission documented violations of economic and social rights, it recommended restricting reparations to victims of violations of civil and political rights.[159] Even the more recently established Tunisian Truth and Dignity Commission faced a rollback of its remit on corruption as a result of political pressure.[160] Moreover, in September 2017, after two years of controversial debate, Tunisia's parliament approved the Law for Reconciliation in the Economic and Financial Areas that granted amnesty to officials accused of corruption during the regime of President Ben Ali.[161] Despite recent efforts to broaden the discourse and practice, transitional justice continues to emphasise violations of civil and political rights and episodes of physical violence.[162]

b Preference for Liberal Democracy

The liberal characteristic of transitional justice discourse is also evident in the preference for liberal democracy. Liberal democracy – where law restrains state power, government is democratically elected and there is separation of powers – is regarded as the ideal endpoint of the transition. Accordingly, transitional justice polices are geared towards some form of liberal democratic

158 Clara Sandoval, Leonardo Filippini and Roberto Vidal, 'Linking Transitional Justice and Corporate Accountability' in Sabine Michalowski (ed), *Corporate Accountability in the Context of Transitional Justice* (Routledge, 2013) 22. See also Charles P Abrahams, 'Lessons from the South African Experience' in Sabine Michalowski (ed), *Corporate Accountability in the Context of Transitional Justice* (Routledge, 2013).

159 Comissão de Acolhimento, Verdade e Reconciliação, *Chega! The Final Report of the Timor-Leste Commission for Reception, Truth and Reconciliation* (CAVR 2006), c 7.9, 46–48, c 12, 40–41. See also Evelyne Schmid, *Taking Economic, Social and Cultural Rights Seriously in International Criminal Law* (Cambridge University Press, 2015) 8–9.

160 Tarek Amara, 'Tunisia Parliament Approves Controversial Amnesty for Ben Ali-era Corruption' *Reuters* (September 2017) www.reuters.com/article/us-tunisia-politics-corruption/tunisia-parliament-approves-controversial-amnesty-for-ben-ali-era-corruption-idUSKCN1BO218, accessed 30 July 2018. For the law's background, see Rim El Gantri, 'Tunisia in Transition: One Year after the Creation of the Truth and Dignity Commission' (ICTJ, 2015) www.ictj.org/sites/default/files/ICTJ-Briefing-Tunisia-TJLaw-2015.pdf, accessed 30 July 2018; Carlotta Gall, 'In Tunisia, a Mission of Justice and a Moment of Reckoning' *New York Times* (November 2015) www.nytimes.com/2015/11/07/world/africa/in-tunisia-a-mission-of-justice-and-a-moment-of-reckoning.html, accessed 30 July 2018.

161 ICTJ, *Tunisia: Draft Law On Reconciliation in Economic and Financial Areas Approved by Cabinet Meeting* (2015) www.ictj.org/news/tunisia-draft-law-reconciliation-economic-and-financial-areas-approved-cabinet-meeting, accessed 4 May 2018.

162 See Mallinder, Wills and Hansen, *Economic Liberalism, Democracy, and Transitional Justice* (n 145) for a recent formulation of this point of view.

state.[163] While non-liberal regimes sometimes use mechanisms and concepts of transitional justice, the discourse favours liberal democracy.[164]

The preference for liberal democracy is evidenced in transitional justice's relationship with the concept of the rule of law. Transitional justice policies are widely supposed to strengthen the rule of law.[165] Like other concepts discussed earlier, the exact meaning of the rule of law is subject to contestation. In its most minimalist expression, the rule of law refers to a regime where everybody, including the state, is bound by law. While this concept can accommodate a variety of ideological perspectives, it is usually 'thickened' with features of a particular political ideology.[166] In transitional justice discourse, these features are decidedly liberal. As the UN Special Rapporteur on the Promotion of Truth, Justice, Reparation and Guarantees of Non-Recurrence has noted, the UN has opted for a rich understanding of the notion of rule of law that includes political and democratic rights.[167] In this vein, the 2004 UNSG Transitional Justice Report defines the rule of law as

> a principle of governance in which all persons, institutions and entities, public and private, including the State itself, are accountable to laws that are publicly promulgated, equally enforced and independently adjudicated, and which are consistent with international human rights norms and standards. It requires, as well, measures to ensure adherence to the principles of supremacy of law, equality before the law, accountability to the law, fairness in the application of the law, separation of powers, participation in decision-making, legal certainty, avoidance of arbitrariness and procedural and legal transparency.[168]

[163] Christine Bell, Colm Campbell and Fionnuala Ní Aoláin, 'Justice Discourses in Transition' (2004) 13 *Social & Legal Studies* 305. See also de Greiff, 'Theorizing Transitional Justice' (n 35); Balint, Evans and McMillan, 'Rethinking Transitional Justice, Redressing Indigenous Harm' (n 43); Andrieu, 'Political Liberalism after Mass Violence' (n 52); Dustin Sharp, 'Interrogating the Peripheries: The Preoccupations of Fourth Generation Transitional Justice' (2013) 26 *Harvard Human Rights Journal* 149.

[164] See Hansen, 'The Vertical and Horizontal Expansion of Transitional Justice' (n 6).

[165] 2004 UNSG Transitional Justice Report, paras 2–3 (n 17); UNHRC Resolution 18/7 (n 19), preamble; UNGA 'Report of the Special Rapporteur on the Promotion of Truth, Justice, Reparation and Guarantees of Non-Recurrence' (13 September 2012) UN Doc A/67/368, paras 23–67; European Union, I(d) (n 79); UN Approach to Transitional Justice 3 (n 82). For a more critical view of their relationship, see Pádraig McAuliffe, 'Transitional Justice and the Rule of Law: The Perfect Couple or Awkward Bedfellows?' (2010) 2 *Hague Journal on the Rule of Law* 127.

[166] Randall Peerenboom, 'Human Rights and Rule of Law: What's the Relationship?' (2005) 36 *Georgetown Journal of International Law* 1. See also Pádraig McAuliffe, *Transitional Justice and Rule of Law Reconstruction: A Contentious Relationship* (Routledge, 2013).

[167] UNGA 'Report of the Special Rapporteur on the Promotion of Truth, Justice, Reparation and Guarantees of Non-Recurrence', para 12 (n 165).

[168] 2004 UNSG Transitional Justice Report, para 6 (n 17). See also Guidance Note of the Secretary-General: United Nations Approach to Rule of Law Assistance (30 April 2008).

The separation of powers, equality before the law and independent adjudication, among others, are crucial aspects of liberal democracy. In seeking to strengthen the rule of law, thus understood, transitional justice policies effectively promote liberal democracy.

This preference for democracy is in line with the general consensus of states which has emerged over the last quarter of a century. Notably, the UN General Assembly in its Millennium Declaration (2000) committed to spare no effort to promote democracy.[169] Five years later, its World Summit Outcome Document reaffirmed that democracy is a universal value that reinforces, and is reinforced by, human rights.[170]

Transitional justice's preference for liberal democracy appears most conspicuously in policies of institutional reform. These reforms, aimed at preventing the recurrence of violence, are often animated by a liberal spirit that favours democratic institutions. For instance, the European Union (EU) supports justice and security sector reform that is 'consistent with democratic norms, rule of law values, good governance principles and respect for human rights'.[171] The UN Special Rapporteur on the Promotion of Truth, Justice, Reparation and Guarantees of Non-Recurrence, has recommended transitional states consider reforming their constitution enshrining 'the principles of the separation of powers, the independence of the judiciary and the non-partisan role of the security forces'.[172] These reforms are directed at constructing liberal democratic institutions.

c Sympathy for Capitalism

A third feature of the liberal characteristic of the discourse of transitional justice is its sympathy for capitalism. Historically, liberalism developed alongside capitalism. Classical liberalism has defended private property, the market and capitalism.[173] Some modern liberals have downplayed the importance of

169 UNGA Resolution 55/2 'United Nations Millennium Declaration' (18 September 2000) UN Doc A/RES/55/2, para 24.

170 UNGA Resolution 60/1'World Summit Outcome' (16 September 2005) UN Doc A/RES/60/1, para 119. This view was reiterated in UNGA Resolution 64/155 'Strengthening the Role of the United Nations in Enhancing Periodic and Genuine Elections and the Promotion of Democratization' (18 December 2009) UN Doc A/RES/64/155.

171 European Union (n 79), IV (9).

172 UNHRC 'Report of the Special Rapporteur on the Promotion of Truth, Justice, Reparation and Guarantees of Non-Recurrence' (7 September 2015) UN Doc A/HRC/30/42, para 110.

173 See Adam Smith, *An Inquiry into the Nature and Causes of the Wealth of Nations* (Roy Hutcheson Campbell, Andrew Skinner and William Todd eds, Clarendon Press, 1976); John Stuart Mill, *On Liberty* (Jean Bethke Elshtain, David Bromwich and George Kateb eds, Yale

economic market freedom and have argued for equality and redistributive policies and but still within a capitalist framework.[174] As Jeremy Waldron notes, liberals are attracted to markets.[175] While liberalism as a political theory could harbour a different economic system, in practice, all liberal political regimes have been capitalist.[176] In transitional justice discourse, this sympathy for capitalism is manifested in three ways.

First, the discourse of transitional justice predominantly examines responses to past widespread or systematic violence adopted in capitalist societies, neglecting communist practices. From criminal trials in Chile[177] to the truth commission in Kenya,[178] to reparations in Colombia[179] to a memorial in Croatia,[180] the discourse concentrates on measures implemented in countries with market-based economies. For instance, only 6 out 241 articles published in the *International Journal of Transitional Justice* (2.48 per cent) mention responses adopted by communist regimes, and even these do it briefly.[181] Sometimes the violence might have taken place in a country with a socialist planned economy, but the responses examined are those adopted after

University Press, 2003); von Hayek, *The Road to Serfdom* (n 138); Milton Friedman, *Capitalism and Freedom* (University of Chicago Press, 1963); Robert Nozick, *Anarchy, State, and Utopia* (Basic Books, 1974).

174 See, eg, Rawls, *A Theory of Justice* (n 139); Dworkin, *Sovereign Virtue* (n 139). See also Mallinder, Wills and Hansen, *Economic Liberalism, Democracy, and Transitional Justice* (n 145).

175 Waldron, 'Theoretical Foundations of Liberalism' 60 (n 138).

176 Wendy Brown, 'Neo-Liberalism and the End of Liberal Democracy' (2003) 7 *Theory & Event*.

177 Cath Collins, *Post-Transitional Justice: Human Rights Trials in Chile and El Salvador* (Pennsylvania State University Press, 2010).

178 Stephen Brown, 'The National Accord, Impunity, and the Fragile Peace in Kenya' in Chandra Lekha Sriram and others (eds), *Transitional Justice and Peacebuilding on the Ground: Victims and Ex-Combatants* (Routledge, 2013).

179 Pamina Firchow, 'Must Our Communities Bleed to Receive Social Services? Development Projects and Collective Reparations Schemes in Colombia' (2013) 8 *Journal of Peacebuilding & Development* 50.

180 Clark, 'Reconciliation through Remembrance?' (n 30).

181 IJTJ, '*International Journal of Transitional Justice*' (n 23). The articles are: Kora Andrieu, 'An Unfinished Business: Transitional Justice and Democratization in Post-Soviet Russia' (2011) 5 *International Journal of Transitional Justice* 198; Victor Igreja, 'Multiple Temporalities in Indigenous Justice and Healing Practices in Mozambique' (2012) 6 *International Journal of Transitional Justice* 404; Christiane Wilke, 'Remembering Complexity? Memorials for Nazi Victims in Berlin' (2013) 7 *International Journal of Transitional Justice* 136; Victor Igreja, 'Amnesty Law, Political Struggles for Legitimacy and Violence in Mozambique' (2015) 9 *International Journal of Transitional Justice* 239; Peter Manning, 'Reconciliation and Perpetrator Memories in Cambodia' (2015) 9 *International Journal of Transitional Justice* 386; Ilya Nuzov, 'The Dynamics of Collective Memory in the Ukraine Crisis: A Transitional Justice Perspective' (2017) 11 *International Journal of Transitional Justice* 132.

economic liberalisation, as is the case with Eastern European countries.[182] This neglect of communist practices of transitional justice is evidently related to the pervasiveness of capitalist economic systems in the last quarter of a century. Yet not even works with a historical outlook engage much with responses to past widespread or systematic violence adopted in socialist countries, as is further discussed in Chapters 4 and 5. In this negative manner, transitional justice discourse assumes and reinforces the naturalness of capitalism.[183]

Second, transitional justice policies are often implemented alongside programmes of economic liberalisation. In recent years, transitional justice has become an integral component of liberal peacebuilding efforts.[184] The UN Security Council has defined peacebuilding as encompassing a range of political, developmental, humanitarian and human rights programmes 'aimed at preventing the outbreak, recurrence or continuation of armed conflict'.[185] Peacebuilding programmes usually follow a liberal recipe of holding elections, building democratic institutions and market liberalisation.[186] Therefore, transitional justice programmes are carried out together with reforms to foster a growing capitalist economy. In places as diverse as Guatemala, Cambodia, Liberia, El Salvador and Bosnia Herzegovina, market liberalisation policies, often by prescription of international financial institutions, were applied alongside mechanisms of transitional justice in the context of UN missions.[187] The linkage of transitional justice and capitalism in liberal peacebuilding is illustrated by the UN Peacebuilding Support Office, which supports transitional

[182] See, eg, David Kosar, 'Lustration and Lapse of Time: "Dealing with the Past" in the Czech Republic' (2008) 4 *European Constitutional Law Review* 460; Andrew Beattie, 'An Evolutionary Process: Contributions of the Bundestag Inquiries into East Germany to an Understanding of the Role of Truth Commissions' (2009) 3 *International Journal of Transitional Justice* 229; Czarnota (n 27).

[183] Makau Mutua, 'The Transformation of Africa: A Critique of Rights in Transitional Justice' in Ruth Margaret Buchanan and Peer Zumbansen (eds), *Law in Transition: Human Rights, Development and Transitional Justice* (Hart, 2014).

[184] European Union IV (10) (n 79); UN Approach to Transitional Justice 6 (n 82). See also Chandra Lekha Sriram and others, *Transitional Justice and Peacebuilding on the Ground: Victims and Ex-Combatants* (Routledge, 2013).

[185] UNSC Presidential Statement 5 (20 February 2001) UN Doc S/PRST/2001/5, 1. For peacebuilding in general, Ho-Won Jeong, *Peacebuilding in Postconflict Societies: Strategy and Process* (Lynne Rienner Publishers, 2005).

[186] For liberal peacebuilding, Roland Paris, *At War's End: Building Peace after Civil Conflict* (Cambridge University Press, 2004).

[187] Ibid. For a number of case studies on economic liberalism and transitional justice, see Mallinder, Wills and Hansen, *Economic Liberalism, Democracy, and Transitional Justice* (n 145).

justice programmes as a component of peacebuilding and collaborates with the World Bank in liberal economic reform in the target countries.[188]

Third, by not engaging with the economic sphere, transitional justice discourse implicitly supports capitalism. As far as transitional justice is concerned, the economic structure is left as it is, or subject to the liberalising programmes referred to earlier. Since the discourse addresses policies carried out either in capitalist countries or in countries in the process of becoming capitalist, the 'economic invisibility' of transitional justice, as Zinaida Miller has called it, effectively entails tacit endorsement of that prevailing economic system.[189]

In these three ways, by concentrating on capitalist countries, being part of liberal and capitalist peacebuilding efforts and not engaging with the economic sphere, transitional justice supports capitalism. Summing up the three dimensions of transitional justice's liberal characteristic: it favours liberal rights, liberal democracy and liberal capitalism.

5 *Multilevel*

A fifth characteristic of transitional justice discourse is that it operates at multiple levels. While the discourse is global, it examines processes that take place at the international, regional, national and local levels.[190] The mechanisms employed include international criminal tribunals,[191] regional human rights courts,[192] national policies,[193] and local – community-based – initiatives.[194] The latter encompass memorials, reconciliation processes, dispute resolution initiatives and truth-finding mechanisms established independently

[188] United Nations Peacebuilding Support Office, 'Annual Report' (2013); United Nations-World Bank Partnership Framework for Crisis and Post-Crisis Situations (25 October 2008); Mary Morrison and Shani Harris, 'Working with the World Bank Group in Fragile and Conflict-Affected Situations: A Resource Note for United Nations Staff' (2015) http://documents.worldbank.org/curated/en/922311467999664758/pdf/99008-WP-Box393181B-PUBLIC-Working-with-the-WBG-final1.pdf, accessed 30 July 2018. See also Sharp, 'Bridging the Gap' (n 22).

[189] Miller, 'Effects of Invisibility' (n 80).

[190] Hansen, 'The Vertical and Horizontal Expansion of Transitional Justice' (n 6). See also Jon Elster, *Closing the Books: Transitional Justice in Historical Perspective* (Cambridge University Press, 2004).

[191] See, eg, Kirsten Campbell, 'The Laws of Memory: The ICTY, the Archive, and Transitional Justice' (2013) 22 *Social & Legal Studies* 247.

[192] See, eg, Eva Brems, 'Transitional Justice in the Case Law of the European Court of Human Rights' (2011) 5 *International Journal of Transitional Justice* 282.

[193] See, eg, Kathryn Sikkink, 'From Pariah State to Global Protagonist: Argentina and the Struggle for International Human Rights' (2008) 50 *Latin American Politics and Society* 1.

[194] See, eg, Kieran McEvoy and Lorna McGregor, *Transitional Justice from Below: Grassroots Activism and the Struggle for Change* (Hart, 2008).

of the state at the local level. Moreover, actors from all levels contribute to the discourse, such as international organisations, national institutions and community-based groups. The multiple levels of transitional justice are not rigid strata. On the contrary, this 'multilayered reality exhibits an increasingly complex set of relationships among the local, national and international planes'.[195] National NGOs join forces with their international counterparts to influence policies at the international level[196] and international NGOs and UN institutions cooperate with national and community-based groups. In sum, the discourse of transitional justice has a complex multilevel character.

6 *State-Centric*

A sixth characteristic of the discourse of transitional justice is that it is state-centric. Transitional justice discourse conceives of the state as the main locus of responses to past widespread or systematic violence. States implement most criminal trials, truth commissions, reparations, vetting processes and institutional reform programmes. Moreover, many transitional justice mechanisms target the state in an attempt to strengthen it. The most obvious examples are programmes of institutional reform, but trials and truth commissions also buttress the state insofar as they seek to bolster the rule of law and state legitimacy.[197] Hence, since the state is both the source and recipient of transitional justice's interventions, the discourse centres on this institution.

The operation of the discourse on multiple levels has not diminished the crucial role of the state. Processes at the international, regional and local levels still depend on the state. International tribunals are set up either by treaties or the UN Security Council; states negotiate and ratify treaties and make decisions in international organisations. Similarly, UN institutions, such as UNDP and OHCHR, require the permission and cooperation of the national state to implement their transitional justice programmes. Local and informal initiatives, such as community memorials and reconciliation ceremonies, have received more attention within the discourse in recent years. They are less reliant on the state, but they are still subject to national laws and administrative oversight. Moreover, local and informal initiatives are often tied in to the state. While the UN has recognised the potential of informal justice

[195] Roht-Arriaza, 'The New Landscape of Transitional Justice' 10 (n 46).
[196] Margaret E Keck and Kathryn Sikkink, *Activists beyond Borders: Advocacy Networks in International Politics* (Cornell University Press, 1998).
[197] McEvoy, 'Beyond Legalism' 422–23 (n 115). See also Balint, Evans and McMillan, 'Rethinking Transitional Justice, Redressing Indigenous Harm' 201 (n 43).

measures to contribute to the rule of law in general, it seeks to integrate them with formal – state-based – systems.[198] The state thus remains at the centre of the discourse of transitional justice.

IV CONCLUSION

This chapter has sought to depict an image of the discourse of transitional justice today. It has argued that transitional justice occupies a distinctive discursive space populated by objects, concepts and actors. The discourse has six characteristics: comparative, technical, teleological, liberal, multilevel and state-centric.

The characteristics provide structure to the discourse by setting parameters for most discussions on transitional justice. They also result in a preference for certain mechanisms and responses. As we will see in the rest of this book, these characteristics determine which mechanisms and responses are included in the history of transitional justice. The six characteristics identified in this chapter have shaped the discourse's choice of the Nuremberg trial as the point of origin of transitional justice (Chapter 4) and of relevant Cold War episodes and responses (Chapter 5).

Yet the characteristics can change. In the same way as concepts and objects are open to contestation and can be redefined, the characteristics can change as new consensuses emerge within the discourse. There are already calls for a transitional justice that is less technical, liberal and state-centric. These alternative approaches can gather momentum and eventually lead to lasting changes within the discourse. As we have seen in this chapter, appeals to incorporate socio-economic issues or give more prominence to victims, once marginal, have become mainstream considerations within transitional justice. The same process could lead to a shift within the discourse that unmoors it from some of the prevailing characteristics.

Having presented a vista of the discourse of transitional justice as it is today, we now turn to its past. The next chapter examines the emergence of the discourse of transitional justice from its tentative beginnings until its consolidation. How did a discourse of transitional justice appear? What historical circumstances influenced this process? What is the origin of the characteristics that it has today? These are the questions we explore next.

198 2011 UNSG Transitional Justice Report, para 39 (n 17); UN Approach to Transitional Justice (n 82). For the relationship of transitional justice and informal justice, see McAuliffe, *Transitional Justice and Rule of Law Reconstruction* (n 166).

3

The Birth of Transitional Justice

Emergence

I INTRODUCTION

In 1979, a group of scholars met at the Graduate Center of the City University of New York to discuss how emerging democracies dealt with the legacy of authoritarian regimes. The questions posed included what to do with the perpetrators and collaborators of the previous regime, how to rehabilitate their victims and how to build a democratic system.[1] The papers presented examined different mechanisms implemented in relation to these questions: criminal trials, vetting of officials, reparations for victims, institutional reform, official apologies and education reform.[2] The convenor of the meetings, John Herz, had advocated for the collective and systematic study of post-dictatorial policies with the purpose of developing a team of experts who would 'stand ready to advise policymakers in countries that emerge from the trauma of dictatorship'.[3]

This project was a pioneer of transitional justice discourse. It examined the same dilemmas and engaged with the same mechanisms. Indeed, Herz's book has been retrospectively called 'the first book to concentrate specifically on the topic of transitional justice'.[4] However, this effort failed to spark a systematic

[1] John H Herz, 'Introduction: Method and Boundaries' in John H Herz (ed), *From Dictatorship to Democracy: Coping with the Legacies of Authoritarianism and Totalitarianism* (Greenwood, 1982) 7–10.

[2] John H Herz, *From Dictatorship to Democracy: Coping with the Legacies of Authoritarianism and Totalitarianism* (Greenwood, 1982).

[3] John H Herz, 'On Reestablishing Democracy after the Downfall of Authoritarian or Dictatorial Regimes' (1978) 10 *Comparative Politics* 559, 562.

[4] Alexandra Barahona de Brito, Carmen González Enríquez and Paloma Aguilar Fernández, 'Bibliographical Survey' in Alexandra Barahona de Brito, Carmen González Enríquez and Paloma Aguilar Fernández (eds), *The Politics of Memory: Transitional Justice in Democratizing Societies* (Oxford University Press, 2001) 316.

discourse, and the volume that resulted from the meetings remains its only enduring legacy. The community of experts ready to advise policymakers did not materialise. Herz's project was indeed pioneering, but it was also inconsequential.

Fast-forward to 2004 and Herz's idea had come to fruition. The United Nations (UN) Secretary-General report 'The Rule of Law and Transitional Justice in Conflict and Post-Conflict Societies' (2004 UNSG Transitional Justice Report) sought to compile the lessons learned by the organisation's experts in the task of helping societies re-establish the rule of law and come to terms with past large-scale abuses.[5] This document also engaged with prosecutions, reparations, institutional reform and vetting of officials. By 2004, the existence of a well-established discourse of transitional justice dealing with the problems discussed in the 1979 meetings was also evidenced by the existence of dedicated international non-governmental organisations (NGOs), such as the International Center for Transitional Justice (ICTJ, founded in 2001),[6] research centres such as the Transitional Justice Institute of the University of Ulster (established in 2003),[7] and numerous books and articles.

The emergence of the discourse of transitional justice has to be historically located between 1979, when John Herz's meetings were held, and 2004, when the UNSG Transitional Justice Report demonstrated the existence of an established discourse. Within this time span, four fundamental events shaped the appearance and development of transitional justice discourse. In 1983, the dictatorship that had ruled Argentina since 1976 came to an end, in the opening act of a series of democratic transitions in Latin America. The new democratic government established a truth commission to investigate enforced disappearances during the dictatorship and sought to prosecute military leaders. In 1989, the Berlin Wall came down, and within months the Soviet Bloc unravelled. The former communist countries of Eastern Europe implemented a series of policies to respond to the legacy of communism. In 1993, the UN Security Council created the International Criminal Tribunal for the former Yugoslavia (ICTY), thus starting a process of development of international criminal justice that culminated with the establishment of the International Criminal Court (ICC) in 2002. In 1995,

5 UNSC 'Report of the Secretary-General on the Rule of Law and Transitional Justice in Conflict and Post-Conflict Societies' (23 August 2004) UN Doc S/2004/616 (2004) (2004 UNSG Transitional Justice Report).

6 Priscilla Hayner, 'International Center for Transitional Justice (ICTJ)' in David Forsythe (ed), *Encyclopedia of Human Rights* (Oxford University Press, 2009).

7 Transitional Justice Institute, 'About' (2016) www.ulster.ac.uk/research-and-innovation/research-institutes/transitional-justice-institute/about, accessed 30 July 2018.

following the end of apartheid, the newly democratic South African parliament created the innovative Truth and Reconciliation Commission (SATRC) to examine the human rights violations of the predecessor regime.

These four events are widely regarded as formative for the emergence and development of transitional justice discourse.[8] As Phil Clark and Nicola Palmer note, Latin America, Eastern Europe and South Africa were the initial sites of transitional justice scholarship and practice, and as such they profoundly shaped the development of the discourse.[9] Despite the prominence of these events, there has not been a systematic exploration of the role that each of these events had in the emergence and development of the discourse.

This chapter follows the process of emergence of the discourse of transitional justice through the Argentine experience, the wave of Eastern European transitions, the rise of international criminal justice and the work of the SATRC. It assesses the specific contribution of each event to transitional justice. The chapter demonstrates that the current characteristics of the discourse stem from its emergence under the influence of these four events.

In order to develop this argument, the first section examines the accountability process that followed the election of the democratic government in Argentina in 1983 and its later influence on transitional justice discourse. Due to the extent of the dictatorship's violence, the ambitious scope of the accountability policy of the successor government and the difficulties it encountered, Argentina's transition became the most influential of the Latin

8 Juan E Méndez, 'Latin American Experiences of Accountability' in Ifi Amadiume and Abdullahi Ahmed An-Na'im (eds), *The Politics of Memory: Truth, Healing, and Social Justice* (ZED Books, 2000) 135; Alexandra Barahona de Brito, Carmen González Enríquez and Paloma Aguilar Fernández, 'Introduction' in Alexandra Barahona de Brito, Carmen González Enríquez and Paloma Aguilar Fernández (eds), *The Politics of Memory: Transitional Justice in Democratizing Societies* (Oxford University Press, 2001) 4–11; Brian Grodsky, 'Re-Ordering Justice: Towards a New Methodological Approach to Studying Transitional Justice' (2009) 46 *Journal of Peace Research* 819, 819; Pádraig McAuliffe, 'From Molehills to Mountains (and Myths?): A Critical History of Transitional Justice Advocacy' (2011) 22 *Finnish Yearbook of International Law* 1, 18–46; Ahmad Nader Nadery, 'Editorial Note: In the Aftermath of International Intervention: A New Era for Transitional Justice?' (2011) 5 *International Journal of Transitional Justice* 171, 173; Jennifer Balint, Julie Evans and Nesam McMillan, 'Rethinking Transitional Justice, Redressing Indigenous Harm: A New Conceptual Approach' (2014) 8 *International Journal of Transitional Justice* 194, 200; Susanne Buckley-Zistel and others, 'Transitional Justice Theories: An Introduction' in Susanne Buckley-Zistel and others (eds), *Transitional Justice Theories* (Routledge, 2014) 1.

9 Phil Clark and Nicola Palmer, 'Challenging Transitional Justice' in Nicola Palmer, Phil Clark and Danielle Granville (eds), *Critical Perspectives in Transitional Justice* (Intersentia, 2012) 15.

American transitions to democracy of the 1980s. The second section explains how the transitions in Eastern Europe following the collapse of the Soviet Bloc gave a sense of purpose to initial discussions on transitional justice. The third section discusses the rise of international criminal justice and the impact that it had on the development of the discourse. The fourth section turns to the SATRC and its role in transforming the tone and scope of transitional justice discourse.

II THE INFLUENCE OF THE ARGENTINE EXPERIENCE

Raúl Alfonsín was sworn president of Argentina on 10 December 1983, bringing to an end seven years of military rule.[10] He had unexpectedly defeated Peronist candidate Italo Luder, whose party had never lost a national election before, on a platform of respect for human rights and prosecutions for military and guerrilla leaders.[11] While Argentina had experienced dictatorships in the past, the series of military juntas that were in power between 1976 and 1983 had carried out a brutal plan to eradicate subversion that targeted anybody with left-leaning views.[12] The tactics employed during this period had included abductions, clandestine detention, systematic torture, enforced disappearances and summary executions.[13] After suffering a humiliating military defeat against the United Kingdom in the 1982 Malvinas/Falklands War, the junta had lost all credibility and had decided to call for democratic elections that Alfonsín won.[14]

[10] Marcos Novaro, *Historia de la Argentina: 1955–2010* (Siglo Veintiuno Editores, 2010) 195.

[11] Alison Brysk, *The Politics of Human Rights in Argentina: Protest, Change, and Democratization* (Stanford University Press, 1994) 62; Yossi Shain, Juan José Linz and Lynn Berat, *Between States: Interim Governments and Democratic Transitions* (Cambridge University Press, 1995) 58. See also Pablo Giussani and Raúl Alfonsín, *¿Por Qué, Doctor Alfonsín?* (Sudamericana/Planeta, 1987) 15–19.

[12] David Pion-Berlin, 'The National Security Doctrine, Military Threat Perception, and the "Dirty War" in Argentina' (1988) 21 Comparative Political Studies 382, 385. See also David Rock, *Argentina 1516–1982: From Spanish Colonization to the Falklands War* (Tauris, 1986) 367–405; Eduardo Anguita and Martín Caparrós, *La Voluntad: Una Historia de la Militancia Revolucionaria en la Argentina* (3rd edn, Grupo Editorial Norma, 1997).

[13] See Jaime Malamud Goti, 'Game without End: State Terror and the Politics of Justice' (University of Oklahoma Press, 1996); Marguerite Feitlowitz, *A Lexicon of Terror: Argentina and the Legacies of Torture* (Oxford University Press 1998); Paul H Lewis, *Guerrillas and Generals: The 'Dirty War' in Argentina* (Praeger, 2002).

[14] David Pion-Berlin, 'The Fall of Military Rule in Argentina: 1976–1983' (1985) 27 *Journal of Interamerican Studies and World Affairs* 55, 56. See also Juan Bautista Yofre, *Fuimos Todos: Cronología de un Fracaso, 1976–1983* (3rd edn, Sudamericana, 2007).

Within days of assuming power, President Alfonsín passed legislation to implement his policy to respond to the violence of the previous regime.[15] Decree 157 provided for the prosecution of the guerrilla leaders, Decree 158 for the prosecution of the junta generals and Decree 187 established an independent commission to investigate enforced disappearances and the abduction of children.[16] The National Commission on the Disappearance of People (Spanish acronym CONADEP) numbered among its members prominent writers, scientists, journalists, religious leaders and politicians.[17] The CONADEP compiled thousands of pages of testimony, visited detention centres and examined prison and police records.[18] After nine months of work, the CONADEP submitted its final report to President Alfonsín on 20 September 1984.[19] It estimated 8,960 enforced disappearances and 380 illegal detention centres.[20] The evidence it gathered was crucial for the later trials.[21]

Prosecuting those responsible for the violence would prove to be more difficult. Initially, Alfonsín's government wanted to have the junta leaders tried by the supreme military tribunal to allow the armed forces to purge themselves and regain legitimacy.[22] But when the supreme military tribunal

[15] Carlos Nino, *Radical Evil on Trial* (Yale University Press, 1996) 71. For a review of Alfonsín's human rights' policy, see Carlos Nino, 'The Human Rights Policy of the Argentine Constitutional Government: A Reply (Mignone, Estlund & Issacharoff, "Dictatorship on Trial: Prosecution of Human Rights Violations in Argentina," 10 *Yale J. Int'l L.* 118, 1984)' (1985) 11 *The Yale Journal of International Law* 217.

[16] Decreto 157/83 13 December 1983; Decreto 158/83 13 December 1983; Decreto 187/83 15 December 1983.

[17] Emilio Crenzel, 'Argentina's National Commission on the Disappearance of Persons: Contributions to Transitional Justice' (2008) 2 *The International Journal of Transitional Justice* 173, 178–79.

[18] Comisión Nacional sobre la Desaparición de Personas CONADEP, *Nunca Mas:(Never Again): A Report* (Faber in association with Index on Censorship, 1986).

[19] Nino, *Radical Evil on Trial* 80 (n 15). See also Emilio A Crenzel, *Memory of the Argentina Disappearances the Political History of Nunca Más* (Routledge, 2012).

[20] CONADEP, *Nunca Mas* 447 (n 18). Some sources say the number of disappeared was much higher, see Alison Brysk, 'The Politics of Measurement: The Contested Count of the Disappeared in Argentina' (1994) 16 *Human Rights Quarterly* 676. However, according to the latest official records of the Argentine Human Rights Secretariat, there were 7,018 victims of enforced disappearances and 1,613 of extrajudicial killings, Secretaría de Derechos Humanos, 'Informe de Investigación sobre Víctimas de Desaparición Forzada y Asesinato, por el Accionar Represivo del Estado y Centros Clandestinos de Detención y otros Lugares de Reclusión Clandestina' (November 2015) 9.

[21] Crenzel, 'Argentina's National Commission on the Disappearance of Persons' (n 17). See also Emilio Crenzel, 'Between the Voices of the State and the Human Rights Movement: Never Again and the Memories of the Disappeared in Argentina' (2011) 44 *Journal of Social History* 1063.

[22] Malamud Goti, 'Game without End' 60 (n 13); Nino, *Radical Evil on Trial* 67–68 (n 15); Decreto 158/83 (n 16).

found that there was no wrongdoing to prosecute, the government referred the cases to the civilian courts.[23] On 9 December 1985, the Federal Criminal Court of Appeals of Buenos Aires convicted five junta leaders of serious crimes under the Argentine Penal Code, including murder, torture and illegal detention.[24] More military perpetrators and some guerrilla leaders were convicted in subsequent trials.[25] While the government wanted to limit the prosecutions to the most senior figures and those who had exceeded their orders,[26] under Argentine law civil parties could initiate criminal proceedings.[27] Since the Penal Procedure Code obliged prosecutors to investigate every single crime,[28] the number of cases skyrocketed as human rights organisations kept bringing new files.[29]

The unintended spread of prosecutions sparked discontent among younger military officers who feared finding themselves in the dock. They staged military uprisings in April 1987, January 1988 and December 1988.[30] These coup attempts were defused through intense negotiation and with the support of troops loyal to the government.[31] To placate the military, the government passed what were later called 'impunity laws'. The 'Full Stop Law' provided

[23] Nino, *Radical Evil on Trial* 78 (n 15); David Pion-Berlin, *Through Corridors of Power: Institutions and Civil-Military Relations in Argentina* (Pennsylvania State University Press, 1997) 82.

[24] *Videla, Jorge Rafael y otros* (Sentencia) Causa 13/84 (9 December 1985) (Federal Criminal Court of Appeals of Buenos Aires). On 30 December 1986, the Federal Supreme Court of Justice confirmed almost all aspects of the appellate court's judgment, *Videla, Jorge Rafael y otros* (Fallo) Causa 13/84 (30 December 1986). For a well-documented contemporaneous account of the trial, see Jorge A Camarasa, Rubén Felice and Daniel González, *El Juicio: Proceso al Horror* (Sudamericana/Planeta, 1985).

[25] See, eg, *Camps, Ramón Juan Alberto y otros* (Sentencia) Causa 44 (2 December 1986) (Federal Criminal Court of Appeals of Buenos Aires); *Obregón Cano, Ricardo Armando* (Apelación) Causa 4230 (29 May 1986) (Federal Criminal Court of Appeals of Buenos Aires); *Firmenich, Mario Eduardo* (Apelación) DJ 1989-2-68 (14 September 1988) (Federal Criminal Court of Appeals of San Martín).

[26] Giussani and Alfonsín, *¿Por Qué, Doctor Alfonsín?* (n 11) 240; Raúl Alfonsín, '"Never Again" in Argentina' (1993) 4 *Journal of Democracy* 15, 17; Malamud Goti, 'Game without End' 60 (n 14).

[27] Ley 2372 Código de Procedimiento Penal (Criminal Procedure Code) 4 October 1888, arts 14; 155; 170.

[28] Ibid, arts 14; 118; 164; 169.

[29] For a contrast of the legal strategies and motivations of the government, the military and human rights organisations, see Mark Osiel, 'The Making of Human Rights Policy in Argentina: The Impact of Ideas and Interests on a Legal Conflict' (1986) 18 *Journal of Latin American Studies* 135.

[30] Deborah Lee Norden, *Military Rebellion in Argentina: Between Coups and Consolidation* (University of Nebraska Press, 1996), chs 5–6.

[31] For President Alfonsín's account of these events, see Giussani and Alfonsín, *¿Por Qué, Doctor Alfonsín?* 242–71, (n 11).

for the termination of all criminal cases related to political violence during the dictatorship whose perpetrators had not been indicted yet.[32] However, by imposing a 60-day deadline, the law caused a rush to file new cases that increased military unrest.[33] The subsequent 'Due Obedience Law' established an unrebuttable presumption that servicemen below the rank of colonel had acted under duress and could not be punished.[34] The president who succeeded Alfonsín – Carlos Menem – pardoned those still in prison, including the junta leaders, in October 1989 and December 1990.[35]

The presidential pardons ended this initial period of accountability for past widespread or systematic violence in Argentina. Instead of trials, the government of President Menem introduced reparation programmes for victims of illegal detention and enforced disappearances.[36] Yet, in 2005, the 'impunity laws' were annulled and a second wave of prosecutions began.[37] As of December 2017, the Argentine civilian courts have indicted 3,123 people for crimes against humanity and have convicted 864.[38]

Other countries in Latin America grappled with similar issues in the 1980s and early 1990s. Autocratic regimes were in power in most countries in the region during the 1970s and well into the 1980s.[39] As these countries underwent democratisation processes, the incoming governments also had to deal

[32] Ley 23492 Extinción de Acciones Penales a Fuerzas Armadas (Extinction of Prosecutions to Armed Forces) 24 December 1986, arts 1–2. See also Jaime Malamud Goti, 'Transitional Governments in the Breach: Why Punish State Criminals?' (1990) 12 *Human Rights Quarterly*.

[33] Nino, *Radical Evil on Trial* 93 (n 15); Ley 23492, art 1 (n 32); Alejandro M Garro, 'Nine Years of Transition to Democracy in Argentina: Partial Failure or Qualified Success?' (1993) 31 *Columbia Journal of Transnational Law* 1, 15.

[34] Ley 23521 Delimita Alcances del Deber de Obediencia Debida (Precises Scope of Due Obedience Duty) 9 June 1987, art 1.

[35] Nino, *Radical Evil on Trial*, 103–4 (n 15); Garro, 'Nine Years of Transition to Democracy in Argentina' 17 (n 33); Francesca Lessa, 'Beyond Transitional Justice: Exploring Continuities in Human Rights Abuses in Argentina between 1976 and 2010' (2011) 3 *Journal of Human Rights Practice* 25.

[36] Ley 24043 Indemnizaciones (Compensation) 2 January 1992; Ley 24411 Desaparición de Personas (Enforced Disappearances) 3 January 1995. For the reaction of the victims to the reparations, see Claire Moon, '"Who'll Pay Reparations on My Soul?" Compensation, Social Control and Social Suffering' (2012) 21 *Social & Legal Studies* 187.

[37] *Simón, Julio Héctor y otros* (Fallo) LL 2005-2-2056 (14 June 2005) (Federal Supreme Court of Justice). See also Margarita O'Donnell, 'New Dirty War Judgments in Argentina: National Courts and Domestic Prosecutions of International Human Rights Violations' (2009) 84 *New York University Law Review*.

[38] CELS, 'Proceso de Justicia: Estadísticas' (2018) www.cels.org.ar/web/estadisticas-delitos-de-lesa-humanidad/, accessed 16 May 2018.

[39] Elin Skaar, Jemima García-Godos and Cath Collins, 'Introduction: The Accountability Challenge' in Elin Skaar, Jemima García-Godos and Cath Collins (eds), *Transitional Justice in Latin America: The Uneven Road from Impunity towards Accountability* (Routledge, 2016) 8.

with the legacy of abuses of the previous regimes. Bolivia's democratic transition took place in 1982,[40] Uruguay's and Brazil's in 1985,[41] Chile's in 1990[42] and Paraguay's in 1992.[43] At the same time, internationally brokered peace processes ended internal armed conflicts in El Salvador (1992)[44] and Guatemala (1996).[45]

All the new democratic governments of these countries adopted different policies to respond to past abuses. Many of them enacted formal or informal amnesties.[46] Truth commissions like CONADEP were established in Bolivia (1982),[47] Uruguay (1985),[48] Chile (1990),[49] El Salvador (1991)[50] and Guatemala (1997).[51] Reparations measures were implemented in Uruguay, Chile, El Salvador, Paraguay, Guatemala and Brazil.[52] However, no other country followed Argentina's example of carrying out extensive prosecutions in the immediate aftermath of the transition. The only other Latin American

40 René Antonio Mayorga, 'Democracy Dignified and an End to Impunity: Bolivia's Military Dictatorship on Trial' in A James McAdams (ed), *Transitional Justice and the Rule of Law in New Democracies* (University of Notre Dame Press, 1997).

41 Alexandra Barahona de Brito, 'Truth and Justice in the Consolidation of Democracy in Chile and Uruguay' (1993) 46 *Parliamentary Affairs* 579; Glenda Mezarobba, 'Brazil: The Tortuous Path to Truth and Justice', in Elin Skaar, Jemima García-Godos and Cath Collins (eds), *Transitional Justice in Latin America: The Uneven Road from Impunity towards Accountability* (Routledge, 2016).

42 Luis Roniger and Mario Sznajder, *The Legacy of Human-Rights Violations in the Southern Cone: Argentina, Chile, and Uruguay* (Oxford University Press, 1999).

43 Cath Collins, 'Paraguay: Accountability in the Shadow of Stroessner' in Elin Skaar, Jemima García-Godos and Cath Collins (eds), *Transitional Justice in Latin America: The Uneven Road from Impunity towards Accountability* (Routledge, 2016).

44 Elena Martínez Barahona and Martha Liliana Gutiérrez Salazar, 'El Salvador: The Difficult Fight against Impunity' in Elin Skaar, Jemima García-Godos and Cath Collins (eds), *Transitional Justice in Latin America: The Uneven Road from Impunity towards Accountability* (Routledge, 2016).

45 Anita Isaacs, 'At War with the Past? The Politics of Truth Seeking in Guatemala' (2010) 4 *International Journal of Transitional Justice* 251.

46 There were amnesties in Peru, Chile, El Salvador, Uruguay, Brazil, Guatemala, see Elin Skaar, Jemima García-Godos and Cath Collins (eds), *Transitional Justice in Latin America: The Uneven Road from Impunity towards Accountability* (Routledge, 2016).

47 Priscilla Hayner, *Unspeakable Truths: Confronting State Terror and Atrocity* (Routledge, 2001) 52.

48 Ibid 53.

49 'Truth Commissions for Chile and El Salvador: A Report and Assessment' (1994) 16 *Human Rights Quarterly* 656.

50 Ibid.

51 Hayner, *Unspeakable Truths* 45 (n 47).

52 Elin Skaar, Jemima García-Godos and Cath Collins, 'Conclusions: The Uneven Road towards Accountability in Latin America' in Elin Skaar, Jemima García-Godos and Cath Collins (eds), *Transitional Justice in Latin America: The Uneven Road from Impunity towards Accountability* (Routledge, 2016) 290.

country that prosecuted a former dictator in the 1980s was Bolivia, where General Luis García Meza and some of his collaborators were tried in a trial that lasted from 1986 to 1993. García Meza was convicted in absentia of 36 counts, including genocide.[53] In other countries, such as Chile, Guatemala, Peru and Uruguay, trials for the crimes of the authoritarian regimes would not take place until the 2000s.[54]

The pioneer Argentine experience during the 1980s of a wide-ranging programme of prosecutions and a truth-finding commission would prove to be very influential for the discourse of transitional justice. In order to understand the role that the Argentine transition had in the appearance of the discourse of transitional justice, it is necessary to examine the discursive panorama before and after the Argentine experience.

1 *Discursive Echo*

Before the Argentine experience, there was not an autonomous discourse of transitional justice – that is, an independent discourse structured around the objects and concepts discussed in the previous chapter. The term 'transitional justice' did not exist at the time.[55] Irrespective of the label, in 1983 there was no common corpus of knowledge about responses to past widespread or systematic violence. There were some isolated books that examined similar issues, mostly related to World War II, but they did not form a distinct field.[56] Merely five years before the Argentine transition, John Herz had lamented the absence of a systematic study of post-dictatorial policies to advise policymakers.[57] Despite the meetings that Herz convened for that purpose and the book with comparative lessons they produced, President Alfonsín and his legal advisors thought that they were treading uncharted territory when designing

[53] The Bolivian Supreme Court relied on a rather lax understanding of genocide as the destruction of a group of politicians and intellectuals; in the case in question, the extrajudicial killing by paramilitary forces of eight political activists, Garcia Meza, Luis y otros (Sentencia) 21 April 1993 (Supreme Court of Justice). See also Mayorga, 'Democracy Dignified and an End to Impunity' (n 40).

[54] Elin Skaar, Jemima García-Godos and Cath Collins, *Transitional Justice in Latin America* (n 46). See also Cath Collins, *Post-Transitional Justice: Human Rights Trials in Chile and El Salvador* (Pennsylvania State University Press, 2010).

[55] Paige Arthur, 'How "Transitions" Reshaped Human Rights: A Conceptual History of Transitional Justice' (2009) 31 *Human Rights Quarterly* 321, 327–30.

[56] See, eg, Otto Kirchheimer, *Political Justice: The Use of Legal Procedure for Political Ends* (Princeton University Press, 1961); Hannah Arendt, *Eichmann in Jerusalem: A Report on the Banality of Evil* (Viking Press, 1964).

[57] Herz, 'On Reestablishing Democracy after the Downfall of Authoritarian or Dictatorial Regimes' (n 3).

their policy to respond to the violence of the previous regime.[58] President Alfonsín afterwards claimed that in 1983 he was not aware of the trial of former military leaders in Greece in 1975.[59] The distant and vastly different Nuremberg trial was the example from which they sought inspiration.[60] Furthermore, the Argentine government elaborated and implemented its policy to respond to the repression of the military regime without the support or advice of international experts. The only foreign scholars who were in any way involved were a group of lawyers and philosophers – including Ronald Dworkin – invited by the government to attend the junta trial.[61]

The discourse of transitional justice did not follow on the heels of the Argentine transition either. An analysis of the discursive resonance that the experience of the investigative commission and the criminal trials generated until 1990 shows that there was not a distinct discourse of transitional justice. The Argentine experiences received significant attention from journalists, area study specialists in South America, lawyers and comparative political scientists. Their analyses, however, remained isolated and fragmented. Argentine and foreign journalists exposed details of the dictatorship and the transition.[62] Specialists on South America examined the roles of the military and the human rights movement.[63] Lawyers commented on legal questions surrounding the trials such as command responsibility,[64] due obedience[65] and the

[58] Interview with Jaime Malamud Goti, legal advisor to President Alfonsín (Buenos Aires, 25 September 2013).

[59] Neil J Kritz, 'The Dilemmas of Transitional Justice' in Neil J Kritz (ed), *Transitional Justice: How Emerging Democracies Reckon with Former Regimes* (United States Institute of Peace Press, 1995) xx.

[60] Interview with Jaime Malamud Goti (n 58).

[61] Owen Fiss, 'The Death of a Public Intellectual' (1995) 104 *The Yale Law Journal* 1187, 1188.

[62] Andrew Graham-Yooll, 'Argentina: The State of Transition 1983–85' (1985) 7 *Third World Quarterly* 573; Horacio Verbitsky, *La Posguerra Sucia: Un Análisis de la Transición* (Editorial Legasa, 1985); Horacio Verbitsky, *Civilians and Military Men: Secret Report of the Transition* (1987); Iain Guest, *Behind the Disappearances: Argentina's Dirty War against Human Rights and the United Nations* (University of Pennsylvania Press, 1990); Martin Edwin Andersen, *Dossier Secreto: Argentina's Desaparecidos and the Myth of the 'Dirty War'* (Westview Press, 1993).

[63] Pion-Berlin, 'The National Security Doctrine, Military Threat Perception, and the "Dirty War" in Argentina' (n 13); Alison Brysk, 'The Political Impact of Argentina's Human Rights Movement: Social Movements, Transition and Democratization' (Stanford University, 1990); Pablo Azcárate and Elizabeth Jelin, 'Memoria y Política: Movimientos de Derechos Humanos y Construcción Democrática' (1991) 1 *América Latina Hoy: Revista de Ciencias Sociales* 29.

[64] Paula Speck, 'The Trial of the Argentine Junta: Responsibilities and Realities' (1987) 18 *University of Miami Inter-American Law Review* 491.

[65] Alejandro M Garro and Henry Dahl, 'Legal Accountability for Human Rights Violations in Argentina: One Step Forward and Two Steps Backward' (1987) 8 *Human Rights Law Journal* 283.

constitutionality of relying on military courts.[66] The legal analyses mostly focused on Argentine domestic law, but they occasionally touched upon questions of international law. Often these lawyers had participated in the transitional process – either as human rights activists, such as Emilio Mignone, or as government officials, as was the case of President Alfonsín's advisors Carlos Nino and Jaime Malamud Goti. Comparative political scientists approached the Argentine experience as part of a larger wave of transitions to democracy that stretched back to the 1970s. For them, Argentina was an example of a 'transition by collapse' where the defeat in the Malvinas/Falklands War had enabled the prosecution of military leaders.[67] Each group examined the Argentine experience from within their disciplinary boundaries, and there was no effort to bring them together.

As more states in the region went through democratisation processes, the isolation of the different disciplines interested in the Argentine experience became less marked. States such as Uruguay and Chile were going through similar problems to those experienced by Argentina earlier. This underscored the possible usefulness of sharing and organising knowledge on how to confront the legacy of widespread or systematic violence. The interaction between people interested in human rights in Latin American countries was facilitated by the international networks that had been in operation since the dictatorships: shared exile and advocacy in international forums had fostered contacts between human rights activists and scholars across South America.[68] The case of Argentina featured heavily in these discussions.

The increasing number of transitions spurred two types of interaction: comparative and multidisciplinary. Analysts who had been working on the Argentine case became interested in the experiences of other states. For example, lawyer Carlos Nino, whose research at first was exclusively

66 Emilio Fermin Mignone, Cynthia Estlund and Samuel Issacharoff, 'Dictatorship on Trial: Prosecution of Human Rights Violations in Argentina' (1984) 10 *The Yale Journal of International Law* 118.

67 Samuel P Huntington, 'Will More Countries Become Democratic?' (1984) 99 *Political Science Quarterly* 193; Scott Mainwaring and Eduardo J Viola, 'Transitions to Democracy: Brazil and Argentina in the 1980s' (1985) 38 *Journal of International Affairs* 193; Guillermo O'Donnell, Philippe C Schmitter and Laurence Whitehead, *Transitions from Authoritarian Rule: Latin America* (Johns Hopkins University Press, 1986); Charles G Gillespie, 'Models of Democratic Transition in South America: Negotiated Reform versus Democratic Rupture' in Diane Ethier (ed), *Democratic Transition and Consolidation in Southern Europe, Latin America and Southeast Asia* (Macmillan, 1990); Samuel P Huntington, *The Third Wave: Democratization in the Late Twentieth Century* (University of Oklahoma Press, 1991).

68 Margaret E Keck and Kathryn Sikkink, *Activists beyond Borders: Advocacy Networks in International Politics* (Cornell University Press, 1998) 90–120. See also Brysk, *The Politics of Human Rights in Argentina* (n 11).

concerned with Argentina, went on to develop comparative approaches.[69] Equally, South America expert David Pion-Berlin shifted from a narrow focus on the Argentine military[70] to writing about transitions in South America.[71] The other type of interaction, across disciplinary boundaries, sought to bring together different perspectives on the common object of responding to past widespread or systematic violence.

An example of the comparative and interdisciplinary trend belatedly inspired by the Argentine experience was a conference held in Maryland in November 1988 with the title 'State Crimes: Punishment or Pardon?' This event, which was organised by the Aspen Institute, gathered people interested in the problem of confronting the human rights violations of a prior regime. The participants included lawyers, journalists, human rights activists, philosophers and political scientists.[72] The meeting was international with participants from Chile, Argentina, the United States, Haiti, Guatemala, Uganda, Brazil, South Korea, Uruguay and South Africa.[73] The delegates discussed different cases of transitions and compared the policies adopted.[74] The events in Argentina, where the 'impunity laws' had recently been passed, influenced the conference.[75] Of the three papers commissioned ahead of the meeting, two drew heavily from the Argentine experience.[76] Argentina was represented by Jaime Malamud Goti as well as human rights activist and lawyer Juan Méndez. Legal scholar Ronald Dworkin and philosopher Thomas Nagel, who had attended the junta trials in 1985, were also present.[77]

69 Compare Nino, 'The Human Rights Policy of the Argentine Constitutional Government' (n 15) with Nino, *Radical Evil on Trial* (n 15).

70 Pion-Berlin, 'The National Security Doctrine, Military Threat Perception, and the "Dirty War" in Argentina' (n 12).

71 David Pion-Berlin, 'To Prosecute or to Pardon? Human Rights Decisions in the Latin American Southern Cone' (1994) 16 *Human Rights Quarterly* 105.

72 Alice H Henkin, 'Conference Report', *State Crimes: Punishment or Pardon* (The Aspen Institute, 1989) 1.

73 Arthur, 'How "Transitions" Reshaped Human Rights' 364–67 (n 55).

74 Henkin, 'Conference Report' 2–6 (n 72).

75 McAuliffe, 'From Molehills to Mountains (and Myths?)' 22 (n 8).

76 Jose Zalaquett, 'Confronting Human Rights Violations Committed by Former Governments: Principles Applicable and Political Constraints', *State Crimes: Punishment or Pardon: Papers and Report of the Conference, November 4–6, 1988, Wye Center, Maryland* (The Aspen Institute, 1989); Jaime Malamud Goti, 'Trying Violators of Human Rights: The Dilemma of Transitional Democratic Governments', *State Crimes: Punishment or Pardon: Papers and Report of the Conference, November 4–6, 1988, Wye Center, Maryland* (The Aspen Institute, 1989).

77 The Aspen Institute, *State Crimes: Punishment or Pardon: Papers and Report of the Conference, November 4–6, 1988, Wye Center, Maryland* (The Aspen Institute, 1989) 95–96.

Paige Arthur has argued that the Aspen Institute conference represented an influential landmark for the development of transitional justice. For her, themes which later would be central in the discourse were discussed there, and key figures of that discourse attended.[78] While this is certainly true, the importance of this conference was not so much due to what happened then and there but due to what followed afterwards. Unlike the meetings organised by John Herz in 1979, the 1988 Aspen Institute conference did have a follow-up. During the Aspen Institute conference, the participants stressed that the event was only a beginning.[79] They were right in that.

While this conference signalled the starting point for multidisciplinary and comparative discussions on transitional justice, it also marked the end of a period. The presidential pardons of 1989–1990 would soon bring to a painful close Argentina's first attempt at dealing with its past. More importantly, the simultaneous end of the Cold War would redefine the global political landscape.

2 *Shaping the Future*

With time, the case of Argentina would prove to be very influential for transitional justice. Although it failed to spark an autonomous discourse, the Argentine transition later became a regular point of reference for transitional justice scholars and practitioners. The Argentine case stood out among other contemporary experiences in Latin America because of the extent and egregiousness of the dictatorship's crimes, the fact that it was one of the earliest democratic transitions and, above all, the dangers of attempting to prosecute members of the former regime.

Argentina's ambitious programme of prosecutions derailed by military pressure sowed the seed of the classic transitional justice debate known as 'peace versus justice'. The question of whether the need to ensure peaceful stability should have primacy over calls for accountability became a dominant theme in the discourse of transitional justice.[80] The Argentine case became the

[78] Arthur, 'How "Transitions" Reshaped Human Rights' 349–55 (n 55).

[79] Henkin, 'Conference Report' 8 (n 72).

[80] See, eg, Miriam J Aukerman, 'Extraordinary Evil, Ordinary Crime: A Framework for Understanding Transitional Justice' (2002) 15 *Harvard Human Rights Journal* 39; Naomi Roht-Arriaza and Javier Mariezcurrena, *Transitional Justice in the Twenty-First Century: Beyond Truth versus Justice* (Cambridge University Press, 2006); Louise Mallinder, 'Can Amnesties and International Justice Be Reconciled?' (2007) 1 *International Journal of Transitional Justice* 208; Chandra Lekha Sriram and Suren Pillay, *Peace versus Justice? The Dilemma of Transitional Justice in Africa* (James Currey, 2010); David P Forsythe, 'Forum: Transitional Justice: The

paradigmatic example of the political risks of extensive prosecutions. Thus, when Diane Orentlicher argued for the existence of a duty under international law to carry out prosecutions for widespread human rights abuses, Carlos Nino replied – using the Argentine example – that the potential political repercussions of criminal trials had to be taken into account.[81] The absence of extensive prosecutions in the transitions to democracy of other countries in the region both underlined the relevance of the 'peace versus justice' debate and the importance of the Argentine experience as a cautionary tale.

The Argentine transition also influenced the discourse of transitional justice through the legacy of the CONADEP – considered the first successful truth commission – and the pioneering use in Argentina of forensic anthropology to examine victims' remains. The model of the CONADEP has been replicated in many other situations[82] and the Argentine Forensic Anthropology Team has worked in more than 30 countries.[83]

More importantly, the Argentine transition and the discussions that followed it presented some of the six characteristics which would later become central for the discourse of transitional justice. First, while the Argentine policymakers were only inspired by the Nuremberg trial, the later discussions evidenced an embryonic penchant for the comparative method. When more Latin American states experienced transitions, authors began to contrast different cases to seek to give advice to newly democratic states.

Second, the Argentine transition relied on technical knowledge. Legal experts designed the human rights policies with a view of attaining predetermined goals. The means later had to be adjusted when the military unrest threatened the stability of the democratic government. Although the Argentine experience was analysed from a variety of disciplinary perspectives, it is impossible to speak of a multidisciplinary discourse at that stage because these

Quest for Theory to Inform Policy' (2011) 13 *International Studies Review* 554; McAuliffe, 'From Molehills to Mountains (and Myths?)' (n 8); Dustin Sharp, 'Interrogating the Peripheries: The Preoccupations of Fourth Generation Transitional Justice' (2013) 26 *Harvard Human Rights Journal* 149.

81 Diane F Orentlicher, 'Settling Accounts: The Duty to Prosecute Human Rights Violations of a Prior Regime' (1991) 100 *The Yale Law Journal* 2537; Carlos Nino, 'The Duty to Punish Past Abuses of Human Rights Put into Context: The Case of Argentina' (1991) 100 *The Yale Law Journal* 2619.

82 Kathryn Sikkink, *The Justice Cascade: How Human Rights Prosecutions Are Changing World Politics* (WW Norton, 2011) 87.

83 Argentine Forensic Anthropology Team, 'EAAF Work by Region and Country' (2018) http://eaaf.typepad.com/eaaf_countries/, accessed 16 May 2018. For the general influence of Argentina in human rights, see Kathryn Sikkink, 'From Pariah State to Global Protagonist: Argentina and the Struggle for International Human Rights' (2008) 50 *Latin American Politics and Society* 1.

contributions remained isolated. In contrast, the legalistic dimension of the technical approach was prominent in Argentina. Law was the dominant technical knowledge used, and it appeared separated from the rest of the social world with its own logic and rules. Lawyers were prominent in the transitional process: President Alfonsín was a lawyer himself and designed the policy with fellow lawyers Nino and Malamud Goti.[84] The prosecution of the junta leaders was the mainstay of this policy. Legalism's influence was extended to the CONADEP, which was not allowed to trespass on the legal sphere. Its primary role was to gather evidence ahead of the trials, and its mandate expressly forbade it from expressing opinions over facts within the exclusive jurisdiction of the judiciary.[85] Even political considerations were justified using legal reasoning and concepts. For instance, Nino defended limiting prosecutions to those responsible for the most serious violations by reference to legal theories of punishment.[86]

The technical dimension of appearing apolitical was only partially present in the Argentine experience. On the one hand, the political debate about how to respond to past widespread or systematic violence was not curtailed by technical knowledge and experts. The electorate had voted for Alfonsín knowing that he had promised to prosecute those responsible for the violence and even the 'impunity laws' were passed after parliamentary debate.[87] Thus, technical knowledge did not crowd out political debate. On the other hand, the technical approach of the mechanisms did dilute the political nature of past violence. Both right-wing military and leftist guerrillas were judged using apolitical technical terms. The courts convicted the military and guerrilla leaders of similar crimes, and the prologue of the CONADEP's report presented a narrative about a terrorism of the left being met by a terrorism of the right.[88] President Alfonsín supported this narrative, known as the theory of the 'two devils', while the victims rejected it for equating the crimes of both parties, irrespective of their politics.[89] This narrative of the equivalence of the leadership of the military and the armed groups coexisted with one of individual victims as passive subjects devoid of any political agency.[90]

84 Fiss, 'The Death of a Public Intellectual' 1190–91 (n 61).
85 Decreto 187/83, art 2 (n 16).
86 Nino, 'The Human Rights Policy of the Argentine Constitutional Government' (n 15).
87 Nino, *Radical Evil on Trial* 65–66, 93–94, 100–01 (n 15).
88 Ernesto Sabato, 'Prologue', *Nunca Mas (Never Again): A Report* (Faber in association with Index on Censorship, 1986) 1.
89 See Alfonsín, '"Never Again" in Argentina' (n 26); Moon, '"Who"ll Pay Reparations on My Soul?' (n 36).
90 See CONADEP, *Nunca Mas* (n 18); Nino, *Radical Evil on Trial*, ch 2 (n 15).

Third, the Argentine case evidenced a teleological framework. The policies implemented to respond to past widespread or systematic violence sought to achieve a set of goals. The Alfonsín government justified the prosecutions and the CONADEP because they would contribute to the goals of accountability, stability, democracy and the rule of law.[91] According to President Alfonsín, the success of the policies implemented would 'ultimately depend on whether their consequences are socially beneficial'.[92] This illustrates the instrumental framework that underpinned the Argentine experience. Commentators also criticised the policies implemented in terms of their contribution to a set of goals. Human rights activist Emilio Mignone criticised President Alfonsín's policy of relying on the military courts for not being conducive to its stated aim of consolidating democracy and the rule of law.[93]

Fourth, the Argentine experience had a liberal imprint manifested in the three dimensions identified in the previous chapter. Both the CONADEP and the criminal trials focused on violations of civil and political rights and instances of physical violence, including enforced disappearances, murder, torture and illegal detention – the type of violence that characterises transitional justice discourse to this day. Neither of the mechanisms addressed socio-economic rights or structural violence. For instance, the complicity of corporate actors in the repression and the economic policy underpinning the military dictatorship were not examined during the transition. Only recently have these areas begun to be examined as part of Argentina's second attempt at transitional justice.[94]

Liberal democracy was the preferred destination for the transition upon which Argentina had embarked. Liberal democracy was conceived as a bulwark that would prevent the recurrence of abuses in the future. The President of the CONADEP, writer Ernesto Sábato, expressed this belief in the prologue to the commission's report where he concluded that

> only democracy … can save a people from horror on this scale, only democracy which can keep and safeguard the sacred, essential rights of man. Only with democracy will we be certain that NEVER AGAIN will events such as these … be repeated in our nation.[95]

[91] Giussani and Alfonsín, *¿Por Qué, Doctor Alfonsín?* 239–40 (n 11). See also Nino's defence of the policies in 'The Human Rights Policy of the Argentine Constitutional Government' (n 15).

[92] Alfonsín, '"Never Again" in Argentina' 18 (n 26).

[93] Mignone, Estlund and Issacharoff, 'Dictatorship on Trial' 143–44 (n 66).

[94] See Wolfgang Kaleck, 'International Criminal Law and Transnational Businesses: Cases from Argentina and Colombia' in Sabine Michalowski (ed), *Corporate Accountability in the Context of Transitional Justice* (Routledge, 2013); Bruno Nápoli, María Celeste Perosino and Walter Bosisio, *La Dictadura del Capital Financiero* (Ediciones Continente, 2015).

[95] Sabato, 'Prologue' 6 (n 88).

Consolidating democracy was so important that it took precedence over other social and political claims. President Alfonsín articulated this priority in his inauguration speech on 10 December 1983 when he said that with democracy 'you can eat, you can educate and you can cure'.[96] From this perspective, democracy enabled socio-economic rights (food, education and health) but also had to be established and consolidated first.

The Argentine transition was also liberal because it did not question capitalism. Although President Alfonsín afterwards recognised that the economic legacy of the dictatorship was as noxious to democracy as was authoritarianism,[97] his administration did not fundamentally change the economic policies carried out by the military. Indeed, there was continuity in terms of a liberal capitalist economic system.[98] The Argentine transition was liberal because all the policies that the Alfonsín government carried out to respond to the legacy of violence concentrated on the political sphere rather than on the economic sphere.

Fifth, in contrast with the discourse of transitional justice today, the Argentine experience was not multilevel. The mechanisms implemented were all national. The military and guerrilla leaders were convicted of common crimes under Argentine domestic law. The transitional policy only touched the international level insofar as the Alfonsín government signed and ratified international human rights treaties as part of its human rights policy.[99] In any case, the ensuing analyses concentrated on national strategies for responding to past widespread or systematic violence. The regional, international and local levels were largely absent.

Sixth, the discussions that followed the Argentine experience were state-centric because they concentrated on state-sponsored responses to past

[96] Raúl Alfonsín, 'Discurso de Asunción ante la Asamblea Legislativa' (Buenos Aires, 10 December 1983) www.parlamentario.com/noticia-68393.html, accessed 31 July 2018. See also Pablo Giussani, *Los Días de Alfonsín* (Legasa, 1986).

[97] Alfonsín, '"Never Again" in Argentina' 85 (n 26).

[98] See Nápoli, Perosino and Bosisio (n 94).

[99] International Covenant on Civil and Political Rights (adopted 16 December 1966 UNGA Resolution 2200A (XXI), entered into force 23 March 1976) 999 UNTS 171 (ICCPR), ratified by Argentina in 1986; International Covenant on Economic, Social and Cultural Rights (adopted 16 December 1966 UNGA Resolution 2200A (XXI), entered into force 3 January 1976) 993 UNTS 3 (ICESCR), ratified by Argentina in 1986; Convention on the Elimination of All Forms of Discrimination against Women (adopted 18 December 1979 UNGA Resolution 34/180, entered into force 3 September 1981) 1249 UNTS 13, ratified by Argentina in 1985; Convention against Torture and Other Cruel, Inhuman or Degrading Treatment or Punishment (adopted 10 December 1984 UNGA Resolution 39/46, entered into force 26 June 1987) 1465 UNTS 85, signed by Argentina in 1985 and ratified in 1986; American Convention on Human Rights (adopted 21 November 1969, entered into force 18 July 1978) 1144 UNTS 123, signed and ratified by Argentina in 1984.

widespread or systematic violence. The responses carried out independently by civil society did not receive much attention.[100] Although some scholars examined the role of human rights activists, they focused on the influence that they had on state policy rather than on their activity beyond the state.[101]

The responses to past authoritarian violence in other Latin American transitions also presented many of these characteristics. The Truth Commission of El Salvador was comparative as it expressly sought to derive lessons from its predecessors in Argentina and Chile.[102] The Uruguayan amnesty was teleological because it was justified as necessary for achieving the goal of completing the transition to democracy.[103] The protracted trial of General García Meza in Bolivia was legalistic and incipiently multilevel insofar as it relied on international law. All of the Latin American transitions to democracy in the 1980s and 1990s were liberal, giving pre-eminence to violations of civil and political rights, striving towards liberal democracy and fostering capitalism.

The Argentine experience was not immediately followed by an autonomous discourse of transitional justice. It nonetheless already presented many of the characteristics that would later mark the discourse. This influential experience helped to shape the discourse when it later emerged.

III EMERGING FROM THE DISAPPOINTMENT OF EASTERN EUROPE

During an interview in 1987, President Alfonsín was asked about the prospects for change in the Soviet Union. He replied that the economic reforms

[100] For instance, the group of victims Madres de Plaza de Mayo (Mothers of Plaza de Mayo) held weekly silent marches to ask for the return of the disappeared and drew human silhouettes in streets and walls to represent them, Inés Vázquez, *Historia de las Madres de Plaza de Mayo: Luchar Siempre, las Marchas de la Resistencia, 1981–2006* (Ediciones Madres de Plaza de Mayo, 2007).

[101] See, eg, David Pion-Berlin, *Through Corridors of Power* (n 23); Garro, 'Nine Years of Transition to Democracy in Argentina' (n 33); Azcárate and Jelin, 'Memoria y Política' (n 63). Alison Brysk went further and examined the impact of human rights groups on social norms; see *The Politics of Human Rights in Argentina* (n 11).

[102] UNSC 'Report of the Commission on the Truth for El Salvador', Annex to the letter dated 29 March 1993 from the Secretary-General addressed to the President of the Security Council UN Doc S/25500, page 17. See also Mark Ensalaco, 'Truth Commissions for Chile and El Salvador: A Report and Assessment' (1994) 16 *Human Rights Quarterly* 656.

[103] Ley 15848 Funcionarios Militares y Policiales, Se Reconoce que ha Caducado el Ejercicio de la Pretensión Punitiva del Estado Respecto de los Delitos Cometidos hasta el 1 de Marzo de 1985 (Military and Police Officers, It Is Recognised That the Exercise of the Punitive Intention of the State Regarding the Crimes Committed until 1 March 1985 Has Lapsed) 22 December 1986, art 1.

introduced by Mikhail Gorbachev might lead in the long run to institutional and political changes.[104] By the long run, surely he did not mean that within two years the seemingly monolithic Communist Bloc would disintegrate. In June 1989, elections were held in Poland that led to the first non-communist government in Eastern Europe in 40 years.[105] Six months later, the only communist party leader still in power in Europe was Gorbachev and he would be gone too, along with the Soviet Union, within 18 months.[106] These unexpected events gave new impetus to discussions on responses to past widespread or systematic violence by adding a practical direction to them. The autonomous discourse of transitional justice grew from these discussions.

In order to make sense of the cataclysmic and unexpected fall of communism, scholars readily incorporated this process into the existing historical narrative of a wave of transitions to democracy.[107] As mentioned when discussing the resonance of the Argentine transition, comparative political scientists – notably Guillermo O'Donnell, Philippe Schmitter and Laurence Whitehead – had been working for some time on the concept of transitions to democracy, which was well established by 1989.[108] This existing framework made it easier to locate the events that followed the fall of the Berlin Wall, however surprising, at the end of that chronological chain of transitions. More importantly, the process of stringing transitions together had a comparative purpose as Adam Przeworski noted in 1991:

> Transitions to democracy occurred in Southern Europe – in Greece, Portugal, and Spain – in the mid 1970s. They were launched in the Southern Cone of Latin America, except for Chile – in Argentina, Brazil, and Uruguay – in the early 1980s. And they were inaugurated in Eastern Europe

[104] Giussani and Alfonsín, *¿Por Qué, Doctor Alfonsín?* 145 (n 11).

[105] Timothy Garton Ash, *We the People: The Revolution of '89 Witnessed in Warsaw, Budapest, Berlin & Prague* (Granta Books, 1990) 19. While since the end of the Cold War many people prefer distinguishing between Central and Eastern Europe, throughout the chapter the region is called Eastern Europe to emphasise the communist legacy. See Timothy Garton Ash, 'The Puzzle of Central Europe' (1999) *The New York Review of Books* www.nybooks.com/articles/1999/03/18/the-puzzle-of-central-europe/, accessed 30 July 2018.

[106] Gordon S Barrass, *The Great Cold War: A Journey through the Hall of Mirrors* (Stanford University Press, 2009) 363.

[107] See, eg, Shain, Linz and Berat, *Between States* 3–4 (n 11).

[108] Guillermo O'Donnell, Philippe C Schmitter and Laurence Whitehead, *Transitions from Authoritarian Rule: Prospects for Democracy* (Johns Hopkins University Press, 1986). For another contemporary project focused on transitions to democracy in developing countries, see Larry Jay Diamond, Juan José Linz and Seymour Martin Lipset, *Politics in Developing Countries: Comparing Experiences with Democracy* (L Rienner Publishers, 1990).

during the 'Autumn of the People' of 1989. Can we draw on the earlier experiences to understand the later ones?[109]

Yet, the transitions in Eastern Europe were markedly different from those in Latin America because they involved both a political and economic transformation. The political change was from a socialist regime to a democracy, and the economic transition was from a planned economy to a market-driven one.[110] In contrast with the Latin American transitions, where the changes were largely restricted to the political sphere; the former communist countries went through 'a vast institutional reorganization of economic life [. . .] involving the steps of privatization, marketization, and stabilization'.[111] These dual political and economic transitions were perceived to be interdependent: the market would buttress democracy and vice versa.[112] Despite this important difference, the previous transitions from authoritarianism to democracy were considered repositories of experience for the countries leaving behind communism.[113]

With the purpose of facilitating the dual transitions, Western states channelled funds and advice to their post-communist counterparts.[114] For them, the most pressing question was how they could assist their former rivals' transition from communism to liberal democracy.[115] As a result of these efforts, the post-communist states 'implement[ed] an intellectual blueprint, a blueprint developed within the walls of American academia and shaped by international financial institutions'.[116] The dual transformation was not a direct external imposition. Timothy Garton Ash, who had first-hand knowledge of opposition groups in several Eastern European countries, noted that there was a 'remarkable underlying consensus' over the general destination of

109 Adam Przeworski, *Democracy and the Market: Political and Economic Reforms in Eastern Europe and Latin America* (Cambridge University Press, 1991) 1.

110 Michael McFaul, 'A Mixed Record, an Uncertain Future' (2001) 12 *Journal of Democracy* 87, 88.

111 Jon Elster, Ulrich Preuss and Claus Offe, *Institutional Design in Post-Communist Societies: Rebuilding the Ship at Sea* (Cambridge University Press, 1998).

112 Przeworski, *Democracy and the Market* ix (n 109); Thomas Carothers, 'Western Civil-Society Aid to Eastern Europe and the Former Soviet Union' (1999) 8 East European Constitutional Review 54, 55.

113 Huntington, *The Third Wave* (n 67) 26–28; Przeworski, *Democracy and the Market* 2–6 (n 109); Juan José Linz and Alfred C Stepan, *Problems of Democratic Transition and Consolidation: Southern Europe, South America, and Post-Communist Europe* (1996) 232–34.

114 Carothers, 'Western Civil-Society Aid to Eastern Europe and the Former Soviet Union' 57–59 (n 112).

115 Garton Ash, *We the People* 150 (n 105).

116 Przeworski, *Democracy and the Market* 7 (n 109).

the transition: a multiparty democracy and an 'economy whose basic engine of growth is the market, with extensive private ownership of the means of production, distribution and exchange'.[117] It was as part of this massive project of re-engineering the political and economic system of the former socialist countries along liberal lines that concerted discussions on responses to past widespread or systematic violence took place.

1 A *Sense of Purpose*

One of the areas of interest concerning the future of former socialist states was how they would respond to their past. After four decades of communist rule, would the newly democratic societies prosecute those responsible for the abuses of the regimes, establish truth commissions, offer reparations to the victims of repression or let bygones be bygones? If the issue of dealing with the past had loomed large in previous transitions to democracy, it was to be expected that it would be the same for the former communist states. The experience of prior transitions provided a road map for the new experience of communist countries moving towards democracy.

The Eastern European transitions reinvigorated and transformed the embryonic transitional justice movement that had started with the Latin American transitions and resulted in the 1988 Aspen Institute conference by giving it a sense of purpose and urgency. Around the discussions sparked by the post-communist transitions, an autonomous discourse of transitional justice began to emerge with specific concepts, objects and actors. People interested in this area started to form an epistemic community, sharing approaches and ideas.

In the aftermath of the collapse of the Soviet Bloc, people from different backgrounds began to work on the question of how post-communist societies were to address their past using a comparative framework.[118] Many echoed the narrative of a wave of democratisation sweeping over the world. Ruti Teitel opens her seminal book *Transitional Justice* with an account of the wave of liberalisation: 'In recent decades, societies all over the world – throughout Latin America, East Europe, the former Soviet Union, Africa – have overthrown military dictatorships and totalitarian regimes for freedom and democracy'.[119] Carlos Nino compares the Eastern European attempts to come to terms with the past with the experiences in Southern Europe, Latin

[117] Garton Ash, *We the People* 151–52 (n 105). See also Przeworski, *Democracy and the Market* 8 (n 109).

[118] Arthur, 'How "Transitions" Reshaped Human Rights' 343 (n 55).

[119] Ruti Teitel, *Transitional Justice* (Oxford University Press, 2000) 3.

America, Asia and Africa.[120] Political scientist Samuel Huntington examined what he called the 'torturer's dilemma': whether to prosecute human rights violators and risk instability or not. He based his analysis on previous transitions, especially Argentina's, and offered practical 'Guidelines for Democratizers'.[121] Fellow political scientist Jon Elster argued that transitional justice takes place in regional waves, and he mentions the examples of Southern Europe, Latin America and the communist states.[122] Journalist Tina Rosenberg also adopted the notion of a democratising wave rolling through regions in different decades before shaking the Soviet Bloc.[123] All these commentators agreed on one thing: issues of transitional justice were comparable across states.

Also at this time, the term 'transitional justice' gained currency as a form of referring to how democratising societies responded to the human rights violations of the previous regime. Ruti Teitel came up with the term in 1991 for a grant proposal for the United States Institute of Peace (USIP). She chose the term because it conveyed the idea the circumstances of each political transition would necessitate modifying the conception of justice.[124] Other people began using the phrase around that time.[125] Notably among them was Neil Kritz of USIP, who used it for the title of his 1995 collected book: *Transitional Justice: How Emerging Democracies Reckon with Former Regimes*.[126] The use of the phrase in this influential book certainly contributed to its dissemination and acceptance.[127]

Neil Kritz's book exemplifies the practical purpose that the post-communist transitions infused on discussions on transitional justice. This three-volume

[120] Nino, *Radical Evil on Trial*, ch 1 (n 15).

[121] Huntington, *The Third Wave* 211–31 (n 67).

[122] Jon Elster, 'Coming to Terms with the Past: A Framework for the Study of Justice in the Transition to Democracy' (1998) 39 *European Journal of Sociology/Archives Européennes de Sociologie* 7, 7.

[123] Tina Rosenberg, 'Overcoming the Legacies of Dictatorship' (1995) 74 *Foreign Affairs* 134, 135; Tina Rosenberg, *The Haunted Land: Facing Europe's Ghosts after Communism* (Vintage, 1995) xix–xx.

[124] Ruti Teitel, 'Global Transitional Justice' (2010) Center for Global Studies, Project on Human Rights, Global Justice & Democracy, Working Paper No 8 www.gmu.edu/centers/globalstudies/publications/hjd/hjd_wp_8.pdf, accessed 26 August 2018, 1; Ruti Teitel, *Transitional Justice* (n 119) 3–9. See also Ruti Teitel, 'Editorial Note-Transitional Justice Globalized' (2008) 2 *International Journal of Transitional Justice* 1; Ruti Teitel, *Globalizing Transitional Justice: Contemporary Essays* (Oxford University Press, 2014). For a discussion on the origin of the term, see Arthur, 'How "Transitions" Reshaped Human Rights' 327–30 (n 55).

[125] For example, Diane Orentlicher discussed the risks and benefits of 'transitional justice' in a book published in 1993, Diane Orentlicher, 'The Role of the Prosecutor in the Transition to Democracy in Latin America' in Irwin P Stotzky (ed), Transition to Democracy in Latin America: The Role of the Judiciary (Westview Press, 1993) 252.

[126] Neil J Kritz, *Transitional Justice: How Emerging Democracies Reckon with Former Regimes* (United States Institute of Peace Press, 1995).

[127] Arthur, 'How "Transitions" Reshaped Human Rights 330 (n 55).

compendium 'on basic questions of "transitional justice"' was the result of a research project of USIP that started in 1991.[128] One of its main themes was 'the extent to which the Central and Eastern Europeans and former Soviets who were just emerging from communist rule could learn any useful lessons from the Latin American transitions of the previous decade'.[129] The lessons of the book were meant to foster democracy and the rule of law.[130]

The project 'Justice in Times of Transition' showed even more this purpose of transferring knowledge across transitions. It was established by the Charter 77 Foundation-New York and held its inaugural meeting in Salzburg, Austria, in March 1992.[131] The project expressly concentrated on how Eastern European leaders could learn from the Latin American transitions.[132] To that end, it gathered forty individuals 'directly involved at the policy-making level in dismantling the security apparatus of the former regimes and formulating policies to deal with implicated individuals'.[133] They came from Poland, Hungary, East Germany, Czechoslovakia, Lithuania and Yugoslavia.[134] This group from post-communist states met with people involved in the Latin American transitions, including President Alfonsín, his legal adviser Jaime Malamud Goti, Chilean Deputy Foreign Minister Roberto Garretón and Uruguayan parliamentarian Rafael Michelini. Experts from the United States and Western Europe attended the conference as well.[135] Although the organisers recognised the differences separating the countries which had undergone transitions, they emphasised that 'each of the new democracies in these regions faces a common and pressing problem: how to deal with individuals who served the former oppressive regimes'.[136] During the conference, participants discussed the role of civil society, the importance of revealing the truth, the validity of amnesties, the role of international law, the legal obstacles to prosecutions and the strategies to confront the past pursued in the post-communist states.[137] In the conclusions of the conference, it was noted that

[128] Charles Duryea Smith, 'Introduction' in Neil J Kritz (ed), *Transitional Justice: How Emerging Democracies Reckon with Former Regimes* (United States Institute of Peace Press, 1995) xvi.
[129] Kritz, 'The Dilemmas of Transitional Justice' xix (n 59).
[130] Duryea Smith, 'Introduction' xv–xvi (n 127).
[131] Mary Albon, 'Project on Justice in Times of Transition: Report of the Project's Inaugural Meeting' in Neil J Kritz (ed), *Transitional Justice: How Emerging Democracies Reckon with Former Regimes* (United States Institute of Peace Press, 1995) 42.
[132] Bronwyn Leebaw, 'The Irreconcilable Goals of Transitional Justice' (2008) 30 *Human Rights Quarterly* 95, 100.
[133] Albon, 'Project on Justice in Times of Transition' 42 (n 130).
[134] Arthur, 'How "Transitions" Reshaped Human Rights' 364–67 (n 55).
[135] Ibid.
[136] Albon, 'Project on Justice in Times of Transition' 42 (n 130).
[137] Albon, 'Project on Justice in Times of Transition' (n 130).

the 'European participants in particular learned some important lessons from the Latin American experience with transitional justice'.[138]

Neil Kritz's book and the Salzburg meeting were important for the appearance of an autonomous discourse of transitional justice for a number of reasons. First, they both expressly sought to transmit knowledge from the Latin American transitions to their post-communist counterparts. This comparative learning process is characteristic of transitional justice discourse. Second, they gathered people from a range of disciplines including law, political science and philosophy. Thus, they advanced a multidisciplinary agenda to approach responses to past widespread or systematic violence. Third, Kritz's book and the Salzburg event counted among their participants and contributors people who would become influential in the discourse of transitional justice, such as Ruti Teitel, Naomi Roht-Arriaza, Diane Orentlicher, Jaime Malamud Goti, Carlos Nino, José Zalaquett, Priscilla Hayner, Jon Elster and Ellen Lutz.[139]

Kritz's *Transitional Justice* prefigured the contours of the discourse. It dealt with the main objects and concepts of the discourse. It examined in detail trials, truth commissions, vetting of officials and reparations. Furthermore, by including excerpts of older works on similar topics, such as Karl Jaspers' 1948 lectures on German guilt, Otto Kirchheimer's 1961 book on political justice and John Herz's 1982 book on dealing with the legacy of authoritarian regimes, Kritz's compendium gave an idea of permanence to the nascent discourse. The cases covered post–World War II experiences, the transitions of Southern Europe in the 1970s, their counterparts in Latin America in the 1980s and the recent events in Eastern Europe thus already foreshadowing which episodes the dominant narrative today considers relevant for transitional justice. Accordingly, Paige Arthur has rightly called Kritz's book a canon of transitional justice literature that was published even before it was clear that a canon was needed. Indeed, one of the purposes of the book is to 'raise the profile of scholarship on transitional justice'.[140] It certainly achieved that goal by giving precision to the discourse's content and giving it historical roots.

In addition to the Salzburg conference and Kritz's compendium, there were other conferences and events focusing on similar problems. For instance, in June 1990, there was a conference in Pécs, Hungary, on how to build institutions in Eastern Europe, where the issue of retribution and reparations

[138] Ibid 54.
[139] Arthur, 'How "Transitions" Reshaped Human Rights' 364–67 (n 55); Kritz, *Transitional Justice* (n 125).
[140] Duryea Smith, 'Introduction' xvii (n 127).

was discussed.[141] The University of Chicago and the Central European University organised a conference in December 1991 in Prague on restitution and retribution in East Central Europe.[142] The Central European University also organised conferences on topics of transitional justice in 1992 and 1993.[143]

These examples show that the collapse of communism sparked an interest in how these societies would respond to their repressive pasts. This interest channelled scholars and funding towards the incipient discursive practice of transitional justice. The purpose of these discussions was to collect the experiences of previous transitions to guide the way of post-communist societies towards democracy. Around these debates, an autonomous discourse of transitional justice began to coalesce.

2 *A Feeling of Disappointment*

One participant in the 1992 Salzburg conference recalls that his Eastern European counterparts did not appear very eager to learn from the Latin American transitions.[144] Perhaps it should come as no surprise, then, that the recipients of the advice relied on their own home-grown mechanisms and did not make much use of those implemented in Latin America.

The Latin American experience in the 1980s and 1990s was marked by two mechanisms, namely criminal trials and truth commissions. Criminal trials were only used in Argentina – with the results described earlier – and Bolivia[145], but the advantages and difficulties of carrying them out still dominated discussions.[146] At the time when the Eastern European states were grappling with the transition, truth commissions had already been established in Argentina, Uruguay, Bolivia, Chile and El Salvador.[147] Despite the lessons of the discourse of transitional justice, neither criminal trials nor truth

[141] Jon Elster, *Closing the Books: Transitional Justice in Historical Perspective* (Cambridge University Press, 2004) ix.

[142] Teitel, *Transitional Justice* vii (n 119); Stephen Holmes, 'Introducing the Center' (1992) 1 *East European Constitutional Review* 13, 14; Dwight Semler, 'From the Center' (1992) 1 *East European Constitutional Review* 30.

[143] Teitel, *Transitional Justice* vii (n 119).

[144] Interview with Jaime Malamud Goti (n 58).

[145] Mayorga, 'Democracy Dignified and an End to Impunity' (n 40).

[146] See, eg, Malamud Goti, 'Transitional Governments in the Breach' (n 32); Pion-Berlin, 'To Prosecute or to Pardon?' (n 71); The Aspen Institute (n 77); Orentlicher (n 81); Nino, 'The Duty to Punish Past Abuses of Human Rights Put into Context' (n 81); Albon, 'Project on Justice in Times of Transition' (n 130).

[147] Priscilla Hayner, *Unspeakable Truths: Confronting State Terror and Atrocity* (Routledge, 2001).

commissions were the main mechanism implemented following the end of communism.

In Eastern Europe, criminal trials were few and far between.[148] No post-communist state had a general policy of prosecutions for human rights violations, as Argentina did. East Germany saw the most trials, aided by its reunification with the Federal Republic of Germany. The reunification meant that West German judges not involved in communism could hear the cases against East German officials.[149] The most serious cases concerned the shooting of people trying to cross the Berlin Wall.[150] The first prosecutions targeted soldiers who had pulled the trigger, and more than 50 of them were convicted in the first 5 years after reunification.[151] In turn, several members of the East German Politburo were indicted for their role in the Berlin Wall shootings. Although the case against the leader of the German Democratic Republic, Erich Honecker, ended due to his poor health,[152] on 16 September 1993 the Berlin Regional Court convicted Politburo members Heinz Kessler, Fritz Streletz and Hans Albrecht of intentional homicide for their role in setting up the system that led to the border shootings.[153] As important as these trials were, they focused on a single aspect of the East German regime.

148 de Brito, González Enríquez and Aguilar Fernández, 'Introduction' 6 (n 8); Elster, *Closing the Books* 117 (n 140); Monika Nalepa, *Skeletons in the Closet: Transitional Justice in Post-Communist Europe* (Cambridge University Press, 2010) 95.

149 Sanya Romeike, 'Transitional Justice in Germany after 1945 and after 1990' (2016) Occasional Paper No 1 International Nuremberg Principles Academy 46.

150 There were more trials for lesser offences, see Gary Bruce, 'East Germany' in Lavinia Stan (ed), *Transitional Justice in Eastern Europe and the Former Soviet Union: Reckoning with the Communist Past* (Routledge, 2008).

151 See Kif Augustine Adams, 'What Is Just? The Rule of Law and Natural Law in the Trials of Former East German Border Guards' (1992) 29 *Stanford Journal of International Law* 271; Micah Goodman, 'After the Wall: The Legal Ramifications of the East German Border Guard Trials in Unified Germany' (1996) 29 *Cornell International Law Journal* 727.

152 A James McAdams, 'Communism on Trial: The East German Past and the German Future' in A James McAdams (ed), *Transitional Justice and the Rule of Law in New Democracies* (University of Notre Dame Press, 1997).

153 LG Berlin Urteil vom 16 September 1993 (527) 2 Js 26/90 Ks (10/92) (Regional Court of Berlin); BGH Urteil vom 26 July 1994 (LG Berlin) 5 StR 98/94 (Federal Court of Justice of Germany). The defendants later took the case to the European Court of Human Rights which found that their trial had not violated the European Convention of Human Rights, *Streletz, Kessler and Krenz* v. *Germany* (2001) Applications Nos 34044/96, 35532/97, 44801/98 ECHR 2001-II (*Streletz, Kessler and Krenz* v. *Germany*). See also A James McAdams, 'The Honecker Trial: The East German Past and the German Future' (1996) 58 *The Review of Politics* 53; Christiane Wilke, 'Law on a Slanted Globe: Traveling Models of Criminal Responsibility for State Violence' (2015) 24 *Social & Legal Studies* 555.

Trials held in other post-communist countries differed even more from the Argentine precedent. In Poland, investigations covered crimes committed during Stalinism in the 1940s, the shooting of strikers in Gdańsk in 1970 and the imposition of the martial law in 1981. Despite this historical breadth, the investigations led to few trials and even fewer verdicts.[154] The slowness of the procedures meant that the highest-profile case against General Wojciech Jaruzelski for ordering the martial law collapsed when he was declared unfit for trial.[155] This contrasted with the Argentine precedent of high-profile convictions for human rights violations less than two years after the transition, albeit later subjected to pardons. In Bulgaria, party leader Todor Zhivkov was convicted in 1992 of embezzlement;[156] in the Czech Republic, some officials were convicted of abuse of power;[157] in Romania, the dictator Nicolae Ceausescu was executed after a summary trial.[158] Some of these trials did not focus on human rights violations; many others failed to reach a verdict and some violated human rights themselves.[159] As Lavinia Stan noted when summing up transitional justice developments in Eastern Europe, 'the slowest progress to date has been registered with regard to the criminal prosecution of former communist officials and secret agents for

[154] Lavinia Stan, 'Poland' in Lavinia Stan (ed), *Transitional Justice in Eastern Europe and the Former Soviet Union: Reckoning with the Communist Past* (Routledge, 2008) 89–91.

[155] Chris Borowski, 'Polish Court: Martial Law Imposed by "Criminal Group"' *Reuters* (12 January 2012) www.reuters.com/article/us-poland-communists-idUSTRE80B1VA20120112, accessed 30 July 2018; 'General Wojciech Jaruzelski – Obituary' *The Telegraph* (25 May 2014) www.telegraph.co.uk/news/obituaries/military-obituaries/10855827/General-Wojciech-Jaruzelski-obituary.html, accessed 30 July 2018.

[156] Human Rights Watch, 'Bulgaria: Human Rights Developments' (1992) www.hrw.org/reports/1993/WR93/Hsw-02.htm, accessed 30 July 2018; 'Ousted Bulgarian Gets 7-Year Term for Embezzlement' *New York Times* (September 1992) www.nytimes.com/1992/09/05/world/ousted-bulgarian-gets-7-year-term-for-embezzlement.html, accessed 30 July 2018; Jamal Benomar, 'Justice after Transitions' (1993) 4 *Journal of Democracy* 3, 6; C Charles Bertschi, 'Lustration and the Transition to Democracy: The Cases of Poland and Bulgaria' (1994) 28 *East European Quarterly* 435, 442–43. However, in 1995 the Court of Appeals ruled that Zhivkov should never have been tried because he enjoyed immunity as head of state, Momchil Metodiev, 'Bulgaria' in Lavinia Stan (ed), *Transitional Justice in Eastern Europe and the Former Soviet Union: Reckoning with the Communist Past* (Routledge, 2008) 163.

[157] Nadya Nedelsky, 'Czechoslovakia and the Czech and Slovak Republics' in Lavinia Stan (ed), *Transitional Justice in Eastern Europe and the Former Soviet Union: Reckoning with the Communist Past* (Routledge, 2008) 57.

[158] Lavinia Stan, 'Romania' in Lavinia Stan (ed), *Transitional justice in Eastern Europe and the Former Soviet Union: Reckoning with the Communist Past* (Routledge, 2008) 142–43. See also Mark Almond, *The Rise and Fall of Nicolae and Elena Ceauşescu* (Chapmans, 1992).

[159] See Adrienne Quill, 'To Prosecute or Not to Prosecute: Problems Encountered in the Prosecution of Former Communist Officials in Germany, Czechoslovakia, and the Czech Republic' (1996) 7 *Indiana International & Comparative Law Review* 165.

their participation in beatings, torture, murder and other gross violations of human rights'.[160]

The main novel mechanism to come out of the Latin American transitions – the truth commission – was even less popular among the post-communist states. The only exception was East Germany, where two commissions were established.[161] In 1992, the unified German parliament created a commission of inquiry to investigate human rights violations during the communist period. After two years of hearing testimony of experts and victims, the commission issued an extensive report that was debated in parliament.[162] A second commission of inquiry continued this work and issued a report in 1999.[163] Later truth commissions were established in Uzbekistan in 1999 and Russia in 2009. These initiatives in former states of the Soviet Union, however, have been accused of being ploys of political manipulation rather than genuine accountability mechanisms.[164]

Instead, the Eastern European states relied primarily on home-grown mechanisms – namely disclosure of secret files, vetting of public officials and restitution of private property. Since the internal secret services of many of these countries held enormous amounts of information on the public, granting access to these files was a simple way of revealing part of the truth about the communist period.[165] Accordingly, the Czech Republic, Poland and Germany put in place programmes to make the secret files available to the public.[166]

160 Lavinia Stan, 'Conclusion: Explaining Country Differences' in Lavinia Stan (ed), *Transitional Justice in Eastern Europe and the Former Soviet Union: Reckoning with the Communist Past* (Routledge, 2008) 260.

161 For a review of the German commissions, see Andrew Beattie, 'An Evolutionary Process: Contributions of the Bundestag Inquiries into East Germany to an Understanding of the Role of Truth Commissions' (2009) 3 *International Journal of Transitional Justice* 229.

162 Deutscher Bundestag, *Materialien Der Enquete-Kommission 'Aufarbeitung von Geschichte Und Folgen Der SED-Diktatur in Deutschland'* (Suhrkamp, 1995).

163 Deutscher Bundestag, *Materialien Der Enquete-Kommission 'Uberwindung Der Folgen Der SED-Diktatur Im Prozeß Der Deutschen Einheit'* (Suhrkamp, 1999).

164 Brian Grodsky, 'Justice without Transition: Truth Commissions in the Context of Repressive Rule' (2008) 9 *Human Rights Review* 281; Kora Andrieu, 'An Unfinished Business: Transitional Justice and Democratization in Post-Soviet Russia' (2011) 5 *International Journal of Transitional Justice* 198.

165 By way of example, in East Germany the secret police (Stasi) had files on half of the adult population, see Hilary Appel, 'Anti-Communist Justice and Founding the Post-Communist Order: Lustration and Restitution in Central Europe' (2005) 19 *East European Politics & Societies* 379, 385.

166 Rosenberg, *The Haunted Land* 5–6, 296–98 (n 123). For the German system, see John Miller, 'Settling Accounts with a Secret Police: The German Law on the Stasi Records' (1998) 50 *Europe-Asia Studies* 305.

Secret files were also used for the main mechanism relied upon in the Eastern European states: lustration.[167] This mechanism, named after the Latin word *lustrare* for ceremonial purification, consists of disqualifying people involved in the previous regime as communist officials or secret informers from public office and positions of influence.[168] Lustration was pioneered in Czechoslovakia, where a law was passed in 1991 banning people who were agents or informers of the security apparatus from taking positions in government, armed forces, parliament, courts, academia and the media.[169] Lustration processes were adopted, in various guises, in many other post-communist states.[170] East Germany (1990),[171] Lithuania (1991), Bulgaria (1992), Estonia (1994), Latvia (1994), Hungary (1994), Albania (1995), Poland (1997), Romania (1991) and Slovakia (2002) all established screening processes to purge people involved with communism.[172] Its widespread use and the relative absence of other forms of accountability underscore that lustration was the dominant transitional justice mechanism in the post-communist states.[173]

Following the end of communism, most states also put in place restitution programmes for private property that the previous regime had nationalised. The governments of East and West Germany issued a joint declaration in June 1990 that stated that confiscated real state would be returned to the former owners or their heirs. Controversially, the declaration expressly

[167] See, eg, Mark S Ellis, 'Purging the Past: The Current State of Lustration Laws in the Former Communist Bloc' (1996) 59 *Law & Contemporary Problems* 181; Jirina Siklova, 'Lustration or the Czech Way of Screening' (1996) 5 *East European Constitutional Review* 57; Roman David, 'Lustration Laws in Action: The Motives and Evaluation of Lustration Policy in the Czech Republic and Poland (1989–2001)' (2003) 28 *Law & Social Inquiry* 387.

[168] Lavinia Stan, 'Introduction: Post-Communist Transition, Justice, and Transitional Justice' in Lavinia Stan (ed), *Transitional Justice in Eastern Europe and the Former Soviet Union: Reckoning with the Communist Past* (Routledge, 2008) 11. See also Natalia Letki, 'Lustration and Democratisation in East-Central Europe' (2002) 54 *Europe-Asia Studies* 529.

[169] Teitel, *Transitional Justice* 164 (n 119); Siklova, 'Lustration or the Czech Way of Screening' 157 (n 166). For the constitutional validity of the Czech lustration process, see David Kosar, 'Lustration and Lapse of Time: "Dealing with the Past" in the Czech Republic' (2008) 4 *European Constitutional Law Review* 460.

[170] For the variations in lustration policies adopted in different countries, see Adam Czarnota, 'Lustration, Decommunisation and the Rule of Law' (2009) 1 *Hague Journal on the Rule of Law* 307.

[171] Although the East Germany vetting process was based on the 1990 unification treaty, it was carried out later. See, Erhard Blankenburg, 'The Purge of Lawyers after the Breakdown of the East German Communist Regime' (1995) 20 *Law & Social Inquiry* 223.

[172] Cynthia M Horne, 'The Impact of Lustration on Democratization in Postcommunist Countries' (2014) 8 *International Journal of Transitional Justice* 496.

[173] Ibid 498. See also Stan, 'Introduction' (n 167).

excluded property seized during the Soviet occupation in 1945–1949.[174] More than one million claims for property restitution were filed in East Germany.[175] In Czechoslovakia, a law allowed owners of real estate that the communists had seized between 1948 and 1989 to claim restitution or compensation.[176] Property nationalised before 1948 was not included to prevent Sudeten Germans expelled after World War II from receiving compensation.[177] The Hungarian restitution law passed in June 1991 did not offer the return of property but indemnification vouchers for property confiscated since 1949.[178]

In Bulgaria, several restitution laws covering industrial, commercial, residential and agricultural land were adopted.[179] All three Baltic states passed property restitution laws in 1990 or 1991. However, the number of claims filed in each country varied, with 840,000 claims in Lithuania, 240,000 in Estonia and 23,000 in Latvia.[180] In this manner, most former communist countries implemented property restitution policies shortly after the transition.

International commentators found the transitional justice trajectory of the post-communist states disappointing. They stressed the scarcity of prosecutions and the difficulties that met those that took place.[181] Lustration policies came under fire for not affording the legal guarantees of due process.[182] Restitution

[174] Joint Declaration of the Governments of the Federal Republic of Germany and the German Democratic Republic on the Settlement of Open Property Questions, June 15, 1990.

[175] David Southern, 'Restitution or Compensation: The Property Question' (1993) 2 *German Politics* 436.

[176] Michael Neff, 'Eastern Europe's Policy of Restitution of Property in the 1990s' (1992) 10 *Dickinson Journal of International Law* 368.

[177] Vojtech Cepl, 'A Note on the Restitution of Property in Post-Communist Czechoslovakia' (1991) 7 *Journal of Communist Studies* 368.

[178] Neff, 'Eastern Europe's Policy of Restitution of Property in the 1990s' (n 175).

[179] *Velikovi* v. *Bulgaria* (2007) Applications Nos 43278/98, 45437/99, 48014/99, 48380/99, 51362/99, 53367/99, 60036/00, 73465/01, and 194/02 ECHR 2007-II, para 117. See also Deyan Kiuranov, 'Assessment of the Public Debate on the Legal Remedies for the Reinstatement of Former Owners and the Realization of Liability for Damages Inflicted by the Totalitarian Regime' in Neil J Kritz (ed), *Transitional Justice: How Emerging Democracies Reckon with Former Regimes* (United States Institute of Peace Press, 1995).

[180] Eva-Clarita Pettai and Vello Pettai, *Transitional and Retrospective Justice in the Baltic States* (Cambridge University Press, 2015).

[181] Ruti Teitel, 'Post-Communist Constitutionalism: A Transitional Perspective' (1994) 26 *Columbia Human Rights Law Review* 167, 180; Peter E Quint, *The Imperfect Union: Constitutional Structures of German Unification* (Princeton University Press, 1997) 196–205; Teitel, *Transitional Justice* 41 (n 119); Noel Calhoun, *Dilemmas of Justice in Eastern Europe's Democratic Transitions* (Palgrave Macmillan, 2004); Elster, *Closing the Books* x (n 140).

[182] Rosenberg, 'Overcoming the Legacies of Dictatorship 152 (n 123); Siklova, 'Lustration or the Czech Way of Screening' 61–62 (n 166); Letki, 'Lustration and Democratisation in East-Central Europe' 541–42 (n 167).

programmes were criticised for excluding some expropriated real estate[183] and depriving good-faith owners of property they have had for a long time.[184]

The hopes that the post-communist transitions had initially engendered in transitional justice advocates were soon replaced by a sense of disappointment. Stephen Holmes, who had attended the 1992 Salzburg conference, captured this feeling of failure particularly well when he wrote in 1994 that, after the impressive international conferences of two or three years before on 'the moral and legal problems associated with disqualification from office, police dossiers, "truth commissions," and screening laws', the impulse for transitional justice had petered out with meagre results.[185] That same year, in a conference in South Africa, the transitional justice experiences in Poland,[186] Bulgaria,[187] and the Czech Republic[188] were all considered disappointing. Despite the effort to transfer lessons from Latin American to Eastern European states, the latter had followed their own way, which was deemed a failure – even by those who had been closely involved in that lesson-learning process.

The feeling of disappointment extended to the wider project of transition to democracy and capitalism of which transitional justice policies were but a part. Ten years after the fall of the Berlin Wall, Thomas Carothers noted that democratization and market reforms were failing in many post-communist states. He pointed out that transitions had ended up 'in banal dictatorships and the bleakest of corrupted statist economies'.[189] In 2009, Polish former dissident Adam Michnik and a participant of the 1992 Salzburg conference noted that the process that began with such high hopes 20 years earlier had become prey of ominous trends that threatened democracy.[190]

183 Southern, 'Restitution or Compensation' (n 174); Cepl, 'A Note on the Restitution of Property in Post-Communist Czechoslovakia' (n 176).

184 Pettai and Pettai, *Transitional and Retrospective Justice in the Baltic States* (n 179).

185 Stephen Holmes, 'The End of Decommunization' (1994) 3 *East European Constitutional Review* 33, 33. In the context of the post-communist transitions, the term decommunization was synonymous with transitional justice, see Stan, 'Introduction' 1 (n 167). Helga Welsh tells a similar story of transitional justice issues being pushed to the backseat in Germany due to more pressing problems, 'When Discourse Trumps Policy: Transitional Justice in Unified Germany' (2006) 15 *German Politics* 137.

186 Wiktor Osiatynski, 'Poland' in Alex Boraine, Janet Levy and Ronel Scheffer (eds), *Dealing with the Past: Truth and Reconciliation in South Africa* (IDASA, 1994) 60.

187 Dimitrina Petrova, 'Bulgaria' in Alex Boraine, Janet Levy and Ronel Scheffer (eds), *Dealing with the Past: Truth and Reconciliation in South Africa* (IDASA, 1994) 76.

188 Karel Schwarzenberg, 'Czech Republic' in Alex Boraine, Janet Levy and Ronel Scheffer (eds), *Dealing with the Past: Truth and Reconciliation in South Africa* (IDASA, 1994) 84.

189 Carothers, 'Western Civil-Society Aid to Eastern Europe and the Former Soviet Union' 56 (n 112).

190 Vaclav Havel and Adam Michnik, 'The Period after 1989' (2009) 15 *Common Knowledge* 319.

The feeling of failure that marked the first practical outlet for discussions on transitional justice did not stop their progress. Commentators found explanations for why former communist states had followed a different path than their Latin American counterparts. The neglect of trials and truth commissions in these countries was blamed on the peculiarities of these transitions. Whereas some commentators emphasised the unique and unprecedented challenges posed by facing simultaneous political and economic transitions,[191] most focused on the characteristics of the prior regime. Thus, the explanations for the absence of widespread prosecutions ranged from the legal obstacles to prosecutions[192] to the length of time elapsed since the worst abuses.[193] As for truth commissions, the indoctrination carried out by the totalitarian regimes made the idea of an officially sanctioned truth unpalatable to the public.[194]

Although it was found disappointing, the experience of the post-communist countries was readily incorporated into transitional justice's growing catalogue of states dealing with past violence. Rather than accepting defeat, the discourse immediately added the Eastern European flagship mechanism – lustration – to the list of practices associated with transitional justice alongside truth commissions, trials and reparations.[195] Restitution of private property was discussed at the time in the context of Eastern Europe and included in Kritz's compendium of transitional justice practices, but it did not feature as prominently in the discourse afterwards.

From then on, transitional justice lost interest in the region that had given it a sense of purpose and a practical outlet. To this day, the former socialist countries of Eastern Europe remain an area of marginal importance for the discourse of transitional justice. The countries of the former Yugoslavia are the only exception, but the discourse examines the later civil wars rather than the legacy of communism. For instance, of 241 articles published in the *International Journal of Transitional Justice* since its creation, only 7 focus

[191] Csaba Varga, *Transition to Rule of Law: On the Democratic Transformation in Hungary* (Project on Comparative Legal Cultures of the Faculty of Law of Loránd Eötvös University: Institute for Legal Studies of the Hungarian Academy of Sciences, 1995); Andrieu, 'An Unfinished Business' (n 163).

[192] Teitel, *Transitional Justice* 41–46 (n 119).

[193] Nino, *Radical Evil on Trial* 122 (n 15). For a recent formulation of this view, see Pettai and Pettai, *Transitional and Retrospective Justice in the Baltic States* 66 (n 180).

[194] Teitel, *Transitional Justice* 93 (n 119); Ruti Teitel, 'Transitional Justice Genealogy' (2003) 16 *Harvard Human Rights Journal* 69.

[195] For example, Teitel, *Transitional Justice* (n 119); Kritz, *Transitional Justice* (n 125).

on Eastern Europe, with the exception of the former Yugoslavia.[196] In contrast, 52 focus on Africa, and 35 focus on Latin America.[197] After the disappointment of the Eastern European transitions, the discourse of transitional justice would concentrate on the possibilities for action offered elsewhere. The brave new world that the collapse of the Soviet Bloc had brought about would allow the discourse to flourish.

3 *The Legacy of the Post-Communist Transitions*

The discussions surrounding the post-communist transitions were influential for the development of the discourse of transitional justice. They generated increasing interaction between commentators that helped to establish an autonomous epistemic community. They also contributed to defining the set of objects and concepts we discussed in the previous chapter.

Nevertheless, at this stage, the discourse of transitional justice was still on fragile footing. For one thing, the 'transitional justice' label was not definitive, and the discourse went by different names including 'retroactive justice',[198] 'historical justice'[199] and 'corrective justice',[200] as well as the more context-specific 'decommunization'.[201] More importantly, the emerging discourse coexisted with rival approaches. Following the break-up of the Soviet Bloc, constitutionalism was perceived as a way of making an institutional and legal break with the past that would usher a democratic future based on the rule of law. This approach to post-communist transitions found institutional backing in the Center for the Study of Constitutionalism in Eastern Europe established in 1990 at the University of Chicago.[202] Not only did this centre organise conferences and workshops, but it also provided advice to post-

[196] Beattie, 'An Evolutionary Process' (n 160); Andrieu, 'An Unfinished Business' (n 163); Christiane Wilke, 'Remembering Complexity? Memorials for Nazi Victims in Berlin' (2013) 7 *International Journal of Transitional Justice* 136; Horne, 'The Impact of Lustration on Democratization in Postcommunist Countries' (n 171); Ilya Nuzov, 'The Dynamics of Collective Memory in the Ukraine Crisis: A Transitional Justice Perspective' (2017) 11 *International Journal of Transitional Justice* 132; Klaus Bachmann and Igor Lyubashenko, 'The Puzzle of Transitional Justice in Ukraine' (2017) 11 *International Journal of Transitional Justice* 297; Raluca Grosescu, 'Judging Communist Crimes in Romania: Transnational and Global Influences' (2017) 11 *International Journal of Transitional Justice* 505.

[197] IJTJ, '*International Journal of Transitional Justice*' (2018) http://ijtj.oxfordjournals.org/, accessed 12 July 2018.

[198] Nino, *Radical Evil on Trial* (n 15).

[199] Holmes, 'The End of Decommunization' (n 184).

[200] Bruce A Ackerman, *The Future of Liberal Revolution* (Yale University Press, 1992).

[201] Holmes, 'The End of Decommunization' (n 184).

[202] Elster, *Closing the Books* xii (n 123); Holmes, 'Introducing the Center' (n 141).

communist states.[203] Like transitional justice, constitutionalism was a response to past widespread or systematic violence, it sought to make a clear break with the past and it was geared towards fostering democracy. Bruce Ackerman's influential book *The Future of Liberal Revolution* encapsulates the challenge that constitutionalism represented to the budding transitional justice discourse.[204] For him, the most important way to consolidate democracy was through a new constitution that marked a clear departure from the communist past. The pre-eminence of constitutionalism made him take issue with what he called 'the mirage of corrective justice'. He maintained that efforts directed at punishing and compensating for past misdeeds risked diverting the society from its main task of preventing a recurrence of the violations through foundational constitution making.[205] Supporters of transitional justice were not remiss to take this challenge. Both Carlos Nino and Ruti Teitel responded that trials and other transitional justice policies could also be foundational.[206]

Crucially, the post-communist transitions and the discussions they sparked presented many of the six characteristics that transitional justice discourse has today. Some of them were already present following the Argentine experience, and others were new. First, the post-communist transitions cemented the comparative method. Following the disintegration of the Soviet Bloc, there were many countries simultaneously experiencing similar processes of political and economic change. These similarities facilitated the comparison of the transitional justice policies adopted in the different former communist states.[207] Since the unexpected post-communist transitions were incorporated into the narrative of a 'third wave' of democratisation, they were readily contrasted with other processes taking place in other regions and times. This led to many comparative works on transitional justice distilling mechanisms and lessons from the diverse experiences of a host of countries.[208] Following

[203] Catherine Behan, 'Center Helps Eastern European Countries Shape Constitutions' *The University of Chicago Chronicle* (7 December 1995) http://chronicle.uchicago.edu/951207/georgia.shtml, accessed 30 July 2018.

[204] Ackerman, *The Future of Liberal Revolution* (n 199).

[205] Ibid 69.

[206] Nino, *Radical Evil on Trial* 128–31 (n 15); Teitel, 'Post-Communist Constitutionalism' (n 180).

[207] See, eg, Helga Welsh comparing the retribution and reconciliation policies in Central and Eastern Europe, 'Dealing with the Communist Past: Central and East European Experiences after 1990' (1996) 48 *Europe-Asia Studies* 413; Ruti Teitel contrasting the dilemmas posed by prosecutions in the post-communist transitions, 'Paradoxes in the Revolution of the Rule of Law' (1994) 19 *The Yale Journal of International Law* 239; and Hilary Appel's comparison of lustration policies (n 164).

[208] The most notable example of this trend is Kritz's compendium, *Transitional Justice* (n 125). See also Nino, *Radical Evil on Trial* (n 15); Teitel, *Transitional Justice* (n 119).

the post-communist transitions, the comparative method became a constant feature of transitional justice discourse.

Second, the discourse surrounding the Eastern European transitions was technical. The transitional justice policies were discussed as the best means to achieve the aim of fostering democracy.[209] Regarding the three dimensions of the technical characteristic, only the legalistic and the apolitical façades were present to varying degrees. As with Argentina, there was not yet a truly multidisciplinary discourse, although people from different disciplines discussed the post-communist transitions. For example, both the Salzburg conference and Neil Kritz's book convoked people from different backgrounds.

The post-communist processes clearly manifested the legalistic dimension of the technical characteristic. Although the main mechanisms for dealing with the past were administrative (lustration, access to files and private property restitution), they were embedded in a constitutional legal system that controlled them. Hence, legal decisions, especially of the newly created constitutional courts, played an important role in enforcing the rule of law, controlling the adherence of prosecutions to legal principles, restricting aspects of the lustration policies and preventing the restitution of property from infringing on legal certainty.[210] Thus these responses were within the legalism spectrum. Legalism was even more pervasive in the discourse that criticised these initiatives for not being legalistic enough. Prosecutions were criticised for not respecting the principle of legality because they targeted conduct that was legal under communism,[211] lustration programmes were condemned for not respecting due process[212] and restitution programmes were found to have infringed on the rights of good-faith owners.[213] Instances that

[209] See, eg, Daniel Friedheim, 'Accelerating Collapse: The East German Road' in Yossi Shain and Juan José Linz (eds), *Between States: Interim Governments and Democratic Transitions* (Cambridge University Press, 1995).

[210] For the role of the Eastern European constitutional courts, Teitel, 'Post-Communist Constitutionalism' (n 180); Kim Lane Scheppele, 'Democracy by Judiciary: Or, Why Courts Can Be More Democratic than Parliaments' in Adam W Czarnota, Martin Krygier and Wojciech Sadurski (eds), *Rethinking the Rule of Law after Communism* (Central European University Press, 2005); Renata Uitz, 'Constitutional Courts and the Past in Democratic Transition' in Adam W Czarnota, Martin Krygier and Wojciech Sadurski (eds), *Rethinking the Rule of Law after Communism* (Central European University Press, 2005).

[211] Adams, 'What Is Just?' (n 150); Goodman, 'After the Wall' (n 150); Teitel, 'Paradoxes in the Revolution of the Rule of Law' (n 208); Ruti Teitel, 'Transitional Jurisprudence: The Role of Law in Political Transformation' (1997) 106 *The Yale Law Journal* 2009.

[212] Siklova, 'Lustration or the Czech Way of Screening' 61–62 (n 166); Letki, 'Lustration and Democratisation in East-Central Europe' 541–42 (n 167).

[213] *Pincová and Pinc* v. *the Czech Republic* (2002) Application No 36548/97 ECHR 2002-VIII, para 60; *Velikovi* v. *Bulgaria*, para 190 (n 178).

departed from legalism, such as the summary trial and execution of Ceausescu and his wife in Rumania, were dismissed as legal travesties.[214] Transitional justice mechanisms were meant to respect the specific rules and principles of the legal realm.

The technical dimension of appearing apolitical was only partially present. International experts were much more involved in the post-communist countries than they had been in Argentina. For instance, several post-Soviet constitutions were drafted with substantial international input.[215] However, as we have seen earlier, post-communist governments adopted their own mechanisms that were subject to political debate and scrutiny. Similarly, the past violence was expressly blamed on communism as a political system. The discourse, on the other hand, did erase some of the political content of the transition. The comparisons with Latin America implied, to a certain extent, an assimilation of the violence of the communist regimes to that of the right-wing dictatorships. This assimilation effectively glossed over the political gulf separating the ideologies that inspired both situations of violence.

Third, the discourse surrounding the post-communist transitions was structured in a teleological framework. The transitional justice policies were supposed to attain various goals such as the rule of law, accountability and democracy. Moreover, these interventions were embedded in a larger architecture of a dual transition towards democracy and capitalism. Hence, the discourse analysing the Eastern European transitional justice policies relied on an instrumentalist logic by which the policies were justified, or not, according to their contribution to certain goals.[216] Even though this characteristic was already present in Argentina, the post-communist transitions added another dimension of teleology: the instrumentality of transitional justice as a discourse. As we have seen, the Eastern European transitions inspired conferences and research projects with the express purpose of using the knowledge of previous transitions to help the former communist countries. Hence, in addition to the goals of the transitional justice policies (accountability, the rule of law, democracy), there were the meta-goals of transitional justice as a discourse in itself (assisting the transitional society to achieve those goals).

[214] Nino, *Radical Evil on Trial* 21–22 (n 15).

[215] The Center for the Study of Constitutionalism in Eastern Europe was prominent in assisting with the drafting of several constitutions. For example, the constitution of Georgia was reportedly drafted at the University of Chicago, Behan (n 202).

[216] See, eg, Daniel Friedheim assessing the trials based on their impact on the rule of law (n 210); or Natalia Letki evaluating lustration programmes according to their contribution to democracy (n 167).

Fourth, the post-communist transitions and the discourse they inspired had a liberal imprint. The dual transitions were meant to replace socialism and a planned economy with liberal democracy and the market.[217] According to experts, the post-communist transitions had to draw clear boundaries between the political and economic spheres in order to foster an autonomous economic system.[218] They were thus advocating for the liberal separation between politics and the economy.

Liberalism was manifested, to varying degrees, in the three dimensions presented in the previous chapter. Some transitional justice mechanisms in Eastern Europe focused on violations of civil and political rights and instances of physical violence, such as the trials held in Germany for the shootings in the Berlin Wall or those in Poland due to the repression of strikes. However, many other mechanisms departed from the norm of the Latin American transitions and concentrated instead on socio-economic issues. There were restitution programmes for private property nationalised by the communist states and trials for embezzlement and abuse of power, and the lustration processes had the socio-economic purpose of barring people who had benefitted during the prior regime from accessing certain positions.[219] This interest in socio-economic aspects of the previous system was related to the fact that part of the public anger against the communist regimes stemmed from their economic policies and the perception that the *nomenklatura* lived much more comfortably than the rest of the population. While this interest in socio-economic issues marks a departure from the emphasis of the discourse on violations of civil and political rights and instances of physical violence, it is nonetheless still liberal. In Eastern Europe's liberal transitions, socio-economic aspects were part of the transitional justice agenda because the previous illiberal economic system was regarded as unjust. The dual transition towards political and economic liberalism was translated into an interest in the perceived economic injustices of the previous communist regime. Tellingly, in later transitions where the previous regime had not been communist, socio-economic issues were not part of the responses to past widespread or systematic violence.

The favoured destination of the post-communist transitions was liberal democracy. Although many dissidents in the former communist countries

[217] Garton Ash, *We the People* 151–52 (n 105).

[218] Elster, Preuss and Offe, *Institutional Design in Post-Communist Societies* 156 (n 111).

[219] Appel, 'Anti-Communist Justice and Founding the Post-Communist Order' 389–94 (n 164). Yet people targeted by these programmes often merely moved to other lucrative jobs in the private sector using their networks to their advantage, see Siklova, 'Lustration or the Czech Way of Screening' 58 (n 166).

were originally sceptical of liberal democracy,[220] once the transitions were on their way, this political system became the common ground between different opposition groups.[221] Therefore, when transitional justice measures were introduced, they were unquestionably meant to foster democratisation.[222] The collapse of the Soviet Bloc cemented the position of liberal democracy as the natural end point of transitions. While before 1989 communism was an option for states in transition, after the fall of the Berlin Wall, liberal democracy became the only legitimate form of government.[223] Accordingly, the discourse of transitional justice that focused on post-communist countries was meant to facilitate democratisation.

Post-communist transitional justice was liberal because it openly supported capitalism as the best economic system. This openness distinguished the post-communist transitions from previous ones in which the support for capitalism had been implicit. In Eastern Europe, the transitional justice policies were imbricated with capitalist reform. Thus the restitution of nationalised property to their pre-communist owners was presented as a privatisation which could 'create a constituency supportive of capitalist reforms, spark entrepreneurship and capital formation, and improve economic growth'.[224] In dealing with a socio-economic grievance of the past, the transitional justice policies were facilitating the advent of the capitalist future.

Fifth, the discourse surrounding the post-communist transitions was not multilevel. As in Argentina, all the examined policies for responding to past widespread or systematic violence operated on the national level. However, the European Court of Human Rights eventually did hear some cases related to transitional justice policies, such as the trial of the members of the East German Politburo for the Berlin Wall shootings[225] and the restitution of private property in the Czech Republic and Bulgaria.[226]

Sixth, the discourse following the Eastern European transitions centred on the state. The responses examined were exclusively those adopted by the state

[220] For example, according to Václav Havel, democracy could be a transitional solution but it was not a political ideal, 'The Power of the Powerless' in John Keane (ed), *The Power of the Powerless: Citizens against the State in Central-Eastern Europe* (Hutchinson, 1985) 91–92. See also Rosenberg, *The Haunted Land* (n 123).

[221] Garton Ash, *We the People* 8 (n 105).

[222] Letki, 'Lustration and Democratisation in East-Central Europe' 534–34 (n 167).

[223] Shain, Linz and Berat, *Between States* 8 (n 11).

[224] Appel, 'Anti-Communist Justice and Founding the Post-Communist Order' 395 (n 164).

[225] *Streletz, Kessler and Krenz* v. *Germany* (n 152).

[226] *Velikovi* v. *Bulgaria* (n 178); *Pincová and Pinc* v. *the Czech Republic* (n 212). See also Eva Brems, 'Transitional Justice in the Case Law of the European Court of Human Rights' (2011) 5 *International Journal of Transitional Justice* 282.

(lustration, trials, restitution of property, parliamentary commissions of inquiry). Only much later were non-state responses to past widespread or systematic violence given some consideration.[227]

Despite the disappointment of the Eastern European transitions, they left behind an emerging discourse that would later blossom. The rise of international criminal justice and the South African transition would contribute to that development. They would also alter the shape of transitional justice, opening it to new perspectives.

IV THE RISE OF INTERNATIONAL CRIMINAL JUSTICE

The creation of the ICTY in 1993 was almost as unexpected as the fall of the Berlin Wall. Projects for an international criminal court had languished in UN forums for decades.[228] The prospects for international criminal justice were so dim that even its staunchest advocates doubted that international criminal courts were feasible at all. In the preface to his Draft International Criminal Code, M. Cherif Bassiouni wrote in 1987 that he did not have great illusions that 'the idea of an international criminal code and an international criminal court will soon become reality'.[229] Even as late as 1991, Carlos Nino conceded that it was idealistic to hope for the establishment of international criminal courts given the state of international law at that time.[230] International criminal tribunals seemed a utopia for the future.[231]

Yet in 1993 the UN Security Council created the ICTY. Acting under Chapter VII of the UN Charter, the Security Council decided to establish an international tribunal to prosecute persons responsible for serious violations of international humanitarian law committed in the territory of the former Yugoslavia.[232] The Security Council granted the ICTY jurisdiction over grave

[227] See Lavinia Stan, *Transitional Justice in Eastern Europe and the Former Soviet Union: Reckoning with the Communist Past* (Routledge, 2008); Lavinia Stan, *Transitional Justice in Post-Communist Romania the Politics of Memory* (Cambridge University Press, 2013).

[228] M Cherif Bassiouni, *A Draft International Criminal Code and Draft Statute for an International Criminal Tribunal* (Martinus Nijhoff Publishers, 1987) 11.

[229] Ibid 7.

[230] Nino, 'The Duty to Punish Past Abuses of Human Rights Put into Context' 2638 (n 66).

[231] Judge Christine Van den Wyngaert, judge of the ICTY and the ICC, has admitted that she never expected to see international criminal courts in her lifetime, 'Victims before International Criminal Courts: Some Views and Concerns of an ICC Trial Judge' (2011) 44 *Case Western Reserve Journal of International Law* 475, 476.

[232] UNSC Resolution 827 (25 May 1993) UN Doc S/RES/827. This resolution followed a previous one requesting the UN Secretary-General to prepare a draft statute for a tribunal, see UNSC Resolution 808 (22 February 1993) UN Doc S/RES/808. A draft of Resolution 808 was introduced by France, UNSC 'Letter dated 10 February 1993 from the Permanent

breaches of the Geneva Conventions of 1949, violations of the laws or customs of war, genocide and crimes against humanity committed between 1 January 1991 and a date to be determined upon the restoration of peace in the former Yugoslavia.[233] Within this jurisdiction, the ICTY had primacy over national courts.[234]

In creating the ICTY, 'the Security Council had shown that the apparently impossible was achievable'.[235] The unexpected creation of the ICTY was facilitated by public pressure stemming from widespread media coverage of the atrocities taking place in the former Yugoslavia[236] and a favourable political juncture within the Security Council which ensured a unanimous vote.[237]

On 8 November 1994, again acting under Chapter VII of the UN Charter, the Security Council created the International Criminal Tribunal for Rwanda (ICTR) to respond to the genocide that had taken place in that country.[238] The ICTR had authority to prosecute genocide, crimes against humanity and violations of Article 3 common to the Geneva Conventions and of Additional Protocol II.[239] The exclusion of other war crimes was due to the characterisation of the Rwandan conflict as internal. The ICTR had jurisdiction to try

Representative of France to the United Nations Addressed to the Secretary-General' UN Doc S/25266. See also Virginia Morris and Michael P Scharf, *An Insider's Guide to the International Criminal Tribunal for the Former Yugoslavia: A Documentary History and Analysis* (Transnational Publishers, 1995), vol 1, 31.

233 Statute of the International Tribunal for the Prosecution of Persons Responsible for Serious Violations of International Humanitarian Law Committed in the Territory of the Former Yugoslavia since 1991, Annex to UNSC Resolution 827 (25 May 1993) UN Doc S/RES/827, arts 2–5, 8. The ICTY closed on 31 December 2017, see Assessment and Report of Judge Carmel Agius, President of the International Tribunal for the Former Yugoslavia', Annex to Letter dated 29 November 2017 from the President of the International Tribunal for the Prosecution of Persons Responsible for Serious Violations of International Humanitarian Law Committed in the Territory of the Former Yugoslavia since 1991 addressed to the President of the Security Council' UN Doc S/2017/1001.

234 Ibid, art 9.

235 James Crawford, 'The Drafting of the Rome Statute' in Philippe Sands (ed), *From Nuremberg to The Hague: The Future of International Criminal Justice* (Cambridge University Press, 2003) 145.

236 Pierre Hazan, *Justice in a Time of War: The True Story behind the International Criminal Tribunal for the Former Yugoslavia* (Texas A & M University Press, 2004) 12–14, 35–36.

237 UNSC Verbatim Record (6 October 1992) UN Doc S/PV/3119; UNSC Verbatim Record (16 November 1992) UN Doc S/PV/3137; UNSC Verbatim Record (22 February 1993) UN Doc S/PV/3175; ibid 37–38. See also Morris and Scharf, *An Insider's Guide to the International Criminal Tribunal for the Former Yugoslavia*, vol 1, 22–35 (n 231); William Schabas, *The UN International Criminal Tribunals: The Former Yugoslavia, Rwanda and Sierra Leone* (Cambridge University Press, 2006) 16–21.

238 UNSC Resolution 955 (8 November 1994) UN Doc S/RES/955.

239 Statute of the International Criminal Tribunal for Rwanda, Annex to UNSC Resolution 955 (8 November 1994) UN Doc S/RES/955, arts 2–4

crimes committed within the territory of Rwanda as well as those committed by Rwandan citizens in neighbouring states.[240] In terms of temporal scope, it covered a period of one calendar year, from 1 January 1994 to 31 December 1994.[241] The ICTR and the ICTY shared their appeals chamber and also shared their prosecutor until 2003 when the Security Council decide to appoint an exclusive prosecutor for the Rwandan tribunal.[242]

In spite of the existing precedent of the ICTY, the ICTR met more resistance at the Security Council than its predecessor. Rwanda, which was occupying a temporary seat at the Security Council, had originally requested the creation of an ad hoc tribunal. However, concerns over the proposed statute – including, inter alia, the temporal jurisdiction of the tribunal, which did not cover the lead-up to the genocide; the fact that the ICTR would share the prosecutor and appeals chamber with the ICTY and the possibility of the seat of the tribunal being outside Rwanda – made Rwanda vote against the resolution. In turn, China abstained, stressing the importance of having the full cooperation of Rwanda.[243]

Although the Security Council did not establish any other international criminal tribunals of the scope and nature of the ICTY and ICTR, international criminal justice continued to develop with the creation of the so-called 'hybrid, mixed or internationalised courts'.[244] These courts combine international and national components. They have mixed staff with international and domestic judges, prosecutors and supporting personnel. They also apply, to varying degrees, international and domestic law. Mixed criminal courts were established in Kosovo (2000), Timor Leste (2000), Sierra Leone (2002), Cambodia (2006) and Lebanon (2006).[245] While all these institutions have mixed benches and staff, they all have different legal bases.[246] The mixed

[240] Ibid, art 7.
[241] Ibid.
[242] UNSC Resolution 1505 (4 September 2003) UN Doc S/RES/1505.
[243] UNSC Verbatim Record (8 November 1994) UN Doc S/PV/3453.
[244] On this type of courts, see Cesare Romano, André Nollkaemper and Jann K Kleffner, *Internationalized Criminal Courts and Tribunals: Sierra Leone, East Timor, Kosovo and Cambodia* (Oxford University Press, 2004); Sarah MH Nouwen, '"Hybrid Courts": The Hybrid Category of a New Type of International Crimes Courts' (2006) 2 *Utrecht Law Review* 190; Sarah Williams, *Hybrid and Internationalised Criminal Tribunals: Selected Jurisdictional Issues* (Hart, 2012).
[245] Daphna Shraga, 'The Second Generation UN-Based Tribunals: A Diversity of Mixed Jurisdictions' in Cesare Romano, André Nollkaemper and Jann Kleffner (eds), *Internationalized Criminal Courts and Tribunals: Sierra Leone, East Timor, Kosovo and Cambodia* (2004); Williams, *Hybrid and Internationalised Criminal Tribunals* (n 243).
[246] Nouwen, 'Hybrid Courts' 200–1 (n 243).

criminal courts in Kosovo and Timor Leste were created by the UN interim administrations, themselves based on Security Council resolutions under Chapter VII, as part of their transitional administration of the territories.[247] The Special Court of Sierra Leone was established by a treaty between the UN and Sierra Leone following a Security Council resolution that did not invoke Chapter VII.[248] A Cambodian law, later complemented by an agreement between the UN and Cambodia, established the Extraordinary Chambers of the Courts of Cambodia (ECCC).[249] The Special Tribunal for Lebanon was created by a Security Council resolution under Chapter VII after Lebanon failed to ratify the agreement it had signed with the UN to establish the tribunal.[250]

While the ad hoc tribunals were beginning to function, negotiations for a permanent international criminal tribunal gathered pace. In 1994, the International Law Commission (ILC) adopted a Draft Statute for an International Criminal Court, and the UN General Assembly established a committee to review it.[251] Negotiations continued and led to a diplomatic conference held

[247] For Kosovo, UNSC Resolution 1244 (10 June 1999) UN Doc S/RES/1244; UN Interim Administration Mission in Kosovo (UNMIK) Regulation No 2000/6 'On the Appointment and Removal from Office of International Judges and International Prosecutors' (15 February 2000) UN Doc UNMIK/REG/2000/6; UNMIK Regulation No 2000/34 (27 May 2000) UN Doc UNMIK/REG/2000/34. For Timor Leste, UNSC Resolution 1272 (15 October 1999) UN Doc S/RES/1272; UN Transitional Authority in East Timor (UNTAET) Regulation No 2000/11 'On the Organization of Courts in East Timor' (6 March 2000) UN Doc UNTAET/REG/2000/11; UNTAET Regulation No 2000/15 'On the Establishment of Panels with Exclusive Jurisdiction over Serious Criminal Offences' (6 June 2000) UN Doc UNTAET/REG/2000/15.

[248] Agreement between the United Nations and the Government of Sierra Leone on the Establishment of a Special Court for Sierra Leone (adopted 16 January 2002, entered into force 12 April 2002) 2178 UNTS 138; UNSC Resolution 1315 (14 August 2000) UN Doc S/RES/1315.

[249] Law on the Establishment of Extraordinary Chambers in the Courts of Cambodia for the Prosecution of Crimes Committed During the Period of Democratic Kampuchea (NS/RKM/1004/006) (Amended 27 October 2004) (Law on the Establishment of the ECCC); Agreement between the United Nations and the Royal Government of Cambodia concerning the prosecution under Cambodian law of crimes committed during the period of Democratic Kampuchea (adopted 6 June 2003, entered into force 29 April 2005) 2329 UNTS 117 (UN-Cambodia Agreement for Khmer Rouge Trials).

[250] UNSC Resolution 1757 (30 May 2007) UN Doc S/RES/1757; *Prosecutor* v. *Salim Jamil Ayyash, Mustafa Amine Badreddine, Hussein Hassan Oneissi and Assad Hassan Sabra* (Decision on the Defence Appeals Against the Trial Chamber's 'Decision on the Defence Challenges to the Jurisdiction and Legality of the Tribunal') STL-11-01/PT/AC/AR90.1 (24 October 2012) Special Tribunal for Lebanon, para 31.

[251] ILC 'Report of the International Law Commission on the Work of its Forty-Sixth Session' (17 February 1995) UN Doc A/RES/49/51; UNGA Resolution 49/53 'Establishment of an International Criminal Court' (9 December 1994) UN Doc A/RES/49/53.

in Rome during June and July 1998.[252] On 17 July 1998, the Rome Statute of the International Criminal Court (Rome Statute) was adopted.[253] The Rome Statute entered into force on 1 July 2002 after receiving 60 instruments of ratification, acceptance, approval or accession.[254] The Rome Statute granted the ICC jurisdiction over genocide, crimes against humanity, war crimes, and – subject to certain conditions – the crime of aggression.[255] As a treaty-based tribunal, the ICC can prosecute crimes committed in the territory of States Parties or by individuals who are nationals of States Parties. However, when the Security Council acting under Chapter VII refers a situation to the ICC, the court can prosecute any crime within the Rome Statute regardless of where or by whom it was committed.[256] The creation of the permanent ICC consolidated the impressive development of international criminal justice in this period.

As former president of the ICTY Judge Theodor Meron has observed, not 'even the most fervent advocates of international tribunals could have predicted their current prominence'.[257] The rise of international and mixed criminal courts of various guises was an unprecedented and momentous development in international law. It led to the technical development of international criminal law and consolidated a body of specialised lawyers and other experts dedicated to this area. This process also had important consequences for the developing discourse of transitional justice.

1 *The Internationalisation of Transitional Justice*

The rise of international criminal justice transformed the discourse of transitional justice by adding an international dimension. Since then, transitional justice discourse has been international because it includes mechanisms operating at the international level and applying international law. Before the creation of the ad hoc tribunals spearheaded the development of

[252] UNGA Resolution 51/207 'Establishment of an International Criminal Court' (17 December 1996) UN Doc A/RES/51/207; UNGA Resolution 52/160 'Establishment of an International Criminal Court' (15 December 1997) UN Doc A/RES/52/160.

[253] For the negotiations, Fanny Benedetti, Karine Bonneau and John Washburn, *Negotiating the International Criminal Court: New York to Rome, 1994–1998* (Martinus Nijhoff Publishers, 2014).

[254] Rome Statute of the International Criminal Court (adopted 17 July 1998, entered into force 1 July 2002) 2187 UNTS 90 (Rome Statute).

[255] Ibid, art 5.

[256] Ibid, art 12(2).

[257] Theodor Meron, 'The Greatest Change in International Law', *The Making of International Criminal Justice* (Oxford University Press, 2011) 75.

international criminal justice, transitional justice was considered a purely national issue, ruled by domestic law. As we have seen, the Argentine transition approached the task of responding to past widespread or systematic violence as a domestic question using national law.[258] The experience of the other Latin American countries was not different. Likewise, during the post-communist transitions, transitional justice was kept within the national sphere. Although at this stage there was an emerging global community of transitional justice experts willing to give advice to the former socialist states, the policies and mechanisms were meant to be adopted at the national level and relying on domestic law. While regional human rights courts became involved in some cases related to the Latin American and Eastern European transitions and some of their decisions would become influential, as examined in Chapter 5, the nature of these bodies as courts of last resort meant that the direct mechanisms of transitional justice remained anchored at the national level.

The unexpected development of international criminal justice opened transitional justice to a new perspective. In the first place, the ad hoc tribunals and the international and mixed criminal courts that followed were immediately ushered into transitional justice's catalogue. In Ruti Teitel's *Transitional Justice*, the ICTY and the ICTR are regarded as contemporary transitional justice mechanisms in the same way as national proceedings.[259] Equally, Carlos Nino discussed the then-nascent ICTY in his *Radical Evil on Trial* together with domestic mechanisms of transitional justice.[260]

Nevertheless, several differences distinguished the ad hoc tribunals from other mechanisms examined by the incipient discourse of transitional justice. First, the ad hoc tribunals were international organs created by the UN rather than national institutions. Second, whereas the other responses examined by

[258] Pádraig McAuliffe, 'From Molehills to Mountains (and Myths?)' (n 9); Par Engstrom, 'Transitional Justice and Ongoing Conflict' in Chandra Lekha Sriram and others (eds), *Transitional Justice and Peacebuilding on the Ground: Victims and Ex-Combatants* (Routledge, 2013). See also Luis Moreno Ocampo, 'The Nuremberg Parallel in Argentina' (1990) 11 *New York Law School Journal of International and Comparative Law* 357.

[259] Teitel, *Transitional Justice* 48 (n 119).

[260] Nino, *Radical Evil on Trial* 26, 186–89 (n 15). See also Dumisa Ntebeza, 'The Struggle for Human Rights: From the UN Declaration of Human Rights to the Present' in Charles Villa-Vicencio and Wilhelm Verwoerd (eds), *Looking Back, Reaching Forward: Reflections on the Truth and Reconciliation Commission of South Africa* (University of Cape Town Press, 2000); Naomi Roht-Arriaza, 'The Role of International Actors in National Accountability Processes' in Alexandra Barahona de Brito, Carmen González Enríquez and Paloma Aguilar Fernández (eds), *The Politics of Memory: Transitional Justice in Democratizing Societies* (Oxford University Press, 2001).

the discourse of transitional justice addressed past violence, when the ICTY was created in early 1993, the conflict in the former Yugoslavia was ongoing. Third, instead of addressing the internal repression of an authoritarian regime, the ICTY tackled atrocity resulting from an armed conflict. Fourth, the ad hoc tribunals adjudicated crimes under international law rather than offences under domestic legislation.

In spite of these differences, the incorporation of the ad hoc tribunals, and the rest of the courts that followed them, into the discourse of transitional justice was successful and permanent. Today these institutions feature regularly in books, journals, conferences and institutions focused on transitional justice. The *Encyclopaedia of Transitional Justice* lists 'international tribunals' as one of the methods, processes and practices of transitional justice, and it has entries on the ICTY, the ICTR, the ICC and many other international and mixed criminal courts and tribunals.[261] The first editorial of the *International Journal of Transitional Justice* discussed the ad hoc tribunals as mechanisms of transitional justice,[262] and 66 per cent of all articles on trials published in that journal focus on international or mixed criminal courts.[263] For the ICTJ, the ad hoc tribunals, the ICC and the mixed criminal courts are transitional justice mechanisms.[264] The 2011 UN Secretary-General report 'The Rule of Law and Transitional Justice in Conflict and Post-Conflict Societies' includes the same courts in its review of transitional justice developments.[265] Similarly, the European Union (EU) regards the ICC and mixed criminal courts as transitional justice institutions.[266] Moreover, expertise in international criminal justice is considered transferrable to transitional justice. For example, the former president of the ICTJ, David Tolbert, used to be the deputy prosecutor of the ICTY, and the former vice president, Paul Seils, was an official of the ICC.[267]

261 Lavinia Stan and Nadya Nedelsky, *Encyclopedia of Transitional Justice* (Cambridge University Press, 2013).

262 IJTJ, 'Editorial Note' (2007) 1 *International Journal of Transitional Justice* 1.

263 IJTJ, '*International Journal of Transitional Justice*' (n 196).

264 ICTJ, 'Criminal Justice' (2018) www.ictj.org/our-work/transitional-justice-issues/criminal-justice, accessed 30 July 2018.

265 UNSC 'Report of the Secretary-General on the Rule of Law and Transitional Justice in Conflict and Post-Conflict Societies' (12 October 2011) UN Doc S/2011/634 (2011 UNSG Transitional Justice Report).

266 European Union 'The EU's Policy Framework on Support to Transitional Justice' (16 November 2015) Annex to Doc 13576/15, II (1), III (1).

267 ICTJ, 'David Tolbert' (2018) www.ictj.org/about/david-tolbert, accessed 30 July 2018; Paul Seils, 'Transitional Justice: Time for a Re-Think' *Open Global Rights* (10 April 2018) www.openglobalrights.org/paul-seils/Transitional-justice-time-for-a-re-think/, accessed 31 July 2018.

The rise of international criminal justice resulted in international and mixed criminal courts becoming policy options for states with an experience of widespread or systematic violence. States can request the creation of international tribunals – as Rwanda,[268] Sierra Leone[269] and Lebanon did –[270] or seek international legal assistance for domestic trials, as Cambodia did.[271] States can also refer situations to the ICC, including those taking place in their own territories,[272] as Uganda,[273] the Democratic Republic of Congo[274] and the Central African Republic[275] have done. The development of international criminal justice has thus established the international as a new realm for transitional justice mechanisms. The discourse of transitional justice quickly claimed this realm as its own. Since then, the formerly fully domestic menu of transitional justice mechanisms also includes international criminal tribunals and international law.

The relationship between international criminal tribunals and other transitional justice initiatives is, however, fraught with tension. International criminal justice is manifestly narrower in its scope and objectives than transitional justice, which is understood as the whole array of possible responses to past widespread or systematic violence. International criminal justice sees violence through the lens of crime definitions under international

268 UNSC 'Letter dated 28 September 1994 from the Permanent Representative of Rwanda to the United Nations addressed to the President of the Security Council' UN Doc S/1994/1115.

269 UNSC 'Letter dated 9 August 2000 from the Permanent Representative of Sierra Leone to the United Nations addressed to the President of the Security Council' UN Doc S/2000/786.

270 UNSC 'Letter dated 13 December 2005 from the Chargé d'affaires of the Permanent Mission of Lebanon to the United Nations addressed to the Secretary-General' UN Doc S/2005/783.

271 UNGA 'Letter dated 21 June 1997 from the First and Second Prime Ministers of Cambodia addressed to the Secretary-General', Annex to the identical letters dated 23 June 1997 from the Secretary-General addressed to the President of the General Assembly and to the President of the Security Council, UN Docs A/51/930, S/1997/48.

272 For self-referrals, Andreas Müller and Ignaz Stegmiller, 'Self-Referrals on Trial: From Panacea to Patient' (2010) 8 *Journal of International Criminal Justice* 1267.

273 ICC 'President of Uganda Refers Situation Concerning the Lord's Resistance Army (LRA) to the ICC' (29 January 2004) Press Release ICC-20040129-44; *Situation in Uganda* (Decision Assigning the Situation in Uganda to Pre-Trial Chamber II) ICC-02/04-1 (5 July 2004). See also Sarah MH Nouwen, *Complementarity in the Line of Fire: The Catalysing Effect of the International Criminal Court in Uganda and Sudan* (Cambridge University Press, 2013) 113.

274 ICC, 'Prosecutor Receives Referral of the Situation in the Democratic Republic of Congo' (19 April 2004) Press Release ICC-OTP-20040419-50; *Situation in the Democratic Republic of Congo* (Decision Assigning the Situation in the Democratic Republic of Congo to Pre-Trial Chamber I) ICC-01/04-1 (5 July 2004).

275 ICC, 'Prosecutor Receives Referral Concerning Central African Republic' (7 January 2005) Press Release ICC-OTP-20050107-86; *Situation in the Central African Republic* (Decision Assigning the Situation in the Central African Republic to Pre-Trial Chamber III) ICC-01/05-1 (19 January 2005).

law and labels perpetrators and victims according to these definitions and available forensic evidence. This tunnel view does not exhaust all possibilities of transitional justice.

Even the principle of complementarity of the ICC, which is meant to give deference to national processes, in fact only contemplates criminal trials as capable of rendering a situation inadmissible before that court.[276] The existence of non-prosecutorial transitional justice policies has no bearing in this regard. As an international criminal law institution, the ICC is only concerned with criminal trials. Moreover, the ICC interprets the principle of complementarity in such a way that makes it hard to challenge the admissibility of a case, even when there are criminal investigations or prosecutions before national courts. By applying the 'same person/same conduct' test to assess whether domestic authorities are investigating or prosecuting the same case,[277] investigations or prosecutions that do not overlap with the specific conduct targeted by the ICC prosecution cannot be wrestled back to national jurisdictions.[278] The assimilation of transitional justice to international criminal justice thus risks precluding other forms of justice to respond to past widespread or systematic violence.[279]

At the same time, international criminal justice sits uncomfortably within transitional justice. It has a historical trajectory that predates transitional justice discourse and a scope that is more contained and focused. Although international criminal justice was reinvigorated with the creation

276 Rome Statute, art 17 (n 253); *Prosecutor* v. *Germain Katanga and Mathieu Ngudjolo Chui* (Judgment on the Appeal of Mr Germain Katanga against the Oral Decision of Trial Chamber II of 12 June 2009 on the Admissibility of the Case) ICC-01/04–01/07–1497 (25 September 2009), paras 85–86. See also *Prosecutor* v. *William Samoei Ruto, Henry Kiprono Kosgey and Joshua Arap Sang* (Judgment on the Appeal of the Republic of Kenya against the Decision of Pre-Trial Chamber II of 30 May 2011 entitled 'Decision on the Application by the Government of Kenya Challenging the Admissibility of the Case Pursuant to Article 19(2)(b) of the Statute) ICC-01/09–01/11–307 (30 August 2011), para 44.

277 *Prosecutor* v. *Saif Al-Islam Gaddafi and Abdullah Al-Senussi* (Judgment on the Appeal of Libya against the Decision of Pre-Trial Chamber I of 31 May 2013 entitled 'Decision on the Admissibility of the case against Saif Al-Islam Gaddafi') ICC-01/11–01/11–547-Red (21 May 2014), para 1.

278 See, eg, *Prosecutor* v. *Simone Gbagbo* (Decision on Côte d'Ivoire's challenge to the admissibility of the case against Simone Gbagbo) ICC-02/11–01/12–47-Red (11 December 2014); *Prosecutor* v. *Simone Gbagbo* (Judgment on the Appeal of Côte d'Ivoire against the decision of Pre-Trial Chamber I of 11 December 2014 entitled 'Decision on Côte d'Ivoire's Challenge to the Admissibility of the Case against Simone Gbagbo') ICC-02/11–01/12–75-Red (27 May 2015).

279 For how the dominance of international criminal law can threaten the diversity of conceptions of justice, see Sarah MH Nouwen and Wouter G Werner, 'Monopolizing Global Justice: International Criminal Law as Challenge to Human Diversity' (2015) 13 *Journal of International Criminal Justice* 157.

of ICTY and ensuing developments, it already existed as a somewhat dormant discourse and had the antecedent of the post–World War II trials that is examined in the next chapter. International criminal justice is also more contained than transitional justice insofar as it concentrates on one discipline (law), one profession (lawyers) and one mechanism (criminal trials). Moreover, the establishment of the various international criminal tribunals discussed earlier led to the development of international criminal law and produced a group of highly specialised lawyers on this area. This fomented further research on international criminal justice. As a result of the historical trajectory, focused scope, professionalisation and attention it attracts, international criminal justice is in some ways too big to fit comfortably under the umbrella of transitional justice. Many international criminal lawyers would not necessarily regard international criminal justice as one among many transitional justice tools but rather as a self-standing discipline and practice.

Alongside the internalisation of transitional justice, the development of international criminal justice marked the expansion of the discourse to violence resulting from armed conflicts. Initially, the discourse of transitional justice concentrated on past widespread or systematic violence enacted by authoritarian regimes. That had been the case with Argentina and other Latin American countries during the 1980s and with Eastern Europe in the early 1990s. As we have seen, these processes were thus inscribed in the 'transitions from authoritarianism to democracy' framework.[280] In contrast, the UN Security Council created the ICTY to respond to an ongoing armed conflict.[281] The ICTR was also established to respond to an armed conflict with the objective of contributing to the maintenance of peace.[282] Most mixed criminal courts such as those in Sierra Leone,[283] Kosovo,[284] Timor Leste[285] and Cambodia[286]

[280] Guillermo O'Donnell, Philippe C Schmitter and Laurence Whitehead, *Transitions from Authoritarian Rule: Latin America* (n 67).

[281] UNSC Resolution 827, para 2 (n 231).

[282] UNSC Resolution 955, preamble (n 237).

[283] UNSC Resolution 1315, preamble.

[284] UNMIK Regulation No 2000/34, preamble (n 248).

[285] UNSC Resolution 1272 (n 247), preamble; UN Doc UNTAET/REG/2000/15, art 3(1).

[286] UN-Cambodia Agreement for Khmer Rouge Trials, preamble (n 247); UNGA Resolution 57/228 'Khmer Rouge trials' (18 December 2002) UN Doc A/RES/57/228, preamble. Although the ECCC has jurisdiction over crimes committed during the Democratic Kampuchea period (1975–1979) that mostly concern offences perpetrated by the Khmer Rouge regime against the Cambodian population, during that time Cambodia was engaged in an armed conflict with Vietnam. War crimes related to this conflict are also within the jurisdiction of the ECCC. See Law on the Establishment of the ECCC, art 2 new (n 248).

had jurisdiction over crimes committed in the context of an armed conflict. Equally, most situations that the ICC has been seized of involved an armed conflict.[287] Because international and mixed tribunals were readily incorporated into transitional justice discourse, so were the situations of armed conflict that these tribunals were addressing. Moreover, while the ICTY and ICTR were being set up, El Salvador and Guatemala were grappling with post-conflict transitions. These transitions taking place in Latin America and implementing truth commissions helped to cement the expansion of transitional justice to armed conflicts.

The incorporation of international and mixed criminal courts addressing armed conflicts into transitional justice also expanded the areas of law associated with this discourse. Since these institutions adjudicate crimes committed in the context of armed conflicts, international and mixed tribunals were granted jurisdiction over war crimes and applied international humanitarian law. War crimes thus became part of the established remit of transitional justice alongside violations of human rights, crimes against humanity and genocide that can occur in peacetime.[288]

The expansion of transitional justice from authoritarian repression to armed conflicts was related to the growing role of the UN in this discourse and practice. The first purpose of the UN is to maintain international peace and security.[289] Due to this mandate, the UN, and particularly the Security Council, would be naturally interested in transitional processes related to armed conflicts that constitute a threat to international peace and security.

[287] See for example, *Prosecutor* v. *Thomas Lubanga Dyilo* (Judgment Pursuant to Article 74 of the Statute) ICC-01/04–01/06–2842 (14 March 2012), para 543 (pertaining to the situation in the Democratic Republic of Congo); *Prosecutor* v. *Jean-Pierre Bemba Gombo* (Judgment Pursuant to Article 74 of the Statute) ICC-01/05–01/08–3343 (21 March 2016), para 663 (pertaining to the situation in the Central African Republic); *Prosecutor* v. *Ahmad Al Faqi Al Mahdi* (Judgment and Sentence) ICC-01/12–01/15–171 (27 September 2016), para 18 (pertaining to the situation in Mali).

[288] For genocide, Convention on the Prevention and Punishment of the Crime of Genocide (adopted 9 December 1948 UNGA Resolution 260 (III) A, entered into force 12 January 1951) 78 UNTS 277 (Genocide Convention); *Prosecutor* v. *Akayesu* (Judgment) ICTR-96–4-T (2 September 1998), paras 497–98. For crimes against humanity, see *Prosecutor* v. *Tadić* (Decision on the Defence Motion for Interlocutory Appeal on Jurisdiction) ICTY-94–1 (2 October 1995), paras 140–41; *Prosecutor* v. *Khieu Samphan, Nuon Chea, Ieng Sary and Ieng Thirith* (Case 002/01 Appeal Judgment) Case 002-F36 (23 November 2016), para 721; Rome Statute (n 253), art 7; M Cherif Bassiouni, *International Criminal Law*, vol 1 (3rd edn, Martinus Nijhoff Publishers, 2008). For human rights see, UN Human Rights Committee, 'General Comment No 31 on (Art. 2) The Nature of the General Legal Obligation Imposed on States Parties to the Covenant' (29 March 2004) UN Doc CCPR/C/21/Rev.1.Add 13.

[289] Charter of the United Nations and Statute of the International Court of Justice (adopted 26 June 1945, entered into force 24 October 1945) 1 UNTS XVI, art 1(1).

As we have seen earlier, the UN was involved in various guises in the establishment of all international and mixed criminal courts and tribunals as well as of the truth commission of El Salvador. With the incorporation of international criminal tribunals and post-conflict transitions into the remit of transitional justice, the UN became more involved in this discourse.

Since then, the UN has continued to participate in the discourse of transitional justice with an emphasis on those situations related to armed conflicts. Thus the UN Secretary-General has submitted reports to the Security Council on 'The Rule of Law and Transitional Justice in Conflict and Post-Conflict Societies' with the purpose of highlighting key issues and lessons learned from the UN's experience in promoting justice and the rule of law in conflict and post-conflict societies.[290] Similarly, while the 'Guidance Note of the Secretary-General on the United Nations Approach to Transitional Justice' includes societies emerging from conflict and repressive rules in its understanding of transitional justice, most of its recommendations relate to post-conflict situations.[291] The focus of the UN on post-conflict transitions combined with its role in international and mixed criminal courts as well as on wider transitional justice initiatives contributed to the expansion of transitional justice discourse in this direction.

2 *Characteristics of International Criminal Justice*

International and mixed criminal courts present many of the six key characteristics of the discourse of transitional justice. These institutions were incorporated into transitional justice, despite the differences highlighted earlier, because they reflected these characteristics. First, the discourse can apply to them its comparative method. The institutional arrangements and jurisprudence of older courts, in particular the ad hoc tribunals, have influenced the design and functioning of later institutions.[292] This process implied distilling lessons from older experiences to apply to other cases in the same way as in the

[290] 2004 UNSG Transitional Justice Report, para 2 (n 5); 2011 UNSG Transitional Justice Report, para 1 (n 264).

[291] Guidance Note of the Secretary-General: United Nations Approach to Transitional Justice' (10 March 2010) (UN Approach to Transitional Justice). Two out of three recommendations are exclusively applicable to post-conflict situations: taking human rights and transitional justice considerations into account during peace processes and coordinating disarmament, demobilization and reintegration with transitional justice initiatives.

[292] Alex Whiting, 'The ICTY as a Laboratory of International Criminal Procedure' in Bert Swart, Alexander Zahar and Göran Sluiter (eds), *The Legacy of the International Criminal Tribunal for the Former Yugoslavia* (Oxford University Press, 2011).

wider discourse of transitional justice. Furthermore, the mixed criminal courts are often compared, although they are sometimes regarded as a monolithic category despite their differences.[293]

Second, international criminal justice is overwhelmingly technical in its legalistic and apolitical dimensions. International and mixed criminal courts stand at the most legalistic end of the spectrum of legalism. Their rise has developed a community of legal experts in international criminal law that regard it as a self-contained system with its own logic. While inherently political in many ways, international and mixed criminal courts depoliticise conflict by focusing on the abstract categories of international criminal law. They turn political conflict into something that can be adjudicated according to law.[294]

Third, international criminal justice is teleological because it is oriented towards the achievement of a set of goals. The founding documents of different tribunals set varying goals for them: putting an end to crimes and contributing to the restoration and maintenance of peace (ICTY),[295] contributing to national reconciliation (ICTR)[296] and putting an end to impunity of perpetrators of the most serious crimes of concern to the international community as well as contributing to their prevention (ICC).[297]

Fourth, international criminal justice has a liberal imprint, especially in the dimension of foregrounding violations of civil and political rights and instances of physical violence. International and mixed criminal courts have jurisdiction over international crimes (eg, genocide, crimes against humanity, war crimes) and, in the case of mixed criminal courts, over some domestic crimes as well. These offences predominantly cover conduct that could also be considered a violation of civil and political rights. While there is conduct that could be both an international crime and a violation of economic, social or cultural rights, such as the war crime of biological experiments that would

[293] Nouwen, 'Hybrid Courts' (n 245). For mixed criminal tribunals as a category, see Steven D Roper and Lilian A Barria, 'Assessing the Record of Justice: A Comparison of Mixed International Tribunals versus Domestic Mechanisms for Human Rights Enforcement' (2005) 4 *Journal of Human Rights* 521; Padraig McAuliffe, 'Hybrid Tribunals at Ten How International Criminal Justice's Golden Child Became an Orphan' (2011) 7 *Journal of International Law & International Relations* 1; Mathias Holvoet and Paul de Hert, 'International Criminal Law as Global Law: An Assessment of the Hybrid Tribunals' (2012) 17 *Tilburg Law Review* 228; Williams, *Hybrid and Internationalised Criminal Tribunals* (n 243).

[294] See Judith Shklar, *Legalism* (Harvard University Press, 1964).

[295] UNSC Resolution 827 (n 231).

[296] UNSC Resolution 955 (n 237).

[297] Rome Statute, preamble (n 253).

violate the right to health,[298] most of the offences under international criminal law overlap more easily with violations of civil and political rights, such as the right to life or physical integrity.[299] The domestic crimes over which some mixed criminal courts have been given jurisdiction mostly overlap with violations of civil and political rights as well. Thus the Special Tribunal for Lebanon has jurisdiction, inter alia, over terrorism, crimes against life and personal integrity;[300] the ECCC over homicide, torture and religious persecution[301] and the Special Court of Sierra Leone over the abuse of girls and the wanton destruction of property.[302] The last offence would be the only exception insofar as it might overlap with the right to housing. As a result of their subject-matter jurisdiction, international and mixed criminal courts concentrate on violations of civil and political rights and instances of physical violence. Despite focusing on the rights preferred by liberalism and being modelled on liberal judicial institutions that seek to respect the principle of legality, it is not as clear that international criminal justice openly supports liberal democracy or capitalism, the other two liberal dimensions discussed in the previous chapter. However, it does concentrate on the political sphere, leaving the economic realm intact.

Fifth, the rise of international criminal justice indeed opened transitional justice discourse to the international level. Since then, mechanisms of transitional justice, albeit restricted to international criminal justice, operate internationally.

Sixth, despite this shift to the international sphere, international criminal justice remains state-centric. The states sitting at the UN Security Council voted to create the ad hoc tribunals, the Rome Statute was negotiated and signed by states and mixed criminal courts were negotiated with the respective states, the exception being those established as part of UN interim administrations. States remain seized with the functioning of international and mixed

[298] Rome Statute, art 8(2)(a)(ii) (n 253); 'Elements of Crimes' Official Records of the Assembly of States Parties to the Rome Statute of the International Criminal Court (First session, New York 3–10 September 2002), Article 8(2)(a)(ii)-3. See also Evelyne Schmid, *Taking Economic, Social and Cultural Rights Seriously in International Criminal Law* (Cambridge University Press, 2015).

[299] See Marcos Zunino, 'Review of Evelyn Schmid's Taking Economic, Social and Cultural Rights Seriously in International Criminal Law' (2015) 74 *Cambridge Law Journal* 624.

[300] Statute of the Special Tribunal for Lebanon, Annex to UNSC Resolution 1757 (30 May 2007) Doc S/RES/1757 (2007), art 2.

[301] Law on the Establishment of ECCC (n 248).

[302] Statute of the Special Court for Sierra Leone, Annexed to the Agreement between the United Nations and the Government of Sierra Leone on the Establishment of a Special Court for Sierra Leone (adopted 16 January 2002, entered into force 12 April 2002) 2178 UNTS 138, art 5.

criminal courts through the UN and the Assembly of States Parties to the Rome Statute. As a result of the heavy involvement of states, while less so than national prosecutions, international criminal justice is state-centric.

The rise of international criminal justice opened an international dimension for the discourse of transitional justice, pushed it towards addressing violence resulting from armed conflict and reflected many of the key characteristics that the discourse has today. Events that took place in South Africa as the pioneer ad hoc tribunals were being set up expanded transitional justice in a different direction.

V THE SOUTH AFRICAN TRANSITION AND THE EXPANSION OF THE DISCOURSE

On 30 January 2015, the South African Minister of Justice and Correctional Services, Michael Masutha, announced that Eugene de Kock had been granted parole.[303] During the hearings of the SATRC, the former police colonel had revealed that he had been involved in more than a hundred acts of murder, torture and fraud against anti-apartheid activists.[304] Even though his confession earned him an amnesty for some of these crimes, de Kock was sentenced in 1996 to 2 life terms and 212 years of imprisonment for those offences not covered by the amnesty provisions.[305] When announcing de Kock's release, Minister Masutha justified it in the 'interests of nation building and reconciliation'.[306] Archbishop Desmond Tutu, who chaired the SATRC, welcomed the announcement as a milestone on the country's road to reconciliation and healing.[307] The confession of de Kock before the SATRC and his release in the name of reconciliation encapsulate what was distinctive

303 Sarah Evans, 'Good Behaviour Paroles de Kock' *Mail & Guardian* (30 January 2015) http://mg.co.za/article/2015–01-30-good-behaviour-pardons-de-kock, accessed 30 July 2018.

304 'South Africa Apartheid Assassin De Kock given Parole' *BBC News* (30 January 2015) http://www.bbc.com/news/world-africa-31054912, accessed 30 July 2018. See also Wilhelm Verwoerd, *Equity, Mercy, Forgiveness: Interpreting Amnesty within the South African Truth and Reconciliation Commission* (Peeters, 2007).

305 On de Kock, see Martin Meredith, *Coming to Terms: South Africa's Search for Truth* (Tina Rosenberg ed, Public Affairs, 1999); Pumla Gobodo-Madikizela, *A Human Being Died That Night: A South African Story of Forgiveness* (Houghton Mifflin, 2004).

306 Ministry of Justice and Correctional Services 'Parole Decisions on Inmates Ferdi Barnard, Eugene Alexander De Kock and Clive Derby Lewis' (30 January 2015) Media Statement www.scribd.com/document/254170044/Media-Statement-on-parole-decisions-on-Ferdi-Barnard-Eugene-Alexander-de-Kock-and-Clive-Derby-Lewis, accessed 30 July 2018.

307 *BBC News* (n 303).

about the South African transition. It was a process that put the accent on reconciliation and nation building.

In 1993, a negotiated settlement between the National Party government of President Frederik de Klerk and the African National Congress (ANC), headed by Nelson Mandela, brought to an end almost 50 years of apartheid after centuries of racial and colonial oppression. In operation since 1948, apartheid was 'a systematic piece of social engineering that embraced every area of life from birth to death',[308] protecting the privileges of the few and marginalising those excluded.[309] Enforcing and defending this system of oppression had led to killings, torture and enforced disappearances. The agreement between the apartheid government and the ANC was prompted by a stalemate in which the government could not crush the armed opposition and the latter could not topple the regime through armed struggle.[310] Following the agreement, an Interim Constitution was adopted in November 1993, and free elections were held in April 1994 that resulted in Nelson Mandela becoming South Africa's first black president.[311]

The 1993 Interim Constitution provided in a postscript that 'amnesty shall be granted in respect of acts, omissions and offences associated with political objectives and committed in the course of the conflicts of the past'.[312] Amnesty for the violence of the apartheid era was a clear demand of the security and police forces which threatened to jeopardise the elections.[313] The new democratic parliament defined the extent of the amnesty through the Promotion of National Unity and Reconciliation Act passed on 17 May 1995, after almost a

308 Alex Boraine, 'Truth and Reconciliation Commission in South Africa Amnesty: The Price of Peace' in Jon Elster (ed), *Retribution and Reparation in the Transition to Democracy* (Cambridge University Press, 2006) 13–14.

309 Ntebeza, 'The Struggle for Human Rights' 16 (n 259).

310 Dale McKinley, *The ANC and the Liberation Struggle: A Critical Political Biography* (Pluto Press, 1997) 80–102.

311 Johnny De Lange, 'The Historical Context, Legal Origins and Philosophical Foundation of the South African Truth and Reconciliation Commission' in Charles Villa-Vicencio and Wilhelm Verwoerd (eds), *Looking Back, Reaching Forward: Reflections on the Truth and Reconciliation Commission of South Africa* (University of Cape Town Press, 2000) 21.

312 Constitution of the Republic of South Africa (1993). For the background to the postscript, see Kader Asmal, 'Discussion on Priorities & Options' in Alex Boraine, Janet Levy and Ronel Scheffer (eds), *Dealing with the Past: Truth and Reconciliation in South Africa* (IDASA, 1994) 139.

313 *Azanian People's Organisation (AZAPO) and Others* v. *President of South Africa and others* 1996 (4) SA 671 (CC), para 19. See also Graeme Simpson, '"Tell No Lies, Claim No Easy Victories": A Brief Evaluation of South Africa's Truth and Reconciliation Commission' in Graeme Simpson and Deborah Posel (eds), *Commissioning the Past: Understanding South Africa's Truth and Reconciliation Commission* (Witwatersrand University Press, 2002) 226; Boraine, 'Truth and Reconciliation Commission in South Africa Amnesty' 302 (n 307).

year of debate.[314] The act provided for the creation of the SATRC that, alongside truth-finding and reparatory functions, would grant amnesty for politically motivated crimes in exchange for full disclosure.[315]

Domestic and foreign antecedents contributed to the idea of having a truth commission in South Africa. The ANC itself had created several fact-finding commissions to investigate abuses in its detention camps. For instance, the 1992 Motsuenyane Commission produced a public report documenting abuse and torture on detainees by ANC cadres.[316] Although these fact-finding institutions differed from an official truth commission, they are often mentioned as antecedents that influenced the SATRC.[317] Two international conferences held in Cape Town in 1994, and organised by the future vice chairman of the SATRC, Alex Boraine, brought external input to the plans for a truth commission.[318] The first one, titled 'Dealing with the Past,' was held in February and gathered scholars and practitioners involved in the Latin American and post-communist transitions. Its purpose was to bring lessons from the experiences of Latin America and Eastern Europe to South Africa.[319] Thus, as Paige Arthur has noted, it included people who had been involved in the Aspen Institute and Salzburg conferences.[320] The second conference took place in July under the title 'Truth and Reconciliation' and had mostly South African participants, including Minister of Justice Dullah Omar.[321] Since on 27 May 1994, it had been announced that there would be a truth commission,[322] the second event concentrated on how to adapt the international experiences to the particularities of the South African context.[323]

314 Lyn Graybill, *Truth and Reconciliation in South Africa: Miracle or Model?* (Lynne Rienner Publishers, 2002) 2.

315 Promotion of National Unity and Reconciliation Act (1995).

316 Kader Asmal, 'Truth, Reconciliation and Justice: The South African Experience in Perspective' (2000) 63 *The Modern Law Review* 1, 11; Hayner, *Unspeakable Truths* (n 146).

317 Asmal, 'Truth, Reconciliation and Justice' (n 315); Alex Boraine, *A Country Unmasked: South Africa's Truth and Reconciliation Commission* (Oxford University Press, 2000) 11.

318 Antjie Krog, *Country of My Skull* (Random House, 1998) 23; Graybill, *Truth and Reconciliation in South Africa* 2 (n 313).

319 Alex Boraine, 'Introduction' in Alex Boraine, Janet Levy and Ronel Scheffer (eds), *Dealing with the Past: Truth and Reconciliation in South Africa* (IDASA, 1994).

320 Arthur, 'How "Transitions" Reshaped Human Rights' 325 (n 55).

321 Alex Boraine, 'Introduction' in Alex Boraine and Janet Levy (eds), *The Healing of a Nation?* (Justice in Transition, 1995) xxiv.

322 Boraine, *A Country Unmasked* 40 (n 316). See also Dullah Omar, 'Building a New Future' in Alex Boraine and Janet Levy (eds), *The Healing of a Nation?* (Justice in Transition, 1995).

323 Katherine Elizabeth Mack, *From Apartheid to Democracy: Deliberating Truth and Reconciliation in South Africa* (The Pennsylvania State University Press, 2014) 24.

According to the 1995 Promotion of National Unity and Reconciliation Act, the objectives of the SATRC were to establish 'as complete a picture as possible of the causes, nature and extent of the gross violations of human rights' by carrying out investigations and holding hearings; to grant amnesty to persons making full disclosure of acts associated with a political objective; to determine the fate of victims, giving them the possibility of relating their own accounts of the violations they suffered and recommending reparations; and to compile a report.[324] Gross violations of human rights were defined as 'the killing, abduction, torture or severe ill-treatment of any person . . . carried out, advised, planned, directed, commanded or ordered, by any person acting with a political motive'.[325] The commission had 18 months to investigate violations committed in the period between March 1960 and 10 May 1994.[326] The deadline was later extended and the interim report was not published until October 1998.[327] From a shortlist prepared by a selection panel, President Mandela appointed 17 commissioners, representing different backgrounds, and Nobel Peace Prize recipient Archbishop Desmond Tutu as chair.[328]

The SATRC consisted of three committees: a Committee on Human Rights Violations, a Committee on Reparation and Rehabilitation and a Committee on Amnesty.[329] The Committee on Human Rights Violations received 22,000 applications and held 50 public hearings throughout the country thus allowing thousands of people to narrate their experiences of abuse.[330] The evidence gathered in this way was crucial for the documentation of violations contained in the report.[331] The committee entrusted with reparations and rehabilitation has been described as the weakest part of the SATRC. Lacking the financial resources to provide reparations and only able

[324] Promotion of National Unity and Reconciliation Act (1995), s 3(1).

[325] Ibid, s 1(1).

[326] Boraine, 'Truth and Reconciliation Commission in South Africa Amnesty' 299 (n 307).

[327] Piers Pigou, 'False Promises and Wasted Opportunities? Inside South Africa's Truth and Reconciliation Commission' in Graeme Simpson and Deborah Posel (eds), *Commissioning the Past: Understanding South Africa's Truth and Reconciliation Commission* (Witwatersrand University Press, 2002) 41.

[328] Boraine, *A Country Unmasked* 73 (n 316). See also Meredith, *Coming to Terms* (n 304).

[329] Promotion of National Unity and Reconciliation Act (1995), s 3(3).

[330] Richard Wilson, *The Politics of Truth and Reconciliation in South Africa: Legitimizing the Post-Apartheid State* (Cambridge University Press, 2001) 21; Simpson, '"Tell No Lies, Claim No Easy Victories"' 229 (n 312). For a case study of a local public hearing, see Hugo Van der Merwe, 'National Narrative versus Local Truths: The Truth and Reconciliation Commission's Engagement with Duduza' in Graeme Simpson and Deborah Posel (eds), *Commissioning the Past: Understanding South Africa's Truth and Reconciliation Commission* (Witwatersrand University Press, 2002).

[331] Wilson, *The Politics of Truth and Reconciliation in South Africa* 21 (n 329).

to make unbinding recommendations, it did not have much impact.[332] The Committee on Amnesty was the most innovative feature of the SATRC. The law tasked this committee with considering and granting applications for amnesty.[333] State officials and supporters of liberation movements could apply for amnesty for acts associated with a political objective. The amnesty would be granted if the applicant had made full disclosure of all relevant facts.[334] When considering applications, the committee could take into account, among other factors, whether the applicant had been following orders and whether the acts committed were proportional to the political objective pursued.[335] Acts committed for personal gain or out of malice were excluded.[336] The amnesty granted had the effect of extinguishing criminal and civil liability for the act in question.[337]

The SATRC differed from previous truth commissions mainly due to its emphasis on reconciliation and its quasi-judicial functions. Rather than merely establishing the factual truth of the human rights violations, the SATRC had the far more ambitious goal of reconciling a nation. As its report notes, the SATRC 'was conceived as part of the bridge-building process designed to help lead the nation away from a deeply divided past to a future founded on the recognition of human rights and democracy'.[338] Due to this ambitious role, the SATRC adopted a language of healing, forgiveness, reconciliation and restorative justice. The SATRC subscribed to a conception of justice that, eschewing retribution, seeks to restore relationships between

332 Ibid 22.

333 For a comprehensive analysis of the amnesty regime and its functioning, see Antje Du Bois-Pedain, *Transitional Amnesty in South Africa* (Cambridge University Press, 2007).

334 Promotion of National Unity and Reconciliation Act (1995), ss 20(1); 20(2).

335 Ibid, s 20(3).

336 Ibid.

337 Ibid, s 20(7). The amnesty process was the object of a constitutional challenge on the grounds that it breached the right to access to justice and was inconsistent with a duty under international law to punish perpetrators of gross human rights violations. The latter challenge was based on a constitutional provision according to which the interpretation of legislation that is consistent with international law should be preferred. The Constitutional Court rejected the claim because by promising amnesty the constitution had already restricted the right to access the courts. However, the court did not examine at length whether the SATRC complied with international law beyond stating that the Geneva Conventions do not apply to non-international conflicts where people need to live together after peace, *Azanian People's Organisation (AZAPO) and Others* v. *President of South Africa and Others*, para 31 (n 312). See also John Dugard, 'Is the Truth and Reconciliation Process Compatible with International Law: An Unanswered Question' (1997) *South African Journal on Human Rights* 258.

338 Truth and Reconciliation Commission of South Africa, *Truth and Reconciliation Commission of South Africa Report* (Macmillan Reference 1999), vol 1, para 2 (SATRC Report). See also Wilson, *The Politics of Truth and Reconciliation in South Africa* (n 329).

victim and perpetrator and to repair the damage suffered.[339] According to the SATRC Report, restorative justice was grounded on Christian and traditional African values.[340] The emphasis on reconciliation was apparent in the public hearings that the SATRC held as a way of promoting engagement and healing. In addition to the human rights and amnesty hearings referred to previously, there were hearings focusing on the role of business, labour, the legal community, religion, media and women.[341] At the same time, the amnesty granting faculty made the SATRC more judicial than its predecessors.[342] Whereas the Argentine CONADEP was expressly barred from expressing opinion on facts within the exclusive jurisdiction of the judiciary, the SATRC was tasked with granting individual amnesties extinguishing criminal and civil responsibility. Accordingly, the Amnesty Committee was composed of judges and legally trained commissioners. In order to carry out its comprehensive mandate, the SATRC had strong subpoena and search and seizure powers.[343]

In addition to the SATRC, there were other measures adopted to respond to the violence of apartheid. As Graeme Simpson has stressed, the SATRC was merely one of a 'full range of vehicles designed to promote restorative justice and build national reconciliation'.[344] Prosecutions were meant to be an important part of the South African transitional justice strategy. The other side of the amnesty policy was that those who did not apply would be prosecuted. Accordingly, there were some criminal trials before, during and after the SATRC.[345] However, many prosecutions failed, and presidential

339 Charles Villa-Vicencio, 'Restorative Justice: Dealing with the Past Differently' in Charles Villa-Vicencio and Wilhelm Verwoerd (eds), *Looking Back, Reaching Forward: Reflections on the Truth and Reconciliation Commission of South Africa* (University of Cape Town Press, 2000) 70.

340 SATRC Report, vol 1, paras 80–88 (n 337).

341 Priscilla Hayner, 'Same Species, Different Animal: How South Africa Compares to Truth Commissions Worldwide' in Charles Villa-Vicencio and Wilhelm Verwoerd (eds), *Looking Back, Reaching Forward: Reflections on the Truth and Reconciliation Commission of South Africa* (University of Cape Town Press, 2000) 37; Graybill, *Truth and Reconciliation in South Africa* 118 (n 313); Wilson, *The Politics of Truth and Reconciliation in South Africa* 35 (n 329).

342 See Emilios A Christodoulidis, '"Truth and Reconciliation" as Risks' (2000) 9 *Social & Legal Studies* 179.

343 Promotion of National Unity and Reconciliation Act (1995), s 29. See also Boraine, 'Truth and Reconciliation Commission in South Africa Amnesty' 304 (n 307); Hayner, 'Same Species, Different Animal' 36 (n 340).

344 Simpson, '"Tell No Lies, Claim No Easy Victories"' (n 312) 225.

345 Boraine, 'Truth and Reconciliation Commission in South Africa Amnesty' 308 (n 307); Paul Gready, *The Era of Transitional Justice: The Aftermath of the Truth and Reconciliation Commission in South Africa and beyond* (Routledge, 2011).

pardons later undermined further that process of accountability.[346] Irrespective of the success of these trials, many commentators consider that the threat of prosecutions was the stick that prompted many perpetrators to come forward and apply for amnesty.[347] The possibility of being brought to trial, albeit in most cases not carried out, buttressed the SATRC. Additionally, South Africa implemented reparations and land reform programmes.[348] Despite this range of mechanisms, it was the SATRC that mostly influenced transitional justice discourse.

1 *Influence of the South African Truth and Reconciliation Commission*

The SATRC influenced transitional justice discourse in a number of ways. First, the experience of the SATRC effectively opened transitional justice to a broader array of disciplines. The SATRC attracted interest from sociology, anthropology, philosophy, psychology and theology. The SATRC 'has been extensively analysed by scholars and commentators from around the world and from almost every discipline of human sciences'.[349] The reason for this multidisciplinary interest lies in the high profile of the South African transition and the characteristics of the SATRC itself. By adopting theological, moral and medical notions of redemption, healing and reconciliation, the SATRC was amenable to debates anchored in other disciplinary approaches. The commission's emphasis on narrative and multiple truths was suitable to examination from disciplinary traditions concerned with linguistics and performance.[350]

[346] See a letter by ICTJ's Vice President condemning pardons, Paul Seils, 'Political Pardons Would Damage the Legacy of South Africa's Truth and Reconciliation Commission' *The Huffington Post* (6 March 2015) www.huffingtonpost.com/paul-seils/political-pardons-would-d_b_6810864.html, accessed 30 July 2018. For prosecutions, Lovell Fernandez, 'Post-TRC Prosecutions in South Africa' in Gerhard Werle (ed), *Justice in Transition: Prosecution and Amnesty in Germany and South Africa* (BWV, 2006).

[347] Verwoerd, *Equity, Mercy, Forgiveness* 15 (n 303); Boraine, 'Truth and Reconciliation Commission in South Africa Amnesty' 208 (n 307); Simpson, '"Tell No Lies, Claim No Easy Victories"' (n 312) 228; Pigou, 'False Promises and Wasted Opportunities?' 55 (n 326).

[348] Chris Colvin, 'Overview of the Reparations Program in South Africa' in Pablo De Greiff (ed), *The Handbook of Reparations* (Oxford University Press, 2008); James Gibson, *Overcoming Historical Injustices: Land Reconciliation in South Africa* (Cambridge University Press, 2009); Cherryl Walker, 'Land, Memory, Reconstruction, and Justice: Perspectives on Land Claims in South Africa' (Ohio University Press, 2010). See also Chapter 5, 211–12.

[349] Andrea Lollini, *Constitutionalism and Transitional Justice in South Africa* (Berghahn Books, 2011) 1.

[350] See, eg, Claire Moon, 'Narrating Political Reconciliation: Truth and Reconciliation in South Africa' (2006) 15 *Social & Legal Studies* 257; Claire Moon, 'Healing Past Violence: Traumatic Assumptions and Therapeutic Interventions in War and Reconciliation' (2009) 8 *Journal of Human Rights* 71; Verwoerd, *Equity, Mercy, Forgiveness* (n 303); Christine Anthonissen,

Moreover, many of the commissioners and staff of the SATRC had backgrounds in theology, philosophy and social sciences.

The multidisciplinary interest that the South African experience sparked broadened the remit of the discourse of transitional justice. Scholars and commentators from the range of disciplines that engaged with the SATRC have continued to participate in transitional justice debates related to other situations and mechanisms. As we have seen, the discourse of transitional justice currently includes contributions from philosophy, history, ethics, education, anthropology, political science, theology, sociology and psychology, among others.[351] The SATRC was instrumental to that disciplinary breadth.

Second, the SATRC succeeded in recasting reconciliation from being a code word for impunity into a desirable goal.[352] Tina Rosenberg summed well the valence that reconciliation had prior to the SATRC during the first Cape Town 1994 conference when she cautioned South Africans to beware of the word reconciliation because it 'can often be confused with recurrence'.[353] In that same forum, future judge of the South African Constitutional Court Albie Sachs conveyed the newly minted conception of that word that would not be a reconciliation to 'bury and forget the past' but a reconciliation assuming responsibility of the past and correcting its injustices.[354] The post-SATRC positive conception of reconciliation has been so successful that it has even percolated into the realm of international criminal justice. For instance, the Appeals Chamber of the ICC has confirmed that reparations should promote reconciliation between the convicted person, the victims and the affected communities.[355]

Discourse and Human Rights Violations (John Benjamins Pub, 2007); Catherine M Cole, *Performing South Africa's Truth Commission: Stages of Transition* (Indiana University Press, 2010); Heidi Grunebaum, *Memorializing the Past: Everyday Life in South Africa after the Truth and Reconciliation Commission* (Transaction Publishers, 2011).

351 Christine Bell, 'Transitional Justice, Interdisciplinarity and the State of the "Field" or "Non-Field"' (2009) 3 *International Journal of Transitional Justice* 5; Dustin Sharp, 'Emancipating Transitional Justice from the Bonds of the Paradigmatic Transition' (2015) 9 *International Journal of Transitional Justice* 150.

352 Moon, 'Narrating Political Reconciliation' (n 307); Judith Renner, *Discourse, Normative Change and the Quest for Reconciliation in Global Politics* (Manchester University Press, 2013).

353 Tina Rosenberg, 'Reconciliation & Amnesty: Latin America' in Alex Boraine, Janet Levy and Ronel Scheffer (eds), *Dealing with the Past: Truth and Reconciliation in South Africa* (IDASA, 1994) 68.

354 Albie Sachs, 'South African Response' in Alex Boraine, Janet Levy and Ronel Scheffer (eds), *Dealing with the Past: Truth and Reconciliation in South Africa* (IDASA, 1994) 128.

355 *Prosecutor* v. *Thomas Lubanga Dyilo* (Amended Order for Reparations) ICC-01/04-01/06-3129-AnxA (3 March 2015), paras 71–72.

Third, the SATRC process helped to consolidate the transitional justice narrative linking the Latin American, Eastern European and South African transitions. South Africans consciously looked to other countries' experiences to inform their transitional justice policy. Whereas the Eastern Europeans were not very interested in the lessons offered by the people involved in the Latin American transitions,[356] the South Africans were eager to do so.[357] Alex Boraine, Vice-Chairperson of the SATRC, recounts how a visit to Eastern Europe in 1992 influenced a group of South Africans in their thinking about dealing with past human rights abuses. Boraine adds that, following a suggestion by Aryeh Neier, he began to look at the Latin American experience as well.[358] Accordingly, he organised the 1994 conference that brought to South Africa people involved in the Eastern European and Latin American transitions. In so doing, as veteran from the Chilean Truth Commission José Zalaquett put it during the conference, South Africa was tapping into a 'pool of world experiences' in dealing with the past.[359] Comparing the South African situation with the experiences in Latin America and Eastern Europe was very popular with practitioners and commentators before, during and after the work of the SATRC.[360] In this manner, the South African process consolidated a narrative joining Latin America with Eastern Europe and South Africa in a 'pool' of transitional experiences.

Fourth, the SATRC led to a widely exported model of transitional justice with truth commissions as its flagship mechanism. Although other mechanisms of transitional justice were implemented in South Africa, the SATRC stood out because of its broad mandate and quasi-judicial functions. Previous commissions occupied more marginal spaces. The SATRC was not a mechanism for gathering evidence for the courts, such as the Argentine CONADEP, or for providing a modicum of truth in the face of blanket amnesty, such as the Chilean commission. The popularity of the SATRC contributed to the prominence of truth commissions in transitional justice discourse. By raising

356 Interview with Jaime Malamud Goti (n 58)
357 Hayner, 'Same Species, Different Animal' (n 340).
358 Boraine, A *Country Unmasked* 14 (n 316); Boraine, 'Introduction' ix (n 321).
359 Jose Zalaquett, 'Why Deal with the Past?' in Alex Boraine, Janet Levy and Ronel Scheffer (eds), *Dealing with the Past: Truth and Reconciliation in South Africa* (IDASA, 1994) 8.
360 See Andre du Toit, 'South African Response' in Alex Boraine, Janet Levy and Ronel Scheffer (eds), *Dealing with the Past: Truth and Reconciliation in South Africa* (IDASA, 1994); Meredith, *Coming to Terms* 19 (n 304); De Lange, 'The Historical Context, Legal Origins and Philosophical Foundation of the South African Truth and Reconciliation Commission' 17 (n 310); Alex Boraine, 'The Language of Potential' in Wilmot James and Linda Van de Vijver (eds), *After the TRC: Reflections on Truth and Reconciliation in South Africa* (Ohio University Press, 2001); Simpson, '"Tell No Lies, Claim No Easy Victories"' (n 312).

the profile of truth commissions and presenting them as a desirable option in their own right, the SATRC installed them as the mechanism most readily associated with transitional justice. The other iconic mechanism of the discourse, the criminal trial, has a trajectory and relevance that exceeds transitional justice discourse. In contrast, truth commissions are exclusively linked with transitional justice.

The people involved in the SATRC facilitated the export of the truth commission model. As the South Africans were keen to learn from prior cases of transitional justice, they were equally forthcoming when it came to exporting their own experience. Alex Boraine was confident in 2000 that 'in the coming months and years many of us who have been directly involved in the TRC will be called upon to assist countries in transition'.[361] The commissioners and staffers of the SATRC wrote prolifically about their experience in that institution.[362] The people involved in the SATRC also travelled to lecture and give advice to Guatemala, Argentina, Northern Ireland, Ethiopia, Rwanda, Bosnia, Serbia and Kosovo.[363]

Some of the people who worked at the SATRC became very prominent in transitional justice circles – particularly Vice Chairperson Alex Boraine, Research Director Charles Villa-Vicencio, and Executive Secretary Paul van Zyl. Charles Villa-Vicencio headed the Institute for Justice and Reconciliation in South Africa that continued the legacy of the SATRC

361 Boraine, *A Country Unmasked* 422 (n 316).

362 Boraine, *A Country Unmasked* (n 316); Desmond Tutu, *No Future without Forgiveness* (Doubleday, 2000); Wendy Orr, 'Reparation Delayed Is Healing Retarded' in Charles Villa-Vicencio and Wilhelm Verwoerd (eds), *Looking Back, Reaching Forward: Reflections on the Truth and Reconciliation Commission of South Africa* (University of Cape Town Press, 2000); Richard Lyster, 'Amnesty: The Burden of Victims' in Charles Villa-Vicencio and Wilhelm Verwoerd (eds), *Looking Back, Reaching Forward: Reflections on the Truth and Reconciliation Commission of South Africa* (University of Cape Town Press, 2000); Janet Cherry, 'Historical Truth: Something to Fight for' in Charles Villa-Vicencio and Wilhelm Verwoerd (eds), *Looking Back, Reaching Forward: Reflections on the Truth and Reconciliation Commission of South Africa* (University of Cape Town Press, 2000); Dumisa Ntsebeza, 'A Lot More to Live for' in Wilmot James and Linda Van de Vijver (eds), *After the TRC: Reflections on Truth and Reconciliation in South Africa* (Ohio University Press, 2001); Frederik Van Zyl Slabbert, 'Truth without Reconciliation' in Wilmot James and Linda Van de Vijver (eds), *After the TRC: Reflections on Truth and Reconciliation in South Africa* (Ohio University Press, 2001); Mary Burton, 'Reparation, Amnesty and a National Archive' in Wilmot James and Linda Van de Vijver (eds), *After the TRC: Reflections on Truth and Reconciliation in South Africa* (Ohio University Press, 2001); Verwoerd, *Equity, Mercy, Forgiveness* (n 303); Pigou, 'False Promises and Wasted Opportunities? (n 326); Charles Villa-Vicencio, *Walk with Us and Listen: Political Reconciliation in Africa* (2009).

363 Boraine, *A Country Unmasked* 73 (n 316). See also Pigou, 'False Promises and Wasted Opportunities? 38 (n 326).

encouraging peaceful transitions focusing on Africa.[364] Alex Boraine and Paul van Zyl, together with Priscilla Hayner, went on to found the influential ICTJ in 2001.[365]

Through the interest it attracted and the vigorous advocacy of some people involved in it, the truth commission, embodied in the SATRC, became a powerful model of transitional justice.[366] As Heidi Grunebaum notes, 'the South African TRC has been held up as a model to be reproduced' with changes to suit the local context.[367] Whereas only 6 truth commissions had functioned in the 10 years that preceded the establishment of the SATRC in 1995, 18 such institutions were created in the 10 years that followed.[368] In most of these countries, the truth commission was the centrepiece of the transitional justice policy.

Despite its success, the SATRC model has been the subject of criticism for its postcolonial connotations. Mahmood Mamdani has argued that by concentrating on the criminal elements of the apartheid regime that committed murder and torture, the SATRC failed to engage with the wider social, political and economic system of oppression built on racial demarcation and colonialism.[369] Moreover, the SATRC process did not entirely reject the apartheid colonial legal system but rather reinforced it by only considering gross human rights violations conduct that was already illegal under the laws of apartheid, such as murder. In contrast, forced removals, which were not against apartheid laws, were left outside the remit of the SATRC.[370] At the same time, the Christian notions of confession and forgiveness that permeated

364 Berkley Center for Religion Peace & World Affairs, 'Charles Villa-Vicencio' (2018) http://berkleycenter.georgetown.edu/people/charles-villa-vicencio, accessed 30 July 2018; 'The Institute for Justice and Reconciliation' (2018) www.ijr.org.za/about-us/, accessed 30 July 2018.

365 Hayner, 'International Center for Transitional Justice (ICTJ)' (n 6).

366 See Kieran McEvoy and Lorna McGregor, 'Transitional Justice from Below: An Agenda for Reasearch, Policy and Praxis' in Kieran McEvoy and Lorna McGregor (eds), *Transitional Justice from Below: Grassroots Activism and the Struggle for Change* (Hart, 2008) 2.

367 Grunebaum 3 (n 349). See also Jan van Eck, 'Reconciliation in Africa?' in Wilmot James and Linda Van de Vijver (eds), *After the TRC: Reflections on Truth and Reconciliation in South Africa* (Ohio University Press, 2001) 86; Deborah Posel and Graeme Simpson, 'The Power of Truth: South Africa's Truth and Reconciliation Commission in Context' in Graeme Simpson and Deborah Posel (eds), *Commissioning the Past: Understanding South Africa's Truth and Reconciliation Commission* (Witwatersrand University Press, 2002) 2; Pigou, 'False Promises and Wasted Opportunities? 83 (n 326).

368 United States Institute of Peace (USIP), 'Truth Commission Digital Collection' (2011) www.usip.org/publications/2011/03/truth-commission-digital-collection, accessed 14 May 2018.

369 Mahmood Mamdani, 'The Truth according to the TRC' in Ifi Amadiume and Abdullahi Ahmed An-Na'im (eds), *The Politics of Memory: Truth, Healing, and Social Justice* (Zed Books, 2000) 180.

370 Ibid.

the SATRC were also a legacy of colonialism in Africa and were not an expression of local culture.[371] The criticism levelled against the SATRC has led several South African commentators to remark that it is more celebrated abroad than domestically.[372]

The appearance of an acclaimed model of transitional justice underpinned by the truth commission helped to unmoor the discourse from purely legal responses. With the SATRC, transitional justice became an alternative to criminal law rather than merely an extension of it in certain circumstances. Thus the truth commission could be considered a transitional justice mechanism on an equal footing with prosecutions, rather than a suboptimal alternative. This cemented the position of criminal trials as one option among a wider repertoire of mechanisms.

By incorporating other disciplines, rehabilitating reconciliation, consolidating the link with other transitions and producing a widely exported model, the SATRC experience transformed the discourse of transitional justice. The variety of disciplinary perspectives contributed to making transitional justice a self-standing discourse independent of the areas of law and politics. The existence of a plurality of mechanisms of transitional justice not necessarily subordinated to criminal law facilitated this process of separation of the discourse. The consolidation of a community of scholars and practitioners working on issues of transitional justice also helped to make the discourse stand on its own feet.

2 *Characteristics of the South African Truth and Reconciliation Commission*

The SATRC and the discussions it generated reflected many of the characteristics of the discourse of transitional justice today. First, the interest of the South Africans in learning from past transitions and their equal eagerness to export their own model evidenced the comparative method. As we have seen, the experience of previous transitions was used to compare them with the South African context, highlighting similarities and differences. Likewise, the experience in South Africa was later compared with other countries facing similar problems. The growing 'pool of world resources' mentioned by

371 Bert Ingelaere, *Inside Rwanda's Gacaca Courts: Seeking Justice after Genocide* (University of Wisconsin Press, 2016).

372 Van Zyl Slabbert 68 (n 361); Wilmot James and Linda Van de Vijver, 'Introduction' in Wilmot James and Linda Van de Vijver (eds), *After the TRC: Reflections on Truth and Reconciliation in South Africa* (Ohio University Press, 2001) 3.

Zalaquett in the first 1994 Cape Town conference was eminently comparative.[373]

Second, the discourse surrounding the SATRC was technical. The SATRC consolidated the dimension of being multidisciplinary. While the development of international criminal justice fomented the growth of a community of lawyers specialised on international criminal law, the SATRC gave impulse to a group of people whose expertise specifically was concerned with transitional justice and truth commissions. This group was multidisciplinary.[374] The creation of the ICTJ by veterans of the SATRC is a testament to the comparative and multidisciplinary legacy of the South African experience. Moreover, since the mandate of the SATRC emphasised reconciliation and the participation of victims, it inspired scholarly engagement from different disciplines that sought to transcend exclusively legal approaches.

The technical characteristic of the South African transition and its attending discourse was also apparent in its legalism. Despite being multidisciplinary, the SATRC was a legalistic institution. Its amnesty committee conducted a quasi-judicial screening process of amnesty applications. In typical legalistic fashion, this process was kept separate from the rest of the SATRC, and only legally trained commissioners and judges could participate in the amnesty committee. Moreover, criminal trials were the stick used to convince perpetrators to participate in the SATRC.

The technical dimension of appearing apolitical was present only in part. The technical character of transitional justice did not completely crowd out political debate because the law creating the SATRC was subject to almost a year of parliamentary discussions.[375] However, the technical knowledge of transitional justice served to occlude part of the political nature of the violence of apartheid. As Mamdani observes, the analogy with the Latin American transitions, which was evident in the Cape Town conferences that prepared the ground for the SATRC, served to obscure what was distinctive of apartheid. Treating apartheid as another dictatorship that had committed gross violations of human rights left out the colonial and racialised politics that underpinned the regime.[376] Thus the technical discourse of transitional justice contributed to expunging part of the politics of the violence of apartheid from the SATRC process.

373 Zalaquett, 'Why Deal with the Past?' 8 (n 358).

374 See Tshepo Madlingozi, 'On Transitional Justice Entrepreneurs and the Production of Victims' (2010) 2 *Journal of Human Rights Practice* 208.

375 Graybill, *Truth and Reconciliation in South Africa* 2 (n 313).

376 Mamdani, 'The Truth According to the TRC' (n 368).

Third, the teleological framework dominant in the Argentine and Eastern European experiences was also present in the SATRC. The truth commission was intended as a conduit for achieving reconciliation and building the nation.[377] Through establishing mechanisms of transitional justice, a series of goals were pursued. Furthermore, the theological references to reconciliation as a future redemption further accentuated the teleological, and even eschatological, character of the South African transition.

Fourth, liberalism infused the South African transition and the discourse surrounding it. This was manifested in the three dimensions identified in the previous chapter. The SATRC emphasised violations of civil and political rights and instances of physical violence. Despite apartheid's structural violence, which imposed marginalisation and poverty on the majority of the population,[378] the SATRC was mandated to concentrate on gross violations of human rights through 'killing, abduction, torture or severe ill-treatment of any person'.[379] The report of the SATRC itself acknowledged that this narrow definition had prevented it from paying more attention to the general policies of apartheid that it had to relegate to providing the context of the violations included in the mandate.[380] Liberal democracy was the favoured destination of the South African transition. Although the ANC had historically held socialist views, the need to gain the backing of businesses, the drying out of the Soviet Union as a source of support and the political compromise of the transition moved the South African transition towards liberalism.[381] Accordingly, the Constitution adopted in 1996 establishes the rule of law as a founding value, includes an extensive bill of rights and protects the right to private property.[382] The liberal influence of the South African transition was also evident in its support for capitalism. By the time of the transition, the ANC government had a market-friendly approach and did not seek the nationalisation of the means of production or a massive redistribution of

377 SATRC Report, vol 1, para 2 (n 337). See also Charles Villa-Vicencio and Wilhelm Verwoerd, *Looking Back, Reaching Forward: Reflections on the Truth and Reconciliation Commission of South Africa* (University of Cape Town Press, 2000); Wilson, *The Politics of Truth and Reconciliation in South Africa* (n 329); Graeme Simpson, *Commissioning the Past: Understanding South Africa's Truth and Reconciliation Commission* (Witwatersrand University Press, 2002).

378 Mahmood Mamdani, 'A Diminished Truth' in Wilmot James and Linda Van de Vijver (eds), *After the TRC: Reflections on Truth and Reconciliation in South Africa* (Ohio University Press, 2001).

379 Promotion of National Unity and Reconciliation Act (1995), s 1.

380 SATRC Report, vol 5, paras 48–49 (n 337).

381 See McKinley, *The ANC and the Liberation Struggle* chs 4–6 (n 309).

382 Constitution of the Republic of South Africa (1996), ss 1(c); 7; 25.

property.[383] Hence, while the SATRC exposed the complicity of some businesses with apartheid and recommended some redistributive measures,[384] capitalism as an economic system was not questioned.[385] Moreover, the SATRC redistributive recommendations were largely ignored and replaced by voluntary contributions from corporations rather than mandatory taxation.[386]

Fifth, while the discourse surrounding the South African transition was not multilevel, it paved the way for the expansion of the discourse of transitional justice towards local level initiatives. The policies examined were those implemented in South Africa at the national level, such as the SATRC. However, the opening of the discourse to a wider array of disciplines that followed the SATRC facilitated the incorporation of local-level responses. A multidisciplinary discourse was certainly more amenable to local practices of justice than an exclusively legalistic one. Contributions from new disciplinary approaches, such as anthropology, coupled with the contemporaneous use of neo-traditional *gacaca* courts to try genocide suspects in Rwanda,[387] brought these local responses into the remit of transitional justice.[388]

Sixth, the discursive echo of the South African transition was undoubtedly state-centric. The SATRC and other responses implemented by the state, such as reparations, dominated accounts of the South African transition. In this way, the South African experience reflected many of the characteristics of the discourse of transitional justice today.

383 McKinley, *The ANC and the Liberation Struggle* 132 (n 309).

384 SATRC Report, vol 5, paras 40–44, vol 4, paras 161–67 (n 337).

385 Simpson, '"Tell No Lies, Claim No Easy Victories"' (n 312); Dustin Sharp, 'Introduction: Addressing Economic Violence in Times of Transition' in Dustin Sharp (ed), *Justice and Economic Violence in Transition* (Springer, 2014).

386 Clara Sandoval, Leonardo Filippini and Roberto Vidal, 'Linking Transitional Justice and Corporate Accountability' in Sabine Michalowski (ed), *Corporate Accountability in the Context of Transitional Justice* (Routledge, 2013) 22; Charles P Abrahams, 'Lessons from the South African Experience' in Sabine Michalowski (ed), *Corporate Accountability in the Context of Transitional Justice* (Routledge, 2013).

387 Timothy Longman, 'Justice at the Grassroots? Gacaca Trials in Rwanda' in Naomi Roht-Arriaza and Javier Mariezcurrena (eds), *Transitional Justice in the Twenty-First Century: Beyond Truth versus Justice* (Cambridge University Press, 2006); Phil Clark, 'Hybridity, Holism, and "Traditional" Justice: The Case of the Gacaca Courts in Post-Genocide Rwanda' (2007) 39 *The George Washington International Law Review* 765.

388 See Kamari Maxine Clarke and Mark Goodale, *Mirrors of Justice: Law and Power in the Post-Cold War Era* (Cambridge University Press, 2010); Alexander Laban Hinton, *Transitional Justice: Global Mechanisms and Local Realities after Genocide and Mass Violence* (Rutgers University Press, 2010).

VI CONCLUSION

The discourse of transitional justice grew around the episodes discussed in this chapter. The Argentine transition with its risky prosecutions and pioneering truth commission sparked the initial discussions. The end of communism in Eastern Europe injected these discussions with a sense of purpose and provided a testing ground. The rise of international criminal justice expanded the discourse of transitional justice towards international responses, international law and armed conflict. The South African transition and the SATRC opened the discourse to more disciplines and galvanised a group of experts in transitional justice as an autonomous field.

The responses to past widespread or systematic violence adopted in these episodes presented many of the key characteristics that the discourse of transitional justice has today. They were technical, legalistic, liberal, state-centric responses that prioritised violations of civil and political rights. The discussions that these responses provoked also reflected some of the characteristics, such as a penchant for the comparative method, multidisciplinarity or inscribing transitional justice into a teleological framework. Since the discourse of transitional justice developed from these responses and discussions, it was shaped by their characteristics. From then onwards, those responses that echoed the characteristics of these influential episodes became the norm for the discourse of transitional justice. It is in this sense that the current characteristics of the discourse can be traced to the four episodes examined in this chapter.

Rupture and contingency marked the process of emergence of transitional over the 20 years covered in this chapter. Rather than a gradual necessary evolution towards a complete transitional justice, the emergence of the discourse owes much to chance. For instance, Raúl Alfonsín won the 1983 presidential elections against the odds. The burning of a coffin with Alfonsín's name during a rally of the opposition the day before the elections antagonised many voters tired of political violence and might have catapulted him to the presidency.[389] As Mark Osiel wrote, it 'would not be an exaggeration to say that if Alfonsín had not been elected President, there would almost certainly have been no trial'.[390] Chance also played a part in the other events discussed.

[389] John Simpson and Jana Bennett, *The Disappeared: Voices from a Secret War* (Robson, 1985) 386; Brysk, *The Politics of Human Rights in Argentina* 61–62 (n 11); Lewis, *Guerrillas and Generals* 195 (n 13); Nino, *Radical Evil on Trial* 66 (n 15); Andersen, *Dossier Secreto* 305 (n 62);.

[390] Osiel, 'The Making of Human Rights Policy in Argentina' 143 (n 29).

The collapse of the Soviet Bloc was a sudden, unexpected and cataclysmic occurrence. Even once the democratic opening took place, not even the Polish opposition leaders expected to defeat the communists in the 1989 elections.[391] Similarly, the competition between France and the United States in the UN Security Council for reaping the political and moral gains of creating a tribunal has been credited with precipitating the establishment of the ICTY.[392] The South African Parliament could have opted for a blanket amnesty to implement the promise of the 1993 Interim Constitution. If any of these chance events had happened differently, there might not be a discourse of transitional justice, or it could be substantially different. In sum, the emergence of transitional justice discourse owes much more to chance and contingency than to preordained evolution.

Once the discourse emerged, a retrospective history of its origin and development was created. The characteristics of the discourse framed that dominant narrative. The situations and mechanisms of the past that were recognised as relevant for that dominant narrative of transitional justice were those that fitted the characteristics. In this fashion, the particular and contingent history of the emergence of the discourse not only shaped how transitional justice is today but also how its past was constructed. The rest of this book concentrates on the prehistory of the discourse of transitional justice. It casts a critical look at the dominant narrative of the origin and descent of the discourse.

391 Garton Ash, *We the People* 25 (n 105).

392 Hazan, *Justice in a Time of War*, ch 2 (n 235).

PART II

Prehistory

4

The Myth of Nuremberg

Origin

I INTRODUCTION

By the middle of the nineteenth century, the biblical account of creation was coming under increasing pressure. As fossils of ancient animals kept cropping up, geological findings seemed to refute the age of the Earth according to the Bible and to lend support to evolutionary theories. English naturalist Philip Henry Gosse found a creative way to reconcile the existence of fossils with the biblical narrative of creation. In his 1857 book *Omphalos* (Greek for navel), Gosse argued that since life is circular, at any point that creation would have happened it would have had to preserve continuity. Logically, there could be no effect without a cause. Hence, although Adam was created as an adult, he must have had a navel or else he would not have been entirely a man. Equally, trees were created with concentric rings and shells with growth lines. Therefore, according to Gosse, fossils of animals that never lived were 'planted' to preserve this continuity.[1] In this way, Earth would have been created in seven days but with a prefabricated history.[2]

Like the Earth for Gosse, the discourse of transitional justice was created with a pre-existing history. Although it did not emerge as a distinct discourse until the end of the Cold War, transitional justice is widely held to have originated in the Nuremberg trial in the aftermath of World War II. Nuremberg thus provides the point of origin of transitional justice. From that origin, and until the emergence of the discourse, several historical episodes have been 'planted', like Gosse's fossils, to preserve the continuity of the narrative. They provide the putative descent of the discourse. The origin (Nuremberg) and the descent (during the Cold War) constitute the prehistory of transitional

[1] Philip Henry Gosse, *Omphalos: An Attempt to Untie the Geological Knot* (John Van Voorst, 1857).

[2] Jorge Luis Borges, 'La Creación y P.H. Gosse', *Otras Inquisiciones* (Emecé, 1971).

justice. It is the historical narrative that was retrospectively created following the emergence of the discourse.

This chapter examines the place that Nuremberg plays in the discourse. It argues that the characteristics of the discourse of transitional justice influenced the choice of Nuremberg as the point of origin. The resulting narrative of the post-war period in transitional justice discourse highlights those episodes that reflected the characteristics and ignores those that did not.

The first section looks into Nuremberg as the origin of transitional justice and describes the role that this historical event plays in the discourse. The second addresses the question of whether Nuremberg can be regarded as a practice of transitional justice. The third argues that Nuremberg was chosen as the point of origin of transitional justice because it reflected many of the discourse's key characteristics. The last section shows how the dominant narrative of the post–World War II period in transitional justice discourse illuminates some aspects of this historical process and obscures others.

II NUREMBERG AS ORIGIN

Most scholars and commentators locate the origin of the modern practice of transitional justice in the policies implemented to respond to the widespread and systematic violence of World War II. As the most referenced origin of transitional justice, 1945 also becomes the starting point of the prehistory of the discourse. While several authors had already held that the post-war period was the point of departure of transitional justice,[3] Ruti Teitel's work has been particularly influential in this regard. The first phase of her historical work on transitional justice 'encompasses the post–World War II model of justice'.[4] Given that it was specifically an account of the origin and development of transitional justice and that it was written by an influential scholar in the

[3] Neil J Kritz, 'The Dilemmas of Transitional Justice' in Neil J Kritz (ed), *Transitional Justice: How Emerging Democracies Reckon with Former Regimes* (United States Institute of Peace Press, 1995) 20; Carlos Nino, *Radical Evil on Trial* (Yale University Press, 1996); Martha Minow, *Between Vengeance and Forgiveness: Facing History after Genocide and Mass Violence* (Beacon Press, 1998) 28; Alexandra Barahona de Brito, Carmen González Enríquez and Paloma Aguilar Fernández, 'Introduction' in Alexandra Barahona de Brito, Carmen González Enríquez and Paloma Aguilar Fernández (eds), *The Politics of Memory: Transitional Justice in Democratizing Societies* (Oxford University Press, 2001) 2–3; Neil J Kritz, 'Where We Are and How We Got Here: An Overview of Developments in the Search for Justice and Reconciliation' in Alice Henkin (ed), *The Legacy of Abuse: Confronting the Past, Facing the Future* (Aspen Institute, 2002) 23; Rama Mani, *Beyond Retribution: Seeking Justice in the Shadows of War* (Polity, 2002) 88.

[4] Ruti Teitel, 'Transitional Justice Genealogy' (2003) 16 *Harvard Human Rights Journal* 69, 72.

discourse, Teitel's narrative helped to install 1945 as the starting point. The repetition of this origin consolidated it in the discourse.[5]

Only two other historical points of departure for transitional justice have been offered: the restoration of democracy in ancient Athens following the oligarchic rule and the emergence of an autonomous discourse of transitional justice in the late 1980s and early 1990s. These alternative dates have not debunked the aftermath of World War II from the established narrative. In the dominant account, the case from classical Greece has become an example of the older roots of some practices of transitional justice but not the origin of the modern phenomenon. The prevalent view is that while 'transitional justice can be dated back to the birth (in classical Athens) of democracy itself, modern conceptions of transitional justice emerge ... in the wake of Second World War'.[6] The later point of origin in the appearance of a distinct discourse from the late 1980s, the one adopted in this book, does not negate the importance of the post-war period as the cradle of some practices of transitional justice. As Pádraig McAuliffe notes, although 'transitional justice as a distinctive, self-conscious policy-making process dates only to the late 1980s, it is widely accepted that the post-World War II trials at Nuremberg, Tokyo and the domestic European trials that complemented them mark the historical starting point of the phenomenon'.[7]

5 Aneta Wierzynska, 'Consolidating Democracy through Transitional Justice: Rwanda's Gacaca Courts' (2004) 79 *New York University Law Review* 1934, 1945; Christine Bell, Colm Campbell and Fionnuala Ní Aoláin, 'Justice Discourses in Transition' (2004) 13 *Social & Legal Studies* 305, 324; Louise Arbour, 'Economic and Social Justice for Societies in Transition' (2007) 40 *New York University Journal of International Law and Politics* 1, 1–2; Christine Bell, Colm Campbell and Fionnuala Ní Aoláin, 'Transitional Justice: (Re)conceptualising the Field' (2007) 3 *International Journal of Law in Context* 81, 82; Zinaida Miller, 'Effects of Invisibility: In Search of the "Economic" in Transitional Justice' (2008) 2 *International Journal of Transitional Justice* 266, 269; Bronwyn Leebaw, 'The Irreconcilable Goals of Transitional Justice' (2008) 30 *Human Rights Quarterly* 95, 98–99; Patricia Lundy and Mark McGovern, 'Whose Justice? Rethinking Transitional Justice from the Bottom Up' (2008) 35 *Journal of Law and Society* 265, 268; Brian Grodsky, 'Re-Ordering Justice: Towards a New Methodological Approach to Studying Transitional Justice' (2009) 46 *Journal of Peace Research* 819, 820; Kora Andrieu, 'Transitional Justice: A New Discipline in Human Rights' (2010) *Online Encyclopedia of Mass Violence* www.sciencespo.fr/mass-violence-war-massacre-resistance/fr/document/transitional-justice-new-discipline-human-rights-0, accessed 30 July 2018; Michael Rothberg, 'Progress, Progression, Procession: William Kentridge and the Narratology of Transitional Justice' (2012) 20 *Narrative* 1, 5.

6 Lundy and McGovern, 'Whose Justice?' (n 5). Even the proponent of the Greek case as the origin of transitional justice considers that the modern history of transitional justice begins in 1945. See Jon Elster, *Closing the Books: Transitional Justice in Historical Perspective* (Cambridge University Press, 2004) 47.

7 Pádraig McAuliffe, 'From Molehills to Mountains (and Myths?): A Critical History of Transitional Justice Advocacy' (2011) 22 *Finnish Yearbook of International Law* 1, 18.

Within the raft of responses to widespread or systematic violence adopted in the wake of World War II, transitional justice discourse concentrates on some of them as constituting its origin. By far the most prominent one is the International Military Tribunal (IMT) that between November 1945 and October 1946 tried 22 Nazi leaders in the city of Nuremberg. The four victorious powers – the United States, the Soviet Union, the United Kingdom and France – created the IMT through the London Agreement.[8] Each of the four signatories of that agreement appointed a judge and a prosecutor. The defence was entrusted to German lawyers. The defendants were the highest-ranking surviving Nazis, including Reich Marshall Hermann Göring, Deputy Party Leader Rudolph Hess, Foreign Minister Joachim von Ribbentrop, and head of the Army High Command Wilhelm Keitel. There were four charges in the indictment: crimes against peace, war crimes, crimes against humanity and participation in the common plan to commit these crimes.[9] Judgment was delivered on 1 October 1946. The IMT found 19 defendants guilty. Twelve were sentenced to death, and 7 were sentenced to prison terms ranging from 10 years to life. Three were acquitted.[10]

Alongside the IMT, the Tokyo trial is sometimes mentioned as also forming part of the origin of the discourse. The International Military Tribunal for the Far East (IMTFE) was created by the Allies to try Japanese war criminals.[11] Sitting in the city of Tokyo, it tried 25 defendants and convicted all of them.[12] 'Most of the literature', Zinaida Miller observes, 'locates the beginning of transitional justice . . . in the post–Second World War Nuremberg and Tokyo

[8] Agreement for the Prosecution and Punishment of the Major War Criminals of the European Axis (adopted and entered into force 8 August 1945) 82 UNTS 279 (London Agreement).

[9] *United States of America, the French Republic, the United Kingdom of Great Britain and Northern Ireland, and the Union of Soviet Socialist Republics against Major War Criminals* (Indictment Number 1) I Nazi Conspiracy and Aggression (Red Series)(Indictment IMT), 13.

[10] *United States of America, the French Republic, the United Kingdom of Great Britain and Northern Ireland, and the Union of Soviet Socialist Republics against Major War Criminals* (Opinion and Judgment) Nazi Conspiracy and Aggression (Red Series) 1 October 1946, 189 (IMT Judgment).

[11] Charter of the International Military Tribunal for the Far East, General Order 1, General Headquarters Supreme Commander of the Allied Forces (19 January 1946) 4 Bevans 20 (as amended 26 April 1946, 4 Bevans 27) (IMTFE Charter).

[12] *United States of America, the Republic of China, the United Kingdom of Great Britain and Northern Ireland, the Union of Soviet Socialist Republics, the Commonwealth of Australia, Canada, the Republic of France, the Kingdom of the Netherlands, New Zealand, India and the Commonwealth of the Philippines* v. *Araki et al* (Judgment of the International Military Tribunal for the Far East) 4 November 1948 in Neil Boister and Robert Cryer (eds), Documents on the Tokyo International Military Tribunal (Oxford University Press, 2008) 598–625 (IMTFE Judgment).

military tribunals set up by the victorious Allies'.[13] However, the IMTFE, as is discussed below, is mentioned much less frequently than its European counterpart.

In addition to the international tribunals, the Allies tried wartime crimes in their respective zones of occupation. The American authorities carried out 12 more trials in the city of Nuremberg between October 1946 and April 1949 under Control Council Law No 10, which provided a uniform basis for the prosecution of war criminals in all occupation zones of Germany.[14] These trials before the Nuremberg Military Tribunal (NMT) focused on the responsibility of various institutions such as the medical profession (Medical Trial),[15] judiciary (Justice Trial),[16] bureaucracy (Ministries Case),[17] military commanders (High Command and Hostage cases),[18] industrialists (IG Farben, Krupp and Flick cases),[19] SS (*Einsatzgruppen*, RuSHA, Pohl cases)[20] and slave

[13] Miller, 'Effects of Invisibility' 269 (n 5).

[14] Control Council Law No 10 'Punishment of Persons Guilty of War Crimes, Crimes against Peace and against Humanity' (20 December 1945) 3 Official Gazette Control Council for Germany 50–55 (1946) (Control Council Law No 10).

[15] *United States of America* v. *Brandt et al (Medical Trial)* II Reports of Trials of War Criminals before the Nuremberg Military Tribunals under Control Council Law No 10 (20 August 1947) Nuremberg Military Tribunal 171.

[16] *United States of America* v. *Altstoetter et al (Justice Trial)* III Reports of Trials of War Criminals before the Nuremberg Military Tribunals under Control Council Law No 10 (3 December 1947) 95.

[17] *United States of America* v. *Von Weizsaecker et al (Ministries Case)*, XIV Reports of Trials of War Criminals before the Nuremberg Military Tribunals under Control Council Law No 10 (13 April 1949) 308 (Ministries Judgment).

[18] *United States of America* v. *Van Leeb et al (High Command Case)* XI Reports of Trials of War Criminals before the Nuremberg Military Tribunals under Control Council Law No 10 (28 October 1948) 462; *United States of America* v. *List et al (Hostage Case)* XI Reports of Trials of War Criminals before the Nuremberg Military Tribunals under Control Council Law No 10 (19 February 1948) 1230.

[19] *United States of America* v. *Krauch et al (IG Farben)* VIII Reports of Trials of War Criminals before the Nuremberg Military Tribunals under Control Council Law No 10 (30 July 1948) 1081 (IG Farben Judgment); *United States of America* v. *Krupp et al (Krupp)* IX Reports of Trials of War Criminals before the Nuremberg Military Tribunals under Control Council Law No 10 (31 July 1948) 1327 (Krupp Judgment); *United States of America* v. *Flick et al (Flick)* VI Reports of Trials of War Criminals before the Nuremberg Military Tribunals under Control Council Law No 10 (22 December 1947) 1187 (Flick Judgment).

[20] *United States of America* v. *Ohlendorf et al (Einsatzgruppen Trial)* IV Reports of Trials of War Criminals before the Nuremberg Military Tribunals under Control Council Law No 10 (9 April 1948) 411; *United States of America* v. *Greifelt et al (RuSHA Case)* V Reports of Trials of War Criminals before the Nuremberg Military Tribunals under Control Council Law No 10 (10 March 1948) 88; *United States of America* v. *Pohl et al* V Reports of Trials of War Criminals before the Nuremberg Military Tribunals under Control Council Law No 10 (3 November 1947) 958.

labour programme (Milch case).[21] The NMT tried 177 defendants, convicting 142 and acquitting 35.[22] The United States also held trials before general military courts, for instance, in the former concentration camp of Dachau where 1,672 defendants were tried between 1945 and 1948.[23] For their part, the British tried 1,085 Germans in military courts held throughout their occupation zone.[24] The most noteworthy of these British trials included those of personnel of the Bergen-Belsen and Auschwitz concentration camps.[25] The Soviets convicted an estimated 40,000 Germans in their occupation zone.[26] Trials were also held in France, Poland, the Netherlands, Hungary, Denmark, Norway and Germany.[27] These post-war trials are mentioned with much less frequency as forming part of the origin of transitional justice than those before the IMT and IMTFE.[28]

The nonjudicial measures that the Allies and liberated countries implemented to respond to the violence of the war are seldom mentioned as being significant for the origin of transitional justice. These initiatives included denazification policies and reparations. As soon as the war was over, the Allies

[21] *United States of America* v. *Erhard Milch* II Reports of Trials of War Criminals before the Nuremberg Military Tribunals under Control Council Law No 10 (16 April 1947) 773.

[22] Jonathan Friedman, 'Law and Politics in the Subsequent Nuremberg Trials, 1946–1949' in Patricia Heberer and Jürgen Matthäus (eds), *Atrocities on Trial: Historical Perspectives on the Politics of Prosecuting War Crimes* (University of Nebraska Press, 2008) 88.

[23] *Trial of Martin Gottfried Weiss et al (the Dachau Concentration Camp Trial)* (Case No. 60) XI Law Reports of Trials of War Criminals (13 December 1945) (General Military Government Court of the United States Zone); Michael J Bazyler and Frank M Tuerkheimer, *Forgotten Trials of the Holocaust* (New York University Press, 2014) 8.

[24] David Cohen, 'Transitional Justice in Divided Germany after 1945' in Jon Elster (ed), *Retribution and Reparation in the Transition to Democracy* (Cambridge University Press, 2006) 63.

[25] Because these trials took place before Control Council Law No 10 was adopted, they were carried out under a Royal Warrant ordering the trial of war crimes, Regulations for the Trial of War Criminals (Royal Warrant 0160/2498 AO 81/1945); *United Kingdom* v. *Kramer et al (Belsen Trial)* (Case No. 10) II Law Reports of Trials of War Criminals (17 November 1945) (British Military Court Luneberg).

[26] Sanya Romeike, 'Transitional Justice in Germany after 1945 and after 1990' (2016) Occasional Paper No 1 International Nuremberg Principles Academy 19. For a lower estimate, see David M Crowe, *War Crimes, Genocide, and Justice: A Global History* (Palgrave Macmillan, 2014) 257.

[27] Ibid ch 8; Cohen, 'Transitional Justice in Divided Germany after 1945' (n 24). For trials in Scandinavia, Hans Fredrik Dahl, 'Dealing with the Past in Scandinavia: Legal Purges and Popular Memories of Nazism and World War II in Denmark and Norway after 1945' in Jon Elster (ed), *Retribution and Reparation in the Transition to Democracy* (Cambridge University Press, 2006). For trials in Germany, Romeike, 'Transitional Justice in Germany after 1945 and after 1990' 15–22 (n 26).

[28] See, eg, de Brito, González Enríquez and Aguilar Fernández, 'Introduction' (n 3); McAuliffe, 'From Molehills to Mountains (and Myths?)' (n 7).

agreed that Nazi party members were to be removed from public office and important private undertakings.[29] Accordingly, the individual occupying powers implemented different denazification policies in their zones.[30] They also passed laws concerning restitution of property.[31] The liberated countries carried out reparation measures including restitutions of property, compensation for material damage and rehabilitation of citizenship and titles.[32]

Out of all these measures, the discourse of transitional justice focuses on the IMT as its origin. For instance, Christine Bell and Catherine O'Rourke note that 'the field of transitional justice is widely accepted as having its origins in the Nuremberg trials'.[33] While most scholars refer to the IMT when they pinpoint Nuremberg as the origin of transitional justice, some others also include the trials that the American NMT held in that city and refer to the Nuremberg trials in plural.[34] The strong association of the IMT with the city lends itself to Nuremberg sometimes being used, metonymically, as a symbol of post-war justice. As Donald Bloxham notes, 'Nuremberg may symbolize all of the Allied trials of war criminals in Europe in the post-war period. Figuratively, it can evoke any trial of war criminals anywhere since 1945.'[35] Despite this degree of conceptual ambiguity, it is the IMT that stands

29 'Protocol of the Proceedings of the Berlin (Potsdam) Conference' (1 August 1945) 3 Bevans 1207, principle 6. See also Cohen, 'Transitional Justice in Divided Germany after 1945' 68–72 (n 24).

30 John H Herz, 'Denazification and Related Policies' in John H Herz (ed), *From Dictatorship to Democracy: Coping with the Legacies of Authoritarianism and Totalitarianism* (Greenwood, 1982) 24. See also Romeike, 'Transitional Justice in Germany after 1945 and after 1990' 22–28 (n 26).

31 Kurt Schwerin, 'German Compensation for Victims of Nazi Persecution' (1972) 67 *Northwestern University Law Review* 489.

32 Michael L Hughes, 'Restitution and Democracy in Germany after Two World Wars' (1995) 4 *Contemporary European History* 1; Istvan Pogany, 'The Restitution of Former Jewish-Owned Property and Related Schemes of Compensation in Hungary' (1998) 4 *European Public Law* 211; Jon Elster, 'Coming to Terms with the Past: A Framework for the Study of Justice in the Transition to Democracy' (1998) 39 *European Journal of Sociology/Archives Européennes de Sociologie* 7, 36–38.

33 Christine Bell and Catherine O'Rourke, 'Does Feminism Need a Theory of Transitional Justice? An Introductory Essay' (2007) 1 *International Journal of Transitional Justice* 23, 24.

34 Wierzynska, 'Consolidating Democracy through Transitional Justice' 1945 (n 5); Bell, Campbell and Ní Aoláin, 'Justice Discourses in Transition' 324 (n 5); Arbour, 'Economic and Social Justice for Societies in Transition' 1–2 (n 5); Andrieu, 'Transitional Justice' 4 (n 5); Bell and O'Rourke, 'Does Feminism Need a Theory of Transitional Justice?' 24 (n 33); Undine Kayser-Whande and Stephanie Schell-Faucon, 'Transitional Justice and Conflict Transformation in Conversation' (2010) 50 *Politorbis* 97, 98.

35 Donald Bloxham, 'Milestone and Mythologies: The Impact of Nuremberg' in Patricia Heberer and Jürgen Matthäus (eds), *Atrocities on Trial: Historical Perspectives on the Politics of Prosecuting War Crimes* (University of Nebraska Press, 2008) 264.

out when scholars make references to Nuremberg as the point of origin of transitional justice.[36]

1 *The Role of Nuremberg*

The role of Nuremberg within transitional justice discourse is threefold: mythological, exemplary and ancestral. Nuremberg operates as a foundational myth for transitional justice. As such, it lends the discourse antiquity and legitimacy. Like the myths that Rome was founded by Aeneas fleeing from Troy, or Britain founded by Trojan Brutus, claiming an origin in Nuremberg allows transitional justice to be inscribed in an older lineage. Thomas Franck has shown how pedigree is a universal form of symbolic validation that confers legitimacy. Establishing a deep-rooted origin to a rule, institution or any other phenomenon, a discourse included, gives it legitimacy and authority.[37] Although the IMT predates the actual emergence of a discourse of transitional justice for almost half a century, harking back to the post-war period adds a veneer of time to the recent discourse. Even as transitional justice was emerging in the 1990s, it could look back to an antecedent – an origin – in Nuremberg. The novelty of the discourse required it to anchor itself to an older, mythical, origin.[38] Transitional justice could thus appear as something rooted and established.

Making Nuremberg the foundational myth of transitional justice not only added antiquity to the discourse but also linked it to a particularly illustrious period. The aftermath of World War II appears as a moment when morality and law rose from the horror of the war.[39] Inscribing the origin of transitional justice in this period linked it with other principled endeavours of the post-war period such as the United Nations (UN) and the Universal Declaration of Human Rights (UDHR).[40] Because the victorious Allies and the liberated countries carried out a wide range of trials and other justice policies at the end

[36] Unless otherwise stated, throughout this chapter Nuremberg is understood as referring to the IMT.

[37] Thomas M Franck, *The Power of Legitimacy among Nations* (Oxford University Press, 1990) 94–98.

[38] For a similar argument, see Anne McClintock, *Imperial Leather* (Routledge, 1995) 358.

[39] Samuel Moyn, 'Substance, Scale, and Salience: The Recent Historiography of Human Rights' (2012) 8 *Annual Review of Law and Social Science* 123, 124.

[40] Charter of the United Nations (adopted 26 June 1945, entered into force 24 October 1945) 1 UNTS XVI; Universal Declaration of Human Rights (adopted 10 December 1948 UNGA Resolution 217 A(III) (UDHR).

of World War II, tracing transitional justice to this period made the budding discourse more solid and relevant.[41]

As with many foundational myths, the IMT is idealised, and its flaws and failings are glossed over. As a consequence, the discourse of transitional justice can avoid engaging with the actual controversies and problems associated with the IMT. The IMT has been criticised mostly on two grounds: first, that it violated the principle of legality by convicting people of offences which were not crimes under international law at the time of being committed,[42] and, second, that it was an instance of victors' justice where the powers sitting in judgment had committed similar crimes but were not prosecuted.[43] While the IMT rejected these arguments as substantial defences, it refrained from convicting the German admirals of waging unlimited submarine warfare on the ground that the Allied navies had done the same.[44] These defects notwithstanding, for transitional justice discourse, Nuremberg is an unmitigated triumph of justice. Nuremberg functions as an idealised, mythical point of origin. In this sense, Ruti Teitel recognised that there was a gap between the idealisation of Nuremberg and its historical reality.[45] After all, nobody believes Britain was actually founded by a Trojan.

The second aspect of Nuremberg's role in transitional justice discourse is exemplary. Nuremberg stands as an archetypical example of two things. First, for transitional justice discourse, it represents a moment when there was political will, resources and support for a comprehensive policy of prosecutions. In the formative experiences of Argentina and South Africa, scholars and practitioners often summoned Nuremberg as an archetypical example of extensive prosecutions that was impossible to follow given the prevailing circumstances in these countries. Carlos Nino argued that in Argentina,

41 See Devin O Pendas, 'Seeking Justice, Finding Law: Nazi Trials in Postwar Europe' (2009) 81 *The Journal of Modern History* 347, 351–52.

42 Hans Kelsen, 'Will the Judgment in the Nuremberg Trial Constitute a Precedent in International Law?' (1947) 1 *International Law Quarterly* 153, 162–63; FB Schick, 'The Nuremberg Trial and the International Law of the Future' (1947) 41 *The American Journal of International Law* 770; Werner Maser, *Nuremberg: A Nation on Trial* (Scribner, 1979) 260–74; Steven Fogelson, 'The Nuremberg Legacy: An Unfulfilled Promise' (1990) 63 *Southern California Law Review* 833, 860–67; Jens David Ohlin, 'On the Very Idea of Transitional Justice' (2007) 8 *The Whitehead Journal of Diplomacy and International Relations* 51, 59–60.

43 Herbert Wechsler, 'The Issues of the Nuremberg Trial' (1947) 62 Political Science Quarterly 11, 25–26; Montgomery Belgion, *Victors' Justice: A Letter Intended to Have Been Sent to a Friend Recently in Germany* (Regnery Co, 1949); Otto Kirchheimer, *Political Justice: The Use of Legal Procedure for Political Ends* (Princeton University Press, 1961) 336–38; Maser, *Nuremberg* 274–80 (n 42).

44 IMT Judgment 138–40 (n 10).

45 Ruti Teitel, *Transitional Justice* (Oxford University Press, 2000) 31.

unlike in post-war Germany, there were no occupying forces to support the trials.[46] Similarly, José Zalaquett affirmed that the Nuremberg model was not fully adequate when perpetrators still wield power, as was the case in Argentina.[47] In a similar vein, in South Africa, the Nuremberg model of wide-ranging trials was considered inappropriate given the power that the security forces still commanded.[48] In this manner, commentators regarded Nuremberg as a desirable example, an ideal type, of a policy of prosecutions for past widespread or systematic violence that was seldom available in transitional situations. Although the majority of the trials for World War II crimes took place elsewhere,[49] for these commentators it was the name of Nuremberg that embodied the example of widespread prosecutions.

Second, Nuremberg is also an example of using international law to respond to past widespread or systematic violence. Advocates of international criminal justice used the example of Nuremberg to generate support for international courts.[50] Since in the aftermath of World War II international law had been used to prosecute those responsible for atrocities, it surely could happen again. The ad hoc tribunals and, later, the International Criminal Court (ICC) were instances where the example of Nuremberg was put into practice. That is why, during the Security Council meetings leading up to the creation of the International Criminal Tribunal for the former Yugoslavia (ICTY), many references were made to the Nuremberg precedent.[51]

The last aspect of Nuremberg's role within transitional justice discourse is ancestral. Claiming Nuremberg as its point of origin allows the discourse to incorporate international criminal tribunals into its remit. Nuremberg is widely regarded as the place where international criminal law was born.[52]

46 Carlos Nino, 'The Duty to Punish Past Abuses of Human Rights Put into Context: The Case of Argentina' (1991) 100 *The Yale Law Journal* 2619, 2623.

47 Jose Zalaquett, 'Balancing Ethical Imperatives and Political Constraints: The Dilemma of New Democracies Confronting Past Human Rights Violations' (1991) 43 *Hastings Law Journal* 1, 1428.

48 John Dugard, 'Is the Truth and Reconciliation Process Compatible with International Law: An Unanswered Question' (1997) *South African Journal on Human Rights* 258, 258; Alex Boraine, *A Country Unmasked: South Africa's Truth and Reconciliation Commission* (Oxford University Press, 2000) 13, 382–83. See also Bronwyn Leebaw, 'Legitimation or Judgment? South Africa's Restorative Approach to Transitional Justice' (2003) 36 *Polity* 23.

49 Of an estimated 95,000 Germans and Austrians convicted of Nazi crimes, only 22 were tried at the IMT and 177 at the NMT, Pendas, 'Seeking Justice, Finding Law' 354 (n 41).

50 Leebaw, 'Legitimation or Judgment?' 27 (n 48).

51 UNSC Verbatim Record (22 February 1993) UN Doc S/PV/3175, 11, 17; UNSC Verbatim Record (25 May 1993) UN Doc S/PV/3217, 6, 11.

52 See Minow, *Between Vengeance and Forgivenes* 48 (n 3); Belinda Cooper, 'Introduction' in Belinda Cooper (ed), *War Crimes: The Legacy of Nuremberg* (TV Books, 1999) 17.

The Nuremberg Charter sought to use international law to try individuals for crimes and introduced the notion of crimes against humanity.[53] The precedent of Nuremberg as the origin of international criminal law was then reinvigorated with the creation of the ad hoc tribunals. Thus, for Judge Theodor Meron, Nuremberg was the 'famous forerunner' of these UN international criminal tribunals that carried its spirit forward.[54]

If the first international criminal tribunal was not merely an instance of transitional justice but, indeed, its origin, transitional justice discourse could appropriate all subsequent international and mixed criminal courts as well. For instance, Carlos Nino begins his account of responses to human rights abuses in Europe with Nuremberg; followed by national post-war prosecutions; the Eichmann trial in Jerusalem; the transitions in Spain, Portugal and Greece in the 1970s; the post-communist transitions and the ICTY.[55] In a similar vein, the first phase of Ruti Teitel's genealogy of transitional justice focuses on Nuremberg; the second revolves around the transitions in Latin America, Eastern Europe and South Africa and the third includes the ad hoc tribunals.[56] These historical narratives of the development of transitional justice include trials before both domestic courts and international tribunals. Placing international and national trials as undifferentiated episodes of a single narrative of transitional justice beginning in Nuremberg has the effect of incorporating all international criminal justice into the discourse. Despite having its own institutions, principles and experts, international criminal justice becomes an instrument of transitional justice. Accordingly, as we have seen in the previous chapter, transitional justice experts, institutions and publications routinely discuss international criminal tribunals. Claiming Nuremberg as the origin of transitional justice facilitated and justified this ancestral incorporation.

The triple role of Nuremberg – mythological, exemplary and ancestral – makes it a crucial event for transitional justice discourse. It anchors the historical narrative of the discourse in a symbolic moment which adds legitimacy, provides an ideal example and allows it to incorporate international criminal justice.

[53] Charter of the International Military Tribunal, Annex to Agreement for the Prosecution and Punishment of the Major War Criminals of the European Axis (adopted and entered into force 8 August 1945) 82 UNTS 279 (Nuremberg Charter). See also Elizabeth Borgwardt, 'Re-Examining Nuremberg as a New Deal Institution: Politics, Culture and the Limits of Law in Generating Human Rights Norms' (2005) 23 *Berkeley Journal of International Law*.

[54] Theodor Meron, 'The Greatest Change in International Law', *The Making of International Criminal Justice* (Oxford University Press, 2011) 75.

[55] Nino, *Radical Evil on Trial* (n 3).

[56] Teitel, 'Transitional Justice Genealogy' (n 4).

III NUREMBERG AS TRANSITIONAL JUSTICE

Although Nuremberg is widely regarded as the point of origin of the discourse, it is still crucial to establish whether it can truly be considered a practice of transitional justice in and of itself. At this stage, it is necessary to return to the distinction between the two dimensions of transitional justice: the historically situated discourse of transitional justice and transitional justice as a descriptive label applicable to practices in the present and in the past. This book defines transitional justice practice in the latter sense as a response to past widespread or systematic violence. This definition can be applied to past practices to see if they can be described as instances of transitional justice, even if they took place decades before a distinct discourse of transitional justice came into being. If a practice fits this definition of response to past widespread or systematic violence, it can retrospectively be considered a practice of transitional justice.

Under the definition adopted in this book, the IMT can be regarded as an instance of transitional justice. According to the London Agreement, the purpose of the IMT was to try the major war criminals for their abominable deeds.[57] It was expressly a response to the violence that the Nazi leadership had unleashed.[58] This violence was undoubtedly widespread and systematic. It was also in the past since Germany surrendered to the Allies on 7 May 1945, and the IMT was established on 8 August 1945.[59]

The IMT trial would fit even narrower definitions of transitional justice that require a link with a political transition[60] or include a limited set of mechanisms.[61] It took place after a regime change and was a criminal trial which is included in any list of transitional justice mechanisms. Hence, the IMT fits the retrospective label of a transitional justice practice.

At the same time, in many ways the IMT diverged from the mechanisms and situations that transitional justice most often addresses. While these differences do not negate the IMT's status as an instance of transitional justice

57 London Agreement, preamble (n 8).

58 'Declaration of German Atrocities' (1 November 1943) 3 Bevans 834 (Moscow Declaration).

59 London Agreement (n 8).

60 Teitel, 'Transitional Justice Genealogy' 69 (n 4); Bell, Campbell and Ní Aoláin, 'Justice Discourses in Transition' 305 (n 5); Elster, *Closing the Books* 1 (n 6); Naomi Roht-Arriaza, 'The New Landscape of Transitional Justice' in Naomi Roht-Arriaza and Javier Mariezcurrena (eds), *Transitional Justice in the Twenty-First Century: Beyond Truth versus Justice* (Cambridge University Press, 2006) 2.

61 Elster, *Closing the Books* 1 (n 6); Roht-Arriaza, 'The New Landscape of Transitional Justice' 2 (n 60).

according to the definition adopted in this book, it is remarkable that in many aspects the originator differed from the norm.

First, the IMT was a response to an international armed conflict. The Nazi atrocities, of course, also included internal repression. The most dramatic example of a state abusing its own nationals is the persecution and extermination of the German Jews and other minorities. But the IMT, which was made possible by the Allied victory, concentrated on wartime violence. The jurisdiction of the IMT included crimes against peace, war crimes and crimes against humanity. All three categories as defined by the Nuremberg Charter required an international armed conflict. Crimes against peace comprised 'planning, preparation, initiation or waging of a war of aggression, or a war in violation of international treaties, agreements or assurances, or participation in a common plan or conspiracy for the accomplishment of any of the foregoing'.[62] All of these acts refer to an international armed conflict. War crimes were defined as 'violations of the laws or customs of war'.[63] Although currently war crimes can be committed during a non-international armed conflict, when the Nuremberg Charter was adopted, they were restricted to armed conflicts of international character.[64] Similarly, while nowadays it is clear that crimes against humanity can be committed during peacetime,[65] the Nuremberg Charter required a nexus with the war for this type of offence.[66] Therefore, the IMT judgment had to connect instances of crimes against humanity, such as the slave labour programme or the concentration camps, with aggressive war.[67] The same requirement of establishing a nexus with the armed conflict precluded the IMT from determining that the murder of political opponents and the persecution of Jews that took place before the beginning of the war constituted crimes against humanity.[68] This shows that the IMT was primarily a response to an international armed conflict.

In contrast, the discourse of transitional justice first developed around a series of experiences where the violence was the result of internal repression

62 Nuremberg Charter, art 6 (n 53).

63 Ibid.

64 *Prosecutor* v. *Tadić* (Decision on the Defence Motion for Interlocutory Appeal on Jurisdiction) ICTY-94-1 (2 October 1995), paras 119–27.

65 Ibid, para 141; *Prosecutor* v. *Khieu Samphan, Nuon Chea, Ieng Sary and Ieng Thirith* (Case 002/01 Appeal Judgement) Case 002-F36 (23 November 2016), para 721; Rome Statute of the International Criminal Court (adopted 17 July 1998, entered into force 1 July 2002) 2187 UNTS 90 (Rome Statute), art 7. See also M Cherif Bassiouni, *International Criminal Law*, vol 1 (3rd edn, Martinus Nijhoff Publishers, 2008).

66 Nuremberg Charter, art 6 (n 53).

67 IMT Judgment, 68, 76, 78 (n 10).

68 Ibid 84.

(Argentina, Eastern Europe). Later, through the incorporation of the ICTY into transitional justice's remit, the discourse examined a response to an armed conflict of mixed character caused by the break-up of a state.[69] Ever since, the discourse of transitional justice has mostly examined situations of internal repression or non-international armed conflicts.[70]

A second difference between contemporary transitional justice and the IMT lies in the latter's focus on the crime of aggression. The IMT's 'real purpose was to try the Nazi leaders for having waged aggressive war'.[71] US Chief Prosecutor Robert Jackson made this clear in the first lines of his opening statement to the IMT when he said that the Allies were using international law to 'meet the greatest menace of our times – aggressive war'.[72] The judgment emphasised the primacy of crimes against peace even further. It claimed that to 'initiate a war of aggression, therefore, is not only an international crime; it is the supreme international crime differing only from other war crimes in that it contains within itself the accumulated evil of the whole'.[73] Although individuals obviously bore the brunt of World War II violence, the overarching narrative of the IMT was one of aggression against states. Conversely, in transitional justice discourse, violence is often characterised as human rights violations directed against individuals. Aggression has not hitherto played a significant role in transitional justice discourse.[74]

The third aspect that distinguishes the IMT from most mechanisms of transitional justice is that the former was an imposition of occupying forces and not an expression of a society responding to its own past. Accordingly, the tribunal set up by the Allies is often regarded as an instance of the victors

69 *Prosecutor* v. *Tadić* (Opinion and Judgment) ICTY-94-1 (7 May 1997), para 569.

70 See Bell, Campbell and Ní Aoláin, 'Justice Discourses in Transition' 306 (n 5).

71 Judith Shklar, *Legalism* (Harvard University Press, 1964) 170. See also Gary Jonathan Bass, *Stay the Hand of Vengeance: The Politics of War Crimes Tribunals* (Princeton University Press, 2000) 173; Kevin Jon Heller, *The Nuremberg Military Tribunals and the Origins of International Criminal Law* (Oxford University Press, 2011).

72 *United States of America, the French Republic, the United Kingdom of Great Britain and Northern Ireland, and the Union of Soviet Socialist Republics against Major War Criminals* (Opening Statement Chief Prosecutor) in I Nazi Conspiracy and Aggression (Red Series) 21 November 1945 114.

73 IMT Judgment 16 (n 10).

74 The inclusion of the crime of aggression among the offences over which the ICC has jurisdiction which has been recently activated by the Assembly of States Parties, albeit only binding for those states that have ratified the relevant amendment, could eventually push aggression into transitional justice's remit. Rome Statute of the International Criminal Court, Rome 17 July 1998, 2187 UNTS 90 (RS), amended by Resolution RC/Res 6 11 June 2010, CN651 2010 Treaties-8, arts 8 *bis*, 15 *bis*, 15 *ter*; Resolution ICC-ASP/16/Res.5 14 December 2017, arts 1–2.

judging their defeated enemies.[75] While only the four victorious powers drafted the Nuremberg Charter and were involved in the trial, 19 other states of the United Nations ratified the Charter.[76] Yet, irrespective of its international standing, the IMT was undoubtedly an external imposition. The reluctance of the Allies to allow the Germans to try the Nazis themselves was a reaction to the German-run Leipzig trials following World War I when only a small number of low-level offenders were prosecuted and were handed lenient sentences to boot.[77] According to Chief Prosecutor Jackson's opening statement, when the war ended, the Allies faced a choice: either 'the victors must judge the vanquished or we must leave the defeated to judge themselves. After the first World War, we learned the futility of the latter course.'[78] Thus German society, with the exception of defence lawyers, played no part in the design or functioning of the IMT. Contrariwise, the discourse of transitional justice initially developed around the responses to past widespread or systematic violence adopted by the societies in question in Latin America and Eastern Europe.[79] While the discourse was later expanded with the incorporation of international criminal justice that can operate without the consent of the state concerned,[80] it is remarkable that the point of origin chosen departed from its formative experiences in this regard.

A fourth difference is that victims did not play a prominent role during the IMT trial. As Mark Osiel notes, at 'Nuremberg there was little testimony by surviving victims of the concentration camps and entirely nothing about their felt experience of life there or its emotional aftermath'.[81] Indeed, only one Jewish victim testified during the trial.[82] This was a consequence of the

75 Maser, *Nuremberg* (n 42).

76 London Agreement (n 8).

77 Bass, *Stay the Hand of Vengeance*, ch 3 (n 71).

78 Opening Statement Chief Prosecutor 116 (n 72).

79 Indeed, some authors restricted the scope of transitional justice to that type of responses, see Harvey M Weinstein and Laurel E Fletcher, 'Violence and Social Repair: Rethinking the Contribution of Justice to Reconciliation' (2002) 24 *Human Rights Quarterly* 573, 574; Elster, 'Coming to Terms with the Past' 1 (n 32).

80 The UN Security Council created the ad hoc tribunals, even against the will of the concerned state in the case of the International Criminal Tribunal for Rwanda, and it can also refer situations to the ICC, Rome Statute, art 13(b) (n 63).

81 Mark Osiel, *Mass Atrocity, Collective Memory, and the Law* (Transaction 1997) 103. See also Annette Weinke, 'West Germany: A Case of Transitional Justice Avant la Lettre?' in Nico Wouters (ed), *Transitional Justice and Memory in Europe (1945–2013)* (Intersentia, 2014).

82 Krista Hegburg, 'The Law Is Such as It Is: Reparations, "Historical Reality," and the Legal Order in the Czech Republic' in Alexander Laban Hinton, Thomas La Pointe and Douglas Irvin-Erickson (eds), *Hidden Genocides: Power, Knowledge, Memory* (Rutgers University Press, 2013), 195.

prosecutorial strategy of relying primarily on documentary evidence obtained from the capture of German archives. Thus, Chief Prosecutor Jackson could boast in his opening statement that there was 'no count of the Indictment that cannot be proved by books and records'.[83] The relegation of victims at the IMT contrasts with the prominence that they are given in transitional justice discourse. As we have seen in Chapter 2, victims are a central actor of transitional justice discourse and the source of its moral legitimacy.

This analysis has shown that while the IMT certainly fits broad definitions of transitional justice, such as the one adopted in this book, it was different in certain aspects from the cases that shaped the emergence of the discourse. This divergence seems to mark it as an unlikely candidate to be regarded as the origin of transitional justice. Other post-war initiatives fall within transitional justice's remit more squarely. For instance, the trials carried out before the Polish Supreme National Tribunals in 1946–1948 or the Auschwitz trial before a German court in Frankfurt in 1963 were home-grown initiatives which focused on atrocities against individuals and featured more victim testimony.[84] However, despite these differences, the discourse of transitional justice regards the Nuremberg tribunal as its point of origin.

IV THE CHOICE OF NUREMBERG AND TRANSITIONAL JUSTICE'S CHARACTERISTICS

The IMT was chosen as the origin of transitional justice because it presented many of the key characteristics of the modern discourse of transitional justice. It was not, as explored earlier, an unproblematic choice. However, in its chosen origin, the discourse found its reflection – allowing it to legitimise and strengthen its characteristics. The IMT was technical, teleological, liberal and state-centric.

First, the IMT was technical in the legalistic and apparently apolitical dimensions. As Chief Prosecutor Jackson famously said at Nuremberg, the victors decided 'to stay the hand of vengeance and voluntarily submit their captive enemies to the judgment of the law'.[85] The IMT tried the senior leaders of Nazi Germany using legal principles, rules and professionals.

[83] Opening Statement Chief Prosecutor, 118 (n 72).

[84] *Trial of Hauptsturmfürher Amon Leopold Goeth* (Case No. 37) VIII Law Reports of Trials of War Criminals (5 September 1946) (Goeth Judgment); *Trial of Obersturmbannfürher Rudolf Franz Ferdinand Hoess* (Case No. 38) VIII Law Reports of Trials of War Criminals (29 March 1947); Devin O Pendas, *The Frankfurt Auschwitz Trial, 1963–1965: Genocide, History, and the Limits of the Law* (Cambridge University Press, 2006); Rebecca Wittmann, *Beyond Justice the Auschwitz Trial* (Harvard University Press, 2005).

[85] Opening Statement Chief Prosecutor 114 (n 72).

Although the IMT has been criticised for not living up to some legalistic standards, it undoubtedly was a legalistic response.[86] Accordingly, for Gary Bass, 'Nuremberg remains legalism's greatest moment of glory'.[87]

The legalism of the IMT served to mask its political nature. An intense period of political negotiations, diplomatic wrangling and mutual concessions preceded the establishment of the IMT. Whereas the Soviets wanted to try the Nazis all along,[88] the British favoured summarily executing the German leadership[89] and the Americans toyed with both options before supporting establishing an international tribunal.[90] The rationale behind the British reluctance to try the Nazi leadership was that it was indeed a political question that should not be entrusted to judges.[91] As Francine Hirsch notes, the creation of the IMT 'was a combination principle, self-interest, and compromise from start to finish'.[92] On the political question of what to do with the German leadership, the Allies eventually chose a legalistic response. Thus, for Judith Shklar, Nuremberg was both legalistic and political. It was 'an act of legalistic statesmanship', of politics resorting to law.[93] The choice of a legalistic response subdued the politics of Nuremberg. The adherence to legal standards meant that some counts of the indictment were rejected and three defendants were acquitted. This was at odds with the Soviet view of the trial as an openly political tool and accordingly the Soviet judge, Major General Nikitchenko, issued a dissenting opinion considering that no defendant should have been acquitted.[94] By choosing a legalistic response that judged the conduct of the German leadership according to legal rules and principles, the Allies made the political issue of dealing with the defeated enemy appear

86 Schick, 'The Nuremberg Trial and the International Law of the Future' (n 42); Maser, *Nuremberg* (n 42); Fogelson, 'The Nuremberg Legacy' (n 42); Ohlin, 'On the Very Idea of Transitional Justice' (n 42).

87 Bass, *Stay the Hand of Vengeance* 203 (n 71).

88 Marina Sorokina, 'People and Procedures: Toward a History of the Investigation of Nazi Crimes in the USSR' (2005) 6 *Kritika: Explorations in Russian and Eurasian History* 797.

89 John Simon, Lord Chancellor 'Major War Criminals Memorandum' (4 September 1944) in Bradley F Smith (ed), The American Road to Nuremberg: The Documentary Record, 1944–1945 (Hoover Institution Press, 1982). See also Francine Hirsch, 'The Soviets at Nuremberg: International Law, Propaganda, and the Making of the Postwar Order' (2008) 113 *American Historical Review* 701.

90 Arieh J Kochavi, *Prelude to Nuremberg: Allied War Crimes Policy and the Question of Punishment* (University of North Carolina Press, 1998); Elizabeth Borgwardt, 'A New Deal for the Nuremberg Trial: The Limits of Law in Generating Human Rights Norms' (2008) 26 *Law and History Review* 679.

91 Simon, 'Major War Criminals Memorandum' 32 (n 89).

92 Hirsch, 'The Soviets at Nuremberg' 729 (n 89).

93 Shklar, *Legalism* 170 (n 71).

94 IMT Judgment 166–78 (n 10).

less openly political. Thus, the IMT was technical in its legalistic and apparently apolitical dimensions.

Second, the IMT was teleological. The Allies created it with the express purpose of trying and punishing 'the major war criminals of the European Axis'.[95] In addition to this specific purpose, according to Chief Prosecutor Jackson, the IMT was part of a wider effort to secure peace and prevent war.[96] The IMT was thus established to achieve a set of goals.

Third, despite the participation of the Soviet Union, the IMT had a liberal imprint. The numerical superiority of liberal Allies in the tribunal ensured that regard was paid to liberal principles such as legality and the presumption of innocence. Moreover, while the IMT did not expressly support liberal democracy or capitalism, it did focus on conduct that could be characterised as violating civil and political rights. Although the Nuremberg trial took place two decades before human rights were divided into civil and political rights and economic, social and cultural rights, the conduct underlying the crimes for which the Nazis were prosecuted would mostly amount to violations of the former category. These violations included murder, extermination and persecution. However, some conduct, such as the slave labour programme and human experimentation could also be characterised as a violation of the socio-economic rights to fair conditions of labour and to health.[97]

Fourth, the IMT was a state-centric response to past widespread or systematic violence. It was created by a treaty negotiated by 4 states and ratified by 19 others. While it tried individuals and not states, almost all of the defendants had been high-ranking officials of Germany. The IMT concentrated on the crime of aggression that can only be committed by those controlling the political and military machinery of a state.[98]

In addition to presenting the characteristics of the later discourse of transitional justice, the IMT trial is a recognisable and renowned historical milestone. The dramatic experience of the Allies coming together to judge the Nazi leadership lent itself to becoming a symbol more than did broader national prosecutions or trials by a single occupying power. The fact that the IMT was created by a treaty and adjudicated questions of international law had a universal scope that made it suitable to be the origin of a discourse with global aspirations. Due to these additional reasons, the IMT was singled out as

[95] Nuremberg Charter, art 1 (n 53).
[96] Opening Statement Chief Prosecutor 171 (n 72).
[97] Evelyne Schmid, *Taking Economic, Social and Cultural Rights Seriously in International Criminal Law* (Cambridge University Press, 2015).
[98] Rome Statute, art 8 *bis*(1) (n 63).

the point of origin of transitional justice from among other post-war responses that also reflected many characteristics of the later discourse, such as trials held by liberated countries. The IMT was much better suited to play the mythological, exemplary and ancestral roles discussed earlier.

Moreover, the IMT had also featured in the formative experiences of the discourse of transitional justice. In Argentina, the 1985 trial of the junta was frequently compared to the Nuremberg trial four decades before.[99] Indeed, President Alfonsín's legal advisors considered the IMT as an antecedent when designing the prosecutorial policy.[100] While in the Eastern European transitions the example of Nuremberg was less present, probably due to the absence of trials and the IMT's associations with the Soviet Union,[101] this antecedent was markedly prominent in the creation of the ICTY, which was celebrated as reviving the precedent of Nuremberg, and the development of international criminal justice.[102] Finally, the antecedent of Nuremberg was invoked in

[99] See James Neilson, 'The Nuremberg Factor Haunts the Junta' *The Observer* (2 May 1982); Martin Andersen, 'Generals Face Judgment in Argentina: Trial of Former Leaders To Open in Argentina' *Washington Post* (21 April 1985); John Tweedy Jr, 'The Argentine "Dirty Wars" Trials: The First Latin American Nuremberg?' (1987) 44 *Guild Practitioner* 15; Luis Moreno Ocampo, 'The Nuremberg Parallel in Argentina' (1990) 11 *New York Law School Journal of International and Comparative Law* 357.

[100] Interview with Jaime Malamud Goti, legal advisor to President Alfonsín (Buenos Aires, 25 September 2013); Jaime Malamud Goti, 'Editorial Note: A Turbulent Past and the Problem with Memory' (2010) 4 *International Journal of Transitional Justice* 153.

[101] Instead parallels were drawn between denazification programmes and lustration, see Vojtech Cepl, 'Ritual Sacrifices' (1992) 1 *East European Constitutional Review* 25; Stephen Holmes, 'The End of Decommunization' 3 *East European Constitutional Review* 33, 33; Tina Rosenberg, 'Overcoming the Legacies of Dictatorship' 74 *Foreign Affairs* 134, 140; Helga A Welsh, 'Dealing with the Communist Past: Central and East European Experiences after 1990' 48 *Europe-Asia Studies* 413, 423.

[102] See, eg, UNSC Verbatim Record 11 (n 50); UNSC Verbatim Record (25 May 1993) UN Doc S/PV/3217, 4, 11; James Podgers, 'Repeating Nuremberg' (1993) 79 *ABA Journal*; 'Not Since Nuremberg' *The Washington Post* (21 August 1994) www.washingtonpost.com/archive/opinions/1994/08/21/not-since-nuremberg/a8f8c897-6634-4f59-92c1-0db63b4b73f7/, accessed 30 July 2018; Theodor Meron, 'The Internationalisation of Criminal Law: Remarks' (1995) 89 *American Society of International Law Proceedings* 297; Marie Ryan, 'Prosecutor of a New Nuremberg' *The Independent* (7 June 1995) www.independent.co.uk/money/spend-save/prosecutor-of-a-new-nuremberg-1585322.html, accessed 30 July 2018; Michael P Scharf, *Balkan Justice: The Story Behind the First International War Crimes Trial since Nuremberg* (Carolina Academic Press, 1997); Charles Trueheart, 'New Kind of Justice: The International Criminal Tribunal for the Former Yugoslavia Is the World's First War-Crimes Tribunal since Nuremberg' (2000) 285 *The Atlantic*. The parallel is often drawn by reference to the seat of the tribunals: 'from Nuremberg to The Hague', see Theodor Meron, 'From Nuremberg to the Hague' (1995) 149 *Military Law Review* 107; Philippe Sands, *From Nuremberg to The Hague: The Future of International Criminal Justice* (Cambridge University Press, 2003); Claire Nielsen, 'From Nuremberg to The Hague: The Civilizing Mission of International Criminal Law' (2008) 14 *Te Mata Koi: Auckland University Law Review* 81; Pascal Chenivesse and

South Africa as a model of prosecutions which was not feasible given the negotiated transition between the ANC and the apartheid government.[103] The fact that the IMT was considered a relevant antecedent in these formative experiences for the discourse, recommended it further to be chosen as the origin of transitional justice.

The choice of Nuremberg as the origin of transitional justice helped to strengthen the technical, teleological, liberal and state-centric characteristics of the discourse. This choice had a number of other consequences that are explored next.

V ILLUMINATED AND OBSCURED ASPECTS OF POST-WAR TRANSITIONAL JUSTICE

According to Michel Foucault's reading of Friedrich Nietzsche, all origins are lowly. While we like to believe that at the origin things were perfect, in reality an attentive look at history is likely to undo any infatuation we might have.[104] This insight applies to transitional justice. A closer examination of the IMT reveals that the putative origin of transitional justice was not a pristine moment bathed 'in the shadowless light of a first morning'.[105] Since it plays such an important role, Nuremberg has been subject to a process of purification. As a symbol, Donald Bloxham notes, parts 'of "Nuremberg" have been inflated, parts marginalized'.[106] As far as transitional justice is concerned, this process meant emphasising the aspects of the IMT and other post-war policies that reflected the characteristics of the discourse and excluding those events that departed from these characteristics from the dominant narrative.

1 *Highlighted Aspects*

Within the discourse of transitional justice, the technical legalistic aspects of Nuremberg are most often emphasised. The IMT appears as a symbol of

Christopher Piranio, 'What Price Justice? On the Evolving Notion of "Right to Fair Trial" from Nuremberg to The Hague' (2011) 24 *Cambridge Review of International Affairs* 403.

[103] Dugard, 'Is the Truth and Reconciliation Process Compatible with International Law' 258 (n 48); Boraine, *A Country Unmasked* 13, 382–83 (n 48).

[104] Michel Foucault, 'Nietzsche, la Généalogie, l'Histoire' in Daniel Defert and François Ewald (eds), *Dits et Écrits, 1954–1988* (Gallimard, 2001), vol 1, 1007; See also Michael Mahon, *Foucault's Nietzschean Genealogy: Truth, Power, and the Subject* (State University of New York Press, 1992) 109.

[105] Michel Foucault, 'Nietzsche, Genealogy, History' in DF Bouchard (ed), *Language, Counter-Memory, Practice: Selected Essays and Interviews* (Cornell University Press, 1977) 143.

[106] Bloxham, 'Milestone and Mythologies' 277 (n 35).

justice, accountability and international law.[107] Most commentators that mention Nuremberg as the origin of transitional justice do not examine the trial in detail and omit the legal irregularities that the IMT suffered from. The few that actually discuss the IMT in more depth actually recognise its shortcomings. For instance, Carlos Nino and Ruti Teitel acknowledge that it was doubtful whether the offences in the Nuremberg Charter were crimes under international law when the accused committed them and that the IMT was selective in prosecuting only German crimes.[108] They also regard the IMT as a political institution.[109] The recognition of the legal problems of the IMT notwithstanding, these authors still consider it a legalistic endeavour which broke new ground in using international law to try individuals.[110] For the discourse, the IMT is primarily a symbol of legalistic transitional justice. This intense focus on legalism means that other instances of transitional justice that are not considered as strongly legalistic have been overlooked or rejected.

The starkest example of this is transitional justice discourse's treatment of the Tokyo IMTFE trial which clearly illustrates the purchase of technical legalism in its account of the post-war period. This tribunal receives much less attention than its European counterpart. While Tokyo is sometimes mentioned in tandem with Nuremberg as the origin of transitional justice, the substance of the trial is hardly touched upon in transitional justice discourse.[111] Even in the broader domain of law, the Tokyo tribunal has attracted much less interest, and more criticism, than the IMT.[112] Apart from a degree of

[107] See, eg, Steven R Ratner and Jason S Abrams, *Accountability for Human Rights Atrocities in International Law: Beyond the Nuremberg Legacy* (Clarendon Press, 1997) xxxi; Mani, *Beyond Retribution* 88 (n 3); Minow, *Between Vengeance and Forgivenes* 27 (n 3); Andrieu, 'Transitional Justice' 4 (n 5); Arbour, 'Economic and Social Justice for Societies in Transition' 1–2 (n 5); Grodsky, 'Re-Ordering Justice' 820 (n 5); Leebaw, 'The Irreconcilable Goals of Transitional Justice' 98–99 (n 5); Lundy and McGovern, 'Whose Justice?' 268 (n 5); Leebaw, 'Legitimation or Judgment? 27 (n 48) 27; Bass, *Stay the Hand of Vengeance* 203 (n 71).

[108] Nino, *Radical Evil on Trial* 161–63 (n 3); Teitel, 'Transitional Justice Genealogy' 73 (n 4); Teitel, *Transitional Justice* 20 (n 45).

[109] Nino, *Radical Evel on Trial* 146 (n 3); Teitel, *Transitional Justice* 29 (n 45).

[110] Nino, *Radical Evil on Trial* 187 (n 3); Teitel, 'Transitional Justice Genealogy' 70 (n 4); Teitel, *Transitional Justice* 31 (n 45).

[111] For the absence of the IMTFE in transitional justice discourse, see Zachary Kaufman, 'Transitional Justice for Tōjō's Japan: The United States Role in the Establishment of the International Military Tribunal for the Far East and Other Transitional Justice Mechanisms for Japan after World War II' (2013) 27 *Emory International Law Review* 755, 755.

[112] For the lack of interest in the IMTFE, the criticism it attracted and why a reappraisal was needed, see the introduction of Neil Boister and Robert Cryer, *The Tokyo International Military Tribunal: A Reappraisal* (Oxford University Press 2008). See also R John Pritchard, 'The International Military Tribunal for the Far East and Its Contemporary Resonances' (1995) 149 *Military Law Review* 25.

Eurocentrism,[113] the fact that the IMTFE was more openly political and less legalistic than the IMT can explain why the Tokyo trial lags far behind in terms of being considered the origin of transitional justice. Unlike the IMT, the IMTFE was not created by treaty but by decree of US General Douglas MacArthur.[114] The United States exerted more ascendancy over the IMTFE than any state over the IMT. General MacArthur appointed all judges of the tribunal which came from 11 Allied states.[115] He also had the power to review the sentences.[116] The political interest of the United States influenced the IMTFE trial in a number of ways. The IMTFE did not prosecute Emperor Hirohito, or even call him as a witness, to ensure stability in occupied Japan where he was considered a divinity.[117] Similarly, the Japanese human experiments and the use of biological weapons in China were not part of the trial because the United States was interested in recruiting the scientists involved in these programmes for its own research.[118] Both the IMT and the IMTFE were

[113] Kim Christian Priemel, 'Consigning Justice to History: Transitional Trials after the Second World War' (2013) 56 *Historical Journal* 553, 569.

[114] The unilateral creation of the IMTFE led some defendants to file writs of habeas corpus before the US judicial system; the Supreme Court, however, found that the IMTFE was an international tribunal because, as Supreme Commander of the Allied Powers, General MacArthur had created it on behalf of the states that had appointed him, see *Hirota* v. *MacArthur* 338 US 197 (1948), 215.

[115] IMTFE Charter, arts 2–3 (n 11). For the judges, Arnold C Brackman, *The Other Nuremberg: The Untold Story of the Tokyo War Crimes Trials* (Morrow, 1987). For a critical analysis written by a judge, Bernard Röling and Antonio Cassese, *The Tokyo Trial and Beyond: Reflections of a Peacemonger* (Polity Press, 1993).

[116] IMTFE Charter, art 17 (n 11).

[117] The French judge, Henri Bernard, pointed out in his dissenting opinion that Emperor Hirohito was 'the principal actor who escaped all prosecution,' *United States of America, the Republic of China, the United Kingdom of Great Britain and Northern Ireland, the Union of Soviet Socialist Republics, the Commonwealth of Australia, Canada, the Republic of France, the Kingdom of the Netherlands, New Zealand, India and the Commonwealth of the Philippines* v. *Araki et al* (Dissenting Opinion of the Member from France) in Neil Boister and Robert Cryer (eds), Documents on the Tokyo International Military Tribunal (Oxford University Press, 2008) 677 (Bernard's Dissent). Without going that far the president of the tribunal, Australian Sir William Webb, also stressed the responsibility of Hirohito for the war, *United States of America, the Republic of China, the United Kingdom of Great Britain and Northern Ireland, the Union of Soviet Socialist Republics, the Commonwealth of Australia, Canada, the Republic of France, the Kingdom of the Netherlands, New Zealand, India and the Commonwealth of the Philippines* v. *Araki et al* (Separate Opinion of the President) in Neil Boister and Robert Cryer (eds), Documents on the Tokyo International Military Tribunal (Oxford University Press, 2008) 638–39. See also Yuma Totani, *The Tokyo War Crimes Trial: The Pursuit of Justice in the Wake of World War II* (Harvard University Asia Center; Distributed by Harvard University Press, 2008) 44.

[118] Jeanne Guillemin, 'National Security, Weapons of Mass Destruction, at the Tokyo War Crimes Trial, 1946–1948' in Kamari Maxine Clarke and Mark Goodale (eds), *Mirrors of Justice:*

political institutions influenced by political considerations. However, in the case of the IMTFE, the political element was much more apparent, and it was widely perceived as such. As US Supreme Court Justice William Douglas put it in a dissenting opinion in 1948, the Tokyo tribunal 'did not sit as a judicial tribunal. It was solely an instrument of political power'.[119]

The judgment rendered on 4 November 1948 convicted all 25 accused, including 7 sentenced to death.[120] However, the French, Indian and Dutch judges dissented.[121] The long dissenting opinion of the Indian judge, Rahadbinod Pal, put in question the legality of the proceedings.[122] He challenged the notion that the category of crimes against peace existed before the war[123] and that there was a conspiracy between the accused.[124] He concluded that all defendants 'must be found not guilty of each and every one of the counts in the indictment'.[125] This opinion distinguishes the IMTFE from the Nuremberg trial where the Soviet judge, while dissenting, did not question the validity of the law applied or the legality of the judgment. The prevailing image of the IMTFE proceedings was negative even among contemporary commentators. In 1950, Georg Schwarzenberger wrote that the 'legal standards – or their absence – of the Tokyo Trial were such as to make lawyers wish to forget all about it at the earliest possible moment'.[126] That negative

Law and Power in the Post-Cold War Era (Cambridge University Press, 2010); Kaufman, 'Transitional Justice for Tōjō's Japan 793 (n 111).

119 *Hirota* v. *MacArthur*, Dissenting Opinion of Justice Douglas, 215 (n 114).

120 IMTFE Judgment 598–625 (n 12).

121 Bernard's Dissent 664 (n 117); *United States of America, the Republic of China, the United Kingdom of Great Britain and Northern Ireland, the Union of Soviet Socialist Republics, the Commonwealth of Australia, Canada, the Republic of France, the Kingdom of the Netherlands, New Zealand, India and the Commonwealth of the Philippines* v. *Araki et al* (Dissenting Opinion of the Member from India) in Neil Boister and Robert Cryer (eds), Documents on the Tokyo International Military Tribunal (Oxford University Press, 2008) 811; *United States of America, the Republic of China, the United Kingdom of Great Britain and Northern Ireland, the Union of Soviet Socialist Republics, the Commonwealth of Australia, Canada, the Republic of France, the Kingdom of the Netherlands, New Zealand, India and the Commonwealth of the Philippines* v. *Araki et al* (Opinion of the Member for the Netherlands) in Neil Boister and Robert Cryer (eds), Documents on the Tokyo International Military Tribunal (Oxford University Press, 2008) 680. See also Borgwardt, 'Re-Examining Nuremberg as a New Deal Institution' 447 (n 53).

122 Dissenting Opinion of the Member from India 838–40 (n 121).

123 Ibid 864–65.

124 Ibid 1302–14.

125 Ibid 1422. See also Elizabeth S Kopelman, 'Ideology and International Law: The Dissent of the Indian Justice at the Tokyo War Crimes Trial' (1991) 23 *New York University Journal of International Law and Politics* 373.

126 Georg Schwarzenberger, 'The Problem of an International Criminal Law' (1950) 3 Current Legal Problems 263, 289. See also Richard H Minear, *Victors' Justice: the Tokyo War Crimes*

perception remained and a legal reappraisal of the IMTFE had to wait until 2008.[127] In transitional justice discourse, the less legalistic and more openly political IMTFE has been relegated to a passing reference.

Transitional justice discourse's post-war narrative highlights those mechanisms that reflected its characteristics. In addition to the IMT, the trials by the occupying powers under Control Council Law No 10 and national prosecutions were legalistic and state-centric endeavours which were presented as apolitical exercises.[128] The denazification programme was also state-centric because it sought to remove Nazi sympathisers from the institutions of the state, but it was not as legalistic as trials. The discourse of transitional justice gives more attention to those mechanisms that reflected the characteristics more faithfully, such as the IMT, and less to those, such as the denazification programme, which departed more from them.

2 *Marginalised Aspects*

In addition to prioritising those mechanisms that reflected more faithfully its characteristics, the discourse of transitional justice has completely marginalised other aspects of the response to the violence of World War II because they departed from these characteristics. Even more than the IMTFE, other crucial elements of post-war transitional justice are completely absent from the established narrative. The obscured stories include the role of the Soviet Union in the IMT and other post-war justice initiatives, the economic dimension of the response to the Nazi atrocities, and the widespread episodes of popular justice that took place after the war. All these excluded processes can be considered practices of transitional justice according to the definition adopted in this book. However, their direct challenge to technical legalism, to the presentation of transitional justice as apolitical, to central tenets of liberalism and to state centrism – characteristics reinforced by the choice of Nuremberg as the origin of the discourse – has led to them being overlooked.

a Soviet Contribution

A first example of the episodes that the discourse of transitional justice has left out of its post-war narrative is the key role that the Soviets played in trials and

Trial (Princeton University Press, 1971). For an analysis of the legal challenges raised by the defendants, see Boister and Cryer, *The Tokyo International Military Tribunal* (n 112).

[127] Boister and Cryer, *The Tokyo International Military Tribunal* (n 112).

[128] See Nino, *Radical Evil on Trial* (n 3); Elster, *Closing the Books* 54–59 (n 6).

denazification processes. The Soviet Union was an important political and legal force behind the creation of the IMT. Already in 1942, the Soviet government had proposed a special international tribunal to try the Nazis.[129] In 1943, they conducted the first Allied war crimes trial in Kharkov.[130] In 1944, one of the foremost Soviet jurists, Aron Traĭnin, wrote a book titled *Hitlerite Responsibility under Criminal Law* in which he argued for the prosecution of the Nazis for committing crimes against peace in launching a war of aggression, as well as examining the concepts of complicity and conspiracy.[131] Traĭnin was part of the Soviet delegation in the negotiation of the IMT's Charter in London and during the Nuremberg trial. As Francine Hirsch shows, Traĭnin's ideas circulated among the Allies and percolated into the Nuremberg Charter which included crimes against peace and conspiracy among its offences.[132] In addition to their role regarding the IMT, the Soviets conducted more trials in their zone of occupation and dismissed more people for having links to the Nazi Party than any other occupying power.[133] Likewise, East Germany convicted twice as many Nazis as West Germany did.[134] They also prosecuted Japanese scientists for testing biological weapons on humans, which the United States did not try at the IMTFE.[135] Finally, the Soviet Union also attempted, unsuccessfully, to have German industrialists extradited to put them to trial.[136]

[129] Sorokina, 'People and Procedures 815 (n 88).

[130] Bazyler and Tuerkheimer, *Forgotten Trials of the Holocaust* ch 1 (n 23); Cohen, 'Transitional Justice in Divided Germany after 1945' 67 (n 24); Ilya Bourtman, '"Blood for Blood, Death for Death": The Soviet Military Tribunal in Krasnodar, 1943' (2008) 22 *Holocaust and Genocide Studies* 246.

[131] AN Traĭnin, *Hitlerite Responsibility under Criminal Law* (Andrey Yanuaryevich Vyshinsky ed, Hutchinson & Co, 1945).

[132] Hirsch, 'The Soviets at Nuremberg' (n 89). The ideas in Traĭnin's book were frequently cited during the London Agreement negotiations, see 'Minutes of Conference Session, June 29, 1945' Report of Robert H. Jackson, United States Representative to the International Conference on Military Trials (Department of State, 1949) 99; 'Minutes of Conference Session, July 19, 1945' Report of Robert H. Jackson, United States Representative to the International Conference on Military Trials (Department of State, 1949) 295, 299; 'Minutes of Conference Session, July 25, 1945' Report of Robert H. Jackson, United States Representative to the International Conference on Military Trials (Department of State, 1949) 379. See also George Ginsburgs, *Moscow's Road to Nuremberg: The Soviet Background to the Trial* (M Nijhoff, 1996).

[133] Romeike, 'Transitional Justice in Germany after 1945 and after 1990' 19, 26 (n 26).

[134] Crowe, *War Crimes, Genocide, and Justice* 257 (n 26).

[135] Jing-Bao Nie, 'The West's Dismissal of the Khabarovsk Trial as "Communist Propaganda": Ideology, Evidence and International Bioethics' (2004) 1 *Journal of Bioethical Inquiry* 32.

[136] Crowe, *War Crimes, Genocide, and Justice* 259 (n 26).

Despite this vigorous participation, transitional justice discourse omits the Soviet contribution or singles it out as being different and less praiseworthy than that of the other powers. Authors either ignore the Soviet role in advocating for the Nuremberg trial and contributing to its legal concepts, or dismiss it as prompted by a desire to use the IMT as a propaganda tool.[137] The mere presence of Soviet judges on the bench is held to have detracted from the credibility of the IMT because of the crimes committed by the Soviet Union.[138] Transitional justice authors distinguish the trials and denazification programmes that the Soviets carried out in their zones of occupation from those of the other powers because they had the political purpose of founding a communist regime.[139] For the established narrative, the role of the Soviets remains 'the Achilles' heel' of the trials.[140] Although the arguments these authors put forward can be compelling, they fail to acknowledge the positive side of the Soviet contribution to post-war justice. Even more, in so doing, they evidence the influence that the characteristics of the discourse of transitional justice have in the narrative of the post-war period.

The Soviet role in post-war justice was at odds with two characteristics of transitional justice discourse: the technical characteristic in its legalistic and apparently apolitical dimensions and the liberal characteristic in its democratic and capitalist dimensions. Since the Soviets did not adhere as closely to legalist principles of due process, transitional justice immediately considers their trials suspect. This attitude is exemplified by Gary Bass, for whom 'Soviet vengeance was utterly unhindered by liberal legalistic norms'.[141] Their efforts are thus invalidated for not respecting legalism. Moreover, the Soviets' explicit use of the trials as a political tool also goes against the discourse's presentation of transitional justice issues as apolitical. For the Soviets, the trials of the Nazis were political didactic exercises in the tradition of the Stalinist show trials against Trotskysts of the 1930s.[142] Transitional justice commentators dismiss

[137] For the first, Borgwardt, 'Re-Examining Nuremberg as a New Deal Institution' (n 53); Osiel, *Mass Atrocity, Collective Memory, and the Law* (n 81). For the second, Bass, *Stay the Hand of Vengeance* 196 (n 71).

[138] Cooper, 'Introduction' 17 (n 52).

[139] Elster, *Closing the Books* 55 (n 6); Cohen, 'Transitional Justice in Divided Germany after 1945' 67 (n 24); Romeike, 'Transitional Justice in Germany after 1945 and after 1990' 12 (n 26).

[140] Hirsch, 'The Soviets at Nuremberg' 701 (n 89) 701.

[141] Bass, *Stay the Hand of Vengeance* 196 (n 71).

[142] Richard Overy, 'The Nuremberg Trials: International Law in the Making' in Philippe Sands (ed), *From Nuremberg to The Hague: The Future of International Criminal Justice* (Cambridge University Press, 2003); Hirsch, 'The Soviets at Nuremberg' (n 89).

the Soviet trials because they did not respect legalism and openly served a political purpose.[143]

The second characteristic of transitional justice discourse that the Soviet participation went against was liberalism. While American, British and French trials and denazification programmes also sometimes departed from legalism and were used as political tools, they were implemented by liberal democracies.[144] Since transitional justice discourse favours liberal democracy and capitalism, the initiatives adopted by socialist countries, or countries on their way to becoming socialist, immediately appear suspect.

b The Economic Dimension of Post-War Responses

Another area that is absent from transitional justice's account of the responses to the violence of World War II is the economic dimension. The Allies believed that the German economy bore responsibility for Nazism's rise to power, wars of aggression and atrocities. The main proponent of this stance was the US government, which was convinced that the highly concentrated German economy with the presence of monopolies and cartels militated against democracy and had led to war.[145] Even before the war, President Roosevelt had linked monopolies with Fascism.[146] In the July 1945 Potsdam Conference, the Allies agreed to decentralise the German economy with 'the purpose of eliminating the present excessive concentration of economic power as exemplified in particular by cartels, syndicates, trusts and other monopolistic arrangements'.[147] Furthermore, the leaders of a number of powerful industrial conglomerates were considered directly responsible for preparing Germany to war through rearmament, sustaining the war effort and participating in the atrocities through slave labour programmes.[148]

143 Elster, *Closing the Books* 55 (n 6); Bass, *Stay the Hand of Vengeance* 196 (n 71); István Deák, 'Political Justice in Austria and Hungary after World War II' in Jon Elster (ed), *Retribution and Reparation in the Transition to Democracy* (Cambridge University Press, 2006).

144 See Belgion, *Victors' Justice* (n 43).

145 Chansoo Cho, 'Manufacturing a German Model of Liberal Capitalism: The Political Economy of the German Cartel Law in the Early Postwar Period' (2003) 10 *Journal of International and Area Studies* 41, 44.

146 Cited in Charles S Maier, 'The Politics of Productivity: Foundations of American International Economic Policy after World War II' (1977) 31 *International Organization* 607, 616.

147 'Protocol of the Proceedings of the Berlin (Potsdam) Conference', principle 12 (n 29).

148 Diarmuid Jeffreys, *Hell's Cartel: IG Farben and the Making of Hitler's War Machine* (Metropolitan Books, 2008) 364. See also Franz Neumann, *Behemoth: The Structure and Practice of National Socialism* (V Gollancz, 1942).

The response to the economic dimension of Nazism included preventive, retributive and restorative policies. The economy would be reformed by breaking up concentrated industries to prevent future wars, those responsible for crimes within the economic sector would be prosecuted and the property confiscated and looted by the Nazis would be restored to their previous owners.[149]

Deconcentration programmes sought to prevent wars by reducing the concentration of the German economy and eliminating monopolies and cartel agreements, thus fostering a free competitive market.[150] This was in line with an American economic policy of free trade in which monopolies were seen with suspicion.[151] American Law 56 and British Ordinance 78, adopted in February 1947, provided for the deconcentration of conglomerates and the prohibition of cartels.[152] Any enterprise employing more than 10,000 people was earmarked for review.[153] Sixty-nine suspicious industrial combines were selected for deconcentration. In 1950, the chemical conglomerate IG Farben was divided into three main companies – Bayer, BASF and Hoechst.[154] The German banking system was reformed to be less concentrated, and the Ruhr coal, iron and steel industry was broken up.[155]

149 Kim Christian Priemel, 'Tales of Totalitarianism: Conflicting Narratives in the Industrialists Cases at Nuremberg' in Kim Christian Priemel and Alexa Stiller (eds), *Reassessing the Nuremberg Military Tribunals: Transitional Justice, Trial Narratives, and Historiography* (Berghahn Books, 2012) 164.

150 John C Stedman, 'The German Decartelization Program: The Law in Repose' (1950) 17 *The University of Chicago Law Review* 441, 443.

151 Luciano Segreto and Ben Wubs, 'Resistance of the Defeated: German and Italian Big Business and the American Antitrust Policy, 1945–1957' (2014) 15 Enterprise & Society 307; Elizabeth Borgwardt, A *New Deal for the World: America's Vision for Human Rights* (Harvard University Press, 2005); Regina Ursula Gramer, 'From Decartelization to Reconcentration: The Mixed Legacy of American-Led Corporate Reconstruction in Germany' in Detlef Junker (ed), *The United States and Germany in the Era of the Cold War, 1945–1990* (Cambridge University Press, 2004).

152 Prohibition of Excessive Concentration of German Economic Power (US Military Government Law No 56) 1947 in *Germany 1947–1949: The Story in Documents* (Department of State, 1950); Prohibition of Excessive Concentration of German Economic Power (British Military Government Ordinance No 78) 1947.

153 Ibid.

154 Jeffreys, *Hell's Cartel* 403 (n 148).

155 Reorganization of German Coal and Iron and Steel Industries (US Military Government Law No 75) 1948 in *Germany 1947–1949: The Story in Documents* (Department of State, 1950), 349; Decentralization of Banks (US Military Government Law No 57 (Revised)) 1949 in Germany 1947–1949: The Story in Documents (Department of State, 1950), 512. See also Stedman, 'The German Decartelization Program' (n 150).

In spite of these efforts, the deconcentration process is widely considered to have failed.[156] The three successors of IG Farben quickly became bigger than they were as a single conglomerate;[157] the banking system, albeit reformed, remained centralised[158] and by 1950 there was retrogression in the deconcentration of the Ruhr industries.[159] A US governmental committee concluded in 1949 that after four years, the decartelisation programme had 'not been effectively carried out'.[160] The failure of the programme has been ascribed to disagreements among the Allies and to the active opposition of American businesses.[161] The only aspect that was belatedly successful was the prohibition of cartels through the passing in 1957 of a law under US pressure.[162]

The retributive arm of the economic post-war policy excluded from transitional justice discourse was the prosecution of those responsible for the Nazi economy. At the IMT, Chief Prosecutor Robert Jackson was determined to expose industrial complicity with the war of aggression.[163] Accordingly, the list of defendants included two Ministers of Economics and Presidents of the Reichsbank (Hjalmar Schacht and Walther Funk) and industrialist Gustav Krupp.[164] Krupp was deemed unfit to stand trial,[165] and Schachts was acquitted because he was dismissed from his senior positions before the start of the

[156] Cho, 'Manufacturing a German Model of Liberal Capitalism' (n 145); Maier, 'The Politics of Productivity' (n 146); Stedman, 'The German Decartelization Program' 442 (n 150); Graham Taylor, 'The Rise and Fall of Antitrust in Occupied Germany, 1945–48' (1979) 11 *Prologue* 23; Segreto and Wubs, 'Resistance of the Defeated' (n 151).

[157] Jeffreys, *Hell's Cartel* 403 (n 148).

[158] Grant Madsen, 'Becoming a State-in-the-World: Lessons Learned from the American Occupation of Germany' (2012) 26 *Studies in American Political Development* 1, 174.

[159] Stedman, 'The German Decartelization Program' 442 (n 150).

[160] Federal Trade Commission 'Report of the Committee Appointed to Review the Decartelization Program in Germany' (Secretary of the Army, 1949) 89 (US) 89.

[161] Cho, 'Manufacturing a German Model of Liberal Capitalism' (n 145); Stedman, 'The German Decartelization Program' (n 150); Segreto and Wubs, 'Resistance of the Defeated' (n 151); Taylor, 'The Rise and Fall of Antitrust in Occupied Germany, 1945–48' (n 156).

[162] Gesetz gegen Wettbewerbsbeschränkungen (Law against Restraints of Competition) 1957. See also Segreto and Wubs, 'Resistance of the Defeated' 331 (n 151).

[163] 'Atrocities and War Crimes: Report from Robert H. Jackson to the President' (7 June 1945) 12 Department of State Bulletin (No 311) 1071 (US), 1074. See also Grietje Baars, 'Capitalism's Victor's Justice? The Hidden Stories behind the Prosecution of Industrialists Post-WWII' in Kevin Jon Heller and Gerry J Simpson (eds), *The Hidden Histories of War Crimes Trials* (Oxford University Press, 2013) 173.

[164] Indictment IMT, appendix A (n 9).

[165] *United States of America, the French Republic, the United Kingdom of Great Britain and Northern Ireland, and the Union of Soviet Socialist Republics against Major War Criminals* (Order of the Tribunal Granting Postponement of Proceedings against Gustav Krupp Von Bohlen) I Nazi Conspiracy and Aggression (Red Series) 15 November 1945 IMT, 91.

war.[166] His successor, Funk, was convicted of planning wars of aggression, war crimes and crimes against humanity due to his role in the slave labour programme, in receiving property seized from people exterminated in concentration camps and in seizing the gold reserves of the Czechoslovakian and Yugoslav national banks. He was sentenced to life imprisonment.[167]

The occupying powers also prosecuted industrialists under Control Council Law No 10. When Krupp was deemed unfit to stand trial and further IMT proceedings were ruled out, the prosecution of industrialists became one of the main reasons for the American NMT.[168] There were three trials of industrialists targeting different combines (IG Farben, Flick and Krupp)[169] and a banker was prosecuted and convicted in the Ministries case.[170] A British military commission tried the manufacturers of the Zyklon B poison used in the gas chambers[171] and the French tried industrialist Hermann Röchling.[172]

The prosecution of the industrialists encountered many difficulties. The IMT acquitted Albert Speer, who was the minister responsible for armaments, of the charge of planning and waging aggressive war. The judgment concluded that Speer's actions 'were in aid of the war effort in the same way that other productive enterprises aid in the waging of war'.[173] In so doing, the IMT set the bar high for the subsequent trials of the industrialists. The judges in the IG Farben Judgment accordingly stated that they left the mark where they found it satisfied that individuals who merely follow the leaders into an aggressive war, like Speer did, should not be held guilty of crimes against peace.[174] Following this precedent, all the industrialists accused before the NMT were acquitted of the charges of crimes against peace.[175] While a

[166] IMT Judgment 134–37 (n 10).

[167] Ibid 131–34.

[168] Baars, 'Capitalism's Victor's Justice?' 173 (n 163).

[169] IG Farben Judgment (n 19); Krupp Judgment (n 19); Flick Judgment (n 19).

[170] Director of the Dresdner Bank Karl Rasche was convicted of participating in the spoliation of property in Holland and Bohemia-Moravia and of being a member of the SS. He was sentenced to seven years imprisonment, Ministries Judgment 784, 862, 868 (n 17).

[171] *Trial of Bruno Tesch et al (Zyklon B)* (Case No. 9) I Law Reports of Trials of War Criminals (8 March 1946) (British Military Court at Hamburg) 93.

[172] *Case* v. *Hermann Röchling et al* XIV Reports of Trials of War Criminals before the Nuremberg Military Tribunals under Control Council Law No 10 (30 June 1948) (General Tribunal of the Military Government of the French Zone of Occupation in Germany) 1075 (Röchling Judgment).

[173] IMT Judgment 156 (n 10).

[174] See IG Farben Judgment 1126–27 (n 19).

[175] IG Farben Judgment 1128 (n 19); *United States of America* v. *Krupp et al (Krupp)* (Order of the Tribunal Acquitting the Defendants of the Charges of Crimes Against Peace) IX Reports of Trials of War Criminals before the Nuremberg Military Tribunals under Control Council Law No 10 (5 April 1948) 390.

French court convicted Röchling of waging aggressive war, the conviction was overturned on appeal based on the IMT precedent.[176]

Moreover, in the IG Farben and Flick cases, the judges accepted the necessity defence in relation to the use of slave labour.[177] They considered that the defendants had no other choice than to comply with the mandates of the Nazi government and accept slave labour in their plants.[178] The charges against IG Farben directors and personnel related to the provision of Zyklon B poison to the death camps and drugs for human medical experimentation were rejected.[179] The majority of judges found that the defendants did not know that the large quantities of Zyklon B and drugs supplied to the concentration camps were used to kill people[180] and conduct illegal experiments.[181] Of the 28 accused in the Flick and IG Farben cases, 17 were fully acquitted. Some defendants, however, were convicted of forced labour because they went beyond necessity and actively participated in the slave labour programmes[182] and of spoliation of property for their role in acquiring property in occupied countries that had been confiscated by German forces or through coerced negotiations.[183] The sentences ranged from 18 months to 7 years.[184] For the prosecutor in the IG Farben case, the sentences were light enough to please a chicken thief.[185]

In the Krupp case, the judges rejected the necessity defence holding inter alia that the defendants were not acting under compulsion or coercion.[186] They considered that if the defendants refused to accept slave labour they would have risked losing their plant or their jobs, not their lives.[187]

[176] Röchling Judgment 1095 (n 172); *Case* v. *Hermann Röchling et al* XIV Reports of Trials of War Criminals before the Nuremberg Military Tribunals under Control Council Law No 10 (25 January 1949) (Superior Military Government Court of the French Occupation Zone in Germany) 1109–10. See also Baars, 'Capitalism's Victor's Justice?' 188 (n 163).

[177] IG Farben Judgment 1174–79 (n 19); Flick Judgment 1200–2 (n 19).

[178] IG Farben Judgment 1175 (n 19); Flick Judgment 1200 (n 19). In IG Farben, Judge Hebert dissented with this finding because he considered that the defendants had moral choice and should be held responsible for participating in the slave labour programme, IG Farben Judgment 1205 (n 19).

[179] IG Farben Judgment 1169–72 (n 19).

[180] Ibid 1169.

[181] Ibid 1172.

[182] IG Farben Judgment 1190, 1192 (n 19); Flick Judgment 1202 (n 19).

[183] Ibid 1156–1157, 1160–1161, 1163, 1165, 1167; Flick Judgment 1208 (n 19).

[184] Ibid 1205–09; Flick Judgment 1223 (n 19).

[185] Josiah Dubois, *The Devil's Chemists* (Beacon Press, 1952) 339.

[186] Krupp Judgment 1438 (n 19).

[187] Ibid 1442–46.

Accordingly, only one defendant was acquitted and the rest convicted of spoliation or slave labour to sentences ranging from 3 to 12 years.[188]

In the trials of economic actors, the rate of acquittals was much higher and the sentences more lenient than in the other cases. A comparison with the rest of the NMT cases shows that the acquittal rate was 34 per cent for the industrialists against 14 per cent for the other defendants. No death sentences or prison terms of more than 12 years were handed to the industrialists. Additionally, in 1950 and 1951, the few industrialists still serving time were released by the US authorities.[189] Even former Minister of Economics Funk, who was sentenced to life by the IMT, was released in 1957.[190]

The reasons for this leniency have to do with a change of heart in the US government inspired by the advent of the Cold War.[191] The trials of the industrialists unfolded against a background of souring relations between the former wartime Allies. Indeed, the verdicts of the IG Farben and Krupp cases were handed out a month after the Soviets started blockading the Western Allies' access to their occupation zones in Berlin in June 1948. By then, US officials were reluctant to set a precedent that might discourage their own industrialists to supply the military.[192] Also, a strong German industry was considered necessary as a bulwark against communism.[193] Moreover, convicting business leaders of international crimes appeared as an indictment of capitalism.[194] Thus, Republican politicians criticised the proceedings and accused the prosecutors of having communist leanings.[195] In addition to this climate inimical to the prosecutions, the judges' sympathies might have been with the industrialists.[196] For example, Judge Morris, who sat in the bench in the IG Farben case, said years later that the industrialists should not have been

188 ibid 1449–52. See also Telford Taylor, 'The Krupp Trial: Fact v. Fiction' (1953) 53 *Columbia Law Review* 197.

189 Priemel, 'Tales of Totalitarianism' 182 (n 149).

190 Telford Taylor, *The Anatomy of the Nuremberg Trials: A Personal Memoir* (Knopf, 1992) 617.

191 Baars, 'Capitalism's Victor's Justice?' 177–78 (n 163). See also Cecelia Goetz, 'The Fifth Annual Ernst C. Steifel Symposium: 1945–1995: Critical Perspectives on the Nuremberg Trials and State Accountability, Panel 1' (1995) 12 *New York Law School Journal of Human Rights* 453.

192 Alberto Zuppi, 'Slave Labor in Nuremberg's IG Farben Case: The Lonely Voice of Paul M. Hebert' (2005) 66 *Louisiana Law Review* 519.

193 Baars, 'Capitalism's Victor's Justice?' 174 (n 163).

194 Ibid 189–90.

195 Donald Bloxham, 'From the International Military Tribunal to the Subsequent Nuremberg Proceedings: The American Confrontation with Nazi Criminality Revisited' (2013) 98 *History* 567, 580.

196 Florian Jessberger, 'On the Origins of Individual Criminal Responsibility under International Law for Business Activity: IG Farben on Trial' (2010) 8 *Journal of International Criminal Justice* 783, 797; Baars, 'Capitalism's Victor's Justice?' 180 (n 163).

tried because they 'were a bunch of eager selfish big businessmen like you would find in any country'.[197]

In addition to the deconcentration programme and the prosecution of economic actors, the occupying powers implemented restorative measures aimed at compensating those whose property had been taken by the Nazis. Already in 1943, 17 Allied states issued a declaration reserving the right to declare invalid any transfers of property in territories under the occupation or control of their enemies.[198] After the end of the war, the Allied powers and liberated countries agreed on the distribution of assets available as reparation from Germany and set principles for the restitution of property taken during occupation.[199] Accordingly, the Western occupying powers passed legislation in their respective zones of occupation, to return property wrongfully acquired to its original owners.[200] For instance, US Military Government Law No 59 had the purpose of effecting the 'speedy restitution of identifiable property . . . to persons who were wrongfully deprived of such property within the period from 30 January 1933 to 8 May 1945 for reasons of race, religion, nationality, ideology or political opposition to National Socialism'.[201] The Soviets, on the other hand, did not establish a property restitution programme but provided victims of the Nazi regime living in their occupation zone with healthcare, work opportunities and preferential procurement of housing, food and consumer goods.[202]

197 Cited in Zuppi 523 (n 192).

198 Inter-Allied Declaration Against Acts of Dispossession Committed in Territories under Enemy Occupation or Control (5 January 1943), Miscellaneous No 1 (1943), Cmd 6418. The Final Act of the 1944 United Nations Monetary and Financial Conference held in Bretton Woods, famous for establishing the World Bank and International Monetary Fund and laying the groundwork for the post-war economic order, also included recommendations aimed at preventing the disposition of looted property and supported its restitution to their lawful owners, United Nations Monetary and Financial Conference Final Act, Bretton Woods (22 July 1944) US Department of State Publication 2187 (1944), VI.

199 Resolution on the Subject of Restitution, Annex to the Final Act of the Paris Conference on Reparation (21 December 1945) Miscellaneous No 1 (1946) Cmd 6721.

200 Restitution of Identifiable Property (US Military Government Law No 59) 1947 in *Germany 1947–1949: The Story in Documents* (Department of State 1950); Ordonnance No 120 du Commandant en Chef Français en Allemagne relative à la restitution des biens ayant fait l'objet d'actes de spoliation (Ordinance No 120 of the French Commander-in-Chief in Germany Concerning the Restitution of Assets Object of Acts of Spoliation) (1947) 119 *Journal Officiel du Commandement en Chef Français en Allemagne* 1219; Restitution of Identifiable Property to Victims of Nazi Oppression (Military Government Law No 59) (1949) 28 Military Government Gazette Germany British Zone of Control 1169.

201 Restitution of Identifiable Property (US Military Government Law No 59) 1947 in *Germany 1947–1949: The Story in Documents* (Department of State, 1950), art 1.

202 Angelika Timm, *Jewish Claims against East Germany: Moral Obligations and Pragmatic Policy* (Central European University Press, 1997) 70.

After the end of occupation, West and East Germany continued the trajectory set by their respective occupying powers. The West German government continued the property restitution process and passed a law that incorporated the laws and ordinances enacted by the occupying states.[203] Between 1959 and 1964, it also entered into bilateral agreements with 12 states for compensating individual claimants in those countries.[204] Moreover, in 1952, West Germany reached an agreement with Israel to compensate the material damage to the Jewish people caused by the Nazis.[205] At the same time, East Germany did not return the assets expropriated by the Nazis to their previous owners but instead nationalised them.[206] It refused to pay compensation to Israel because it did not consider itself a successor to the Nazi regime.[207] The issue of the restitution of assets expropriated by the Nazis was not settled in the post-war period and re-emerged in the 1990s following the reunification of Germany and claims in US courts regarding dormant Jewish accounts in Swiss banks.[208]

The deconcentration programme, the trials of the industrialists and the restitution of property taken by the Nazis can undoubtedly be characterised as transitional justice practices. They were responses to past widespread or systematic violence implemented after conflict. Moreover, trials and institutional reform are two well-established mechanisms of transitional justice. As mentioned in the previous chapter, restitution of property is not as prominent in transitional justice discourse today as the other two mechanisms, but it can still be characterised as a transitional justice practice.

Despite this affinity, the economic dimension has been largely absent from transitional justice accounts. Although John Herz's 1982 book includes a chapter that discusses the deconcentration programme, this was well before

[203] Bundesgesetz zur Regelung der rückerstattungsrechlichen Geldverbindlichkeiten des Deutschen Reichs und gleichgestellter Rechtsträger (Bundesrückerstattungsgesetz – BrüG) (Federal Law on Restitution) 1957. This law incorporated the restitution laws and ordinances passed by occupying forces. See also Schwerin (n 31).

[204] The countries were Luxembourg (1959), Norway (1959), Denmark (1959), Greece (1960), the Netherlands (1960), France (1960), Belgium (1960), Italy (1961), Switzerland (1961), Austria (1961), the United Kingdom (1964) and Sweden (1964). See Thomas Berger, *War, Guilt, and World Politics after World War II* (Cambridge University Press, 2012) 55.

[205] Agreement between the State of Israel and the Federal Republic of Germany, Signed in Luxembourg, on 10 September 1952 (adopted 10 September 1952, entered into force 27 March 1953) 345 UNTS 91. See also Frederick Honig, 'The Reparations Agreement between Israel and the Federal Republic of Germany' (1954) 48 *The American Journal of International Law* 564.

[206] Timm, *Jewish Claims against East Germany* 68 (n 202).

[207] Ibid 67.

[208] See Michael R Marrus, *Some Measure of Justice: The Holocaust Era Restitution Campaign of the 1990s* (University of Wisconsin Press, 2009).

the discourse emerged and its characteristics consolidated.[209] No other scholar followed that tack later. The industrialists' trials do not feature prominently in transitional justice's narratives about World War II prosecutions either. The restitution of property has been the policy of the post-war economic dimension that has generated more interest in transitional justice discourse, at least in its origins. Probably due to the fact that restitution of property was an important aspect of transitional justice policies in the contemporary post-communist transitions, Neil Kritz's 1995 compendium *Transitional Justice: How Emerging Democracies Reckon with Former Regimes* included material related to post-World War II restitution of property.[210] However, this interest in the restitution of property was short-lived. With the shift towards post-conflict situations in contexts in which property restitution seems less urgent, this mechanism largely disappeared from transitional justice's horizon. As William Schabas put it, 'talk of recovering lost assets seems even beyond the irrelevant in the context of poor, developing countries'.[211] Restitution of property has accordingly been largely relegated to a subset of reparations.[212] In this sense, property restitution 'is frequently overlooked by scholars as an integral part of transitional or retrospective justice'.[213] The lack of prominence of property restitution in transitional justice discourse occurs despite its recognition as a right in international law[214] and its frequent inclusion in peace agreements in the context of displacement of people.[215] More generally, despite the interest

[209] Michael Fichter, 'Non-State Organizations and the Problems of Redemocratization' in John Herz (ed), *From Dictatorship to Democracy: Coping with the Legacies of Authoritarianism and Totalitarianism* (Greenwood, 1982).

[210] Neil J Kritz, *Transitional Justice: How Emerging Democracies Reckon with Former Regimes* (United States Institute of Peace Press, 1995).

[211] William Schabas, 'Foreword' in Michael R Marrus, *Some Measure of Justice: The Holocaust Era Restitution Campaign of the 1990s* (University of Wisconsin Press, 2009) xiii.

[212] See UNGA Resolution 60/147 'Basic Principles and Guidelines on the Right to a Remedy and Reparation for Victims of Gross Violations of International Human Rights Law and Serious Violations of International Humanitarian Law' (16 December 2005) UN Doc A/RES/60/147, para 19.

[213] Eva-Clarita Pettai and Vello Pettai, *Transitional and Retrospective Justice in the Baltic States* (Cambridge University Press, 2015). With the recent expansion of transitional justice, there has been some interest in examining the restitution of property from a transitional justice perspective, Liviu Damşa, *The Transformation of Property Regimes and Transitional Justice in Central Eastern Europe: In Search of a Theory* (Springer, 2017).

[214] Case Concerning the Factory at Chorzów (*Germany* v. *Poland*) Claim for Indemnity (Merits) 1928 PCIJ Series A No 17, 47.

[215] For example, Protocol of Agreement between the Government of Rwanda and the Rwandese Patriotic Front on the Repatriation of Rwandese Refugees and the Resettlement of Displaced Persons (signed 9 June 1993), art 4; Protocol III (signed 12 March 1992), General Peace Agreement for Mozambique, Annex to Letter Dated 6 October 1992 from the Permanent

within transitional justice discourse in engaging with the socio-economic dimension of violence, the post-war precedents of the deconcentration programme, industrialists' trials and restitution of property have not gained prominence. The economic dimension of post-war transitional justice is thus largely absent from the narrative of the discourse.[216]

This absence can be explained by the fact that the post-war policies tackling economic aspects departed from the liberal characteristic of transitional justice discourse in two of its dimensions: its emphasis on civil and political rights and its support for capitalism. The deconcentration programme, the industrialists' trials and the restitution of property addressed the role of economic actors in widespread or systematic violence. In contrast, transitional justice discourse normally focuses on violations of civil and political rights, often involving physical violence. By engaging with the economic aspects of the Nazi regime, the deconcentration programme, the industrialists' trials and the restitution of property fell outside transitional justice's usual scope. Some authors seeking to broaden the scope of transitional justice discourse to give more emphasis to social and economic rights are currently challenging this narrow lens.[217]

The second dimension of the liberal character of transitional justice discourse that the economic dimension challenged was its support for capitalism. Although these responses targeting the economic facet of Nazism were animated, as far as the Western Allies were concerned, by a spirit of free market, they also represented an indictment of some aspects of capitalism.[218] As Grietje Baars explains, initially the United States and the Soviet Union saw eye to eye in that German economic imperialism was to blame for the war.[219] For the Soviets, 'the German financial and industrial heads must also be sent

Representative of Mozambique to the United Nations Addressed to the Secretary-General (8 October 1992) UN Doc S/24635, art IV(e); Agreement on Refugees and Displaced Persons, Annex 7 to General Framework Agreement for Peace in Bosnia and Herzegovina (Dayton Agreement) (signed 21 November 1995), Attachment to Letter Dated 29 November 1995 from the Permanent Representative of the United States of America to the United Nations Addressed to the Secretary-General (30 November 1995) UN Docs A/50/790, S/1995/999, art 1(1). See also Scott Leckie, *Housing, Land, and Property Restitution Rights of Refugees and Displaced Persons: Laws, Cases, and Materials* (Cambridge University Press, 2007).

216 See Baars, 'Capitalism's Victor's Justice?' 191 (n 163).

217 See, eg, Sabine Michalowski, *Corporate Accountability in the Context of Transitional Justice* (Routledge, 2013); Hannah Franzki and Maria Carolina Olarte, 'Understanding the Political Economy of Transitional Justice: A Critical Theory Perspective' in Susanne Buckley-Zistel and others (eds), *Transitional Justice Theories* (Routledge, 2014).

218 Segreto and Wubs, 'Resistance of the Defeated' (n 151).

219 Baars, 'Capitalism's Victor's Justice?' 164 (n 163).

for trial as criminals'.[220] The United States was also determined to prosecute the economic actors of Nazism. However, when the frictions between the former Allies mounted, the United States sought to protect all aspects of capitalism. After all, the German combines had trade links with many American companies that were still interested in doing business with them. Further, while IG Farben was Europe's biggest conglomerate, three American corporations – General Motors, US Steel and Standard Oil – were larger.[221] Therefore, the deconcentration programme and the industrialists' trials were still critical enough of capitalism to warrant their being jettisoned. The restitution of property, on the other hand, was less critical of capitalism than the other two responses. Although it concentrated on the economic dimension of the violence and targeted some assets that had been taken by large industries, the restitution of property actually reinforced the respect of private property that is a core principle of capitalism. Given the affinity of the discourse of transitional justice with capitalism, when this discourse emerged, it did not engage with these policies that had blamed aspects of that economic system for World War II, and only partially engaged with the property restitution programme that concentrated on the economic realm rather than on the political sphere.

c Popular Justice

The last aspect of the responses to World War II that transitional justice discourse's accounts have marginalised is the widespread resort to popular justice. As the Allied forces and resistance movements liberated areas occupied by the Nazis, there were thousands of summary executions and other instances of people taking justice in their own hands. What these popular responses had in common was that they departed from transitional justice's legalistic and state-centric characteristics.

In France, at least 8,000 people were executed in the absence of any meaningful legal proceeding.[222] The timing of these summary killings ranged from before the Allied landing in Normandy until well after liberation.[223] The French government estimated that a quarter of the executions were preceded by a tokenistic drumhead trial, whereas the rest dispensed with any formality

220 Traĭnin, *Hitlerite Responsibility under Criminal Law* 85 (n 131).

221 Jeffreys, *Hell's Cartel* 9 (n 148).

222 Henry Rousso, *Vichy: l'Événement, la Mémoire, l'Histoire* (Gallimard 2001) 499. Other estimates set the figure as high as 40,000, Robert Aron, *Histoire de l'Épuration: De l'Indulgence Aux Massacres* (Fayard, 1967) 557.

223 Rousso *Vichy* 499 (n 222).

altogether.[224] The perpetrators of the executions were mostly members of resistance movements, but there were also spontaneous lynchings after liberation.[225] The victims were often people accused of being collaborators or members of Vichy's militias. In the convulsed time of the liberation, resistance movements also executed people for belonging to the aristocratic class, in order to steal their possessions, due to political infighting and to settle personal scores.[226] Gradually, as the new French authorities consolidated their territorial control, this phenomenon died out.[227] Yet the trials carried out by the new French government were a far cry from any legalistic ideal and have been deemed a parody of due process.[228] For instance, famous writer and apologist of the Vichy regime Robert Brasillach was tried in six hours and convicted of the crime of intelligence with the enemy and sentenced to death by a jury of four partisans.[229] Summary executions were by no means an exclusively French phenomenon; in Italy more than 9,000 alleged fascists were killed without trial.[230]

Another form of popular justice after World War II was the widespread phenomenon of 'shorn women' that targeted women accused of 'horizontal collaboration' that is, having a relationship with a German soldier.[231] The women were taken to a public space where they would have their hair shorn. After this humiliating spectacle, the women were paraded through the streets, oftentimes in their underwear or naked, to be jeered at and insulted by the mob. Frequently, they were branded with swastikas or other Nazi insignia and sometimes they were beaten and sexually assaulted.[232] It is estimated that in France alone 20,000 women suffered this scarring punishment between

[224] Cited in Peter Novick, *The Resistance versus Vichy: The Purge of Collaborators in Liberated France* (Constable, 1968) 71.

[225] Henri Amouroux, *Joies et Douleurs du Peuple Libéré: 6 Juin-1er Septembre 1944*, vol 8 (R Laffont, 1988) 539; Novick, *The Resistance versus Vichy* 72 (n 224).

[226] Aron (n 222) 563; Novick, *The Resistance versus Vichy* 72 (n 224); Amouroux, *Joies et Douleurs du Peuple Libéré* 462 (n 225).

[227] Amouroux, *Joies et Douleurs du Peuple Libéré* 541 (n 225).

[228] Ibid 519–27.

[229] For an account of the trial, Alice Yaeger Kaplan, *The Collaborator: The Trial and Execution of Robert Brasillach* (University of Chicago Press, 2000).

[230] Michele Battini, *The Missing Italian Nuremberg: Cultural Amnesia and Postwar Politics* (Stanislao Pugliese ed, Palgrave Macmillan, 2007) 19.

[231] *Femmes tondues* in French. The most comprehensive analysis of this phenomenon is Fabrice Virgili, *Shorn Women: Gender and Punishment in Liberation France* (Berg, 2002).

[232] This was a gendered attack on women's sexuality; no men were punished for having sexual relations with the occupiers, see Rousso, *Vichy* (n 222); Virgili, *Shorn Women* (n 231); Julie Desmarais, *Femmes Tondues: Coupables, Amoureuses, Victimes* (Les Presses de l'Université Laval, 2010).

1943 and 1946.[233] This phenomenon also took place in Belgium, Denmark, Italy and the Netherlands.[234]

Allied troops also engaged in episodes of extrajudicial punishment. When the US army liberated the Dachau concentration camp on 29 April 1945, SS troops who surrendered were immediately executed or turned over to camp inmates who lynched them.[235] Likewise, a former US military intelligence officer has confessed that it was common practice to hand over low-ranking SS personnel who had admitted taking part in atrocities to displaced persons who would lynch them.[236]

The authorities' response to this wave of extralegal and popular justice was mixed. On the one hand, they issued proclamations against this phenomenon, and in some cases punishment was meted out for popular violence. In 1942, the exiled leaders of the occupied countries condemned resorting to 'acts of vengeance on the part of the general public' to punish war criminals.[237] After liberation, the French government passed legislation to stem the wave of popular executions and sought to replace them with state-sponsored legal proceedings.[238] However, the Allies also turned a blind eye to extrajudicial punishment and in some cases even encouraged it. During occupation, radio broadcasts and clandestine publications called on the resistance in France to punish traitors.[239] In 1944, the British Lord Chancellor expressed in a memorandum his hope that the Nazi criminals would be 'disposed of by the people whom they have led to destruction'.[240] Despite the regulations enacted, few people were punished for carrying out extrajudicial punishment. US General Patton refrained from taking any action against the soldiers who executed SS staff when Dachau was liberated, despite receiving a report documenting those killings.[241] The few people that the new French authorities convicted for carrying out executions received lenient sentences,

[233] Virgili, *Shorn Women* 52 (n 231).

[234] Virgili, *Shorn Women* (n 231); Peter Romijn and Erik Schumacher, 'Transitional Justice in the Netherlands after World War II' in Nico Wouters (ed), *Transitional Justice and Memory in Europe (1945–2013)* (Intersentia, 2014).

[235] Bazyler and Tuerkheimer, *Forgotten Trials of the Holocaust* 79 (n 23).

[236] Matthew Brzezinski, 'Giving Hitler Hell' *The Washington Post* (24 July 2005) www.washingtonpost.com/wp-dyn/content/article/2005/07/21/AR2005072101680.html, accessed 30 July 2018.

[237] 'Allied Resolution on German War Crimes' (12 January 1942) II Inter-Allied Review No 1 (1942), 2.

[238] Rousso, *Vichy* (n 222).

[239] Amouroux, *Joies et Douleurs du Peuple Libéré* 470 (n 225).

[240] Simon, 'Major War Criminals Memorandum' 32 (n 89).

[241] Bazyler and Tuerkheimer, *Forgotten Trials of the Holocaust* 79 (n 23).

even for atrocious acts committed for personal motives.[242] This was in contrast with Allied military courts that sentenced German civilians to death for killing downed airmen.[243]

Although these forms of popular justice are problematic, they can be regarded as responses to past widespread or systematic violence. They did not have a legal mandate, they lacked proportionality and they often targeted the guilty and the innocent alike, but they were carried out by the people in reaction to the violence of the war. These instances of popular justice were inspired by the same desire for accountability and abhorrence of impunity that animates many more recognisable forms of transitional justice. Given their popular origin, it can even be argued that they enjoyed a more immediate mandate from the victims than many state-sponsored mechanisms. But in many cases small groups of partisans meted out informal justice without necessarily having genuine popular support. Regardless of their legitimacy and desirability, these practices were instances of transitional justice according to the definition adopted in this book which mirrors most other definitions in being non-normative, as discussed in Chapter 1.

Yet this vast response to wartime violence, popular and unbridled, encouraged or tolerated, justified or illegitimate, has been largely omitted as practices of transitional justice. Most accounts do not even mention popular justice. The few authors that refer to the phenomenon do it as a regrettable event, a spontaneous occurrence that had to be curtailed by the authorities.[244] Hence, negative normative terms are used to denote it. Transitional justice authors call it 'wild justice',[245] 'assassination',[246] or 'private revenge'.[247] However, popular justice is not presented as a mechanism of transitional justice, even

[242] Novick, *The Resistance versus Vichy* 77 (n 224); Amouroux, *Joies et Douleurs du Peuple Libéré* 463 (n 225).

[243] See, eg, *Trial of Erich Heyer et al (The Essen Lynching Case)* (Case No. 8) I *Law Reports of Trials of War Criminals* 1 (22 December 1945) (British Military Court Essen).

[244] Luc Huyse, 'Justice after Transition: On the Choices Successor Elites Make in Dealing with the Past' (1995) 20 *Law & Social Inquiry* 51, 76; Nino (n 3) 12–13; Leebaw, 'The Irreconcilable Goals of Transitional Justice' 14 (n 5); Miriam J Aukerman, 'Extraordinary Evil, Ordinary Crime: A Framework for Understanding Transitional Justice' (2002) 15 *Harvard Human Rights Journal* 39; Elster, *Closing the Books* 56 (n 6); Henry Rousso, 'The Purge in France: An Incomplete Story' in Jon Elster (ed), *Retribution and Reparation in the Transition to Democracy* (Cambridge University Press, 2006); Dahl, 'Dealing with the Past in Scandinavia' (n 27); Romijn and Schumacher, 'Transitional Justice in the Netherlands after World War II' 137 (n 234).

[245] Elster, *Closing the Books* 56 (n 6).

[246] Aukerman, 'Extraordinary Evil, Ordinary Crime' 48 (n 244).

[247] Nino, *Radical Evil on Trial* 11 (n 3).

if negatively assessed.[248] The only exception seems to be Roy Macridis, who in 1982 included the French post-war executions alongside other responses to the past.[249] But this was before the discourse emerged with its characteristics, and since then nobody has engaged with popular justice in this manner. By way of example, Marc Baruch's recent case study of post-war transitional justice in France does not mention popular justice.[250] Even authors that concentrate on recent popular responses to widespread violence do not link them to the wave of popular justice that followed World War II. Mihaela Mihai's analysis of popular responses to impunity in Argentina and Juan Espíndola Mata's discussion of public shaming of Stasi informants in Germany after reunification do not mention the antecedent of the post-war.[251]

Post-war popular justice challenged transitional justice's technical legalism and state-centrism. These social practices did away with any regard for due process and impartiality. They did not follow written legal norms, they were often carried out by openly partisan groups, their conclusions were predetermined and they did not allow the accused to defend themselves. The sentences imposed frequently did not bear any proportion with the alleged fault. Indeed, popular justice represents the antithesis of legalism. Popular justice equally departs from transitional justice's state-centric approach. The instances of popular justice, both summary executions and shorn women, took place beyond state control and authority. People were taking justice in their own hands. The wave of popular justice that followed the end of World War II breached legalism and undermined the centrality of the state.

In sum, the established narrative of the post-war period in transitional justice discourse highlights some aspects and downplays others. As the origin of transitional justice, the legalistic and state-centric traits of the IMT are emphasised while its political valence and legal problems are often glossed

[248] For instance, Jon Elster explicitly excluded cases of private justice from his transitional justice framework, 'Coming to Terms with the Past' 16 (n 32).

[249] Roy C Macridis, 'France: From Vichy to the Fourth Republic' in John H Herz (ed), *From Dictatorship to Democracy: Coping with the Legacies of Authoritarianism and Totalitarianism* (Greenwood, 1982) 171–72.

[250] Marc Olivier Baruch, 'Changing Things so Everything Stays the Same: The Impossible "épuration" of French Society, 1945–2000' in Nico Wouters (ed), *Transitional Justice and Memory in Europe (1945–2013)* (Intersentia, 2014). In contrast, the case study of the Netherlands in the same volume mentions that the Dutch authorities managed to contain most instances of private justice, Romijn and Schumacher, 'Transitional Justice in the Netherlands after World War II' 137 (n 234).

[251] Mihaela Mihai, *Negative Emotions and Transitional Justice* (Columbia University Press, 2016); Juan Espíndola Mata, *Transitional Justice after German Reunification: Exposing Unofficial Collaborators* (Cambridge University Press, 2015).

over. Those attending post-war responses that do not conform to the characteristics of the discourse of transitional justice receive less attention. Hence, the Soviet participation, the economic dimension and instances of popular justice are largely absent from transitional justice discourse.

VI CONCLUSION

For over two decades, the discourse of transitional justice has regarded Nuremberg as its fountainhead. This chapter examined the role that this starting point plays in transitional justice discourse. It demonstrated that the IMT was chosen as the origin because it reflected the characteristics that the discourse inherited from its process of emergence. The retrospective choice of the IMT reinforced these characteristics. Therefore, the resulting established narrative of the post-war period concentrates on those responses that reflect the characteristics. This led to the exclusion of many other instances of transitional justice. Like Gosse's planted fossils, the prehistory of the origin of transitional justice was created to suit the characteristics of the later discourse.

The influence of the characteristics in the writing of the history of transitional justice extends beyond the confines of the post-war experience and into the 40 years that separate the international trial of the Nazi leaders at Nuremberg from the national trial of the military junta in Buenos Aires. This temporal space between the putative origin and the actual emergence of transitional justice constitutes its descent. The dominant narrative dictates that the Cold War stalemate froze any attempts of transitional justice during this period. The following chapter looks into those lost 40 years and shows how the narrative that starts at Nuremberg illuminates some aspects and ignores others, depending on whether they reflect the characteristics of transitional justice discourse.

5

The Cold War Impasse

Descent

I INTRODUCTION

'Will they be drawn into the Communist camp? Or will the great experiments in self-government that are now being made in Asia and Africa ... prove so successful ... that the balance will come down in favour of freedom and order and justice?'[1] This fragment from British Prime Minister Harold MacMillan's 1960 'Wind of Change' speech, famous for heralding the final break-up of the British Empire, encapsulates the two historical processes that overshadowed the four decades that separate the Nuremberg trial from the emergence of the discourse of transitional justice: the Cold War antagonism and decolonisation. The confrontation between capitalism and communism loomed so large in 1960 that the risk of the newly independent colonies becoming socialist was one of the British Prime Minister's primary concerns. The Cold War antagonism and decolonisation, however, have not entered the ken of transitional justice discourse. For the discourse, the period between the International Military Tribunal (IMT) trial and the collapse of the Soviet Bloc was predominantly empty of significant developments.

This chapter examines the treatment of the Cold War period by the discourse of transitional justice. It shows how the narrative of the history of transitional justice illuminates certain aspects and leaves others in the shadows. For the discourse of transitional justice, the period between its mythical origin among the smouldering ruins of Nuremberg and its actual emergence as an autonomous discourse around the jubilant rubble of the Berlin Wall constitute its descent. The discourse traces this pedigree according to its current

[1] Harold Macmillan, 'Address to Members of Both Houses of the Parliament of the Union of South Africa' (Cape Town, 3 February 1960) https://web-archives.univ-pau.fr/english/TD2doc1.pdf, accessed 30 July 2018.

characteristics. It records those ancestors that reflected them; it leaves those that did not unacknowledged.

The first part of the chapter focuses on the discourse's dominant account of transitional justice during the Cold War. It looks critically at the few events and responses of this period that the discourse has addressed. It explores the developments in international law that took place between 1946 and 1989, as well as the three situations that historical accounts of transitional justice mention amidst the general aridness of the Cold War: the transitions in Portugal, Greece and Spain in the mid-1970s.

The second part of the chapter turns to those episodes that have been completely left out of the narrative. Whereas the first section probes the consistency of the existing account, the second exposes its blind spots. In particular, it engages with the wars that the superpowers fought by proxy, the end of empire and decolonisation and the transitions towards non-liberal regimes. These three processes kindled different types of societal responses to past widespread or systematic violence that have not been acknowledged by the discourse of transitional justice. This is explained by the fact that these responses did not reflect the current characteristics of the discourse; indeed, this is another indicator of the purchase of the characteristics in the establishment of the dominant narrative of the history of transitional justice.

II THE LOST FORTY YEARS

For most accounts of transitional justice's history, the period of the Cold War is a barren space. Its defining feature is that the development of transitional justice was arrested by the ideological and political stalemate between the United States and its allies and the countries of the Soviet Bloc. Between 1946 and 1989, trials like those examined in the previous chapter were not possible, and international criminal justice came to a hiatus. The only exceptions were prosecutions in national courts of crimes linked to World War II and the responses following the transitions to democracy of Portugal, Greece and Spain in the mid-1970s.[2] While Paige Arthur has criticised this account for 'collapsing decades of history',[3] no significant attention has been paid to the developments that took place in this historical period. Transitional justice discourse's narrative of the Cold War is, thus, one of paralysis of international

[2] As for the 1985 trial in Argentina, the discourse ranks it as part of the post–Cold War period, Ruti Teitel, 'Transitional Justice Genealogy' 16 *Harvard Human Rights Journal* 69, 75.

[3] Paige Arthur, 'How "Transitions" Reshaped Human Rights: A Conceptual History of Transitional Justice' (2009) 31 *Human Rights Quarterly* 321, 342.

criminal justice and general emptiness, the only exception being the pioneering democratisation in Southern Europe.

The main aspect that the discourse's dominant account emphasises is the paucity of instances of transitional justice during the Cold War. From this perspective, the justice source that sprung in the post-war period was forced underground by the *realpolitik* of the Cold War and resurfaced only at the end of this conflict. According to Ruti Teitel, with 'the Cold War and its balance of power came a related political equilibrium and an impasse for transitional justice'.[4] This view is so influential that it has become the 'traditional historical presentation' of transitional justice.[5] Even those who do not expressly claim that there were no instances of transitional justice during the Cold War nonetheless move seamlessly from Nuremberg to the end of the 1980s and the demise of the Cold War.[6] As a consequence of this prevalent narrative, the period has not been thoroughly examined in transitional justice discourse.

The discourse's barren account of the Cold War primarily rests on the lack of progress in the development of international criminal law and the absence of international tribunals. Commentators contrast this period with the extensive prosecutions that followed the end of World War II and find it wanting. They emphasise, like Martha Minow, 'the enormous gap in time between the Nuremberg trials and any comparable effort to prosecute war crimes in international settings'.[7] The antagonism of the Cold War blocked the possibility of establishing a permanent international criminal court modelled on the IMT. This led to the Nuremberg precedent being dormant for decades.[8] As a consequence of the lack of progress in international criminal justice, the period became of marginal interest for transitional justice scholars.

4 Ruti Teitel, 'The Law and Politics of Contemporary Transitional Justice' (2005) 38 *Cornell International Law Journal* 837, 839.

5 Pádraig McAuliffe, 'From Molehills to Mountains (and Myths?): A Critical History of Transitional Justice Advocacy' (2011) 22 *Finnish Yearbook of International Law* 22. See also Martha Minow, *Between Vengeance and Forgiveness: Facing History after Genocide and Mass Violence* (Beacon Press, 1998); Kora Andrieu, 'Transitional Justice: A New Discipline in Human Rights' (2010) *Online Encyclopedia of Mass Violence* www.sciencespo.fr/mass-violence-war-massacre-resistance/fr/document/transitional-justice-new-discipline-human-rights-0, accessed 30 July 2018; Kamari Maxine Clarke and Mark Goodale, 'Introduction: Understanding the Multiplicity of Justice' in Kamari Maxine Clarke and Mark Goodale (eds), *Mirrors of Justice: Law and Power in the Post-Cold War Era* (Cambridge University Press, 2010); Kathryn Sikkink, *The Justice Cascade: How Human Rights Prosecutions Are Changing World Politics* (WW Norton, 2011).

6 For a more recent example, Laurel Fletcher, 'Editorial Note' (2015) 9 *International Journal of Transitional Justice* 1, 2.

7 Minow, *Between Vengeance and Forgiveness* 27(n 5).

8 Sikkink, *The Justice Cascade* 5 (n 5).

According to this narrative, with the deadlock in the international arena precluding the Nuremberg model, only national responses to past atrocities were possible.[9] National prosecutions for World War II crimes continued throughout the Cold War. These ranged from the trials before the Polish Supreme National Tribunal between 1946 and 1948;[10] the prosecution of the SS official in charge of the final solution, Adolf Eichmann, in Jerusalem in 1961;[11] the Auschwitz trial in Frankfurt in 1963[12] and the trial in France of Klaus Barbie in 1987.[13] However, for transitional justice discourse, these cases are part of the extended post-war period rather than Cold War phenomena.[14] Equally, the discourse considers the 1983 Argentine and other Latin American transitions (Bolivia in 1982, Uruguay and Brazil in 1985) post-Cold War experiences, despite preceding the crumbling of the Soviet Bloc by several years.[15] The only cases taking place during the Cold War that have been addressed by the discourse of transitional justice as such are the transitions in Southern Europe in the mid-1970s.[16]

9 Teitel, 'Transitional Justice Genealogy' 76 (n 2).

10 *Trial of Hauptsturmfürher Amon Leopold Goeth* (Case No. 37) VIII Law Reports of Trials of War Criminals (5 September 1946) (Supreme National Tribunal); *Trial of Oberstumbannfürher Rudolf Franz Ferdinand Hoess* (Case No. 38) VIII Law Reports of Trials of War Criminals (29 March 1947) (Supreme National Tribunal). See also Mark A Drumbl, '"Germans Are the Lords and Poles Are the Servants": The Trial of Arthur Greiser in Poland, 1946', *The Hidden Histories of War Crimes Trials* (Oxford University Press, 2013).

11 *Attorney General* v. *Adolf Eichmann* (Judgment) Criminal Case No. 40/61 (11 December 1961) 36 International Law Reports 5 (District Court of Jerusalem); *Attorney General* v. *Adolf Eichmann* (Judgment) Criminal Appeal No 336/61 (29 May 1962) 36 *International Law Reports* 277 (Supreme Court of Israel). See also Hannah Arendt, *Eichmann in Jerusalem: A Report on the Banality of Evil* (Viking Press, 1964).

12 Rebecca Wittmann, *Beyond Justice the Auschwitz Trial* (Harvard University Press, 2005); Devin O Pendas, *The Frankfurt Auschwitz Trial, 1963–1965: Genocide, History, and the Limits of the Law* (Cambridge University Press, 2006).

13 *Barbie* (Arrêt) N° de pourvoi 87–84240 (3 June 1988) (Cassation Court Criminal Chamber). See also Golsan Richard, 'Crimes-against-Humanity Trials in France and Their Historical and Legal Context: A Retrospective Look' in Patricia Heberer and Jürgen Matthäus (eds), *Atrocities on Trial: Historical Perspectives on the Politics of Prosecuting War Crimes* (University of Nebraska Press, 2008).

14 See, eg, Carlos Nino, *Radical Evil on Trial* (Yale University Press, 1996) 14–16; Alexandra Barahona de Brito, Carmen González Enríquez and Paloma Aguilar Fernández, 'Introduction' in Alexandra Barahona de Brito, Carmen González Enríquez and Paloma Aguilar Fernández (eds), *The Politics of Memory: Transitional Justice in Democratizing Societies* (Oxford University Press, 2001) 3; Sikkink, *The Justice Cascade* 96–98 (n 5).

15 Teitel, 'Transitional Justice Genealogy' 75 (n 2).

16 Carlos Nino mentions the atrocities of the Khmer Rouge in Cambodia, of Idi Amin in Uganda, Ferdinand Marcos in the Philippines, Hissein Habré in Chad and Mariam Mengistu in Ethiopia but very briefly. Moreover, any transitional justice measures taken to address these violations were implemented at least in the mid-1980s. *Radical Evil on Trial* 29–32 (n 14).

The tryptic of transitions in Portugal, Greece and Spain is the centrepiece of transitional justice's narrative during the Cold War. They link the post-war trials with the Latin American transitions of the 1980s. In Portugal, middle-ranking officers dissatisfied with the protracted colonial wars in Africa staged a coup on 25 April 1974 that brought to an end 46 years of dictatorship.[17] In Greece, following the disastrous Cyprus campaign against Turkey, the leaders of the armed forces initiated negotiations in July 1974 to transfer power to civilians after seven years of military rule.[18] In Spain, the death of Francisco Franco, dictator for 36 years, in November 1975 initiated a process of democratisation that ended with the adoption of a democratic Constitution in 1978.[19] According to the transitions paradigm, the third wave of democratisation starts with the break-up of the authoritarian regimes in these Southern European countries.[20] As such, transitional justice discourse has examined the different ways in which they responded to the legacy of previous authoritarian regimes. The widespread trials in Greece, the purges in Portugal and the total amnesty in Spain have featured in the transitional justice literature since the emergence of the discourse.[21] With time, these transitions have become entrenched as part of the historical narrative of transitional justice.[22]

[17] Kenneth Maxwell, 'The Emergence of Portuguese Democracy' in John H Herz (ed), *From Dictatorship to Democracy: Coping with the Legacies of Authoritarianism and Totalitarianism* (Greenwood, 1982) 235.

[18] P Nikoforos Diamandouros, 'Regime Change and the Prospects for Democracy in Greece: 1974–1983' in Guillermo O'Donnell, Philippe C Schmitter and Laurence Whitehead (eds), *Transitions from Authoritarian Rule: Southern Europe* (Johns Hopkins University Press, 1986).

[19] Juan José Linz and Alfred C Stepan, *Problems of Democratic Transition and Consolidation: Southern Europe, South America, and Post-Communist Europe* (1996) 89–90.

[20] Samuel P Huntington, *The Third Wave: Democratization in the Late Twentieth Century* (University of Oklahoma Press, 1991) 3.

[21] See Neil J Kritz, *Transitional Justice: How Emerging Democracies Reckon with Former Regimes* (United States Institute of Peace Press 1995); Nino, *Radical Evil on Trial* (n 14); A McAdams, *Transitional Justice and the Rule of Law in New Democracies* (A James McAdams ed, University of Notre Dame Press, 1997); Alexandra Barahona de Brito, Carmen González Enríquez and Paloma Aguilar Fernández, *The Politics of Memory: Transitional Justice in Democratizing Societies* (Oxford University Press, 2001).

[22] For mentions of the Southern European transitions as part of transitional justice's history, Eric A Posner and Adrian Vermeule, 'Transitional Justice as Ordinary Justice' (2004) 117 *Harvard Law Review* 761; Chandra Lekha Sriram, 'Transitional Justice Comes of Age: Enduring Lessons and Challenges' (2005) 23 *Berkeley Journal of International Law* 506, 506; Naomi Roht-Arriaza, 'The New Landscape of Transitional Justice' in Naomi Roht-Arriaza and Javier Mariezcurrena (eds), *Transitional Justice in the Twenty-First Century: Beyond Truth versus Justice* (Cambridge University Press, 2006) 2; Brian Grodsky, 'Re-Ordering Justice: Towards a New Methodological Approach to Studying Transitional Justice' (2009) 46 *Journal of Peace Research* 819, 821; Thomas O Hansen, 'Transitional Justice: Toward a Differentiated Theory' (2011) 13 *Oregon Review of International Law* 1, 4; McAuliffe, 'From Molehills to Mountains (and Myths?)' 19–21

In this manner, for transitional justice discourse, the Cold War is a period of emptiness, dominated by the lack of development of international criminal law, with the exception of the Southern European transitions. The rest of this section examines critically this account of transitional justice in the Cold War.

1 *International Criminal Law Arrested, International Human Rights Law Freed*

The discourse's established account of transitional justice during the Cold War pivots around the absence of progress in international criminal justice. In effect, the onset of the Cold War quickly blocked initiatives to establish a permanent international criminal court. Although in 1948 the United Nations (UN) General Assembly tasked the International Law Commission (ILC) to study the desirability and possibility of establishing a court to try crimes under international law, this proposal came to nought.[23] In 1950, the ILC produced a report in which both Special Rapporteurs expressed the desirability of an international criminal court, but one concluded that the international community was not yet ripe for such an institution.[24] The report was shelved, and there was no further significant progress in the matter.[25] The issue of international criminal justice would not re-emerge in earnest until after the end of the Cold War, prompted by the conflict in the former Yugoslavia.[26] Therefore, it is true that the Cold War was an inauspicious period for international criminal justice in that there were no significant international legal developments or any international prosecutions.

Nevertheless, the Cold War period was fundamental for the development of another area of international law. During these 40 years, international human

(n 5); Elena Andreevska, 'Transitional Justice and Democratic Change: Key Concepts' (2013) 20 *Lex et Scientia* 54, 56; Judith Renner, 'The Local Roots of the Global Politics of Reconciliation: The Articulation of "Reconciliation" as an Empty Universal in the South African Transition to Democracy' (2014) 42 *Millennium – Journal of International Studies* 263, 283.

[23] UNGA Resolution 260 B (III) (9 December 1948) UN Doc A/RES/3/260. See also UNGA Resolution 95(1) 'Affirmation of the Principles of International Law Recognized by the Charter of the Nurnberg Tribunal' (11 December 1946) UN Doc A/RES/1/95.

[24] ILC 'Report of the International Law Commission on the Question of International Criminal Jurisdiction' (1950), UN Doc A/CN.4/20 (1950), reprinted in *Yearbook of the International Law Commission* 1950, vol II, 8.

[25] James Crawford, 'The Drafting of the Rome Statute' in Philippe Sands (ed), *From Nuremberg to The Hague: The Future of International Criminal Justice* (Cambridge University Press, 2003) 119.

[26] See Chapter 3, 97–101.

rights law grew from a somewhat vague concept to a global regime buttressed by international conventions, international institutions and a vigorous advocacy movement.[27] This phenomenon had an impact on countries' attempts to come to terms with the past and paved the way for the emergence of transitional justice at the end of the Cold War.

The main instruments codifying international human rights law were negotiated and adopted in the decades that followed the end of World War II. From the 1948 Universal Declaration of Human Rights (UDHR) to the Convention on the Rights of the Child, adopted in 1989, the Cold War period witnessed the development of the bulk of the international human rights legal regime.[28] Regional human rights arrangements developed in parallel during this period.[29] This progressive process of codification took place entirely against the backdrop of the Cold War.

In addition to these legal developments, the global human rights advocacy movement was born during the Cold War period. In 1953 there were 33 international human rights organisations; by 1993 their number had grown to 190.[30] Most notable among them, Amnesty International was founded in

[27] Diane F Orentlicher, 'Settling Accounts: The Duty to Prosecute Human Rights Violations of a Prior Regime' (1991) 100 *The Yale Law Journal* 2537, 2560.

[28] Universal Declaration of Human Rights (adopted 10 December 1948 UNGA Resolution 217 A(III) (UDHR); Convention on the Prevention and Punishment of the Crime of Genocide (adopted 9 December 1948 UNGA Resolution 260 (III) A, entered into force 12 January 1951) 78 UNTS 277 (Genocide Convention); International Convention on the Elimination of All Forms of Racial Discrimination (adopted 21 December 1965 UNGA Resolution 2106 (XX), entered into force 4 January 1969) 660 UNTS 195; International Covenant on Civil and Political Rights (adopted 16 December 1966 UNGA Resolution 2200A (XXI), entered into force 23 March 1976) 999 UNTS 171 (ICCPR); International Covenant on Economic, Social and Cultural Rights (adopted 16 December 1966 UNGA Resolution 2200A (XXI), entered into force 3 January 1976) 993 UNTS 3 (ICESCR); Convention on the Elimination of All Forms of Discrimination against Women (adopted 18 December 1979 UNGA Resolution 34/180, entered into force 3 September 1981) 1249 UNTS 13; Convention against Torture and Other Cruel, Inhuman or Degrading Treatment or Punishment (adopted 10 December 1984 UNGA Resolution 39/46, entered into force 26 June 1987) 1465 UNTS 85; Convention on the Rights of the Child (adopted 20 November 1989 UNGA Resolution 44/25, entered into force 2 September 1990) 1577 UNTS 3.

[29] European Convention for the Protection of Human Rights and Fundamental Freedoms (adopted 4 November 1950, entered into force 3 September 1953) 213 UNTS 221; American Convention on Human Rights (adopted 21 November 1969, entered into force 18 July 1978) 1144 UNTS 123; African Charter on Human and Peoples' Rights (adopted 27 June 1981, entered into force 21 October 1986) 1520 UNTS 217.

[30] Kathryn Sikkink and Jackie Smith, 'Infrastructures for Change: Transnational Organizations, 1953–93' in Sanjeev Khagram, James V Riker and Kathryn Sikkink (eds), *Restructuring World Politics: Transnational Social Movements, Networks, and Norms* (University of Minnesota Press, 2002) 30.

1961 and Human Rights Watch in 1979.[31] While the legal regime of international human rights grew steadily throughout the Cold War period, the global advocacy movement gained particular momentum during the 1970s.[32]

Two processes that took place during this decade were particularly influential in the development of the human rights movement: the Helsinki Final Act and the wave of repression in Latin America. The Conference on the Security and Co-operation in Europe (CSCE) involved negotiations between 33 European states from both sides of the Iron Wall, as well as Canada and the United States.[33] After two and a half years, the Helsinki Final Act was agreed in 1975.[34] One of its principles was 'respect for human rights and fundamental freedoms, including the freedom of thought, conscience, religion or belief'.[35] Although the document was not legally binding, it ignited monitoring organisations in the West and added human rights language to political claims in the Soviet Bloc. As Václav Havel explained in 1977, in 'the "dissident movements" of the Soviet Bloc, the defence of human beings usually takes the form of a defence of human and civil rights as they are entrenched in various official documents'.[36] The organisations founded to monitor compliance with the Helsinki Final Act established transnational contacts and formed a global network that collected information, recorded abuses and lobbied the socialist countries until the end of the Cold War.[37] At the same time, the repression carried out by right-wing regimes in Latin America during the 1970s pushed many activists to exile. These Chilean, Argentine and Uruguayan political exiles became involved in the work of international human rights organisations abroad and drew attention to the situation in their countries.[38] Exiles and

[31] Stephen Hopgood, *Keepers of the Flame: Understanding Amnesty International* (Cornell University Press, 2006) 1, 140.

[32] For the development of human rights in the 1970s, Samuel Moyn, *The Last Utopia: Human Rights in History* (Belknap, 2010).

[33] William Korey, *The Promises We Keep: Human Rights, the Helsinki Process, and American Foreign Policy* (St Martin's Press, 1993) 1.

[34] See Daniel Charles Thomas, *The Helsinki Effect: International Norms, Human Rights, and the Demise of Communism* (Princeton University Press, 2001) 66–87.

[35] 'Conference on Security and Co-operation in Europe Final Act, Helsinki' (1 August 1975), principle VII.

[36] Václav Havel, 'The Power of the Powerless' in John Keane (ed), *The Power of the Powerless: Citizens against the State in Central-Eastern Europe* (Hutchinson, 1985) 69.

[37] Sarah B Snyder, *Human Rights Activism and the End of the Cold War: A Transnational History of the Helsinki Network* (Cambridge University Press, 2011) x.

[38] For Argentina, Margaret E Keck and Kathryn Sikkink, *Activists beyond Borders: Advocacy Networks in International Politics* (Cornell University Press, 1998). For Chile, Darren Hawkins, 'Human Rights Norms and Networks in Authoritarian Chile' in Sanjeev Khagram, James V Riker and Kathryn Sikkink (eds), *Restructuring World Politics: Transnational Social Movements, Networks, and Norms* (University of Minnesota Press, 2002). For Uruguay, Vania

domestic activists found that human rights offered a useful language to get international support.[39]

Lastly, during the Cold War period, and in particular from the late 1970s, human rights became an important part of foreign policy. In the first place, the legally binding International Covenant on Civil and Political Rights (ICCPR) and International Covenant on Economic, Social and Cultural Rights (ICESCR) came into force in 1976.[40] Moreover, the adoption of the 1975 Helsinki Final Act raised the profile of human rights in East and West relations.[41] Crucially, President Carter made human rights an integral part of US foreign policy. Presidential Directive NSC-30 of 1978 stated that promoting the observance of human rights should 'be a major objective of U.S. foreign policy'.[42] To that end, it instructed officials to resort to all diplomatic tools and to use international aid as a means to reward or punish foreign countries depending on their human rights record.[43] The combinations of these three factors – the development of international human rights law, the growth of a global advocacy movement and the adoption of human rights as a foreign policy concern – contributed to establishing human rights as a universal language that states are required to speak to have credibility.[44] As Michael Ignatieff notes, even 'oppressive states feel obliged to engage in rhetorical deference toward human rights instruments'.[45]

The development of international human rights that took place during the Cold War paved the way for transitional justice discourse. The international human rights legal architecture that grew in this period was an instrumental part of early debates on transitional justice. During the 1988 Aspen Institute conference, the participants discussed the ICCPR, the Genocide Convention and the Convention against Torture.[46] In an influential 1991 article, Diane Orentlicher argued for a duty to prosecute human rights violations based on international human rights treaties, including the Genocide Convention, the

Markarian, *Left in Transformation: Uruguayan Exiles and the Latin American Human Rights Networks, 1967–1984* (Routledge, 2005).

39 Luis Roniger and Mario Sznajder, *The Legacy of Human-Rights Violations in the Southern Cone: Argentina, Chile, and Uruguay* (Oxford University Press, 1999) 38–51.

40 ICCPR on 23 March and ICESCR on 3 January (see note 28).

41 Thomas, *The Helsinki Effect* 87 (n 34). See also Korey, *The Promises We Keep* (n 33).

42 Presidential Directive/NSC-30 (17 February 1978) (US) 1.

43 Ibid 2.

44 de Brito, González Enríquez and Aguilar Fernández, 'Introduction' 22 (n 14).

45 Michael Ignatieff, 'Human Rights as Polictics and Idolatry' in Amy Gutmann (ed), *Human Rights as Politics and Idolatry* (Princeton University Press, 2001) 7.

46 Alice H Henkin, 'Conference Report', *State Crimes: Punishment or Pardon* (The Aspen Institute, 1989) 4.

Convention against Torture, the ICCPR and the American and European regional conventions on human rights.[47] Judicial bodies based on international human rights treaties have also influenced transitional justice discourse. For example, the Inter-American Court of Human Rights' decisions in the Velásquez Rodríguez case, which determined the existence of a duty to investigate violations of rights protected by the American convention, and the Barrios Altos case, which found that amnesty provisions were incompatible with the convention, are landmark decisions for the development of international standards of transitional justice practice.[48] Transitional justice discourse has relied heavily on the international human rights regime developed between 1948 and 1989.

Even more importantly, transitional justice discourse appeared as an outcrop of the wider human rights movement that gained prominence in the 1970s. The human rights organisations that during the Latin American dictatorships monitored violations and lobbied for political change turned their attention towards accountability and punishment once democracy was restored. In Argentina, human rights organisations founded by the relatives of the disappeared such as *Centro de Estudios Legales y Sociales* (Centre of Legal and Social Studies; CELS) and *Madres de Plaza de Mayo* (Mothers of Plaza de Mayo) began advocating against amnesty and for prosecutions as soon as the dictatorship relaxed its grip.[49] Human rights activists and scholars participated in the debates that helped shape the discourse of transitional justice. People like Aryeh Neier of Human Rights Watch, Juan Méndez of America's Watch, Diane Orentlicher and José Zalaquett were present at the

47 Orentlicher, 'Settling Accounts' (n 27).

48 *Velásquez Rodríguez* v. *Honduras* (Judgment) IACtHR Series C No 4 (29 July 1988), paras 174–76; *Aguirre* v. *Peru (Barrios Altos Case)* (Judgment) IACtHR Series C No 83 (3 September 2001), para 43. For discussions within the discourse of transitional justice, Naomi Roht-Arriaza, 'State Responsibility to Investigate and Prosecute Grave Human Rights Violations in International Law' (1990) 78 *California Law Review* 451; Orentlicher, 'Settling Accounts' (n 27); Louise Mallinder, *Amnesty, Human Rights and Political Transitions: Bridging the Peace and Justice Divide* (Hart, 2008); Jo-Marie Burt, 'Guilty as Charged: The Trial of Former Peruvian President Alberto Fujimori for Human Rights Violations' (2009) 3 *International Journal of Transitional Justice* 384; David P Forsythe, 'Forum: Transitional Justice: The Quest for Theory to Inform Policy' (2011) 13 *International Studies Review* 554; Pádraig McAuliffe, 'The Roots of Transitional Accountability: Interrogating the "Justice Cascade"' (2013) 9 *International Journal of Law in Context* 106.

49 CELS, *Autoamnistia: Legalizar la Impunidad* (1982) www.cels.org.ar/common/documentos/autoamnistia.pdf, accessed 30 July 2018; Inés Vázquez, *Historia de las Madres de Plaza de Mayo: Luchar Siempre, las Marchas de la Resistencia, 1981–2006* (Ediciones Madres de Plaza de Mayo, 2007).

Aspen Institute conference.[50] During the conference, Zalaquett noted that 'dealing with transitional political situations is a new area of human rights practice'.[51] The 1992 'Justice in Times of Transition' conference in Salzburg included Latin American and Eastern European human rights experts and activists.[52] A similar constituency was very active during the South African transition, attending the Cape Town conferences in 1994 and being involved in the Truth and Reconciliation Commission (SATRC).[53]

International human rights organisations also became involved in the emerging transitional justice discourse. While Amnesty International was founded to lobby for the release of prisoners of conscience, by the 1990s it was, ironically enough, advocating against amnesty laws and in favour of prosecutions for human rights violations.[54] Human Rights Watch had a similar stance.[55] Significantly, Neil Kritz's seminal book *Transitional Justice: How Emerging Democracies Reckon with Former Regimes* included policy statements of these two human rights organisations.[56] The human rights movement that developed during the Cold War period was thus fundamental for transitional justice discourse.[57]

Furthermore, the vast scope of the language of human rights provided transitional justice discourse with the common denominator that allowed it to encompass a broad spectrum of widely different situations. With the

[50] The Aspen Institute, *State Crimes: Punishment or Pardon: Papers and Report of the Conference, November 4–6, 1988, Wye Center, Maryland* (The Aspen Institute 1989) 95–96. Juan Méndez would replace Alex Boraine as the president of the ICTJ, ICTJ, 'Juan E. Méndez' (2018) www.ictj.org/about/juan-e-méndez, accessed 30 July 2018.

[51] Jose Zalaquett, 'Confronting Human Rights Violations Committed by Former Governments: Principles Applicable and Political Constraints', *State Crimes: Punishment or Pardon: Papers and Report of the Conference, November 4–6, 1988, Wye Center, Maryland* (The Aspen Institute, 1989) 26.

[52] Arthur, 'How "Transitions" Reshaped Human Rights' 364–67 (n 3).

[53] Alex Boraine, *A Country Unmasked: South Africa's Truth and Reconciliation Commission* (Oxford University Press, 2000) 16–18, 25–29, 77–81. See also Alex Boraine, Janet Levy and Ronel Scheffer, *Dealing with the Past: Truth and Reconciliation in South Africa* (IDASA, 1994); Alex Boraine and Janet Levy, *The Healing of a Nation?* (Justice in Transition, 1995).

[54] Amnesty International, 'Policy Statement on Impunity' in Neil J Kritz (ed), *Transitional Justice: How Emerging Democracies Reckon with Former Regimes* (United States Institute of Peace Press, 1995).

[55] Human Rights Watch, 'Policy Statement on Accountability for Past Abuses' in Neil J Kritz (ed), *Transitional Justice: How Emerging Democracies Reckon with Former Regimes* (United States Institute of Peace Press, 1995).

[56] Amnesty International, 'Policy Statement on Impunity' (n 54); Human Rights Watch, 'Policy Statement on Accountability for Past Abuses' (n 55).

[57] See Bronwyn Leebaw, 'The Politics of Impartial Activism: Humanitarianism and Human Rights' (2007) 5 *Perspectives on Politics* 223.

development of human rights as an advocacy movement and foreign policy concern, human rights acquired a meaning that went beyond legal strictures. In this broader sense, human rights denote a general concern 'for the humane treatment of individuals and certain groups'.[58] This label includes international human rights law strictly defined, as well as international humanitarian law, aspects of international criminal law and broader ethical and policy considerations related to the humane treatment of individuals and groups. International human rights law in the narrow sense is already quite ample due to its universality and equal applicability in peacetime and during armed conflict.[59] In its broader extralegal sense, human rights cover almost all aspects of social life from expression, justice, policing, education, politics and health. As such, human rights are used as a language to express all sorts of political and ethical claims. This broadness of human rights as a language makes it possible to characterise different situations taking place in a diversity of contexts as a violation of these rights. Transitional justice discourse has taken advantage of the amplitude of human rights in this broader sense to smooth over the differences separating the situations and mechanisms it examines. Hence, the international prosecution before the IMT of crimes committed mostly during wartime has been retrospectively labelled as a human rights trial.[60] The same label was attached to the trials by national courts in Greece in 1974 and in Argentina in 1985, as well as to the trials before the International Criminal Tribunal for the former Yugoslavia (ICTY).[61] These instances relied on different types of law, domestic and international. Whereas the IMT and the ICTY mostly adjudicated on questions of international criminal law and humanitarian law, the Greek and Argentine courts relied solely on domestic criminal law. International human rights law was not the primary source of law of any of these trials. Nonetheless, they are considered human rights trials using the broader sense that exceeds international human rights law. In this manner, the broad language of human rights provides the gel that brings these

[58] Roger O'Keefe, 'State Immunity and Human Rights: Heads and Walls, Hearts and Minds' (2011) 44 *Vanderbilt Journal of Transnational Law* 999, 1003.

[59] See UDHR (n 28); UN Human Rights Committee, 'General Comment No 31 on (Art. 2) The Nature of the General Legal Obligation Imposed on States Parties to the Covenant' (29 March 2004) UN Doc CCPR/C/21/Rev.1.Add 13. For the applicability of human rights law in armed conflict, *Legality of the Threat or Use of Nuclear Weapons* (Advisory Opinion) 8 July 1996 International Court of Justice (ICJ), para 25; *Legal Consequences of the Construction of a Wall in the Occupied Palestinian Territory* (Advisory Opinion) 4 July 2004 ICJ, para 106; *Case Concerning Armed Activities on the Territory of the Congo (DRC* v. *Uganda)* (Judgment) 19 December 2005 ICJ, para 216.

[60] Nino, *Radical Evil on Trial* 187 (n 14).

[61] Ibid 20, 26, 187.

situations together. The appearance of a language of human rights with such universality and scope allowed these responses to be joined together.

Without the development of human rights as a legal regime, advocacy movement, foreign policy interest and global language, the discourse of transitional justice would probably not have emerged in its current form.[62] The discourse relies heavily on these manifestations of human rights. Without international human rights law, transitional justice discourse would have lacked part of its legal armature; without the human rights movement, the activists behind its emergence would have been missing; without a global language, the unifying force covering national and international law would have been lost. Therefore, although during the Cold War the progress of international criminal justice was arrested, the progress made in human rights in this period enabled the appearance of the discourse of transitional justice.

2 *National Trials in Southern Europe*

The democratic transitions that took place in Portugal, Greece and Spain in the 1970s are the other landmark in the otherwise desolate historical account of transitional justice during the Cold War. While they currently do not elicit much examination in transitional justice discourse and are mostly a historical anecdote,[63] a closer look at them yields several insights about the dominant narrative and how it privileges those episodes that reflect the characteristics of the discourse.

On 25 April 1974, a small group of Portuguese middle-ranking officers, the Armed Forces Movement (MFA), staged a coup against the government of Marcello Caetano. Economic recession and the protracted colonial wars that Portugal was relentlessly waging in Angola, Mozambique and Guinea-Bissau prompted the rebellion.[64] The coup brought to an end the dictatorial New State regime which had been in power since 1926. The National Salvation Junta – composed of the radical MFA and more moderate forces within the military – assumed power. They immediately removed the president, cabinet

[62] See Sikkink, *The Justice Cascade* 96–125 (n 5).

[63] Sikkink, *The Justice Cascade* (n 5). The only exception would be Spain, where renewed efforts to revert the amnesty policy have attracted some attention. See Paloma Aguilar, 'Judiciary Involvement in Authoritarian Repression and Transitional Justice: The Spanish Case in Comparative Perspective' (2013) 7 *International Journal of Transitional Justice* 245; Jonah Rubin, 'Transitional Justice against the State: Lessons from Spanish Civil Society-Led Forensic Exhumations' (2014) 8 *International Journal of Transitional Justice* 99.

[64] Maxwell, 'The Emergence of Portuguese Democracy' 235 (n 17).

ministers, leaders of the single party, and high-ranking generals. The deposed officials were allowed to go into exile despite popular pressure to put them to trial.[65] The Portuguese people also carried out spontaneous purges: workers removed industrialists, and students expelled academics associated with the previous regime. This popular reaction prompted the junta to pass regulations to purge the public administration.[66]

Measures implemented to respond to the previous regime became more drastic after the most radical elements of MFA seized control in March 1975. They ended the wars in Africa and adopted a revolutionary programme. They nationalised large industry, the banking and insurance sectors, and promised to expropriate great landed estates.[67] In this effervescent context, the purges in the armed forces, public servants, and universities were deepened.[68] Following popular pressure to try the members of the Political Police (PIDE), a law was passed retroactively criminalising membership of that organisation.[69] The penalties ranged from 2 to 12 years of imprisonment depending on the rank, participation in the repression and individual responsibility.[70] Many officers went into exile and were tried in absentia. Although PIDE had held 12,000 people in prison between 1945 and 1973 and had resorted to torture, its death toll was relatively low, with 11 deaths in custody in Portugal over that period.[71] In fact, by far the worst abuses of PIDE forces took place in the colonies, but these were not taken into account when assessing the degree of responsibility of each officer.[72]

The revolutionary measures were rolled back after moderate elements within the armed forces staged a countercoup against the radicals on 25 November 1975. Many of those purged were reinstated in their positions,

[65] António Costa Pinto, 'Settling Accounts with the Past in a Troubled Transition to Democracy: The Portuguese Case' in Alexandra Barahona de Brito, Carmen González Enríquez and Paloma Aguilar (eds), *The Politics of Memory: Transitional Justice in Democratizing Societies* (Oxford University Press, 2001) 71–72.

[66] Decreto-lei 277/74 (25 June 1974). See also Filipa Raimundo and António Costa Pinto, 'From Ruptured Transition to Politics of Silence: The Case of Portugal' in Nico Wouters (ed), *Transitional Justice and Memory in Europe (1945–2013)* (Intersentia, 2014).

[67] Maxwell, 'The Emergence of Portuguese Democracy' 237 (n 17).

[68] Decreto-lei 123/75 (11 March 1975). See also Costa Pinto, 'Settling Accounts with the Past in a Troubled Transition to Democracy' 72–74 (n 65).

[69] Lei 8/75 (25 July 1975).

[70] Ibid, art 6.

[71] Sikkink, *The Justice Cascade* 52 (n 5).

[72] Filipa Alves Raimundo, 'The Double Face of Heroes: Transitional Justice towards the Political Police (PIDE/DGS) in Portugal's Democratization, 1974–1976' (MA thesis, University of Lisbon, 2007) 67.

and the radical elements were themselves removed.[73] The nationalisation process was reverted and expropriated land returned to the owners.[74] The prosecution of PIDE officers was also stemmed with legislation ordering the release of some in pretrial detention and incorporating extenuating circumstances. Most convictions were of low-ranking officers who received sentences of less than six months.[75] The election of a moderate socialist government on 15 July 1976 consolidated Portugal's path towards liberal democracy and dissipated the imminent threat of communism.[76]

The Greek transition was, in most respects, different. Rather than the passage from an authoritarian regime, through a revolutionary period, to a social-democracy, in Greece a military dictatorship was replaced by a conservative democratic government. The disastrous invasion of Cyprus and the ensuing military defeat against Turkey prompted the collapse of the colonels' regime, which had been in power since 1967. The same military leaders who had accepted the colonels' junta removed them and gave power back to civilians in July 1975. Former conservative premier Constantine Karamanlis returned from exile and became the president. Karamanlis retired senior military officers and purged the ministries. Those who had lost their positions because of their opposition to the junta were reinstated.[77]

On the heels of assuming power, the Karamanlis government put to trial those responsible for the abuses of the previous regime. There were three types of trials. First, the 5 ringleaders of the 1967 coup together with 44 other officers were tried for treason and insurrection in July–August 1975. Eighteen were convicted. Three received death sentences, which Karamanlis commuted to life imprisonment.[78] Second, between August and September 1975, eighteen military police officers were tried for torture in proceedings that exposed the systematic use of torture by the junta. According to an Amnesty International report, another 100 to 400 torture trials took place at the time.[79] The last type of trial targeted those responsible for the crackdown of a protest at Athens

73 Raimundo and Costa Pinto, 'From Ruptured Transition to Politics of Silence' (n 66).

74 Maxwell, 'The Emergence of Portuguese Democracy' 239–40 (n 17).

75 Alves Raimundo, 'The Double Face of Heroes' 86 (n 72).

76 Maxwell, 'The Emergence of Portuguese Democracy' 241 (n 17). For transitional justice in Portugal after the consolidation of democracy, see Raimundo and Costa Pinto, 'From Ruptured Transition to Politics of Silence' (n 66).

77 Harry J Psomiades, 'Greece: From the Colonels' Rule to Democracy' in John H Herz (ed), *From Dictatorship to Democracy: Coping with the Legacy of Authoritarianism and Totalitarianism* (Greenwood, 1982) 263.

78 Ibid 264.

79 Amnesty International, *Torture in Greece: The First Torturers' Trial 1975* (Amnesty International Publications, 1977) 75–78.

Polytechnic University in November 1973.[80] The defendants included junta leaders as well as army and police officers.[81] Twenty individuals were found guilty, and 12 were acquitted.[82] This programme of extensive prosecutions was remarkably quick. The whole criminal accountability process took less than 18 months.[83]

The last Southern European transition took place in Spain. The death of dictator Francisco Franco in 1975, spurred a process of gradual democratisation. Franco had been in power since 1939, when he overthrew the Republican government after three years of civil war. In July 1976, King Juan Carlos appointed conservative politician Adolfo Suárez as prime minister.[84] Suárez legalised the communist party and allowed it to compete in Spain's June 1977 legislative elections, which were the first since 1936.[85] The following year a democratic constitution was drafted and was overwhelmingly accepted by the public in a referendum.

During the transition, there was a tacit agreement among political parties to avoid any calls for justice for the crimes of the dictatorship.[86] Thus the issue was not discussed during the 1977 elections.[87] In October 1977, the Suárez government passed an amnesty law.[88] The law released political prisoners and precluded trials. It also rehabilitated some civil servants who had lost their jobs.[89] The public almost unanimously supported the amnesty.[90] The memory of the civil war has been credited with prompting the public to eschew trials. They wanted to avoid polarisation and were suspicious of

80 Sikkink, *The Justice Cascade* 48–49 (n 5).

81 Psomiades, 'Greece: From the Colonels' Rule to Democracy' 265 (n 77).

82 Nicos C Alivizatos and P Nikiforos Diamandouros, 'Politics and the Judiciary in the Greek Transition to Democracy' in A James McAdams (ed), *Transitional Justice and the Rule of Law in New Democracies* (University of Notre Dame Press, 1997) 46.

83 Diamandouros, 'Regime Change and the Prospects for Democracy in Greece: 1974–1983' (n 18).

84 Edward Malefakis, 'Spain and Its Francoist Heritage' in John Herz (ed), *From Dictatorship to Democracy: Coping with the Legacy of Authoritarianism and Totalitarianism* (Greenwood, 1982) 226.

85 Linz and Stepan, *Problems of Democratic Transition and Consolidation* 96–98 (n 19).

86 Omar G Encarnación, *Democracy without Justice in Spain: The Politics of Forgetting* (University of Pennsylvania Press, 2014) 27.

87 Ibid 55.

88 Ley 46/1977 de Amnistía (Amnesty) (15 October 1977). See also Malefakis, 'Spain and Its Francoist Heritage' 226–27 (n 84).

89 Paloma Aguilar, 'Justice, Politics and Memory in the Spanish Transition' in Alexandra Barahona de Brito, Carmen González Enríquez and Paloma Aguilar (eds), *The Politics of Memory: Transitional Justice in Democratizing Societies* (Oxford University Press, 2001) 102.

90 Sikkink, *The Justice Cascade* 57 (n 5).

political trials, which were common during the civil war.[91] In addition to the amnesty, the government implemented moderate measures to reform the armed forces, and reparations were provided in the form of pensions for the relatives of those fallen in the civil war.[92]

The political contexts, the preceding violence and the mechanisms implemented in these three cases were different. In Portugal, in the wake of long-term repression, revolutionary officers carried out extensive purges, economic reform and trials applying criminal law retroactively. In Greece, following a shorter but more intense period of state-sponsored violence, those responsible were tried in regular criminal proceedings. In Spain, at the end of a long dictatorship whose worst abuses had taken place in the distant past, amnesties and political reform prevailed. The only element that these cases had in common was that they were in the same region and saw the eventual replacement of dictatorial regimes by liberal democracies.

The Southern European transitions became instances of transitional justice only retroactively, once the discourse emerged. At the time, commentators saw them as different countries going through different political processes, influenced by different domestic and international circumstances. Several authors have emphasised the contingent factors influencing the occurrence and outcome of the transitions.[93] Moreover, the transitional justice policies adopted – trials, purges and amnesties – were not regarded, in these countries or abroad, as foundational moments for the new regimes, such as was the case in Argentina or South Africa later on. The trials that took place in Portugal and Greece are not well known in these countries today. In Greece, these trials were inscribed in a lengthy tradition of political trials rather than as transitional human rights focused measures.[94] In Portugal, the purges and trials carried out during the revolutionary period were later reversed and forgotten.[95] Neither did these processes, apart from the Greek trials which are discussed later, inspire much international debate at the time. These

[91] Aguilar, 'Justice, Politics and Memory in the Spanish Transition' 103 (n 89). See also Sikkink, *The Justice Cascade* 57–58 (n 5).

[92] Aguilar, 'Justice, Politics and Memory in the Spanish Transition' (n 89). For transitional justice measures in later years, see Paloma Aguilar and Clara Ramírez-Barat, 'Amnesty and Reparations without Truth or Justice in Spain' in Nico Wouters (ed), *Transitional Justice and Memory in Europe (1945–2013)* (Intersentia, 2014).

[93] Linz and Stepan, *Problems of Democratic Transition and Consolidation* 89–90 (n 19); António Costa Pinto, 'Authoritarian Legacies, Transitional Justice and State Crisis in Portugal's Democratization' (2006) 13 Democratization 173, 174–75; Maxwell, 'The Emergence of Portuguese Democracy' 231–32 (n 17).

[94] Sikkink, *The Justice Cascade* 46 (n 5).

[95] Raimundo and Costa Pinto, 'From Ruptured Transition to Politics of Silence' (n 66).

practices did not influence later transitions until they were rescued from their relative obscurity by the autonomous discourse of transitional justice once it emerged.[96] For instance, in 1983, Argentine President Alfonsín did not know about the Greek trials of the military junta.[97]

It was through the transitions to the democracy paradigm that the Southern European experiences were retrospectively incorporated into transitional justice discourse. The comparative approach of scholars focusing on political transitions inspired them to link the events that had taken place in Portugal, Greece and Spain in the previous decade with later democratisation processes in Latin America and elsewhere. From this perspective, this trio of transitions was the beginning of the third wave of democratisation that reached the end of the Cold War.[98] Since the transitions paradigm was influential in the formative debates of transitional justice discourse,[99] the Southern European cases were incorporated into the latter's inventory of relevant case studies. For example, comparative political scientist John Herz included the Southern European cases in his 1982 book and later participated in the 1988 Aspen Institute conference. As is examined further later, other Cold War cases of transitional justice that did not reflect the characteristics of the discourse were not included.

The Southern European transitions illustrate how the development of human rights during the Cold War period transformed how the widespread or systematic violence of the previous regime was characterised. These transitions took place in the mid-1970s at the time when human rights were gaining traction through the legal, social and political developments described in the previous section. However, human rights were yet to achieve the prominence they would have later on. Accordingly, human rights featured intermittently in the Southern European transitions. In Portugal, human rights language was absent from both the revolutionary period and the following moderate

96 See de Brito, González Enríquez and Aguilar Fernández, 'Introduction' (n 14).

97 See Chapter 3, 67–68.

98 Guillermo O'Donnell, Philippe C Schmitter and Laurence Whitehead, *Transition from Authoritarian Rule: Southern Europe* (Johns Hopkins University Press, 1986); Diane Ethier, *Democratic Transition and Consolidation in Southern Europe, Latin America and Southeast Asia* (Macmillan, 1990); Juan J Linz, 'Transitions to Democracy' (1990) 13 *The Washington Quarterly* 143; Huntington, *The Third Wave* (n 20); Yossi Shain, Juan José Linz and Lynn Berat, *Between States: Interim Governments and Democratic Transitions* (Cambridge University Press, 1995); Linz and Stepan, *Problems of Democratic Transition and Consolidation* (n 19).

99 Arthur, 'How "Transitions" Reshaped Human Rights' 343–48 (n 3). See also Juan E Méndez, 'In Defense of Transitional Justice' in A James McAdams (ed), *Transitional Justice and the Rule of Law in New Democracies* (University of Notre Dame Press, 1997).

government.[100] As Kathryn Sikkink notes, 'human rights was not part of the common discourse at that time. The debate was not about human rights but about revolution and counter-revolution.'[101] In Spain, it was constitution making rather than human rights that was prominent.[102] In Greece, human rights played a more important, albeit still modest, role. Since Greece was a member of the Council of Europe, in 1967, some other members referred the situation in that country to the European Commission of Human Rights, which found that Greece was in violation of many articles of the European Convention on Human Rights.[103] Later, during the transition, the extensive prosecutions for torture clearly targeted human rights violations and were carefully followed by Amnesty International, which issued a report supporting them.[104] When the Argentine transition occurred ten years later, human rights had already become a universal language. Thus, 'in contrast with the debate over transitional justice in the Southern European transitions of the 1970s, in Latin America the discussion was clearly framed in terms of universal human rights'.[105]

The discourse's selection of the Southern European cases as valid instances of transitional justice, and the way it depicts them, underscores the purchase of its current characteristics. First, the political transitions in Portugal, Greece and Spain were well-suited for the comparative method. Since they took place within a short lapse of time, in countries with similar characteristics but that followed different courses of action, they were amenable to be contrasted and compared.

Second, what groups the Southern European transitions together is that they resulted in liberal democratic and capitalist regimes. Nevertheless, this liberal outcome was not at all clear in the Portuguese case. During the revolutionary period when the radical officers of the MFA held sway and nationalisations and agrarian reform were on the political agenda, it seemed as if Portugal might move towards communism. This led to the United States and Western European countries vigorously supporting moderate elements in

100 See Kenneth Maxwell, 'Regime Overthrow and the Prospects for Democratic Transitions in Portugal' in Guillermo O'Donnell, Philippe C Schmitter and Laurence Whitehead (eds), *Transitions from Authoritarian Rule: Southern Europe* (Johns Hopkins University Press, 1986); Costa Pinto, 'Settling Accounts with the Past in a Troubled Transition to Democracy' (n 65); Alves Raimundo, 'The Double Face of Heroes' (n 72).

101 Sikkink, *The Justice Cascade* 53 (n 5).

102 Aguilar, 'Justice, Politics and Memory in the Spanish Transition' 115–16 (n 89).

103 *Greek Case* (1970) Applications Nos 3321/67, 3322/67, 3323/67, 3344/67 12 Yearbook of the European Convention on Human Rights.

104 Sikkink, *The Justice Cascade* 50 (n 5); Amnesty International, *Torture in Greece* (n 79).

105 de Brito, González Enríquez and Aguilar Fernández, 'Introduction' 23 (n 14).

Portugal.[106] Once Portugal eventually was set on a democratic and capitalist course, this contingent outcome was naturalised as the start of the wave of democratisation. This happened only once the communist threat had been avoided. In addition to highlighting the liberal imprint of the Southern European transitions in its democratic and capitalist dimension, the established narrative of the discourse of transitional justice concentrates on violations of civil and political rights and, in particular, instances of physical violence. Hence, the Greek junta violence – including torture, prolonged detention and harsh repression of protests – is considered the most severe. In contrast, the discourse depicts the Portuguese regime as less repressive, despite the inequality and backwardness that characterised the New State, not to mention the widespread abuses that took place in the extensive Portuguese colonies.

Third, among the policies implemented in the Southern European transitions, the discourse of transitional justice discourse emphasises those that were more legalistic and marginalises those that departed from that characteristic. The contrast between the Greek and Portuguese cases illustrates this differentiation. The Greek experience with legalistic prosecutions commended by Amnesty International appears as the most influential case. Conversely, the Portuguese trials following the retroactive criminalisation of membership to PIDE are little known in transitional justice discourse.[107]

Fourth, the discourse equally highlights state-centric responses and dismisses practices not supported by the state. The spontaneous purges occurring in Portugal during the revolutionary period are not prominent in the discourse, and they are dismissed as illegitimate responses. For instance, the scholar who has written most extensively on transitional justice in Portugal, António Costa Pinto, calls the purges 'savage' and 'wildcat'.[108] These adjectives clearly express condemnation for these popular practices and marks them as illegitimate because they were not state sponsored and did not respect legalism. This preference for legalistic and state-centric responses shows the implicit normative valence of transitional justice discourse, despite the use of value-free definitions.

The dominant narrative of the history of transitional justice during the Cold War is shaped by the key characteristics. The Southern European transitions

[106] Maxwell, 'The Emergence of Portuguese Democracy' 240 (n 17).

[107] See Sikkink, *The Justice Cascade* (n 5); Nico Wouters, 'The Use of History in the Field of Transitional Justice: A Critical Introduction' in Nico Wouters (ed), *Transitional Justice and Memory in Europe (1945–2013)* (Intersentia, 2014).

[108] Costa Pinto, 'Settling Accounts with the Past in a Troubled Transition to Democracy' (n 65) 66, 73, 76–79; Costa Pinto, 'Authoritarian Legacies' 184, 187, 190 (n 93).

are included because they resulted in capitalist and liberal democracies. The policies that the discourse underscores are those that conform to its characteristics. At the same time, other responses to legacies of widespread or systematic violence that occurred in the Cold War period have been completely excluded from this narrative.

III MISSING HISTORIES, EXCLUDED MECHANISMS

Three crucial historical processes that took place between the end of World War II and 1989 are absent from the discourse's dominant account of transitional justice during this period: the proxy wars between the United Statess and the Soviet Union, the decolonisation process and the many transitions to non-liberal regimes. First, whereas the confrontation between the two opposing superpowers never erupted into direct warfare, it did kindle armed conflicts throughout the world in which at least one of the belligerents was supported by either the United States or the Soviet Union, depending on its political orientation. Second, the period covered by the Cold War also witnessed the final break-up of colonial empires. In 1945, most of Africa and large swathes of Asia were under European control. By 1989, colonial empires with direct rule from the metropolis were a relic from the past. Third, while the 'third wave' referred to transitions to liberal democracies, as was the case in Southern Europe, during the Cold War period there were also many non-liberal transitions. From Cuba in 1959, to Burkina Faso in 1983, many countries experienced political changeovers that did not lead to liberal regimes.

These three processes – the proxy wars, decolonisation and non-liberal transitions – involved responses to past widespread or systematic violence. Probably because most of these responses did not conform to the most common transitional justice mechanisms and did not reflect the discourse's characteristics, they have hitherto been omitted from the dominant account of the history of transitional justice. The rest of this chapter examines each one of these processes, showing how the transitional justice measures adopted there, which have been marginalised from the established narrative of the discourse, did not reflect the discourse's six key characteristics.

1 *Proxy Wars and the Russell Tribunal*

The Cold War between the United States and the Soviet Union was fought primarily in foreign lands. The superpowers vied for global supremacy and competed to attract other countries to their respective political and economic systems. Once the battle lines were solidified in Europe, with the continent neatly divided by the Iron Curtain into capitalist American allies and communist Soviet supporters, the superpower competition moved to the so-called Third World.[109] As Yuri Andropov, who would rise to be head of state of the Soviet Union, prophesised in 1965, the 'future competition with the United States will take place not in Europe, and not in the Atlantic Ocean. It will take place in Africa, and in Latin America. We will compete for every piece of land, for every country'.[110] For their part, Third World governments and rebel groups tried to play the Cold War antagonism to their benefit, seeking the support of superpowers keen to forestall the threat of them turning over to their rival.

The war was anything but cold in these places. The proxy wars in Korea, El Salvador, Vietnam, Angola, Ethiopia, Afghanistan and Mozambique were bitterly fought and caused thousands of casualties and widespread suffering.[111] Conflicts were so endemic during the Cold War period that, according to Eric Hobsbawm, there 'was hardly a year between 1948 and 1989 without a fairly serious armed conflict somewhere'.[112] The violence inspired, or exacerbated, by the Cold War also included cases of internal repression. For instance, the military dictatorships that spread around Latin America in the 1970s and 1980s were seen from the United States as containing the threat of communism.[113] As a result of the global scope of the Cold War and the use of proxies, most of the casualties of this long confrontation occurred far from Washington and Moscow, and most of the victims were neither American nor Soviet.[114]

Transitional justice discourse has examined some episodes of this Cold War–related violence. The four influential cases that we examined in Chapter 3 had Cold War elements. The Argentine trials targeted the internal violence perpetrated by the right-wing military against a perceived communist threat. Internal repression in Eastern Europe and the shooting of people crossing the Berlin Wall were justified in the strife against the West.[115] The

[109] This division happened quite soon after the end of the war. Winston Churchill coined the term 'Iron Curtain' in a speech delivered on 5 March 1946, 'The Sinews of Peace' (Westminster College, Fulton, Missouri) www.winstonchurchill.org/resources/speeches/235-1946-1963-elder-statesman/120-the-sinews-of-peace, accessed 30 July 2018.

[110] Cited in Gordon S Barrass, *The Great Cold War: A Journey through the Hall of Mirrors* (Stanford University Press, 2009) 187.

[111] See Odd Arne Westad, *The Global Cold War: Third World Interventions and the Making of Our Times* (Cambridge University Press, 2005).

[112] Eric Hobsbawm, *Age of Extremes: The Short Twentieth Century, 1914–1991* (Abacus, 1995) 251.

[113] Westad, *The Global Cold War*, ch 4 (n 111).

[114] Barrass, *The Great Cold War* 2 (n 110).

[115] Tina Rosenberg, *The Haunted Land: Facing Europe's Ghosts after Communism* (Vintage, 1995) 269–76.

civil wars in Yugoslavia that were precipitated by the demise of communism sparked the rise of international criminal justice with the creation of the ICTY. Apartheid South Africa was a key actor in the Cold War confrontation and fought proxy wars in Angola and Namibia against communist armed groups.[116] Transitional justice discourse has also engaged to a greater or lesser extent with other conflicts with Cold War elements such as the civil wars in El Salvador,[117] Guatemala,[118] Peru[119] and Mozambique,[120] as well as the repression in Ethiopia,[121] Chile[122] and South Korea.[123] Yet, in all these cases, the focus has overwhelmingly been on domestic perpetrators. In contrast, the discourse of transitional justice has relegated the role of the superpowers to the background at best, or omitted it altogether at worst.[124]

Transitional justice discourse has neglected even more those conflicts where the superpowers intervened directly. It has not examined at length the war that the United States fought in Vietnam between 1965 and 1975 or the Soviet intervention in Afghanistan between 1979 and 1989.[125] The

[116] See Westad, *The Global Cold War*, ch 6 (n 111).

[117] UNSC 'Report of the Commission on the Truth for El Salvador', Annex to the letter dated 29 March 1993 from the Secretary-General addressed to the President of the Security Council UN Doc S/25500. See also Mark Ensalaco, 'Truth Commissions for Chile and El Salvador: A Report and Assessment' (1994) 16 *Human Rights Quarterly* 656; Cath Collins, *Post-Transitional Justice: Human Rights Trials in Chile and El Salvador* (Pennsylvania State University Press, 2010).

[118] Anita Isaacs, 'At War with the Past? The Politics of Truth Seeking in Guatemala' (2010) 4 *International Journal of Transitional Justice* 251; Madeleine Fullard and Nicky Rousseau, 'Truth Telling, Identities, and Power in South Africa and Guatemala' in Paige Arthur (ed), *Identities in Transition: Challenges for Transitional Justice in Divided Societies* (Cambridge University Press, 2011).

[119] Jemima García-Godos, 'Victim Reparations in the Peruvian Truth Commission and the Challenge of Historical Interpretation' (2008) 2 *International Journal of Transitional Justice* 63; Burt, 'Guilty as Charged' (n 48).

[120] Victor Igreja, 'Amnesty Law, Political Struggles for Legitimacy and Violence in Mozambique' (2015) 9 *International Journal of Transitional Justice* 239.

[121] Kjetil Tronvoll, Charles Schaefer and Girmachew Alemu Aneme, *The Ethiopian Red Terror Trials: Transitional Justice Challenged* (James Currey, 2009).

[122] Roniger and Sznajder, *The Legacy of Human-Rights Violations in the Southern Cone* (n 39); Cath Collins, 'Human Rights Trials in Chile during and after the "Pinochet Years"' (2010) 4 *International Journal of Transitional Justice* 67.

[123] Kritz, *Transitional Justice* (n 21); Terence Roehrig, *The Prosecution of Former Military Leaders in Newly Democratic Nations: The Cases of Argentina, Greece and South Korea* (McFarland, 2002).

[124] For instance, the Guatemalan truth commission mentioned the role of external actors as part of the context in which the civil war was fought, Comisión para el Esclarecimiento Histórico, *Guatemala Memoria del Silencio* (F&G Editores, 1999). See also Rosemary Nagy, 'Transitional Justice as Global Project: Critical Reflections' (2008) 29 *Third World Quarterly* 275.

[125] See Westad, *The Global Cold War*, chs 5 and 8 (n 111).

discourse has only engaged with two responses related to the Vietnam War. But these responses tackled narrow aspects of the widespread and systematic violence that swept through Indochina during the Cold War period.

A first response to the Vietnam War that some transitional justice scholars have briefly touched upon is the prosecution of US servicemen for the notorious massacre of civilians that took place in 1968 in My Lai village in South Vietnam.[126] In 1970, an army inquiry found that up to 400 unarmed civilians had been killed by US troops in that village and that the events had been covered-up by various military authorities. The report submitted a list of suspects to be court-martialled.[127] Although 25 men were charged with crimes in relation to the My Lai massacre, only one conviction ensued, with the rest of the charges being dropped or the suspects acquitted.[128] In 1971, platoon commander Lieutenant William Calley was convicted of the premeditated murder of no fewer than 22 Vietnamese civilians and was sentenced to life imprisonment.[129]

The My Lai proceedings were related to a single event and targeted low and middle-ranking officers. The responsibility for the massacre stopped at Lieutenant Calley. The court martial, departing from the standard of military responsibility under which an American military commission had convicted Japanese General Yamashita in 1945, acquitted Lieutenant Calley's commanding officer, Captain Medina. While Yamashita was convicted because he failed to prevent troops under his command from committing war crimes without requiring knowledge of the crimes,[130] in the Medina case the jury was instructed that a conviction required actual knowledge of the crimes.[131] Even Lieutenant Calley was treated with leniency. Many people regarded Calley as

[126] Nino, *Radical Evil on Trial* 26–28 (n 14); Ruti Teitel, *Transitional Justice* (Oxford University Press, 2000) 35.

[127] Department of the Army 'Report of the Department of the Army Review of the Preliminary Investigations into the My Lai Incident' (14 March 1970) (US).

[128] Joanna Bourke, *An Intimate History of Killing: Face-to-Face Killing in Twentieth-Century Warfare* (Basic Books, 1999) 196.

[129] *US* v. *Calley* 22 USCMA 534 (1973). See also J Holmes Armstead, 'The United States vs William Calley: An Opportunity Missed' (1983) 10 *Southern University Law Review* 205.

[130] *In re* Yamashita 327 US 1 39 (1946) (Supreme Court). See also Telford Taylor, *Nuremberg and Vietnam: An American Tragedy* (Bantam Books, 1971); Ann Marie Prévost, 'Race and War Crimes: The 1945 War Crimes Trial of General Tomoyuki Yamashita' (1992) 14 *Human Rights Quarterly* 303; Bruce D Landrum, 'The Yamashita War Crimes Trial: Command Responsibility Then and Now' (1995) 149 *Military Law Review* 293.

[131] *US* v. *Medina* CM 427162 (ACMR 1971) reported in Kenneth Howard, 'Command Responsibility for War Crimes' (1972) 21 *Journal of Public Law* 7, 10–12. See also Michael Smidt, 'Yamashita, Medina, and Beyond: Command Responsibility in Contemporary Military Operations' (2000) 164 *Military Law Review* 155.

a hero and opposed his trial. A song made in his support sold 200,000 copies, and a poll showed that nearly 80 per cent of Americans disapproved of the trial.[132] Following an appeal, Calley was released on parole in 1974.[133] While they were the most notorious, the My Lai trials were not the only court martials for war crimes during the Vietnam War. Between January 1965 and September 1973, 36 cases of alleged war crimes by US Army troops were tried by court martials with 20 of them, involving 31 servicemen, leading to convictions.[134] These trials targeted individual servicemen mostly for wilful murder or assault of protected persons or mutilation of dead bodies.[135] Transitional justice discourse has not engaged with these further trials. In sum, the discourse of transitional justice has examined briefly only one Vietnam War case concerning a single massacre and resulting in the conviction of a low-ranking officer.

The second response related to the Vietnam War that the discourse of transitional justice has engaged with is the prosecution of Khmer Rouge officials before the Extraordinary Chambers in the Courts of Cambodia (ECCC).[136] The proxy war in Vietnam spilled over borders and affected neighbouring Cambodia. The United States bombed Vietnamese targets and Khmer Rouge positions in Cambodia during the Vietnam War. They also supported the military government of Lon Nol, while China and Vietnam provided weapons to Cambodian revolutionaries.[137] In 1975, the Khmer Rouge toppled the Lon Nol regime and implemented a Maoist programme to refashion Cambodia into an agrarian society, while exterminating political opponents, religious leaders, intellectuals and professionals. Between 1.5 and

[132] Bourke, *An Intimate History of Killing* 182–83 (n 128). See also William Thomas Allison, *My Lai: An American Atrocity in the Vietnam War* (Johns Hopkins University Press, 2012).

[133] Armstead, 'The United States vs William Calley' (n 129); Allison, *My Lai: An American Atrocity in the Vietnam War* (n 132).

[134] George Prugh, *Law at War: Vietnam 1964–1973* (Department of the Army, 1975) 74.

[135] Ibid 76.

[136] See, eg, James Gibson, Jeffrey Sonis and Sokhom Hean, 'Cambodians' Support for the Rule of Law on the Eve of the Khmer Rouge Trials' (2010) 4 *International Journal of Transitional Justice* 377; Randle C DeFalco, 'Accounting for Famine at the Extraordinary Chambers in the Courts of Cambodia: The Crimes against Humanity of Extermination, Inhumane Acts and Persecution' (2011) 5 *International Journal of Transitional Justice* 142; Maria Elander, 'The Victim's Address: Expressivism and the Victim at the Extraordinary Chambers in the Courts of Cambodia' (2013) 7 *International Journal of Transitional Justice* 95; Julie Bernath, '"Complex Political Victims" in the Aftermath of Mass Atrocity: Reflections on the Khmer Rouge Tribunal in Cambodia' (2016) 10 *International Journal of Transitional Justice* 46.

[137] John Ciorciari and Anne Heindel, *Hybrid Justice: The Extraordinary Chambers in the Courts of Cambodia* (University of Michigan Press, 2014) 1.

2 million people died during the Khmer Rouge regime.[138] Its reign came to an end when the Vietnamese army and Cambodian rebels invaded Cambodia in January 1979.[139] The ECCC was created in 2006 to try senior leaders of the Khmer Rouge regime and those most responsible for genocide, crimes against humanity, grave breaches of the Geneva Conventions, and crimes under the Cambodian Penal Code committed between 17 April 1975 and 6 January 1979.[140] Since the ECCC's jurisdiction is confined to the crimes committed by the Khmer Rouge regime in Cambodia between these dates, it cannot adjudicate the earlier conflict in Vietnam and Cambodia or the role of external actors such as the United States and China. This broader picture is at best relegated to providing the historical context of the cases.[141] Therefore, the second response related to the Vietnam War that the discourse of transitional justice has addressed tackles only one aspect of the Indochina conflicts.

a The Russell Vietnam War Crimes Tribunal

While the discourse of transitional justice has engaged with these two narrow responses to the violence related to the Vietnam War, it has ignored a mechanism with a much more ambitious scope.[142] The International War Crimes Tribunal was established in 1967 at the initiative of Bertrand Russell to expose the action of the United States in Vietnam.[143] Initially, the British

[138] Ibid 2.
[139] The responses adopted after the Vietnamese invasion are examined in the following section.
[140] Agreement between the United Nations and the Royal Government of Cambodia concerning the prosecution under Cambodian law of crimes committed during the period of Democratic Kampuchea (adopted 6 June 2003, entered into force 29 April 2005) 2329 UNTS 117; Law on the Establishment of Extraordinary Chambers in the Courts of Cambodia for the Prosecution of Crimes Committed during the Period of Democratic Kampuchea (NS/RKM/1004/006) Amended 27 October 2004, art 3.
[141] For instance, the ECCC judgment in case 002/01 briefly discussed the US bombing of Cambodia as a possible justification for the Khmer Rouge policy of evacuating cities, *Prosecutor v. Khieu Samphan, Nuon Chea, Ieng Sary and Ieng Thirith* (Case 002/01 Judgment) Case 002-E313 (7 August 2014), paras 153–56. Yet defendant Nuon Chea argued in his closing submissions that he was prevented from presenting evidence concerning the historical context, including the American bombings of Cambodia between 1969 and 1973, *Prosecutor v. Khieu Samphan, Nuon Chea, Ieng Sary and Ieng Thirith* (Closing Submissions in Case 002/01) Case 002-E295/6/3 (26 September 2013), paras 51–55.
[142] Fragments of this section were originally published by Oxford University Press as Marcos Zunino, 'Subversive Justice: The Russell Vietnam War Crimes Tribunal and Transitional Justice' (2016) 10 *International Journal of Transitional Justice* 211.
[143] Bertrand Russell, 'Opening Statement to the First Tribunal Session' in John Duffett (ed), *Against the Crime of Silence: Proceedings of the Russell International War Crimes Tribunal, Stockholm, Copenhagen* (Bertrand Russell Peace Foundation, 1968). Self-appointed tribunals

philosopher, then 94 years old, had envisaged a tribunal of prestigious figures based in Paris which would try US President Lyndon Johnson for international crimes committed in the conduct of the Vietnam War. The tribunal would be modelled on the IMT, but, being independent of any state or international organisation, it would be unable to enforce its verdict. Its purpose would be to influence public opinion to force the United States to end the war.[144] Legislation forbidding insults to foreign heads of state resulted in the tribunal changing the kind of responsibility the tribunal addressed. Wary that discussing the potential individual criminal responsibility of President Johnson could fall foul of the law, the organisers opted for examining the state responsibility of the United States and its allies instead. When the French government refused to provide assistance with visas, the organisers decided to move the seat of the tribunal to Stockholm.[145]

The Russell Tribunal had a panel of 22 members including French philosophers Jean-Paul Sartre and Simone de Beauvoir, American Black Power activist Stokely Carmichael, German playwright Peter Weiss, former Mexican President Lázaro Cárdenas, Italian lawyer Lelio Basso, Scottish trade unionist Lawrence Daly and Yugoslav historian Vladimir Dedijer. Due to his age, Russell was appointed honorary president of the tribunal, with Sartre occupying the executive presidency.

Unsurprisingly, the United States and North Vietnam had contrasting attitudes toward the Russell Tribunal. The government of North Vietnam lauded it as 'the first international tribunal of the masses to try the crimes of aggression committed by U.S. imperialism in Vietnam'.[146] It facilitated visas for witnesses and investigators and provided funding for the tribunal's fact-finding trips.[147] Conversely, the United States refused to participate. In August 1966, when Russell was preparing the tribunal, he wrote to President Johnson asking him to appear in his own defence or to nominate a representative.[148] Since the US government had decided to play down the Russell Tribunal to

which seek to influence public opinion are called different names: civil society tribunals, unofficial tribunals, mock tribunals, citizens' tribunals or people's tribunals. In this chapter, they are referred to as unofficial tribunals.

144 Harish C Mehta, 'North Vietnam's Informal Diplomacy with Bertrand Russell: Peace Activism and the International War Crimes Tribunal' (2012) 37 *Peace & Change* 64, 65.

145 Arthur Jay Klinghoffer and Judith Apter Klinghoffer, *International Citizens' Tribunals: Mobilizing Public Opinion to Advance Human Rights* (Palgrave, 2002) 120.

146 Radio Hanoi, cited in ibid 132.

147 Mehta, 'North Vietnam's Informal Diplomacy with Bertrand Russell 68–71 (n 144).

148 Bertrand Russell, 'Letter from Russell to Johnson, 25 August 1966' in John Duffett (ed), *Against the Crime of Silence: Proceedings of the Russell International War Crimes Tribunal, Stockholm, Copenhagen* (Bertrand Russell Peace Foundation, 1968).

avoid giving it publicity, there was no reply to the request.[149] Once the tribunal was set up, Sartre invited again the US to send a representative; Secretary of State Dean Rusk then responded that he had no intention of 'playing games with a 94-year-old Briton'.[150]

During its eight days of sessions in Stockholm in May 1967, the Russell Tribunal covered most aspects of the war in Vietnam and in neighbouring countries. It heard expert testimonies on international law, on the medical effects of US weapons and on the consequences of the destruction of dikes and irrigations systems. Witnesses were brought from Vietnam and Cambodia to narrate their experiences of the war. Victims showed their wounds, burns and scars and were examined by doctors. While there was not a defence to cross-examine the witnesses, the panel questioned them. The verdict rendered on 10 May 1967 found that the United States had committed acts of aggression against Vietnam; that it was guilty of deliberate bombardment of civilian targets and that it had violated the sovereignty of Cambodia. It also found Australia, New Zealand and South Korea guilty of being accomplices to the aggression against Vietnam.[151]

Further sessions held in Roskilde, Denmark, expanded the scope of the enquiry further, examining allegations of torture, use of prohibited weapons, infringement of Laos' sovereignty and genocide.[152] During these hearings, three former US army servicemen gave testimony about widespread torture and killings of Vietnamese prisoners. On 1 December 1967, the Russell Tribunal found that the United States had committed aggression against Laos;[153] that it had used prohibited weapons and that it had subjected prisoners of war to treatment unlawful under the laws of war. Most notably, it found the United States guilty of genocide against the people of Vietnam. The verdict also extended the complicity of aggression to Thailand, the Philippines

[149] Mehta, 'North Vietnam's Informal Diplomacy with Bertrand Russell 79–80 (n 144).

[150] Arthur W Blaser, 'How to Advance Human Rights without Really Trying: An Analysis of Nongovernmental Tribunals' (1992) 14 *Human Rights Quarterly* 339, 362.

[151] International War Crimes Tribunal, 'Verdict of the Stockholm Session' in John Duffett (ed), *Against the Crime of Silence: Proceedings of the Russell International War Crimes Tribunal, Stockholm, Copenhagen* (Bertrand Russell Peace Foundation, 1968).

[152] On 30 August 1967, a chapter of the tribunal set up in Tokyo had found Japan guilty of aggression, International War Crimes Tribunal, 'Combined Report on the Complicity of Japan in the Vietnam War: Testimony by the Japanese Committee' in John Duffett (ed), *Against the Crime of Silence: Proceedings of the Russell International War Crimes Tribunal, Stockholm, Copenhagen* (Bertrand Russell Peace Foundation, 1968).

[153] The bombing of Cambodia referred to earlier took place later on the war.

and Japan.[154] The Russell Tribunal did not succeed in ending the war, which continued until 1975. But it managed to gain broad media coverage, and the evidence it gathered was later used by opponents of the war, especially once the news of the 1968 My Lai massacre transpired.[155]

The Russell Tribunal on the Vietnam War can be considered an instance of transitional justice.[156] According to the definition adopted in this book, a transitional justice practice refers to responses to past widespread or systematic violence. The Vietnam War undoubtedly entailed widespread and systematic violence, and the Russell Tribunal was designed as a response to that violence. Although the Russell Tribunal issued its verdicts whilst the Vietnam War was still unfolding, it addressed past violence in the sense of examining events which had already occurred.[157] Moreover, some scholars have recognised unofficial tribunals modelled after the Russell initiative as transitional justice mechanisms.[158]

The discourse, however, mentions only the Russell Tribunal as a footnote and not as a transitional justice mechanism.[159] This is despite the expansion of mechanisms associated with transitional justice and a growing interest in historical antecedents. Even those who engage with later unofficial tribunals that were inspired by the Russell Tribunal often do not make reference to the

154 International War Crimes Tribunal, 'Summary and Verdict of the Second Session' in John Duffett (ed), *Against the Crime of Silence: Proceedings of the Russell International War Crimes Tribunal, Stockholm, Copenhagen* (Bertrand Russell Peace Foundation, 1968) 643–50.

155 For the impact of the tribunal, Wilfrid Fleischer, 'U.S. Is "Guilty" Says "Tribunal"' *The Washington Post* (10 May 1967); Roland Huntford, 'War Victims at Russell Tribunal' *The Observer* (7 May 1967); 'Russell "Tribunal" Hears a U.S. Negro' *New York Times* (26 November 1967); Caroline Moorehead, *Bertrand Russell: A Life* (Sinclair-Stevenson, 1992). For the use of the evidence, Edward F Sherman, 'Betrand Russell and the Peace Movement: Liberal Consistency or Radical Change' in George Nakhnikian (ed), *Bertrand Russell's Philosophy* (Duckworth, 1974); Richard Falk, 'War, War Crimes, Power, and Justice: Toward a Jurisprudence of Conscience' (2013) 21 *Transnational Law & Contemporary Problems* 667.

156 For the Russell Tribunal and transitional justice in general, see Zunino, 'Subversive Justice' (n 142).

157 See Chapter 1, 5.

158 Louis Bickford, 'Unofficial Truth Projects' (2007) 29 *Human Rights Quarterly* 994; Lavinia Stan, 'Tribunal of Opinion' in Lavinia Stan and Nadya Nedelsky (eds), *Encyclopedia of Transitional Justice* (Cambridge University Press, 2013), vol 1; Lavinia Stan, *Transitional Justice in Post-Communist Romania the Politics of Memory* (Cambridge University Press, 2013); Binoy Kampmark, 'Citizens' War Crimes' Tribunals' (2014) 33 *Social Alternatives* 5.

159 Minow, *Between Vengeance and Forgiveness* 28 (n 5); Emilios A Christodoulidis, '"Truth and Reconciliation" as Risks' (2000) 9 *Social & Legal Studies* 179, 184; Arthur, 'How "Transitions" Reshaped Human Rights' 342 (n 3).

precursor.[160] The Russell Tribunal thus remains mostly invisible for transitional justice discourse.[161]

The discourse of transitional justice has also ignored other unofficial tribunals modelled on the Russell initiative, even when they referred to situations normally examined by the discourse. In 1974, the Bertrand Russell Peace Foundation set up the Russell Tribunal on Latin America that exposed the atrocities of the then military regimes in Chile, Bolivia and Uruguay.[162] In 1977, the Humberto Delgado Popular Tribunal, inspired by the Russell initiative, was set up in Portugal to mobilise public opinion for the condemnation of the former regime and the prosecution of PIDE military police.[163] The Humberto Delgado Popular Tribunal concluded that the Oliveira Salazar regime and PIDE had committed crimes against humanity, war crimes and genocide. It also held that the former regime had systematically violated the economic, social and cultural rights of the Portuguese and the colonised peoples.[164] In Argentina, months after the last remaining junta prisoners were pardoned in 1990, an unofficial Tribunal Against Impunity was held in Buenos Aires with international figures to try to keep the issue of the crimes of the dictatorship in the public agenda.[165] The discourse has not regarded any of these initiatives as transitional justice practices.

The reason for the Russell Tribunal's obscurity within the discourse of transitional justice is that it went against many of the characteristics that lie at the core of that discourse today. The first characteristic that the Russell Tribunal ran counter to was technical legalism. The Russell Tribunal disregarded legal values and broke down the barrier separating the legal sphere from the rest of the social world. The Russell Tribunal openly violated basic principles of law. It stated that its purpose was to deliver an impartial

[160] See Bickford, 'Unofficial Truth Projects' (n 158); Stan, 'Tribunal of Opinion' (n 158).

[161] Without explicitly using a transitional justice framework, there are a few notable exceptions such as Klinghoffer and Klinghoffer, *International Citizens' Tribunals* (n 145); Blaser, 'How to Advance Human Rights without Really Trying' (n 150); Craig Borowiak, 'The World Tribunal on Iraq: Citizens' Tribunals and the Struggle for Accountability' (2008) 30 *New Political Science* 161; Falk, 'War, War Crimes, Power, and Justice' (n 155).

[162] William Jerman, *Repression in Latin America: A Report on the First Session of the Second Russell Tribunal, Rome, April 1974* (Spokesman Books, 1975).

[163] Tribunal Civico Humberto Delgado, 'Julgar a PIDE, Condenar O Fascismo: Decisão Final' (1978) https://ephemerajpp.com/2017/04/04/tribunal-civico-humberto-delgado/, accessed 30 July 2018, 1–2. See also Raimundo and Costa Pinto, 'From Ruptured Transition to Politics of Silence' (n 66).

[164] Tribunal Civico Humberto Delgado, 'Julgar a PIDE, Condenar O Fascismo: Decisão Final' 31–32 (n 163).

[165] Marguerite Feitlowitz, *A Lexicon of Terror: Argentina and the Legacies of Torture* (Oxford University Press, 1998) 128–33.

judgment,[166] but the members of the panel were all open critics of the US intervention in Vietnam. Russell asserted that the conclusions of the tribunal were 'built out of the evidence',[167] but the 'Aims and Objectives of the International War Crimes Tribunal' already held that the United States was using 'sadistically designed' weapons.[168] This neglect of legal principles was not casual but deliberate. Bertrand Russell made it clear when he opened the Stockholm session: 'Our Tribunal is not a group of disembodied formalists, quibbling over definitions'.[169] For Judith Shklar, having a refined system of formal definitions is one of the characteristics of legalism.[170] Here the tribunal was openly challenging it.

The Russell initiative also rejected legalism by breaching the barrier that keeps the legal sphere in isolation. The Russell Tribunal appropriated legal forms and language. It called itself a tribunal, investigated crimes and issued verdicts, thus breaking into the privative sphere of law. Lawyers are entrusted to minister the law. Accordingly, while some nonjudicial transitional justice mechanisms can include non-lawyers, such as truth commissions, judicial proceedings are the exclusive purview of lawyers. Yet the tribunal was composed of philosophers, writers, scientists and historians, not just revealing the truth but passing legal judgment. People used quotation marks to signal that the tribunal's use of legal concepts was regarded as spurious. For the press, the '"judges"'[171] of the '"Tribunal"'[172], were going to '"try"' the US and declare it '"guilty"'.[173] Similarly, both British Prime Minister Harold Wilson and French President Charles de Gaulle used quotation marks to refer to the tribunal.[174]

166 International War Crimes Tribunal, 'Aims and Objectives of the International War Crimes Tribunal' in John Duffett (ed), *Against the Crime of Silence: Proceedings of the Russell International War Crimes Tribunal, Stockholm, Copenhagen* (Bertrand Russell Peace Foundation, 1968).

167 Bertrand Russell, 'Closing Address to the Stockholm Session' in John Duffett (ed), *Against the Crime of Silence: Proceedings of the Russell International War Crimes Tribunal, Stockholm, Copenhagen* (Bertrand Russell Peace Foundation, 1968) 310.

168 International War Crimes Tribunal, 'Aims and Objectives of the International War Crimes Tribunal' 14 (n 166).

169 Russell, 'Opening Statement to the First Tribunal Session' 49 (n 143).

170 Judith Shklar, *Legalism* (Harvard University Press, 1964) 2.

171 'Reluctance to Allow Mock Trial' *The Guardian* (6 October 1966).

172 *New York Times* (n 155).

173 W Granger Blair, 'Russell Discusses His Plan for "War-Crime Trial"' *New York Times* (17 November 1966).

174 Harold Wilson, 'Harold Wilson to Bertrand Russell, 14 March, 1967' in John Duffett (ed), *Against the Crime of Silence: Proceedings of the Russell International War Crimes Tribunal, Stockholm, Copenhagen* (Bertrand Russell Peace Foundation, 1968); Charles de Gaulle, 'Letter from de Gaulle to Sartre' in John Duffett (ed), *Against the Crime of Silence: Proceedings*

The second characteristic of transitional justice discourse that the Russell Tribunal was at odds with was its liberal imprint. The tribunal emphasised economic and social rights and denounced capitalism. Bertrand Russell extended the understanding of the crime of aggression to include economic aspects. For him, the world market was a form of aggression in which prices were set by rich countries to exploit the nations of Africa, Asia and Latin America.[175] Moreover, capitalism was to blame for the war. For Sartre, the expansionism of capitalism pushed the United States to subject the whole world to its markets. Accordingly, in Sartre's view, the United States was waging war in Vietnam to incorporate this country into the capitalist system. From this perspective, The US intervention was an 'expression of the economic infrastructure of that power, its political objectives and the contradictions of its present situation'.[176] The Russell Tribunal thus ran counter to the liberal imprint of transitional justice discourse.

The last characteristic of the later discourse of transitional justice that the Russell Tribunal did not reflect was state-centrism. The Russel Tribunal was created and run independently of any state. Hence, it could not derive power from it. More crucially, it sought the legitimacy of its judicial function beyond the state. The tribunal's president, Jean-Paul Sartre, claimed that the source of the tribunal's legitimacy was the people who had the right to set up tribunals. He also expressed a desire that the masses across borders could unite to impose on states a genuine 'Court of the People'[177]. The idea of the masses bypassing the institutions of the state was a challenge not only to its monopoly over the administration of justice but also to its relevance. The French government's reaction to the intention of hosting the tribunal in Paris showcases how it considered that the unofficial initiative was defying its monopoly of justice. In a letter to Sartre, President de Gaulle wrote that Russell and his friends 'intend to give a juridical form to their investigations and the semblance of a verdict to their conclusions. I have no need to tell you that justice of any sort, in principle

of the Russell International War Crimes Tribunal, Stockholm, Copenhagen (Bertrand Russell Peace Foundation, 1968).

175 Bertrand Russell, 'Message from Bertrand Russell to the Tribunal' in John Duffett (ed), *Against the Crime of Silence: Proceedings of the Russell International War Crimes Tribunal, Stockholm, Copenhagen* (Bertrand Russell Peace Foundation, 1968) 38.

176 Jean-Paul Sartre, 'On Genocide' in John Duffett (ed), *Against the Crime of Silence: Proceedings of the Russell International War Crimes Tribunal, Stockholm, Copenhagen* (Bertrand Russell Peace Foundation, 1968) 612.

177 Jean-Paul Sartre, 'Jean Paul Sartre's Inaugural Statement to the Tribunal' in John Duffett (ed), *Against the Crime of Silence: Proceedings of the Russell International War Crimes Tribunal, Stockholm, Copenhagen* (Bertrand Russell Peace Foundation, 1968) 42.

as in execution, emanates from the State."[178] Sartre replied that justice deriving exclusively from the state completely subjugated the legal machinery to it. For him, justice had to find its source both in the state and in the people. The Russell Tribunal thus challenged the primacy of the state in judicial matters.

The proxy wars, the conflict in Vietnam and the novel mechanism created in response to this conflict have been largely marginalised from the history of transitional justice. The Russell Tribunal was a practice of transitional justice that went against many of the characteristics that the discourse has today and is accordingly ignored.

2 *Decolonisation and the Land Question*

During the Cold War period, another momentous process unfolded. The centuries-old European colonial empires were finally dismantled. The end of empire reconfigured the international landscape with the arrival of scores of new sovereign states.[179] Membership to the UN bears witness to the scope of decolonisation in the Cold War period. When the UN was founded in 1945 it had 51 members; in 1991 it counted 166.[180] The process of decolonisation that trebled the number of sovereign states was as protracted in its gestation over decades of struggle as its denouement was sudden. Between 1955 and 1965, 36 former colonies or protectorates became independent.[181] This took place at the height of the Cold War. As a historical process, decolonisation was distinct from the Cold War. European overseas empires dated from Portugal's maritime expansion in the fifteenth century. The process of decolonisation itself can be stretched back to the independence of Haiti in 1804.[182] Yet since the end of empire coincided with the height of the global confrontation between the United States and the Soviet Union, the decolonised states became inevitably enmeshed in that conflict.[183]

178 De Gaulle, 'Letter from de Gaulle to Sartre' 28 (n 174).

179 The demise of empires and the attending dramatic increase in the number of independent lead Frederick Cooper to signal the aftermath of World War II as the true beginning of the Westphalian system of sovereign nation-states, *Colonialism in Question: Theory, Knowledge, History* (University of California Press, 2005) 188–90.

180 UN, *Growth in United Nations Membership, 1945–Present* (2018) www.un.org/en/sections/member-states/growth-united-nations-membership-1945-present/index.html, accessed 30 July 2018.

181 Westad, *The Global Cold War* 88 (n 111).

182 See Cyril Lionel Robert James, *The Black Jacobins: Toussaint l'Ouverture and the San Domingo Revolution* (Allison and Busby, 1989).

183 See Frantz Fanon, *The Wretched of the Earth* (Grove Press: Distributed by Publishers Group West, 2004) 52–57.

Decolonised countries inherited a legacy of widespread and systematic violence. In many instances, colonies gained independence only after a long armed struggle.[184] Torture, massacre and collective punishments marked these conflicts and counter-insurgency operations. As Martin Shipway notes, 'none of the various colonial combatants in these quintessentially "dirty wars" ... was untouched by the stain of abusive and transgressive violence'.[185] If the decolonisation process itself was not violent, a hurried exit or divisions exacerbated during the colonial period often led to internecine conflict soon after independence. This was the case with the Indian partition that left between half a million and a million dead and the war that ensued following the Belgian departure from Congo.[186] In addition to the bouts of violence that accompanied or followed decolonisation, the colonial experience itself had entailed innumerable abuses, systematic discrimination, cultural repression and entrenched inequality. This structural but very palpable violence of colonialism was the main legacy with which decolonised countries continued to grapple well after becoming independent.[187]

Transitional justice discourse has not engaged in depth with the violence of decolonisation and the policies instituted to respond to the legacy of colonialism. Indeed, the colonial violence recounted earlier has not spurred trials, truth commissions or reparations, especially in the metropolises. The discourse of transitional justice has not examined either colonialism as a process or the responses adopted in the decolonised countries.[188] Instead, transitional justice discourse has been concerned at length with the widespread or systematic violence that erupted after the colonisers left. It has examined the extermination by the Khmer Rouge but not the French colonial war in Indochina; it has looked into the physical violence that marked the end of the apartheid regime in South Africa but not the centuries of racialised

[184] The French fought full-blown wars for their empire in Algeria and Indochina. As was discussed earlier in this chapter, the Portuguese tried to hold on to their empire by fighting colonial wars in Angola, Mozambique and Guinea. The British used the military to combat the Mau Mau insurrection in Kenya and during the Malaya emergency, see MPK Sorrenson, *Land Reform in the Kikuyu Country: A Study in Government Policy*, (Oxford University Press, 1967); John Springhall, *Decolonization since 1945: The Collapse of European Overseas Empires* (Palgrave, 2001); Martin Shipway, *Decolonization and Its Impact: A Comparative Approach to the End of the Colonial Empires* (Blackwell Pub, 2008).

[185] Shipway, *Decolonization and Its Impact* 163 (n 184).

[186] Springhall, *Decolonization since 1945* (n 184); Frederick Cooper, *Africa since 1940: The Past of the Present* (Cambridge University Press, 2002) 83.

[187] See Mahmood Mamdani, 'Beyond Settler and Native as Political Identities: Overcoming the Political Legacy of Colonialism' (2001) 43 *Comparative Studies in Society and History* 651.

[188] See Nagy, 'Transitional Justice as Global Project: Critical Reflections' (n 124).

settlement that preceded it; it has discussed the Rwandan genocide but has relegated the colonial policies that paved the way to it to the background. Transitional justice discourse's neglect of the violence of colonialism remains, despite some recent calls to pay more attention to it.[189]

The policies that the newly independent countries carried out to confront the violence of colonialism differed from the mechanisms that transitional justice normally studies. As Paige Arthur has persuasively shown, the decolonised governments chose to deal with the past mainly in a socio-economic way.[190] The new leaders wanted to redress decades of exploitation through redistribution and development. Influential post-colonial writer Franz Fanon had already announced in his 1961 book *The Wretched of the Earth* that decolonisation meant that the last should now be first.[191] That maxim resonated during the processes of decolonisation. Those who were relegated and exploited during colonialism would now be prosperous and lead the country. The process of decolonisation thus involved a series of policies that were part of responding to the widespread or systematic violence of the past through reforming the unjust structures of colonial rule. In many ways, newly independent states dealt with their violent colonial past by looking towards a better future. Indonesian President Ahmed Sukarno encapsulated this forward-looking attitude in his speech at the historic 1955 Bandung Conference that congregated Asian and African leaders: 'Let us not be bitter about the past, but let us keep our eyes firmly on the future.'[192]

The first measure that confronted the colonial past was decolonisation itself. Again according to Fanon, achieving independence brought moral reparation and dignity to the colonised peoples.[193] Putting first those who were last naturally required those who used to be first to cede their places. Millions of European colonial administrators and settlers left following

[189] Ismael Muvingi, 'Sitting on Powder Kegs: Socioeconomic Rights in Transitional Societies' (2009) 3 *International Journal of Transitional Justice* 163; Stiina Loytomaki, 'The Law and Collective Memory of Colonialism: France and the Case of "Belated" Transitional Justice' (2013) 7 *International Journal of Transitional Justice* 205; Khanyisela Moyo, 'Mimicry, Transitional Justice and the Land Question in Racially Divided Former Settler Colonies' (2015) 9 *International Journal of Transitional Justice* 70; Hakeem Yusuf, 'Colonialism and the Dilemmas of Transitional Justice in Nigeria' (2018) 12 *International Journal of Transitional Justice* 257.

[190] Arthur, 'How "Transitions" Reshaped Human Rights' 341–42 (n 3).

[191] Fanon, *The Wretched of the Earth* 3 (n 183).

[192] Cited in Vijay Prashad, *The Darker Nations: A People's History of the Third World* (New Press; Distributed by WW Norton, 2007) vii.

[193] Fanon, *The Wretched of the Earth* 40 (n 183).

decolonisation. In Algeria, the majority of European settlers numbering almost a million and a half people returned to France after independence.[194] Once Congo became independent, it is estimated that 60,000 out of a total of 80,000 settlers left.[195] Thirty thousand white settlers left Kenya following decolonisation. In 1975, Portugal was flooded with 800,000 returnees from their African colonies, including nine-tenths of European settlers in Angola.[196] Although many settlers remained, especially in countries such as Kenya and in the apartheid states of South Africa and Rhodesia, this massive exodus enabled the formerly colonised people to occupy positions in public administration and business, thus taking control of their own countries.[197] The process of replacing the governmental bureaucracies had economic consequences as well. For instance, according to Stephen Orvis, the Kenyanisation of the public sector, especially in the higher echelons, was the 'most dramatic economic effect of independence' because it increased the employment and wages of skilled Kenyan labour.[198] The departure of the colonial rulers and settlers and their replacement with local people was part of the process of making the last first and responding to the colonial violence.

Development was a second way of redressing the colonial past that the newly independent states pursued. After World War II, the colonial powers had started to develop the infrastructure and economy of their dependencies as a last bid to keep their empires together. The independent governments continued along the same path.[199] They hoped that by developing the infrastructure and the economy of their countries they would be able to provide their citizens with the prosperity denied to them during colonial rule. By increasing the size of the economy, development would raise the standard of living without needing to redistribute wealth. The policies of decolonised countries were thus shaped by a vision of development.[200]

[194] Muriel Evelyn Chamberlain, *The Longman Companion to European Decolonisation in the Twentieth Century* (Longman, 1998) 162; Springhall, *Decolonization since 1945* 156 (n 184).
[195] Shipway, *Decolonization and Its Impact* 222 (n 184).
[196] Costa Pinto, 'Authoritarian Legacies' 190 (n 93); Cooper, *Africa since 1940* 141 (n 186).
[197] Colonial empires differed in how they approached the process of decolonisation regarding colonial bureaucracies. For example, whereas the British carried out a nation-building strategy through the progressive incorporation of local staff into public service, the Belgian civil servants left abruptly without training Congolese successors, John Hargreaves, *Decolonization in Africa* (Longman, 1988) 119; Cooper, *Africa since 1940* 164 (n 186).
[198] Stephen Walter Orvis, *The Agrarian Question in Kenya* (University Press of Florida, 1997) 33.
[199] Hargreaves, *Decolonization in Africa* 113 (n 197).
[200] Cooper, *Africa since 1940* 86 (n 186).

a Land Reform

Land reform was a third pervasive measure used to respond to the colonial past that has not been examined at length in transitional justice discourse. The dispossession of land and resources had been a key aspect of colonialism.[201] Accordingly, most governments of the decolonised states pursued policies to redress that dispossession. This was the ultimate measure to put first those who were last. In many countries, these redistributive policies were inspired by the egalitarian promise of socialism with the Soviet Union as its living example.[202] The question of land reform was particularly acute in those countries which had received, due to their geographical conditions, large numbers of European settlers. Settlers had mostly concentrated in areas that were good for agriculture and not subject to malaria, such as the Eastern African highlands and Southern Africa. In those countries where the struggle for independence succeeded completely and most settlers left, such as Angola or Mozambique, the question of land was quickly resolved. On the contrary, in those countries where significant numbers remained – such as Kenya, Namibia, Zimbabwe and South Africa – the question of redistributing land lingered on.[203] Land reform, however, transcends the process of decolonisation during the Cold War. The land question has fuelled conflicts and violence throughout the world. Agrarian reform programmes have been carried out in countries that were not immediately emerging from colonialism – such as Mexico (1911), Bolivia (1953), Cuba (1959), Colombia (1961), Chile (1962), and Nicaragua (1979).[204] Moreover, questions of land restitution to indigenous peoples have cropped up in most settler states, from Canada to New Zealand.[205]

The governments of the newly independent states pursued various methods of land reform, underpinned by diverging political and economic perspectives, to respond to the legacy of colonialism. Independent Kenya opted for

[201] Derick Fay and Deborah James, 'Giving Land Back or Righting Wrongs? Comparative Issues in the Study of Land Restitution' in Cherryl Walker and others (eds), *Land, Memory, Reconstruction, and Justice: Perspectives on Land Claims in South Africa* (Ohio University Press, 2010).

[202] See Prashad, *The Darker Nations* (n 192).

[203] Sam Moyo, 'The Land Question in Southern Africa: A Comparative Review' in Ruth Hall and Lungisile Ntsebeza (eds), *The Land Question in South Africa: The Challenge of Transformation and Redistribution* (HSRC Press, 2007).

[204] Robert Alexander, *Agrarian Reform in Latin America* (Macmillan, 1974); William C Thiesenhusen, *Searching for Agrarian Reform in Latin America* (Unwin Hyman, 1989); Jaime Wheelock, *La Reforma Agraria Sandinista: 10 Años de Revolución en el Campo* (Editorial Vanguardia, 1990).

[205] See Fay and James, 'Giving Land Back or Righting Wrongs?' (n 201).

market-driven land redistribution with voluntary transfers of land, together with land tenure reform, to strengthen private property. The reform of land tenure was initiated during the last years of colonial rule. While for most of the colonial era economic development was based on European immigrant farming,[206] after the Mau Mau uprising the British implemented a plan to replace communal tenure with individual freeholds to create an African middle class and increase productivity.[207] The independent government continued with this policy.[208] Regarding land redistribution, as part of the decolonisation process, the British government negotiated with the Kenyan authorities a series of programmes for buying land from European settlers where African peasants would be resettled.[209] These programmes allowed those settlers who wanted to leave a possibility of selling their land while they created an opportunity for Africans to access land. The initial programmes aimed at commercial farming benefitted mostly Kenyan elites who thus acquired a vested interest in the stability of private ownership.[210] Later programmes sought to purchase land to redistribute among landless and unemployed households, but they were hampered by financial shortfalls and rising land prices. Moreover, the government's priority shifted from redistribution to development, leading to an emphasis on commercial farmers rather than small-hold peasants.[211] Eventually, large swathes of the redistributed landed ended up being transferred to wealthy African businessmen.[212] These market-based restitutions programmes were criticised by many Kenyan nationalists who held that Africans should not have to pay for the land that was stolen from them. However, President Jomo Kenyatta opposed the resettled farmers not repaying their loans.[213]

Other decolonised countries relied on more radical methods of land reform. Tanzania under Julius Nyerere followed a path of forced nationalisation of land and collectivisation of the agricultural system. Likewise, in Mozambique, the large colonial estates were converted into state farms which were collectively exploited.[214] These policies were evidently more

[206] Sorrenson, *Land Reform in the Kikuyu Country* 55 (n 184).
[207] Orvis, *The Agrarian Question in Kenya* 31 (n 198).
[208] Ibid 33.
[209] Wolfgang Reinhard, *A Short History of Colonialism* (Manchester University Press, 2011) 261.
[210] Cooper, *Africa since 1940* 174–75 (n 186).
[211] Orvis, *The Agrarian Question in Kenya* 35 (n 198). See also John Harbeson, *Nation-Building in Kenya: The Role of Land Reform* (Northwestern University Press, 1973) 146.
[212] Hargreaves, *Decolonization in Africa* 210 (n 197).
[213] Harbeson, *Nation-Building in Kenya* 331 (n 211).
[214] Henry Bernstein, 'Agrarian Questions of Capital and Labour: Some Theory about Land Reform (and a Periodisation)' in Ruth Hall and Lungisile Ntsebeza (eds), *The Land Question in South Africa: The Challenge of Transformation and Redistribution* (HSRC Press, 2007) 34.

effective in redistributing land in a shorter period of time, but people resisted the forced collectivisation, and the total agricultural output fell.[215]

In Zimbabwe, Namibia and South Africa where decolonisation was delayed, the land question lingered on unresolved.[216] When in 1980 the first majority government took office in Zimbabwe after 15 years of civil war, almost all large-scale commercial farming was in European hands.[217] While land redistribution was a key demand of the liberation movement, the compromise reached to end the war proscribed the expropriation of land.[218] The new government, with British financial support, launched a land resettlement programme that bought land from willing European sellers. Although some land was thus distributed, the new regime sought to preserve the high-output agricultural sector which relied on large European-owned estates.[219] In 2000, following occupations of white commercial farms,[220] the government implemented a radical programme of 'Fast Track' land redistribution.[221] While this programme changed the agricultural landscape from large-scale to small-scale farms, the productivity fell, some farmers were violently evicted, and government officials benefitted from the redistribution.[222] When Namibia finally gained independence in 1990, market-led redistribution programmes were carried out. In 2004, the government announced a programme of land expropriation but offered owners compensation.[223] In South Africa, land reform was a crucial tenet of the African National Congress (ANC). From 1994, the government implemented a programme of subsidies to buy land at market price.[224] But it failed. Even though its goal was to transfer 30 per cent of farming land in 5 years, 10 years later it had only transferred 4 per cent.[225]

[215] Cooper, *Africa since 1940* 143–44 (n 186).
[216] Moyo, 'The Land Question in Southern Africa' 62 (n 203).
[217] Chris Alden, *Land, Liberation and Compromise in Southern Africa* (Ward Anseeuw and Inc Ebrary eds, Palgrave Macmillan, 2009); Ian Scoones, *Zimbabwe's Land Reform: Myths & Realities* (Jacana Media, 2010).
[218] Sam Moyo, *Land and Agrarian Reform in Zimbabwe beyond White-Settler Capitalism* (CODESRIA, 2013) 2.
[219] Cooper, *Africa since 1940* 138 (n 186).
[220] Moyo, 'The Land Question in Southern Africa' (n 203) 77.
[221] Prosper Bvumiranayi Matondi, *Zimbabwe's Fast Track Land Reform* (Zed Books, 2012).
[222] Ibid; Alden, *Land, Liberation and Compromise in Southern Africa* (n 217).
[223] Alden, *Land, Liberation and Compromise in Southern Africa* 147–48 (n 217).
[224] Alden, *Land, Liberation and Compromise in Southern Africa* (n 217).
[225] Ruth Hall, 'Transforming Rural South Africa? Taking Stock of Land Reform' in Ruth Hall and Lungisile Ntsebeza (eds), *The Land Question in South Africa: The Challenge of Transformation and Redistribution* (HSRC Press, 2007) 88–89.

The ANC government also carried out a programme of restitution of land but only for those who had been dispossessed after 1913.[226]

Despite being pervasive responses to the violence of colonialism, the discourse of transitional justice has not engaged with the land reform policies implemented after decolonisation. They are certainly not included in the narrative of transitional justice during the Cold War. More generally, land reform is not regarded as a relevant mechanism of transitional justice. Of recent years, some authors have shown interest in examining land questions within a transitional justice framework in situations already well established in the discourse's horizon, such as South Africa, Colombia or Rwanda.[227] However, these recent efforts do not necessarily inscribe the issue of land reform today in the narrative of colonial violence and the land reform processes that followed decolonisation. In spite of these isolated and localised endeavours, the overall question of land redistribution as a response to the widespread and systematic violence of colonialism has not been addressed in the discourse of transitional justice.[228]

The explanation for this neglect is that land reform ran counter to the technical and liberal characteristics of the discourse of transitional justice. Although colonial powers and foreign donors tried to present land reform as a technical question related to agricultural productivity, in the countries in question it was considered an openly political matter. In the decolonising countries, the unfair distribution of land was linked to the injustice of colonialism and was a problem to be resolved by political means. By way of example, in Kenya, land redistribution was a source of political contention, sparking debates over whether European settlers should be paid for their land.[229] In this context, the violence of colonialism and the way to redress it were presented not in technical apolitical terms but as intrinsically political issues. The land reform policies also departed from the technical legalistic dimension of the discourse of transitional justice. Programmes of land reform as a response to past violence implied a preference for policy interventions to produce social

[226] Restitution of Land Rights Act (1994).

[227] See, eg, James Gibson, *Overcoming Historical Injustices: Land Reconciliation in South Africa* (Cambridge University Press, 2009); Luis Jorge Garay Salamanca, *Memoria y Reparación: Elementos para una Justicia Transicional pro Víctima* (Universidad Externado de Colombia, 2012); Helen Hintjens, 'Land Reform, Social Justice, and Reconstruction: Challenges for Post-Genocide Rwanda' in Dick W Simpson and Cassandra Rachel Veney (eds), *African Democracy and Development: Challenges for Post-Conflict African Nations* (Lexington Books, 2013).

[228] See Muvingi, 'Sitting on Powder Kegs: Socioeconomic Rights in Transitional Societies' (n 189).

[229] Harbeson, *Nation-Building in Kenya* 122–34 (n 211).

change rather than relying on judicial institutions. While land tenure reform was in the legalistic spectrum insofar as it involved reforming the law regulating land, other policies openly defied legalism. The forcible expropriations and nationalisation of land carried out in Tanzania, Mozambique and Zimbabwe disregarded legal certainty and undermined the rule of law.

Land reform did not reflect transitional justice discourse's liberal imprint either. Land reform concentrates on the economic sphere rather than on the institutional realm in which transitional justice policies normally operate.[230] It emphasises violations of socio-economic rights and structural violence rather than violations of civil and political rights and instances of physical violence. Because the newly independent states perceived that the most insidious legacy of colonialism was the unjust socio-economic structure, they implemented measures such as land redistribution and eschewed trials or reparations programmes.[231] Many programmes of land reform also questioned the capitalist dimension of the discourse's liberal imprint. They were implemented in decolonised countries that followed socialist paths with centrally controlled economies. These programmes rejected private property and nationalised land.

Decolonisation was a defining historical process of the latter half of the twentieth century. It shaped the world in which we live today and in which transitional justice discourse emerged. Colonial rule entailed widespread and systematic violence both in terms of oppressive structures and instances of physical abuse. But the responses adopted to respond to this violence remain absent from the historical narrative of transitional justice discourse.

3 *Non-Liberal Transitions and Popular Tribunals*

The last process that historical accounts of transitional justice practices during the Cold War have overlooked is the spate of political transitions to non-liberal regimes. When transitional justice discourse emerged, it was inscribed in the paradigm of a 'third wave' of transitions to democracy. However, while the Cold War lasted, societies transitioning from an authoritarian or conflict-ridden past could opt for a socialist future as much as for a

[230] See Hannah Franzki and Maria Carolina Olarte, 'Understanding the Political Economy of Transitional Justice: A Critical Theory Perspective' in Susanne Buckley-Zistel and others (eds), *Transitional Justice Theories* (Routledge, 2014).

[231] At the same time, in the context of decolonisation, it was impossible to bring to court those colonial officials who had committed the abuses or have access to sufficient funds to finance reparation programmes for victims of physical violence.

liberal democratic one. In other words, for each Greece or Argentina, there was a Vietnam or Cuba.

The discourse of transitional justice has not addressed the responses to past widespread or systematic violence that these non-liberal regimes carried out. As Thomas Hansen notes, 'the scholarship appears to lack interest in these cases of non-liberal transitions'.[232] Even Hansen himself, while recognising that the responses adopted following non-liberal transitions have been overlooked, does not regard them as relevant historical examples but, rather, as warning signs that the established mechanisms of transitional justice can be appropriated by illiberal and repressive states. This section examines the responses to past widespread or systematic violence that were implemented in the aftermath of non-liberal political transitions in order to show that they were excluded because they ran counter to the key characteristics of the discourse of transitional justice.

Between 1945 and 1989, scores of states embarked on non-liberal transitions. Most were animated by some strand of Marxist thought and looked for inspiration and support from the Soviet Union and other communist countries. Those in Eastern Europe were part of the opening act of the Cold War and were carried out on the back of Soviet military occupation. Other non-liberal transitions took place in states coming out of a process of decolonisation or that at one stage had been colonised. Cuba under Fidel and Raúl Castro (from 1959), Mozambique with the Mozambique Liberation Front (FRELIMO) (1975–1990), Ghana under Flight-Lieutenant Rawlings (1981–1993), Nicaragua after the Sandinista revolution (1979–1990) and Burkina Faso with Thomas Sankara (1983–1987) all experimented with variants of socialism. While these states received material and ideological support from the Soviet Union, they adapted socialist institutions to fit their own contexts.[233] Being further away from the Soviet Union and, in some cases, having less geopolitical value, these states could pursue their own path to socialism with more freedom than those behind the Iron Curtain.

All these countries faced comparable difficulties. They had inherited unequal and unjust economic and social structures from their colonial past. In the face of these challenges, revolutionary governments sought to reform the entire economic, social, political and legal fabric of society. While liberal

[232] Thomas O Hansen, 'Transitional Justice: Toward a Differentiated Theory' (2011) 13 *Oregon Review of International Law* 1, 15. For an early example of this attitude to non-liberal transitions, see Charles Duryea Smith, 'Introduction' in Neil J Kritz (ed), *Transitional Justice: How Emerging Democracies Reckon with Former Regimes* (United States Institute of Peace Press, 1995) xvi.

[233] See Prashad, *The Darker Nations* (n 192).

reforms operate under the assumption that changes at the institutional level would free the forces of the market and civil society,[234] their socialist counterparts seek to engineer the complete transformation of society. Rather than being limited to political-institutional reform, the latter also aim to transform the socio-economic structure as well.[235] For instance, the government of Thomas Sankara in Burkina Faso 'sought nothing else than a total reconstruction of Burkinabe society through a massive redistribution of the country's wealth'.[236] This reconstruction implied a response to the widespread or systematic violence of the previous regimes; a violence that was not only direct and physical but also structural and pervasive.

In order to redress the widespread or systematic violence of the past, these societies implemented a series of policies. Many of them focused on the economic sphere. They nationalised key industries, thus concentrating the manufacturing capacity in the hands of the state. The degree of nationalisation varied. Cuba nationalised great industries in 1960 and during the following decade proceeded to nationalise smaller businesses.[237] Starting in 1979, the Sandinistas in Nicaragua implemented a more moderate programme that nonetheless saw the nationalisation of financial, insurance and mining businesses.[238] During these transitions, the governments tackled the unequal distribution of land by carrying out policies of agrarian reform. Instead of relying on market-led models, countries following non-liberal paths opted for expropriating or nationalising land. In Burkina Faso, all the land which until then had been communal was nationalised in 1984.[239] Similarly, in Mozambique, where during the colonial times the best land had been reserved for Portuguese settlers, the FRELIMO government nationalised all land in 1979.[240] Other non-liberal revolutions were less radical. For instance, while redistribution of land was one of the pillars of the Sandinista revolution

[234] See, eg, Pádraig McAuliffe, 'Transitional Justice's Expanding Empire: Reasserting the Value of the Paradigmatic Transition' (2011) 2 *Journal of Conflictology* 32, 38–39.

[235] See Carlos María Vilas, *The Sandinista Revolution: National Liberation and Social Transformation in Central America* (Monthly Review Press, 1986) 152–64.

[236] Victor Le Vine, *Politics in Francophone Africa* (Lynne Rienner Publishers, 2004) 149.

[237] Víctor Figueroa Albelo, *Economía Política de la Transición al Socialismo: Experiencia Cubana* (Editorial de Ciencias Sociales, 2009) 261–69.

[238] Frente Sandinista de Liberación Nacional, 'Entrevista de Sepla con Gladys Zalaquet, Representante del FSLN', *Nicaragua, Elementos Históricos, Estratégicos y Tácticos de la Revolución* (Seminario Permanente sobre Latino América, 1979) 20–22; James McDonald and Marjorie Zatz, 'Popular Justice in Revolutionary Nicaragua' (1992) 1 *Social & Legal Studies* 283, 286.

[239] Ernest Harsch, *Thomas Sankara: An African Revolutionary* (Ohio University Press, 2014) 97.

[240] Albie Sachs and Gita Honwana Welch, *Liberating the Law: Creating Popular Justice in Mozambique* (Zed Books, 1990) 27.

in Nicaragua, the Sandinistas refrained from nationalising all land. Instead, they reduced large estates and consolidated land tenure.[241]

The responses to the widespread or systematic violence of the previous regimes also tackled the social fabric and governance institutions. Revolutionary governments in Nicaragua, Cuba and Mozambique implemented policies to redress gender imbalances and injustice.[242] In Burkina Faso, Sankara carried out an ambitious plan to promote the emancipation of women. He raised the minimum age for marriage, instituted divorce, established widows' right to inherit and tried to erradicate ingrained practices such as female genital mutilation and forced marriage.[243] Traditional forms of governance were also at the receiving end of the reforms carried out in some of the transitions coming out of colonialism. Local chiefs were considered backwards and socially repressive, especially where they had been incorporated into the colonial administration. Accordingly, during these socialist transitions, their authority was diminished. Hence, in Burkina Faso, their role in allocating land was removed, and in Mozambique, chieftaincy was abolished.[244]

Many of these economic measures failed, and some of the novel governance structures became sources of oppression themselves. Some of these regimes committed abuses so egregious that they became the subject of transitional justice processes later on. For instance, the communist-inspired Khmer Rouge toppled an authoritarian regime in 1975 and went on to commit such abuses that, 30 years later, the ECCC was established to try some of its leaders. Likewise, coming into power after a revolution in 1974, the socialist Ethiopian Derg regime was responsible for the 'Red Terror' of 1977–1978, which claimed the lives of thousands of people. This violence was the subject of wide-ranging prosecutions between 1994 and 2007 in which some of the Derg leaders were convicted of genocide.[245] Irrespective of their political content, effectiveness and even abusiveness, the responses to past widespread or systematic violence adopted following non-liberal transitions can be considered practices of transitional justice. These responses fit the definition of

[241] Wheelock, *La Reforma Agraria Sandinista* 71–76 (n 204); Carlos Fonseca Terán, *El Poder, la Propiedad, Nosotros: La Revolución Sandinista y el Problema del Poder en la Transformación Revolucionaria de la Sociedad Nicaragüense* (Editorial Hispamer, 2005) 330–32.

[242] See Vilas, *The Sandinista Revolution*, ch 7(n 235).

[243] Harsch, *Thomas Sankara: An African Revolutionary* 79–84 (n 239).

[244] Ibid 97–98; Juan Obarrio, *The Spirit of the Laws in Mozambique* (University of Chicago Press, 2014) 46–47.

[245] See Firew Kebede Tiba, 'The Mengistu Genocide Trial in Ethiopia' (2007) 5 *Journal of International Criminal Justice* 513; Firew Kebede Tiba, 'Mass Trials and Modes of Criminal Responsibility for International Crimes: The Case of Ethiopia' in Kevin Jon Heller and Gerry J Simpson (eds), *The Hidden Histories of War Crimes Trials* (Oxford University Press, 2013).

transitional justice practice adopted in this book as well as any other definition of transitional justice that does not include normative requirements.

a Popular Tribunals

Following non-liberal transitions, many revolutionary governments established popular tribunals to respond to the violence of past regimes. Socialist governments – for example, in Cuba, Ghana, Burkina Faso, Nicaragua, Mozambique and Cambodia – created popular tribunals that included judges who were not legally trained, had a pedagogical purpose and rejected legal formalism.[246] The logic underlying these experiments was expressed by the Minister of Interior of the Nicaraguan Sandinista regime: 'We have to fight to bring about, in the short term, popular justice, to incorporate the wisdom of the masses in the administration of justice.'[247] As we shall see, popular tribunals were similar to two mechanisms normally associated with transitional justice: criminal trials and institutional reform.

Two types of popular tribunals were adopted following non-liberal transitions, namely revolutionary tribunals and people's tribunals. Revolutionary tribunals were established as emergency institutions during the rebellion or shortly after its success as temporary courts to deal with the legacy of the previous regime. They were usually composed of military officers or militiamen, and their proceedings were summary. They dealt with serious offences committed by the previous regime and imposed heavy penalties. Once the new regime became established and its formal institutions were strengthened, the revolutionary tribunals were normally replaced by ordinary courts. The people's tribunals, by contrast, were permanent institutions created to deal with special types of offences that incorporated ordinary people into the administration of justice. People's tribunals often applied innovative and not overly severe penalties. However, in some cases, the differences between these two types of tribunals eroded when revolutionary tribunals became permanent or when people's tribunals were used for political offences.

[246] During the presidency of Salvador Allende in Chile, there was an attempt to create popular courts that was blocked by the legislature. See Jack Spence, 'Institutionalizing Neighborhood Courts: Two Chilean Experiences' in Richard Abel (ed), *The Politics of Informal Justice* (Academic Press, 1982). The Constitution of Cambodia under the Khmer Rouge contemplated the creation of popular courts, Constitution du Kampuchea Democratique (Constitution of Democratic Kampuchea) (1975). However, no judicial system functioned during this regime, see Case 002/01 Judgment, para 238 (n 141).

[247] Tomás Borge, 'Justice in Nicaragua Is No Longer the Same' in Bruce Marcus (ed), *Nicaragua: The Sandinista People's Revolution: Speeches by Sandinista Leaders* (Pathfinder Press, 1985) 267.

The creation of both types of popular tribunals was underpinned by both pragmatic and ideological reasons. Revolutionary governments resorted to lay judges because of a shortfall of lawyers and qualified judges. This was a result of most legally trained people going into exile,[248] colonial officers returning to the metropolis[249] or general lack of state resources.[250] For instance, following independence, there were only 25 qualified lawyers in the whole of Mozambique.[251] Moreover, the revolutionary governments considered the existing court structure inadequate either because of the sheer number of cases to be processed or because the courts were sympathetic to the previous regime.[252] In this context, bypassing, or replacing, the ordinary courts with an alternative structure that was not confined to existing qualified personnel or restricted by legal procedures appeared conducive to the ends of the revolutionary regimes.

Popular tribunals were also supported by ideological reasons. According to Marxist theory, the law was an expression of the existing relations of production under capitalism. Once a society had attained communism, class antagonism and exploitation would disappear, and with them many crimes related to greed and inequality would no longer occur.[253] Socialist law was just a temporary stage necessary until the dictatorship of the proletariat gave way to communism. From this perspective, while ordinary courts were distrusted as instruments of bourgeois law, popular tribunals had the potential of integrating more citizens into the revolutionary process as well as modifying social patterns.[254] The pedagogic and socialisation purpose of these institutions was particularly prominent in people's courts because they included ordinary citizens in the decision-making process and targeted social offenses such as laziness at work and neighbourly quarrels. In African countries, the previous legal regime was rejected not only as an embodiment of capitalism but also as a relic of colonial oppression. The first president of Ghana, Kwame Nkrumah, had denounced the Ghanaian legal system as 'made for

[248] This happened in Cuba; see Luis Salas, 'The Emergence and Decline of the Cuban Popular Tribunals' (1983) 17 *Law & Society Review* 587, 598.

[249] In Mozambique, see Sachs and Welch, *Liberating the Law* 58 (n 240).

[250] This was the case in Burkina Faso, see Harsch, *Thomas Sankara: An African Revolutionary* 61–62 (n 239).

[251] Barbara Isaacman and Allen Isaacman, 'A Socialist Legal System in the Making: Mozambique before and after Independence' in Richard Abel (ed), *The Politics of Informal Justice* (Academic Press, 1982) 304.

[252] 'The Emergence and Decline of the Cuban Popular Tribunals' 597–98 (n 248).

[253] Valeria Vegh Weis, *Marxism and Criminology: A History of Criminal Selectivity* (Brill, 2017) 15.

[254] Salas, 'The Emergence and Decline of the Cuban Popular Tribunals' 603–5 (n 248).

application to an imperialist and colonial purpose'.[255] Similarly, for Thomas Sankara, there were two forms of law: the neocolonial reactionary law he replaced and the revolutionary law of the people.[256] For him, people's courts were 'sounding the death knell of Roman law; they are playing the swan song of the alien Napoleonic social law that has marginalized so very many of our people'.[257]

Popular tribunals were instances of transitional justice in two distinct ways. First, they directly adjudicated the violence of the previous regimes. Several of the experiments in popular justice implemented after non-liberal transitions were set up to try those considered responsible for the violence of the previous regime. Second, popular tribunals sought to redress the legacy of violence of the past by changing states' institutions and social practices. By incorporating the masses into the administration of justice and rejecting the legal order of the previous regime, they sought a break with the past. In this sense, they were akin to programmes of institutional reform that target the judiciary to prevent the recurrence of violence.[258] Although they departed in many ways from recognised criminal trials and judicial reform programmes, popular tribunals were undoubtedly responses to the past widespread or systematic violence of the previous regime. Therefore, they have to be regarded as mechanisms of transitional justice according to the definition adopted in this book and most definitions that do not have a normative element.

The first type of popular tribunal comprises the revolutionary tribunals that many victorious socialist guerrillas set up to try elements in the regime they had defeated. Immediately following victory, Fidel Castro's troops began carrying out revolutionary trials of military and civilian personnel of the Fulgencio Batista regime.[259] They were composed of a mixed bench of professional judges and soldiers and militiamen. Initially, these revolutionary tribunals heard cases of murder and torture but later also heard counter-revolutionary offences (eg, overthrowing government, embezzlement by

[255] Cited in Roger Gocking, 'Ghana's Public Tribunals: An Experiment in Revolutionary Justice' (1996) 95 *African Affairs* 197, 201.

[256] Thomas Sankara, 'The People's Revolutionary Courts: 3 January 1984', *Thomas Sankara Speaks: The Burkina Faso Revolution, 1983–87* (Pathfinder Press, 1988) 60.

[257] Ibid 61.

[258] See, eg, Marcos Zunino, 'Releasing Transitional Justice from the Technical Asylum: Judicial Reform in Guatemala Seen through Techne and Phronesis' (2011) 5 *International Journal of Transitional Justice* 99.

[259] Francisco José Moreno, 'The Cuban Revolution v Batista's Pilots' in Theodore Lewis Becker (ed), *Political Trials* (Bobbs-Merrill, 1971) 95–96.

public officials).[260] Following the Sandinista overthrow of Anastasio Somoza in Nicaragua, Special Tribunals with mixed professional and lay judges were set up to try the more than 7,000 National Guardsmen, members of the government and collaborators in detention.[261] In the fifteen months they functioned, they tried 5,500 cases, imposing prison sentences ranging from a few months to 30 years.[262] In 1983, when the civil war against the Contras intensified, the Sandinista regime established the Anti-Somocist Popular Tribunals, which also had mixed panels and tried Somoza supporters for war crimes and crimes against humanity.[263]

Some of these revolutionary tribunals created to try people associated with the previous regime relegated lawyers even further. In Mozambique, in 1979 the FRELIMO government set up Revolutionary Military Tribunals composed of military officers to try a wide range of offenses from treason and rebellion to insulting the ruling party.[264] Following the Vietnamese invasion of Cambodia in 1979, the new Cambodian regime set up the People's Revolutionary Tribunal to address the crimes of the Khmer Rouge leaders.[265] Only 1 of the 11 members of the tribunal had legal training, and its president was the Minister of Propaganda.[266] The tribunal convicted Khmer Rouge leaders Pol Pot and Ieng Sary of genocide and sentenced them to death in absentia.[267]

260 Jesse Berman, 'The Cuban Popular Tribunals' (1969) 69 *Columbia Law Review* 1317, 1333–34; Erik Luna, 'Cuban Criminal Justice and the Ideal of Good Governance' (2004) 14 *Transnational Law & Contemporary Problems* 529, 556–58.

261 Robert Steinberg, 'Judicial Independence in States of Emergency: Lessons from Nicaragua's Popular Anti-Somocista Tribunals' (1986) 18 *Columbia Human Rights Law Review* 359, 369.

262 McDonald and Zatz, 'Popular Justice in Revolutionary Nicaragua' 291 (n 238).

263 Decreto N° 1233 Ley de Tribunales Populares Antisomocistas (Law of Anti-Somocist Popular Tribunals) 11 April 1983. See also Steinberg, 'Judicial Independence in States of Emergency' (n 261).

264 Human Rights Watch, 'Mozambique: New Constitution Protects Basic Rights but Political Prisoners Still Suffer Unfair Trials' (1991) www.hrw.org/reports/pdfs/m/mozambq/mozambiq912.pdf, accessed 30 July 2018.

265 People's Revolutionary Council of Kampuchea Decree Law No 1 Establishment of People's Revolutionary Tribunal at Phnom Penh to Try the Pol Pot-Ieng Sary Clique for the Crime of Genocide (15 July 1979). See also Ciorciari and Heindel, *Hybrid Justice* 18–19 (n 137).

266 People's Revolutionary Council of Kampuchea Decree Law No 4 Appointment of Presiding Judge and Alternate (20 July 1979); People's Revolutionary Council of Kampuchea Decree Law No 25 Appointment of Members of the Tribunal (20 July 1979). See also Evan Gottesman, *Cambodia after the Khmer Rouge: Inside the Politics of Nation Building* (Yale University Press, 2003).

267 Judgment of the Revolutionary People's Tribunal held in Phnom Penh from 15 to 19 August 1979 in Howard Nike, John Quigley and Kenneth Robinson (eds), *Genocide in Cambodia: Documents from the Trial of Pol Pot and Ieng Sary* (University of Pennsylvania Press, 2000) 523. Later, Ieng Sary challenged his prosecution by the ECCC on the basis of his 1979 trial by the People's Revolutionary Tribunal and the subsequent pardon he received. The Trial Chamber

Popular tribunals of this first type were instances of transitional justice because they directly adjudicated the violence of the previous regimes. The Cuban revolutionary tribunals convicted members of the Batista air force of genocide for bombing civilian targets.[268] The Cambodian People's Revolutionary Tribunal also tried and convicted Khmer Rouge leaders of genocide.[269] In turn, the Nicaraguan Special Tribunals and Anti-Somocist Popular Tribunals tried members of Somoza's National Guard for war crimes and crimes against humanity.[270] In doing so, they operated as the paradigmatic transitional trial bringing to justice those responsible for the violations of the previous regime, albeit without respecting liberal standards of due process and featuring lay judges.

This first type of popular tribunal has been the subject of intense criticism. Revolutionary tribunals are condemned for being political instruments and for not ensuring minimum judicial guarantees. The enormity of the crimes committed by the Khmer Rouge in Cambodia notwithstanding, the Cambodian People's Revolutionary Tribunal convicted Pol Pot and Ieng Sary after only five days of trial. For this reason, the ECCC considered that the revolutionary tribunal was not impartial or independent and concluded that its decisions were incapable of producing valid legal effects.[271] The Nicaraguan Special Tribunals and Anti-Somocist Popular Tribunals were consistently condemned by the Inter-American Commission on Human Rights for not allowing for judicial review, not granting enough time for the preparation of the defence and not issuing reasoned decisions.[272] The Mozambican Revolutionary Military Tribunals have also been criticised for lacking independence and not being subject to appeal.[273] Despite its clear shortcomings,

rejected the objection because the proceedings before the People's Revolutionary Tribunal were not conducted in accordance with the requirements of due process, and the *ne bis in idem* principle did not apply to trials before internationalised tribunals, *Prosecutor* v. *Khieu Samphan, Nuon Chea, Ieng Sary and Ieng Thirith* (Decision on Ieng Sary's Rule 89 Preliminary Objections [Ne bis in idem and Amnesty and Pardon]) Case 002-E51/15 (3 November 2011), paras 30–36.

268 For an account of this trial, Moreno, 'The Cuban Revolution v Batista's Pilots' (n 259).

269 Judgment of the Revolutionary People's Tribunal 549 (n 267).

270 McDonald and Zatz, 'Popular Justice in Revolutionary Nicaragua' 290–92 (n 238).

271 *Prosecutor* v. *Khieu Samphan, Nuon Chea, Ieng Sary and Ieng Thirith*, para 30 (n 267).

272 Inter-American Commission on Human Rights 'Report on the Situation of Human Rights in the Republic of Nicaragua' (30 June 1981) OEA/Ser.L/V/II.53 Doc 25, c IV, s D; Inter-American Commission on Human Rights 'Annual Report of the Inter-American Commission on Human Rights 1988–1989 (18 September 1989) OEA/Ser.L/V/II.76 Doc 10, c V.

273 Human Rights Watch, 'Mozambique: New Constitution Protects Basic Rights but Political Prisoners Still Suffer Unfair Trials' (n 264).

revolutionary tribunals are mechanisms of transitional justice according to most definitions that do not have normative content.

Permanent people's tribunals constitute the second type of popular justice institution implemented after non-liberal transitions. These people's courts were inspired by the Soviet Comrades' Courts that were non-professional lower courts with civil and criminal jurisdiction.[274] These experiments in popular participation in the administration of justice were first used in the 1920s, disappeared during Stalinism and were revived in 1959 with a focus on prevention and education.[275] Soviet Comrades' Courts sought to 'prevent violations of law and offenses detrimental to society, to educate people by means of persuasion and social pressure, and to create conditions of intolerance toward any anti-social acts'.[276]

People's tribunals were introduced in Cuba in 1962. They heard minor cases such as torts up to a certain amount, juvenile delinquency, petty crime and personal quarrels.[277] The lay judges of its panels received basic legal training and assistance from law students.[278] The Sandinistas in Nicaragua also established people's courts but with mixed panels. They created Agrarian Tribunals to adjudicate on disputes concerning the redistribution of land[279] and introduced a pilot plan to try criminal cases.[280] Most of these people's tribunals imposed innovative sentences which included public censure, educational improvement (eg, completing secondary education) and prohibition of certain activities (eg, attending bars).[281]

The people's tribunals implemented in African countries following socialist inspired transitions departed more from the Soviet model of the Comrades' Courts and were used for more serious crimes. In Ghana, in 1982, the government of Flight-Lieutenant Rawlings established Public Tribunals with mixed panels to try criminal offences.[282] They were meant to reject legal

[274] René David and John N Hazard, *Le Droit Soviétique: Les Données Fondamentales du Droit Soviétique* (Librairie Générale de Droit et de Jurisprudence, 1954) 278; Harold Berman and James Spindler, 'Soviet Comrades' Courts' (1963) 38 *Washington Law Review* 842.

[275] Gordon Smith, 'Popular Participation in the Administration of Justice in the Soviet Union: Comrades' Courts and the Brezhnev Regime' (1973) 49 *Indiana Law Journal* 238.

[276] Statute on Comrades' Courts, Edict of the Presidium of the Supreme Soviet of the RSFSR (3 July 1961), No 26, Item 371 in Zigurds L Zile, *Ideas and Forces in Soviet Legal History: A Reader on the Soviet State and Law* (Oxford University Press, 1992), art I.

[277] Berman, 'The Cuban Popular Tribunals' 1321–22 (n 260).

[278] Salas, 'The Emergence and Decline of the Cuban Popular Tribunals' 588 (n 248).

[279] McDonald and Zatz, 'Popular Justice in Revolutionary Nicaragua' 292–94 (n 238).

[280] Ibid 294–95. See also Borge, 'Justice in Nicaragua Is No Longer the Same' (n 247).

[281] Berman, 'The Cuban Popular Tribunals' 1329–32 (n 260).

[282] Gocking, 'Ghana's Public Tribunals' 204 (n 255).

formalism and operate on the basis of the rules of natural justice.[283] They imposed harsh penalties, including death sentences.[284] In Burkina Faso, Thomas Sankara established Popular Revolutionary Tribunals in 1983 to try cases of political and economic crimes committed by civil servants or public officials.[285] They sought to punish crimes of corruption and embezzlement while they educated the public on moral values. The panels included one legally trained magistrate, one member of the security forces, and five laypersons.[286] The FRELIMO government in Mozambique carried out the most wide-ranging experiment of people's tribunals. Legal reform in 1978 replaced the Portuguese colonial judicial system with an innovative system of people's tribunals with lay judges in all courts.[287] While local courts were entirely composed of lay judges, higher courts had mixed benches.[288]

People's tribunals were transitional justice measures because they sought to respond to the violence of the past by reforming the institutions of the state and changing social practices.[289] Whereas the revolutionary tribunals were ad hoc solutions imbued with a particular ideological content that rejected the legal system of the previous regime, people's tribunals were created with the express objective of reforming institutions and shaping social attitudes. The Cuban, Nicaraguan, Burkinabe and Mozambican people's tribunals sought to redefine the legal system and re-educate the public. They rejected how justice had been done in the past and wanted to make the administration of justice more democratic and pedagogic. The Cuban tribunals sought to transform bourgeois cultural patterns;[290] the Nicaraguan project aimed at socialising the lay participants;[291] the Burkinabe tribunals had the

[283] Human Rights Watch, 'Ghana: Revolutionary Injustice: Abuse of the Legal System under the PNDC Government' (1992) www.hrw.org/reports/pdfs/g/ghana/ghana921.pdf, accessed 30 July 2018.

[284] For instance, in 1987 the Ghanaian Public Tribunals sentenced 61 persons to death for armed robbery; Gocking, 'Ghana's Public Tribunals' 213 (n 255).

[285] Le Vine, *Politics in Francophone Africa* 149 (n 236).

[286] Harsch, *Thomas Sankara: An African Revolutionary* 62 (n 239).

[287] Lei da Organização Judiciária nº 12/78 (Law of Judicial Organisation) (2 December 1978). See also Sachs and Welch, *Liberating the Law* 46–48 (n 240).

[288] Isaacman and Isaacman, 'A Socialist Legal System in the Making' 311–14 (n 251); João Carlos Trindade and João Pedroso, 'The Judicial System: Structure, Legal Education and Legal Training' in Boaventura De Sousa Santos, João Carlos Trindade and Maria Paula Meneses (eds), *Law and Justice in a Multicultural Society: The Case of Mozambique* (Council for the Development of Social Science Research in Africa, 2006) 115–17.

[289] Some people's tribunals also tried members of the previous regime (eg, the first trial of the Burkinabe people's tribunal was against former president Sangoulé Lamiana for corruption), see Sankara, 'The People's Revolutionary Courts' (n 256).

[290] Salas, 'The Emergence and Decline of the Cuban Popular Tribunals' 603 (n 248).

[291] McDonald and Zatz, 'Popular Justice in Revolutionary Nicaragua' 295 (n 238).

purpose of infusing public life with morality[292] and the Mozambican courts had an educational and participatory role.[293] The people's tribunals were institutions that responded to the violence of the past by trying to establish a new emancipatory order. They were judicial reform programmes that did not follow liberal normative blueprint.

These experiments in popular justice were eventually abandoned. In Cuba, as the revolution became more institutionalised, both the revolutionary and people's tribunals were abolished.[294] By the 1970s, the legal profession had been rehabilitated, and the ordinary court system had been purged from representatives of the previous regime. Still, the ordinary judicial system features mixed benches with professional and lay judges.[295] In Nicaragua, the revolutionary tribunals were dissolved as part of the peace process, and the people's tribunals were never fully implemented due to lack of funding.[296] The Mozambican Constitution of 1990 abandoned popular justice but retained lay judges.[297] By the end of the 1980s, the Ghanaian Public Tribunals were so sullied by corruption scandals and criticised for inflicting harsh punishments that they became a liability for a government which wanted to appear responsible.[298] The Burkinabe experiment came to an end when Sankara was ousted and executed in 1987.[299] Once these tribunals outlived their pragmatic purpose or the ideology they embodied, they were dissolved.

While meeting the definition of transitional justice, popular tribunals have usually been omitted from historical accounts of transitional justice because they did not embody, or explicitly they rejected, many of the current characteristics of the discourse. First, popular tribunals were at odds with the technical characteristic of transitional justice in its legalistic and apparently

[292] Harsch, *Thomas Sankara: An African Revolutionary* 61 (n 239).
[293] Sachs and Welch, *Liberating the Law* 10–11 (n 240).
[294] Harold Berman and Van Whiting, 'Impressions of Cuban Law' (1980) 28 *American Journal of Comparative Law* 475, 477–79.
[295] Salas, 'The Emergence and Decline of the Cuban Popular Tribunals' 610 (n 248).
[296] Steinberg, 'Judicial Independence in States of Emergency' (n 261); McDonald and Zatz, 'Popular Justice in Revolutionary Nicaragua' (n 238).
[297] Constituição da República de Moçambique (Constitution of the Republic of Mozambique) (1990), art 160(1). See also Trindade and Pedroso, 'The Judicial System' 120–28 (n 288); Maria Paula Meneses, 'Powers, Rights and Citizenship: The "Return" of the Traditional Authorities in Mozambique' in Tom Bennett and others (eds), *African Perspectives on Tradition and Justice* (Intersentia, 2012).
[298] Gocking, 'Ghana's Public Tribunals' 218 (n 255).
[299] Le Vine, *Politics in Francophone Africa* 149–50 (n 236). See also Valère Somé, *Thomas Sankara: l'Espoir Assassiné* (L'Harmattan, 1990).

apolitical dimensions. Popular tribunals were intended to simplify the law and the procedure to make them less esoteric and more accessible to the public.[300] Their proponents considered that legal technicalities severed the link between the people and justice. Accordingly, the Sandinistas sought to 'attain expedited and simple justice; to put an end to antiquated and annoying procedures and phraseology'.[301] The Ghanaian Public Tribunals were designed not to be 'fettered by technical rules'.[302] In Burkina Faso, Sankara denounced the irony of a country with 95 per cent illiteracy and a legal regime that held that ignorance of the law was no excuse.[303] For him, law was consciously written in a confusing, esoteric and elitist language which separated it from the people.[304]

Not only did the supporters of popular tribunals reject legal principles, but they also did not conceive of the legal realm as separate from the rest of the social world. The revolutionary governments wanted to include ordinary citizens in the administration of justice and to make law simple enough to be applied by anybody. Lawyers were seen as the personification of the legalism of the prior regime they wanted to supersede. Therefore, in Cuba the legal training of judges was kept to the minimum because professionalism could lead to a return to legal formalism.[305] Sankara openly defied 'jurists and other scholars – formalists obsessed by procedures and protocol – [to] be indignant and scandalized'.[306] The Sandinistas held lawyers in an even dimmer light. According to their Minister of Interior, they had been 'trained to exploit the unwary and to share the gains of robbers and thieves'.[307] The leaders of these regimes wanted to replace the existing legalistic systems with new simplified and popular legal orders.

The popular tribunals equally ran counter to transitional justice's technical dimension of being presented as apolitical. Instead of relying on technical legalism to present the violence as apolitical, popular tribunals emphasised the political aspects of the cases they heard. Many of the revolutionary tribunals were expressly created to have jurisdiction over political cases, such as the Cuban Revolutionary Tribunals and the Nicaraguan Anti-Somocist Popular

300 Sachs and Welch, *Liberating the Law* 10–12 (n 240).
301 Borge, 'Justice in Nicaragua Is No Longer the Same' 267 (n 247).
302 Gocking, 'Ghana's Public Tribunals' 197 (n 255).
303 Sankara, 'The People's Revolutionary Courts' (n 256).
304 Ibid 59.
305 Salas, 'The Emergence and Decline of the Cuban Popular Tribunals' 600 (n 248).
306 Sankara, 'The People's Revolutionary Courts' 57 (n 256).
307 Borge, 'Justice in Nicaragua Is No Longer the Same' 267 (n 247).

Tribunals.[308] Moreover, popular tribunals always placed the cases in a political context. For example, the Cambodian People's Revolutionary Tribunal showcased the political motivation of the atrocities and the support that the Khmer Rouge regime had received from external actors.[309] People's tribunals, such as the Mozambican courts, also located the cases within a broader political, social and economic background.[310] Equally, for Sankara, people's tribunals should 'publicly bring to light and expose the entire hidden social and political side of the crimes perpetrated against the people'.[311]

In their functioning and purpose, the people's tribunals were expressly political. This was a consequence of the socialist legal outlook. For the socialist revolutionaries, law was a political instrument of the ruling class used for maintaining power and extracting economic resources.[312] They also believed that the administration of justice was an eminently political task. Therefore, the appointment of judges was always political. The revolutionary tribunals were staffed with military or political leaders of the victorious revolution. In the people's tribunals, judges were appointed by political institutions which usually screened the candidates for their political commitment to the revolution. For instance, in Mozambique, judges were appointed according to their revolutionary knowledge.[313] In sum, popular justice rejected the technical characteristic in dismissing legalism and being openly political.

A second tension with the characteristics of transitional justice discourse can be found in the popular tribunal's rejection of liberalism. As the creatures of non-liberal transitions, the experiments on popular justice opposed liberalism. As a consequence, they were at odds with the three dimensions of the liberal characteristic of transitional justice discourse, namely an emphasis on violations of civil and political rights and episodes of physical violence, preference for liberal democracy and support for capitalism. First, popular courts put the focus on economic, social and cultural rights and instances of structural violence. Some of them examined socio-economic issues directly: the Burkinabe tribunals adjudicated on cases of economic crime, and the

[308] Decreto N° 1074 Ley sobre el Mantenimiento del Orden y Seguridad Pública (Law on Public Order and Security) 6 July 1982 (Nicaragua); Salas, 'The Emergence and Decline of the Cuban Popular Tribunals' 597 (n 248); Steinberg, 'Judicial Independence in States of Emergency' 382 (n 261); Decreto N° 1233 (n 262).

[309] This was an exercise of political point scoring of the Vietnamese liberators of Cambodia against China; see Judgment of the Revolutionary People's Tribunal 545–49 (n 267).

[310] Isaacman and Isaacman, 'A Socialist Legal System in the Making' 314–15 (n 251).

[311] Sankara, 'The People's Revolutionary Courts' 56–57 (n 256).

[312] Luna, 'Cuban Criminal Justice and the Ideal of Good Governance' 536–37 (n 260).

[313] Sachs and Welch, *Liberating the Law* 46 (n 240).

Nicaraguan agrarian tribunals on land redistribution. Furthermore, as attempts to reform the social and economic fabric of society, these initiatives transcended the episodes of physical violence of the previous regimes and engaged with the wider legacy of colonialism and authoritarianism. Second, being infused with Marxist and postcolonial ideology, the creators of these institutions did not conceive of liberal democracy as the ideal destination of political change. The purpose of the popular tribunals was to educate the public for a socialist regime. Third, popular justice initiatives did not endorse capitalism as the preferred economic system but actually denounced it.

The third characteristic of transitional justice discourse that popular tribunals did not present was its state-centrism. Even though they were organs created by the state, since they were staffed by ordinary citizens and were less formalistic, they were, to a certain extent, more independent than ordinary courts. Revolutionary tribunals were a consequence of the upheaval of revolutions, and people's courts of the ideological effervescence that followed them. Once the socialist regimes became more established and institutionalised, popular tribunals were replaced by more formal institutions where legalism and lawyers played a more leading role. As James McDonald and Marjory Zatz observe, 'as regimes become stable, there is frequently an increase in legal professionalism and a decline in citizen participation'.[314] The strengthening of the revolutionary states led to the withering of the pragmatic and ideological reasons underpinning popular justice. But popular tribunals started out as less state-centric than ordinary courts. In this manner, popular tribunals were at odds with many of the key characteristics of the later discourse of transitional justice.

Many of the experiments of popular justice, particularly the revolutionary tribunals, were a source of abuse and oppression. Many of the regimes that established them also failed to live up to the ideals that had inspired the revolutions. However, popular tribunals were undoubtedly practices of transitional justice that have been omitted from the discourse's historical narrative due to its implicit normative content.

IV CONCLUSION

This chapter has critically examined the dominant history of transitional justice that presents the Cold War as a landscape desolate of transitional justice and has argued that what the dominant narrative has included and

[314] McDonald and Zatz, 'Popular Justice in Revolutionary Nicaragua' 297 (n 238).

excluded, emphasised and understated, reflects the current characteristics of transitional justice discourse. The chapter has shown that although international criminal law indeed did not thrive during this period, other regimes fundamental for the emergence of transitional justice – in particular, international human rights law – did develop between 1945 and 1989. It has also demonstrated that the characteristics of the discourse shaped the choice and presentation of the only Cold War cases that the discourse of transitional justice mentions: the transitions in Portugal, Greece and Spain in the 1970s. The dominance of these characteristics has also resulted in the exclusion of the Cold War proxy wars, the process of decolonisation and the non-liberal transitions from the dominant account of transitional justice, together with their specific mechanisms: the Russell Tribunal, land reform programmes and popular tribunals.

After the Cold War, transitional justice discourse emerged in a world which had been shaped by superpower rivalry, the development of human rights, proxy wars, decolonisation and liberal and non-liberal transitions. The people involved in the four foundational moments examined in Chapter 3 wrote their own histories but under conditions inherited from the Cold War period. As this chapter has argued, the retroactive gaze that the discourse set on that period, however, was coloured by the characteristics it inherited from its post-Cold War process of emergence.

6

Conclusion

I RECAPITULATION

Transitional justice has become the dominant approach for engaging with societies' responses to past widespread or systematic violence. It includes a growing number of mechanisms for addressing abuses in an expanding list of situations with an experience of violence. This book has sought to critically examine the history of transitional justice. Its main finding is that the present and the past of transitional justice have been shaped by characteristics inherited from the historical emergence of an autonomous discourse of transitional justice in the 1990s. These characteristics have determined which responses to past widespread or systematic violence are considered appropriate and relevant.

Chapter 2 mapped the discursive space of transitional justice today, describing its objects, concepts and key actors. It argued that the discourse has six characteristics that operate as its frame of reference, influencing which situations and mechanisms are considered relevant. Transitional justice is comparative, technical (with multidisciplinary, legalistic and apolitical dimensions), teleological, liberal (manifested in an emphasis on violations of civil and political rights, a preference for liberal democracy and support for capitalism), multilevel and state-centric.

Chapter 3 looked into the emergence of the discourse of transitional justice. It followed the impact of four paradigmatic developments: the Argentine trials and truth commission, the Eastern European transitions, the rise of international criminal justice and the Truth and Reconciliation Commission of South Africa (SATRC). It contended that the six characteristics that the discourse of transitional justice has today can be traced to the influence of those four developments and the discussions they inspired.

The rest of the book addressed the prehistory of transitional justice. It reviewed the dominant account of the history of transitional justice that precedes its emergence as an autonomous discourse. It showed how the current characteristics of the discourse framed this narrative, highlighting those episodes that reflected them and marginalising those that did not. Chapter 4 examined the place of Nuremberg as the point of origin of transitional justice. It argued that the International Military Tribunal plays a mythological, exemplary and ancestral role in transitional justice discourse. It also demonstrated that the characteristics of the discourse shaped which transitional justice practices of the aftermath of World War II were emphasised and which were omitted from existing accounts.

Chapter 5 examined the period of time between Nuremberg and the emergence of the discourse. It challenged the dominant account of the Cold War as a barren period for transitional justice. It showed the importance of the development of human rights in that period and how the current characteristics of the discourse framed its retroactive treatment of the democratic transitions in Southern Europe. The chapter also argued that the responses to past widespread or systematic violence implemented after the proxy wars, decolonisation and non-liberal transitions have been marginalised from the discourse of transitional justice because they did not conform to its six characteristics.

This book has demonstrated the existence, source and influence of the characteristics of transitional justice discourse. It has also challenged existing historical accounts of transitional justice and uncovered a number of missing mechanisms and practices for responding to past widespread or systematic violence. The remaining pages discuss some common themes that cut across individual chapters, the implications of the findings of this study for transitional justice and wider implications for the development of ideas.

II CROSS-CUTTING THEMES

There are several themes that, like common threads, appear throughout the tapestry of the book. They are evidence of consistent ideas in the prehistory, history and present of the discourse of transitional justice. These include the normativity of transitional justice, its relationships with the socio-economic sphere and informal mechanisms.

1 *Implicit Normativity of Transitional Justice*

The characteristics of the discourse of transitional justice betray an implicit normativity. The historical conditions of emergence of the discourse in the

1990s left a lasting normative imprint that repeatedly manifests itself in the selection of episodes and mechanisms considered relevant. The most clearly normative among the six characteristics are the technical legalistic, liberal and state-centric. They are the consequence of not only the four developments that influenced the emergence of the discourse of transitional justice discussed in Chapter 3 but also of the general zeitgeist of that period. The discourse of transitional justice emerged at a historical moment when liberalism reigned as the unchallenged ideology, technical and legalistic solutions based on multilateralism were on the rise and the state bore the ultimate responsibility for upholding rights and justice. As a child of this age, the nascent discourse of transitional justice developed with these values ingrained.

Episodes and mechanisms of post–World War II, the Cold War, the period of emergence of the discourse of transitional justice and the present have been filtered out of the narrative because they ran counter to these characteristics. Spontaneous expressions of popular justice, unofficial tribunals, land reform programmes and popular tribunals were non-legalistic, non-liberal or non-state-centric initiatives that did not fit the normative frame of reference that transitional justice inherited from its process of emergence.

This shows that while the definitions of transitional justice might be apparently devoid of normative content, the discourse has an implicit set of values that frame and restrict what options are available. Accordingly, transitional justice cannot be considered a value-free discourse but is rather one with a distinct normative imprint in which legalism, state-centrism and, especially, liberalism loom large.

2 *Transitional Justice and the Economic Sphere*

The discourse of transitional justice is generally loath to engage with the economic sphere. Faithful to its liberal imprint, transitional justice is mainly concerned with situations, policies and mechanisms pertaining to the political arena of democracy, government and the rule of law rather than the economic sphere of property, labour, production and distribution. This is manifested in the type of violence recognised as warranting transitional justice's intervention (overwhelmingly physical violence and violations of civil and political rights) and in the change that transitional justice's initiatives are expected to bring about (largely limited to legal-institutional change). Hence, the economic dimension of the responses to the violence of World War II and the socio-economic policies decolonising countries adopted, including land reform, have been left out of the narrative of transitional justice.

The focus of transitional justice discourse on the political realm is a consequence of three interrelated factors: its liberal imprint, the situations that prompted and influenced its emergence and its development as an outcrop of the human rights advocacy movement. Liberalism establishes a separation between the political and economic spheres, and the former is the site of government, politics and the law where transitional justice operates. The four formative developments for the emergence of the discourse of transitional justice that were discussed in Chapter 3 influenced the discourse's focus on situations of physical violence and violations of civil and political rights and legal and institutional change. Lastly, as an outgrowth of the human rights advocacy movement, transitional justice inherited its preoccupations and priorities. These not only involve an emphasis on civil and political rights but also an option for progressive and moderate change relying on liberal law and institutions. The human rights advocacy movement gained prominence during the 1970s at a moment when the promises of radical change, from decolonisation, to the radical left, to the non-aligned movement were on the wane.[1] At this point in time, many intellectuals and activists turned to human rights and the protection of the civil and political rights of the individual.[2] This last, and moderate, utopia implied an abdication of grander collective aspirations of social justice and emancipation and a retrenchment towards the individual.[3] Transitional justice discourse emerged within this moderate matrix, and even with its slow expansion towards structural violence and economic, social and cultural rights it still has difficulty in aiming for structural and emancipatory change.

The relationship of transitional justice with the thorny issue of property illustrates the purchase of liberalism and the reluctance to seek structural socio-economic change. The restitution of property taken by the Nazis or nationalised by communist regimes has been considered an instance of transitional justice, albeit it has not been given substantial importance. In contrast, land reform in the context of decolonisation has been absent in transitional justice discourse. The restitution of property, while it involves

[1] Samuel Moyn, 'Substance, Scale, and Salience: The Recent Historiography of Human Rights' (2012) 8 *Annual Review of Law and Social Science* 123. See also Vijay Prashad, *The Darker Nations: A People's History of the Third World* (New Press; Distributed by WW Norton, 2007).

[2] Paige Arthur, 'How "Transitions" Reshaped Human Rights: A Conceptual History of Transitional Justice' (2009) 31 *Human Rights Quarterly* 321, 339.

[3] See Samuel Moyn, *The Last Utopia: Human Rights in History* (Belknap, 2010). See also David Kennedy, *A World of Struggle: How Power, Law, and Expertise Shape Global Political Economy* (Princeton University Press 2016); Samuel Moyn, *Not Enough: Human Rights in an Unequal World* (Harvard University Press, 2018).

engaging with the economic sphere, reinforces liberal property rights and signifies a return to the pre-violence status. Land reform programmes also concern the economic sphere, but instead of reinforcing liberal property rights, they undermine them by subordinating property to a social end. Instead of seeking a return to the past, land reform aims to overcome past and future violence by a fair distribution of land. The erosion of liberal rights and the aspiration of structural change mark land reform as even more foreign for transitional justice discourse than property restitution.

3 *Definition of Violence*

The definition of violence adopted is fundamental for the framing of transitional justice. As discussed in Chapter 2, the experience of violence triggers the intervention of transitional justice and brings a situation within its remit. A broader definition expands the ambit of transitional justice and allows for a wider array of mechanisms suitable to respond to such violence. Conversely, a narrower definition limits its scope and circumscribes the potential mechanisms to those that can address the violence included.

This book defined the violence forming the object of transitional justice as 'past widespread or systematic violence'. This is a broad definition but it still qualifies the violence by requiring it to be in the past and to reach a certain threshold of extension or organisation. Other definitions opt to make past human rights violations or atrocity the object of transitional justice. Defining transitional justice's object by reference to human rights violations, effectively ties the remit of transitional justice to that of human rights law. The definition ultimately adopted determines what countries, situations, mechanisms, victims and perpetrators end up within the reach of transitional justice.

The definition of violence is even more crucial in transitional justice mechanisms and policies. The SATRC was tasked with concentrating on gross violations of human rights through 'killing, abduction, torture or severe ill-treatment of any person'.[4] This narrow definition excluded a significant part of the violence of the apartheid regime. Conversely, during the decolonisation process the violence was understood as including structural discrimination and oppression.[5] The Rome Statute defines the violence the International Criminal Court (ICC) can adjudicate on as the crime of genocide, crimes

4 Promotion of National Unity and Reconciliation Act (1995), s 1.

5 Frantz Fanon, *The Wretched of the Earth* (Grove Press: Distributed by Publishers Group West, 2004) 52–57.

against humanity, war crimes and the crime of aggression.[6] Anything beyond those categories is outside its jurisdiction. The Russell Vietnam War Crimes Tribunal also used the legal figures of the crime of genocide and the crime of aggression but expanded them to include cultural genocide and aggression through economic means that are beyond the jurisdiction of the ICC.[7] Whether the violence that is the object of transitional justice is limited to killing, torture or severe ill treatment or includes structural discrimination and oppression will determine who are the victims and perpetrators, what mechanisms are available and what their goals should be. Equally, whether the scope of the crime aggression is limited to acts involving the use of armed force or includes economic behaviour would determine a different list of situations, defendants and victims. How the violence that warrants the intervention of transitional justice is defined and understood has enormous implications for the scope, mechanisms and aspirations of transitional justice.

4 *Informal Mechanisms and Non-State Actors*

Alongside the recognised state-sponsored mechanisms of transitional justice, there are other responses to past widespread or systematic violence that are implemented by non-state actors. States intitutions normally carry out trials, truth commissions, reparations and institutional reform programmes. As the discourse of transitional justice expands, practices implemented by non-state actors are also incorporated into its remit. These include conventional mechanisms that the state usually implements, such as truth commissions,[8] as well as other ways of responding to past widespread or systematic violence, such as art or performance activism.[9]

This book has shown that non-state actors have been carrying out responses to past widespread or systematic violence throughout the history and prehistory of the discourse of transitional justice. The wave of popular justice that followed the end of World War II, unofficial tribunals such as Russell's

[6] Rome Statute of the International Criminal Court, Rome 17 July 1998, 2187 UNTS 90 (RS), amended by Resolution RC/Res 6 11 June 2010, CN651 2010 Treaties-8, art 5.

[7] Marcos Zunino, 'Subversive Justice: The Russell Vietnam War Crimes Tribunal and Transitional Justice' (2016) 10 *International Journal of Transitional Justice* 211.

[8] David Androff, 'Can Civil Society Reclaim Truth? Results from a Community-Based Truth and Reconciliation Commission' (2012) 6 *International Journal of Transitional Justice* 296.

[9] Peter D. Rush and Olivera Simić, *The Arts of Transitional Justice: Culture, Activism, and Memory after Atrocity* (Springer, 2014); Arnaud Kurze, '#WarCrimes #PostConflictJustice #Balkans: Youth, Performance Activism and the Politics of Memory' (2016) 10 *International Journal of Transitional Justice* 451.

Vietnam initiative, revolutionary tribunals held by insurgent armed groups and the spontaneous purges in Portugal were all responses to past widespread or systematic violence where the state was not the protagonist. However, these informal mechanisms have been left out of the dominant narrative due to transitional justice's state-centrism and the fact that these practices often did not reflect other characteristics either.

It is important to acknowledge this parallel popular history of transitional justice that mirrors the official history where state actors monopolise the centre stage. Some of these informal responses to past widespread or systematic violence were themselves a source of abuse. Some popular practices – such as unofficial tribunals, demonstrations, unofficial memorials and public shaming of perpetrators – continue to this day. These contemporary continuators could reclaim and learn from the positive examples of the popular tradition of transitional justice that spans decades of activism across the world.

III IMPLICATIONS FOR TRANSITIONAL JUSTICE TODAY

Revealing the influence of the characteristics of the discourse allows scholars and practitioners to be aware of them and how they colour the lens of transitional justice. Many initiatives adopted to respond to past widespread or systematic violence that do not reflect the characteristics of the discourse of transitional justice have been disregarded by it. Being aware of the implicit normativity of the discourse of transitional justice can lead to more open discussions about its role and purpose.

Acknowledging the framing process opens the door for other possible and actual responses to past widespread or systematic violence that are not constrained by the characteristics of the discourse. Transitional justice responses can be less technically oriented, and political questions can be more openly addressed. A transitional justice discourse that is not dominated by legalism could facilitate innovative responses to past violence that are legitimate and beneficial. The discourse could also be less goal-oriented and recognise the importance of the processes regardless of quantifiable results. Letting go of the state-centric filter could add support to the myriad of ways in which communities deal with past violence. Transitional justice discourse could also look beyond the liberal model. The full dimension of violence, physical and structural, could be examined. Violations of economic, social and cultural rights could be given as much weight as those of civil and political rights. The prevalence of liberal democracy and capitalism does not need to banish other possible forms of political and economic organisation.

There is already movement in that direction. There is a growing scholarship on community-based initiatives that are less state-centric and legalistic.[10] Equally, there is increasing pressure to incorporate socio-economic issues from corruption to inequality in transitional justice discussions and mechanisms.[11] The link between transitional justice and liberal democracy and capitalism is also being put in question.[12] These scholarly and advocacy trends are finding some resonance in some states and international organisations. Some recent truth commissions, such as those of Kenya and Tunisia, had corruption built into their remit.[13] The 2010 'United Nations Approach to Transitional Justice' recognises the need to address the root causes of the conflict including violations of economic, social and cultural rights.[14]

These developments could eventually lead to the modification or abandonment of some of the characteristics of the discourse. They were linked to its historical emergence and have proved to be durable and influential over the last 20 years. However, as we have seen in Chapter 2, the characteristics are open to change. If other views on transitional justice become prevalent, the current characteristics could give way to different ones.

An awareness of the characteristics that frame transitional justice should not entail an outright dismissal of them. As useful as it could be to explore beyond them, some extant characteristics present clear advantages. Legalism has been successful in reining in the punitive power of the state and in preventing arbitrariness. Thus, putting in question the force of legalism and thinking about other options for confronting the past does not mean advocating for show trials or revolutionary tribunals which can be a source of indiscriminate

[10] Kieran McEvoy and Lorna McGregor, *Transitional Justice from Below: Grassroots Activism and the Struggle for Change* (Hart, 2008); Simon Robins, 'Towards Victim-Centred Transitional Justice: Understanding the Needs of Families of the Disappeared in Postconflict Nepal' (2011) 5 *International Journal of Transitional Justice* 75.

[11] Ruben Carranza, 'Plunder and Pain: Should Transitional Justice Engage with Corruption and Economic Crimes?' (2008) 2 *International Journal of Transitional Justice* 310; Ismael Muvingi, 'Sitting on Powder Kegs: Socioeconomic Rights in Transitional Societies' (2009) 3 *International Journal of Transitional Justice* 163; Louise Arbour, 'Economic and Social Justice for Societies in Transition' (2007) 40 *New York University Journal of International Law and Politics* 1; Sam Szoke-Burke, 'Not Only "Context": Why Transitional Justice Programs Can No Longer Ignore Violations of Economic and Social Rights' (2015) 50 *Texas International Law Journal* 465.

[12] Hannah Franzki and Maria Carolina Olarte, 'Understanding the Political Economy of Transitional Justice: A Critical Theory Perspective' in Susanne Buckley-Zistel and others (eds), *Transitional Justice Theories* (Routledge, 2014).

[13] Isabel Robinson, 'Truth Commissions and Anti-Corruption: Towards a Complementary Framework?' (2014) 9 *International Journal of Transitional Justice* 33.

[14] Guidance Note of the Secretary-General: United Nations Approach to Transitional Justice (10 March 2010).

punishment and unbridled repression. The state has also been the vehicle for some effective transitional justice mechanisms. Accordingly, validating community-based initiatives does not require maintaining that the state has no role to play in transitional justice. Civil and political rights protect crucial aspects of human dignity. Hence, broadening the gaze of transitional justice to include violations of economic, social and cultural rights should not lead to ignoring or relegating episodes of physical violence. Yet a broader transitional justice discourse not bound by the characteristics could benefit from further insights and experiences.

Accepting that the characteristics of the discourse have shaped historical accounts of transitional justice can lead to a re-examination of these narratives. The economic dimension of the post-war policies, the participation of the Soviets and the spate of popular justice could gain a more prominent role in historical accounts of transitional justice after World War II. Likewise, emphasising the development of human rights, the proxy wars, decolonisation, and non-liberal transitions could reverse the view of the Cold War as an empty period for transitional justice. This could lead to a rehabilitation of some of the transitional justice responses that were adopted in those forgotten episodes.

Applying a broader lens to history could enrich the present of transitional justice discourse. Many of the overlooked historical practices of transitional justice have continuators today. They were not historical dead ends but have inspired similar undertakings. There are contemporary programmes of economic reform and prosecutions targeting corporate actors. The Russell Tribunal has inspired dozens of unofficial tribunals aimed at influencing public opinion. The land question continues to haunt many countries. By taking into account hitherto occluded historical precedents, advocates and opponents of less legalistic, more community-based and more socio-economic-focused practices of transitional justice can bolster their arguments.

IV WIDER IMPLICATIONS FOR THE HISTORY OF IDEAS

The main finding of this book has wider implications for the history of ideas. The discourse of transitional justice was shaped by the historical conditions amidst which it emerged. These conditions left a lasting imprint on the discourse in the form of characteristics that framed which social practices it recognised as relevant and valid. This insight can be extended to other discourses and fields.

Discourses and ideas are historically situated. They are not timeless. They appear at a particular moment influenced by the prevailing historical conditions. These social, economic, political, epistemological and philosophical circumstances shape the contours and content of the discourses, concepts and ideas.[15] Some of these historical conditions are epochal and affect in various forms all ideas that emerge at the time. Other conditions are more specific and only influence particular ideas depending on their own process of emergence. However, there are always links between specific and epochal conditions.

The conditions of emergence of a particular idea or discourse are a combination of both types of conditions. Amongst the conditions of emergence of transitional justice, the predominance of liberalism as the prevailing political and economic ideology is clearly an epochal condition. In contrast, the creation of the ad hoc criminal tribunals that opened an international dimension for transitional justice is a more specific condition but still linked to the epochal heyday of multilateralism that followed the end of the Cold War rivalry. The establishment of the SATRC with quasi-judicial functions and nation-building objectives is a condition that is even more specific to transitional justice but also related to epochal processes of democratisation.

Other discourses and ideas that appeared during the same period as transitional justice would have been influenced by the same epochal conditions as well as by conditions specific to their process of emergence. For example, the responsibility to protect and genocide prevention discourse was shaped by similar epochal conditions to transitional justice, such as liberalism and multilateralism, but also by conditions specific to it such as the Rwanda and Srebrenica genocides and the 2005 World Summit where the principle of the responsibility to protect was endorsed.[16]

Contingency and rupture are integral to the development of discourses and ideas. The conditions of emergence should not be understood as dictating a gradual evolution towards the completion of a preordained idea. As discussed in the conclusion to Chapter 3, contingency plays a crucial role in the process of emergence of ideas or discourses. Epochal conditions themselves can be triggered by contingent events such as the assassination of Archduke Franz

[15] Michel Foucault examined the historical origins of madness, clinical medicine, prisons and sexuality. See Michel Foucault, *Folie et Déraison: Histoire de la Folie à L'Âge Classique* (Plon, 1961); Michel Foucault, *Naissance de la Clinique: Une Archéologie du Regard Médical* (Presses Universitaires de France, 1963); *Michel Foucault, Surveiller et Punir: Naissance de la Prison* (Gallimard, 1975); Michel Foucault, *Histoire de la Sexualité* (Gallimard, 1976).

[16] See UNGA Resolution 60/1 'World Summit Outcome' (16 September 2005) UN Doc A/RES/60/1, paras 138–39; David Chandler, 'The Responsibility to Protect? Imposing the 'Liberal Peace' (2004) 11 *International Peacekeeping* 59; Alex Bellamy and Ruben Reike, 'The Responsibility to Protect and International Law' (2010) 2 *Global Responsibility to Protect* 267; Cedric Ryngaert and Nico Schrijver, 'Lessons Learned from the Srebrenica Massacre: From UN Peacekeeping Reform to Legal Responsibility' (2015) 62 *Netherlands International Law Review* 219.

Ferdinand or Alexander Fleming's accidental discovery of penicillin. Personal decisions, such as Ruti Teitel's choice of the name 'transitional justice', may influence the specific historical conditions of a particular discourse or idea.[17] The emergence of discourses and ideas is thus the result of a combination of historical conditions, agency and contingency.

Discourses and ideas are not static, and they change over time. The blend of historical conditions particular to a discourse or idea helps to mould its contour and content during its process of emergence. However, later historical developments would also influence the discourse or idea. For instance, the historical conditions prevailing when the discourse of human rights emerged at the end of World War II were markedly different than those during the 1970s when the human rights advocacy movement gained momentum and those at the end of the Cold War when they became a universal language that all states use. The human rights discourse necessarily changed as it navigated those different historical periods with diverging social, economic, political, epistemological and philosophical circumstances. Discourses or ideas with an even longer historical span such as democracy or politics would have been subject to the influence of a countless succession of historical conditions. Discourses and ideas also change through the action of people and institutions that propose new meanings and reformulate existing ideas. As new consensuses emerge on the meaning of certain concepts, often influenced by historical conditions, the content and contours of a discourse or idea change.

The model presented in this book of a discourse shaped by the historical conditions of its emergence can be applied to other discourses or ideas. Interrogating the process by which a certain discourse or idea emerged could help to understand better its current form and its implicit normative framework.

This book began by describing some disparate scenes of different practices taking place in different places: a traditional reconciliation ceremony in Uganda, an international criminal trial in the Netherlands, a truth commission's hearing in the Solomon Islands and a human rights memorial in Argentina. They are held together by the discourse that recognises them as relevant practices of transitional justice. The history of the emergence of this discourse and the retrospective narrative of its origin explain why these widely diverging practices are considered examples of the same phenomenon while other comparable responses to past widespread or systematic violence are not.

[17] See Chapter 3, 80.

Bibliography

Abrahams CP, 'Lessons from the South African Experience' in Sabine Michalowski (ed), *Corporate Accountability in the Context of Transitional Justice* (Routledge, 2013).

Ackerman BA, *The Future of Liberal Revolution* (Yale University Press, 1992).

Adams KA, 'What Is Just? The Rule of Law and Natural Law in the Trials of Former East German Border Guards' (1992) 29 *Stanford Journal of International Law* 271.

'African Transitional Justice Research Network' (2016) www.transitionaljustice.org.za/, accessed 17 April 2016.

Aguilar P, 'Justice, Politics and Memory in the Spanish Transition' in Alexandra Barahona de Brito, Carmen González Enríquez and Paloma Aguilar (eds), *The Politics of Memory: Transitional Justice in Democratizing Societies* (Oxford University Press, 2001).

'Judiciary Involvement in Authoritarian Repression and Transitional Justice: The Spanish Case in Comparative Perspective' (2013) 7 *International Journal of Transitional Justice* 245.

Aguilar P and Ramírez-Barat C, 'Amnesty and Reparations without Truth or Justice in Spain' in Nico Wouters (ed), *Transitional Justice and Memory in Europe (1945–2013)* (Intersentia, 2014).

Aiken N, *Identity, Reconciliation and Transitional Justice: Overcoming Intractability in Divided Societies* (Routledge, 2013).

'Rethinking Reconciliation in Divided Societies: A Social Learning Theory of Transitional Justice' in Susanne Buckley-Zistel and others (eds), *Transitional Justice Theories* (Routledge, 2014).

Ainley K, 'Evaluating the Evaluators: Transitional Justice and the Contest of Values' (2017) 11 *International Journal of Transitional Justice* 421.

Albelo VF, *Economía Política de la Transición al Socialismo: Experiencia Cubana* (Editorial de Ciencias Sociales, 2009).

Albon M, 'Project on Justice in Times of Transition: Report of the Project's Inaugural Meeting' in Neil J Kritz (ed), *Transitional Justice: How Emerging Democracies Reckon with Former Regimes* (United States Institute of Peace Press, 1995).

Alden C, *Land, Liberation and Compromise in Southern Africa* (Palgrave Macmillan, 2009).

Alexander R, *Agrarian Reform in Latin America* (Macmillan, 1974).
Alfonsín R, 'Discurso de Asunción Ante la Asamblea Legislativa' (Buenos Aires, 10 December 1983) www.parlamentario.com/noticia-68393.html, accessed 31 July 2018.
'"Never Again" in Argentina' (1993) 4 *Journal of Democracy* 15.
Alivizatos NC and Diamandouros PN, 'Politics and the Judiciary in the Greek Transition to Democracy' in A James McAdams (ed), *Transitional Justice and the Rule of Law in New Democracies* (University of Notre Dame Press, 1997).
Allison WT, *My Lai: An American Atrocity in the Vietnam War* (Johns Hopkins University Press, 2012).
Almond M, *The Rise and Fall of Nicolae and Elena Ceauşescu* (Chapmans, 1992).
Alvargonzález D, 'Multidisciplinarity, Interdisciplinarity, Transdisciplinarity, and the Sciences' (2011) 25 *International Studies in the Philosophy of Science* 387.
Alves Raimundo F, 'The Double Face of Heroes: Transitional Justice towards the Political Police (PIDE/DGS) in Portugal's Democratization, 1974–1976' (MA thesis, University of Lisbon, 2007).
Amara T, 'Tunisia Parliament Approves Controversial Amnesty for Ben Ali-era Corruption' *Reuters* (September 2017) www.reuters.com/article/us-tunisia-politics-corruption/tunisia-parliament-approves-controversial-amnesty-for-ben-ali-era-corruption-idUSKCN1BO218, accessed 4 May 2018.
Amnesty International, *Torture in Greece: The First Torturers' Trial 1975* (Amnesty International Publications, 1977).
'Policy Statement on Impunity' in Neil J Kritz (ed), *Transitional justice: How Emerging Democracies Reckon with Former Regimes* (United States Institute of Peace Press, 1995).
Amouroux H, *Joies et Douleurs du Peuple Libéré: 6 Juin-1er Septembre 1944*, vol 8 (R Laffont, 1988).
Andersen M, 'Generals Face Judgment in Argentina: Trial of Former Leaders to Open in Argentina' *Washington Post* (21 April 1985).
Dossier Secreto: Argentina's Desaparecidos and the Myth of the 'Dirty War' (Westview Press, 1993).
Andrieu K, 'Transitional Justice: A New Discipline in Human Rights' (2010) Online Encyclopedia of Mass Violence www.sciencespo.fr/mass-violence-war-massacre-resistance/fr/document/transitional-justice-new-discipline-human-rights-0, accessed 30 July 2018.
Andrieu K, 'An Unfinished Business: Transitional Justice and Democratization in Post-Soviet Russia' (2011) 5 *International Journal of Transitional Justice* 198.
'Dealing with a "New" Grievance: Should Anticorruption Be Part of the Transitional Justice Agenda?' (2012) 11 *Journal of Human Rights* 537.
'Political Liberalism after Mass Violence: John Rawls and a "Theory" of Transitional Justice' in Susanne Buckley-Zistel and others (eds), *Transitional Justice Theories* (Routledge, 2014).
Androff D, 'Can Civil Society Reclaim Truth? Results from a Community-Based Truth and Reconciliation Commission' (2012) 6 *International Journal of Transitional Justice* 296.
Anguita E and Caparrós M, *La Voluntad: Una Historia de la Militancia Revolucionaria en la Argentina* (3rd edn, Grupo Editorial Norma, 1997).

Anker K, 'Symptoms of Sovereignty? Apologies, Indigenous Rights and Reconciliation in Australia and Canada' in Ruth Margaret Buchanan and Peer Zumbansen (eds), *Law in Transition: Human Rights, Development and Transitional Justice* (Hart, 2014).

An-Na'im AA, 'Editorial Note: From the Neocolonial "Transitional" to Indigenous Formations of Justice' (2013) 7 *International Journal of Transitional Justice* 197.

Anthonissen C, *Discourse and Human Rights Violations* (John Benjamins, 2007).

Appel H, 'Anti-Communist Justice and Founding the Post-Communist Order: Lustration and Restitution in Central Europe' (2005) 19 *East European Politics & Societies* 379.

Arbour L, 'Economic and Social Justice for Societies in Transition' (2007) 40 *New York University Journal of International Law and Politics* 1.

Arendt H, *Eichmann in Jerusalem: A Report on the Banality of Evil* (Viking Press, 1964).

Arenhovel M, 'Democratization and Transitional Justice' (2008) 15 *Democratization* 570.

Argentine Forensic Anthropology Team, 'EAAF Work by Region and Country' (2018) http://eaaf.typepad.com/eaaf_countries/, accessed 16 May 2018.

Aron R, *Histoire de l'Epuration: De l'Indulgence aux Massacres* (Fayard, 1967).

Arthur P, 'How "Transitions" Reshaped Human Rights: A Conceptual History of Transitional Justice' (2009) 31 *Human Rights Quarterly* 321.

'Introduction: Identities in Transition' in Paige Arthur (ed), *Identities in Transition: Challenges for Transitional Justice in Divided Societies* (Cambridge University Press, 2011).

Asmal K, 'Discussion on Priorities & Options' in Alex Boraine, Janet Levy and Ronel Scheffer (eds), *Dealing with the Past: Truth and Reconciliation in South Africa* (IDASA, 1994).

'Truth, Reconciliation and Justice: The South African Experience in Perspective' (2000) 63 *The Modern Law Review* 1.

Aukerman MJ, 'Extraordinary Evil, Ordinary Crime: A Framework for Understanding Transitional Justice' (2002) 15 *Harvard Human Rights Journal* 39.

Azcárate P and Jelin E, 'Memoria y Política: Movimientos de Derechos Humanos y Construcción Democrática' (1991) 1 *América Latina Hoy: Revista de Ciencias Sociales* 29.

Baars G, 'Capitalism's Victor's Justice? The Hidden Stories Behind the Prosecution of Industrialists Post-WWII' in Kevin Jon Heller and Gerry J Simpson (eds), *The Hidden Histories of War Crimes Trials* (Oxford University Press, 2013).

Babo-Soares D, 'Nahe Biti: The Philosophy and Process of Grassroots Reconciliation (and Justice) in East Timor' (2004) 5 *The Asia Pacific Journal of Anthropology* 15.

Bachmann K and Lyubashenko I, 'The Puzzle of Transitional Justice in Ukraine' (2017) 11 *International Journal of Transitional Justice* 297.

Baines E, 'The Haunting of Alice: Local Approaches to Justice and Reconciliation in Northern Uganda' (2007) 1 *International Journal of Transitional Justice* 91.

'Spirits and Social Reconstruction after Mass Violence: Rethinking Transitional Justice' (2010) 109 *African Affairs* 409.

Balint J, Evans J and McMillan N, 'Rethinking Transitional Justice, Redressing Indigenous Harm: A New Conceptual Approach' (2014) 8 *International Journal of Transitional Justice* 194.

Barrass GS, *The Great Cold War: A Journey through the Hall of Mirrors* (Stanford University Press, 2009).

Baruch MO, 'Changing Things so Everything Stays the Same: The Impossible "épuration" of French Society, 1945–2000' in Nico Wouters (ed), *Transitional Justice and Memory in Europe (1945–2013)* (Intersentia, 2014).

Bass GJ, *Stay the Hand of Vengeance: The Politics of War Crimes Tribunals* (Princeton University Press, 2000).

'Reparations as a Noble Lie' in Melissa Williams, Rosemary Nagy and Jon Elster (eds), *Transitional Justice* (New York University Press, 2012).

Bassiouni MC, *A Draft International Criminal Code and Draft Statute for an International Criminal Tribunal* (Martinus Nijhoff Publishers, 1987).

International Criminal Law, vol 1 (3rd edn, Martinus Nijhoff Publishers, 2008).

Battini M, *The Missing Italian Nuremberg: Cultural Amnesia and Postwar Politics* (Stanislao Pugliese ed, Palgrave Macmillan, 2007).

Bazyler MJ and Tuerkheimer FM, *Forgotten Trials of the Holocaust* (New York University Press, 2014).

Beattie A, 'An Evolutionary Process: Contributions of the Bundestag Inquiries into East Germany to an Understanding of the Role of Truth Commissions' (2009) 3 *International Journal of Transitional Justice* 229.

Behan C, 'Center Helps Eastern European Countries Shape Constitutions' *The University of Chicago Chronicle* (7 December 1995) http://chronicle.uchicago.edu/951207/georgia.shtml, accessed 30 July 2018.

Belgion M, *Victors' Justice: A Letter Intended to Have Been Sent to a Friend Recently in Germany* (Regnery Co, 1949).

Bell C, 'Transitional Justice, Interdisciplinarity and the State of the "Field" or "Non-Field"' (2009) 3 *International Journal of Transitional Justice* 5.

Bell C, Campbell C and Ní Aoláin F, 'Justice Discourses in Transition' (2004) 13 *Social & Legal Studies* 305.

'Transitional Justice: (Re)Conceptualising the Field' (2007) 3 *International Journal of Law in Context* 81.

Bell C and O'Rourke C, 'Does Feminism Need a Theory of Transitional Justice? An Introductory Essay' (2007) 1 *International Journal of Transitional Justice* 23.

Bellamy A and Reike R, 'The Responsibility to Protect and International Law '(2010) 2 *Global Responsibility to Protect* 267.

Benedetti F, Bonneau K and Washburn J, *Negotiating the International Criminal Court: New York to Rome, 1994–1998* (Martinus Nijhoff Publishers, 2014).

Benomar J, 'Justice after Transitions' (1993) 4 *Journal of Democracy* 3.

Berger T, *War, Guilt, and World Politics after World War II* (Cambridge University Press, 2012).

Berkley Center for Religion Peace & World Affairs, 'Charles Villa-Vicencio' (2016) http://berkleycenter.georgetown.edu/people/charles-villa-vicencio, accessed 30 July 2018.

Berman H and Spindler J, 'Soviet Comrades' Courts' (1963) 38 *Washington Law Review* 842.

Berman H and Whiting V, 'Impressions of Cuban Law' (1980) 28 *American Journal of Comparative Law* 475.

Berman J, 'The Cuban Popular Tribunals' (1969) 69 *Columbia Law Review* 1317.

'"Complex Political Victims" in the Aftermath of Mass Atrocity: Reflections on the Khmer Rouge Tribunal in Cambodia' (2016) 10 *International Journal of Transitional Justice* 46.

Bernstein H, 'Agrarian Questions of Capital and Labour: Some Theory about Land Reform (and a Periodisation)' in Ruth Hall and Lungisile Ntsebeza (eds), *The Land Question in South Africa: The Challenge of Transformation and Redistribution* (HSRC Press, 2007).

Bertschi CC, 'Lustration and the Transition to Democracy: The Cases of Poland and Bulgaria' (1994) 28 *East European Quarterly* 435.

Bickford L, *Transitional Justice* (Macmillan Reference, 2004).

'Unofficial Truth Projects' (2007) 29 *Human Rights Quarterly* 994.

Blankenburg E, 'The Purge of Lawyers after the Breakdown of the East German Communist Regime' (1995) 20 *Law & Social Inquiry* 223.

Blaser AW, 'How to Advance Human Rights without Really Trying: An Analysis of Nongovernmental Tribunals' (1992) 14 *Human Rights Quarterly* 339.

Bloxham D, 'Milestone and Mythologies: The Impact of Nuremberg' in Patricia Heberer and Jürgen Matthäus (eds), *Atrocities on Trial: Historical Perspectives on the Politics of Prosecuting War Crimes* (University of Nebraska Press, 2008).

'From the International Military Tribunal to the Subsequent Nuremberg Proceedings: The American Confrontation with Nazi Criminality Revisited' (2013) 98 *History* 567.

Bobbio N, *Liberalism and Democracy* (Verso, 2005).

Boister N and Cryer R, *The Tokyo International Military Tribunal: A Reappraisal* (Oxford University Press, 2008).

Boraine A, 'Introduction' in Alex Boraine, Janet Levy and Ronel Scheffer (eds), *Dealing with the Past: Truth and Reconciliation in South Africa* (IDASA, 1994).

'Introduction' in Alex Boraine and Janet Levy (eds), *The Healing of a Nation?* (Justice in Transition, 1995).

A Country Unmasked: South Africa's Truth and Reconciliation Commission (Oxford University Press, 2000).

'The Language of Potential' in Wilmot James and Linda Van de Vijver (eds), *After the TRC: Reflections on Truth and Reconciliation in South Africa* (Ohio University Press, 2001).

'Truth and Reconciliation Commission in South Africa Amnesty: The Price of Peace' in Jon Elster (ed), *Retribution and Reparation in the Transition to Democracy* (Cambridge University Press, 2006).

Boraine A and Levy J, *The Healing of a Nation?* (Justice in Transition, 1995).

Boraine A, Levy J and Scheffer R, *Dealing with the Past: Truth and Reconciliation in South Africa* (IDASA, 1994).

Borge T, 'Justice in Nicaragua is no Longer the Same' in Bruce Marcus (ed), *Nicaragua: The Sandinista People's Revolution: Speeches by Sandinista Leaders* (Pathfinder Press, 1985).

Borges JL, *Ficciones* (Emecé, 1971).

'La Creación Y P.H. Gosse', *Otras Inquisiciones* (Emecé, 1971).

Borgwardt E, *A New Deal for the World: America's Vision for Human Rights* (Harvard University Press, 2005).

'Re-Examining Nuremberg as a New Deal Institution: Politics, Culture and the Limits of Law in Generating Human Rights Norms' (2005) 23 *Berkeley Journal of International Law*.

'A New Deal for the Nuremberg Trial: The Limits of Law in Generating Human Rights Norms' (2008) 26 *Law and History Review* 679.

Borowiak C, 'The World Tribunal on Iraq: Citizens' Tribunals and the Struggle for Accountability' (2008) 30 *New Political Science* 161.

'Polish Court: Martial Law Imposed by "Criminal Group"' *Reuters* (12 January 2012) www.reuters.com/article/us-poland-communists-idUSTRE80B1VA20120112, accessed 30 July 2018.

Bourke J, *An Intimate History of Killing: Face-to-Face Killing in Twentieth-Century Warfare* (Basic Books, 1999).

Brackman AC, *The Other Nuremberg: The Untold Story of the Tokyo War Crimes Trials* (Morrow, 1987).

Bradley M, 'More than Misfortune: Recognizing Natural Disasters as a Concern for Transitional Justice' (2017) 11 *International Journal of Transitional Justice* 400.

Brems E, 'Transitional Justice in the Case Law of the European Court of Human Rights' (2011) 5 *International Journal of Transitional Justice* 282.

Brown S, 'The National Accord, Impunity, and the Fragile Peace in Kenya' in Chandra Lekha Sriram and others (eds), *Transitional Justice and Peacebuilding on the Ground: Victims and Ex-Combatants* (Routledge, 2013).

Brown W, 'Neo-Liberalism and the End of Liberal Democracy' (2003) 7 *Theory & Event*.

Bruce G, 'East Germany' in Lavinia Stan (ed), *Transitional Justice in Eastern Europe and the Former Soviet Union: Reckoning with the Communist Past* (Routledge, 2008).

Brysk A, 'The Political Impact of Argentina's Human Rights Movement: Social Movements, Transition and Democratization' (Stanford University, 1990).

The Politics of Human Rights in Argentina: Protest, Change, and Democratization (Stanford University Press, 1994).

'The Politics of Measurement: The Contested Count of the Disappeared in Argentina' (1994) 16 *Human Rights Quarterly* 676.

Brzezinski M, 'Giving Hitler Hell' *The Washington Post* (24 July 2005) www.washingtonpost.com/wp-dyn/content/article/2005/07/21/AR2005072101680.html, accessed 30 July 2018.

Buckley-Zistel S, 'Narrative Truths: On the Construction of the Past in Truth Commissions' in Susanne Buckley-Zistel and others (eds), *Transitional Justice Theories* (Routledge, 2014).

'Transitional Justice Theories: An Introduction' in Susanne Buckley-Zistel and others (eds), *Transitional Justice Theories* (Routledge, 2014).

'New Release "Perpetrators and Perpetration of Mass Violence"' (2018) 117 *TJnetwork Digest*.

Buckley-Zistel S and Schäfer S, *Memorials in Times of Transition* (Intersentia, 2014).

Burnet JE, '(In)Justice: Truth, Reconciliation, and Revenge in Rwanda's Gacaca' in Alexander Laban Hinton (ed), *Transitional Justice: Global Mechanisms and Local Realities after Genocide and Mass Violence* (Rutgers University Press, 2010).

Burt JM, 'Guilty as Charged: The Trial of Former Peruvian President Alberto Fujimori for Human Rights Violations' (2009) 3 *International Journal of Transitional Justice* 384.

Burton M, 'Reparation, Amnesty and a National Archive' in Wilmot James and Linda Van de Vijver (eds), *After the TRC: Reflections on Truth and Reconciliation in South Africa* (Ohio University Press, 2001).

Calhoun N, *Dilemmas of Justice in Eastern Europe's Democratic Transitions* (Palgrave Macmillan, 2004).

Camarasa JA, Felice R and González D, *El Juicio: Proceso al Horror* (Sudamericana/ Planeta, 1985).

'Cambridge Transitional Justice Research Network' (2016) www.ctjrn.law.cam.ac.uk/, accessed 30 July 2018.

Campbell C and Ni Aolain F, 'The Paradox of Transition in Conflicted Democracies' (2005) 27 *Human Rights Quarterly* 172.

Campbell K, 'The Gender of Transitional Justice: Law, Sexual Violence and the International Criminal Tribunal for the Former Yugoslavia' (2007) 1 *International Journal of Transitional Justice* 411.

'The Laws of Memory: The ICTY, the Archive, and Transitional Justice' (2013) 22 *Social & Legal Studies* 247.

Carothers T, 'Western Civil-Society Aid to Eastern Europe and the Former Soviet Union' (1999) 8 *East European Constitutional Review* 54.

Carranza R, 'Plunder and Pain: Should Transitional Justice Engage with Corruption and Economic Crimes?' (2008) 2 *International Journal of Transitional Justice* 310.

Cassese A, 'Reflections on International Criminal Justice' (1998) 61 *Modern Law Review* 1.

CELS, *Autoamnistia: Legalizar La Impunidad* (1982) www.cels.org.ar/common/documentos/autoamnistia.pdf, accessed 30 July 2018.

'Proceso de Justicia: Estadísticas' (2018) www.cels.org.ar/web/estadisticas-delitos-de-lesa-humanidad/, accessed 16 May 2018.

'Centre for Transitional Justice and Post-Conflict Reconstruction' (2018) http://tjcentre.uwo.ca/index.html, accessed 30 July 2018.

Cepl V, 'A Note on the Restitution of Property in Post-Communist Czechoslovakia' (1991) 7 *Journal of Communist Studies* 368.

'Ritual Sacrifices' (1992) 1 *East European Constitutional Review*.

Chamberlain ME, *The Longman Companion to European Decolonisation in the Twentieth Century* (Credo Reference ed, Longman, 1998).

Chandler D, 'The Responsibility to Protect? Imposing the 'Liberal Peace' (2004) 11 *International Peacekeeping* 59.

Chenivesse P and Piranio C, 'What Price Justice? On the Evolving Notion of "Right to Fair Trial" from Nuremberg to The Hague' (2011) 24 *Cambridge Review of International Affairs* 403.

Cherry J, 'Historical Truth: Something to Fight for' in Charles Villa-Vicencio and Wilhelm Verwoerd (eds), *Looking Back, Reaching Forward: Reflections on the Truth and Reconciliation Commission of South Africa* (University of Cape Town Press, 2000).

Cho C, 'Manufacturing a German Model of Liberal Capitalism: The Political Economy of the German Cartel Law in the Early Postwar Period' (2003) 10 *Journal of International and Area Studies* 41.

Christodoulidis E and Veitch S, 'Reconciliation as Surrender: Configurations of Responsibility and Memory' in François Du Bois and Antje Du Bois-Pedain (eds), *Justice and Reconciliation in Post-Apartheid South Africa* (Cambridge University Press, 2008).

Christodoulidis EA, '"Truth and Reconciliation" as Risks' (2000) 9 *Social & Legal Studies* 179.

Churchill WSL, 'The Sinews of Peace' (Fulton, Missouri, 5 March 1946) www.winstonchurchill.org/resources/speeches/235-1946-1963-elder-statesman/120-the-sinews-of-peace, accessed 30 July 2018.

Ciorciari, John and Heindel A, *Hybrid Justice: The Extraordinary Chambers in the Courts of Cambodia* (University of Michigan Press, 2014).

Clarke KM and Goodale M, 'Introduction: Understanding the Multiplicity of Justice' in Kamari Maxine Clarke and Mark Goodale (eds), *Mirrors of Justice: Law and Power in the Post-Cold War Era* (Cambridge University Press, 2010).

Mirrors of Justice: Law and Power in the Post-Cold War Era (Cambridge University Press, 2010).

Clark JN, 'Reconciliation through Remembrance? War Memorials and the Victims of Vukovar' (2013) 7 *International Journal of Transitional Justice* 116.

Clark P, 'Hybridity, Holism, and "Traditional" Justice: The Case of the Gacaca Courts in Post-Genocide Rwanda' (2007) 39 *The George Washington International Law Review* 765.

Clark P and Kaufman ZD, *After Genocide: Transitional Justice, Post-Conflict Reconstruction and Reconciliation in Rwanda and Beyond* (C Hurst, 2008).

Clark P and Palmer N, 'Challenging Transitional Justice' in Nicola Palmer, Phil Clark and Danielle Granville (eds), *Critical Perspectives in Transitional Justice* (Intersentia, 2012).

Cohen D, 'Transitional Justice in Divided Germany after 1945' in Jon Elster (ed), *Retribution and Reparation in the Transition to Democracy* (Cambridge University Press, 2006).

Cole CM, *Performing South Africa's Truth Commission: Stages of Transition* (Indiana University Press, 2010).

Cole E, 'Transitional Justice and the Reform of History Education' (2007) 1 *International Journal of Transitional Justice* 115.

Collins C, *Post-Transitional Justice: Human Rights Trials in Chile and El Salvador* (Pennsylvania State University Press, 2010).

'Human Rights Trials in Chile During and After the "Pinochet Years"' (2010) 4 *International Journal of Transitional Justice* 67.

'The End of Impunity? "Late Justice" and Post-Transitional Prosecutions in Latin America' in Nicola Palmer, Phil Clark and Danielle Granville (eds), *Critical Perspectives in Transitional Justice* (Intersentia, 2012).

'Paraguay: Accountability in the Shadow of Stroessner' in Elin Skaar, Jemima García-Godos and Cath Collins (eds), *Transitional Justice in Latin America: The Uneven Road from Impunity towards Accountability* (Routledge, 2016).

Colvin C, 'Overview of the Reparations Program in South Africa' in Pablo De Greiff (ed), *The Handbook of Reparations* (Oxford University Press, 2008).

Comisión para el Esclarecimiento Histórico, *Guatemala Memoria del Silencio* (F&G Editores, 1999).

CONADEP, *Nunca Mas:(Never Again): A Report* (Faber in association with Index on Censorship, 1986).

Cooper B, 'Introduction' in Belinda Cooper (ed), *War Crimes: The Legacy of Nuremberg* (TV Books, 1999).

Cooper F, *Africa since 1940: The Past of the Present* (Cambridge University Press, 2002).

Colonialism in Question: Theory, Knowledge, History (University of California Press, 2005).

Costa Pinto A, 'Settling Accounts with the Past in a Troubled Transition to Democracy: The Portuguese Case' in Alexandra Barahona de Brito, Carmen González Enríquez and Paloma Aguilar (eds), *The Politics of Memory: Transitional Justice in Democratizing Societies* (Oxford University Press, 2001).

'Authoritarian Legacies, Transitional Justice and State Crisis in Portugal's Democratization' (2006) 13 *Democratization* 173.

Crawford J, 'The Drafting of the Rome Statute' in Philippe Sands (ed), *From Nuremberg to The Hague: The Future of International Criminal Justice* (Cambridge University Press, 2003).

Crenzel E, 'Argentina's National Commission on the Disappearance of Persons: Contributions to Transitional Justice' (2008) 2 *The International Journal of Transitional Justice* 173.

'Between the Voices of the State and the Human Rights Movement: Never Again and the Memories of the Disappeared in Argentina' (2011) 44 *Journal of Social History* 1063.

Crenzel EA, *Memory of the Argentina Disappearances the Political History of Nunca Más* (Routledge, 2012).

Crocker DA, 'Reckoning with Past Wrongs: A Normative Framework' (1999) 13 *Ethics & International Affairs* 43.

Crowe DM, *War Crimes, Genocide, and Justice: A Global History* (Palgrave Macmillan, 2014).

Czarnota A, 'Lustration, Decommunisation and the Rule of Law' (2009) 1 *Hague Journal on the Rule of Law* 307.

Dahl HF, 'Dealing with the Past in Scandinavia: Legal Purges and Popular Memories of Nazism and World War II in Denmark and Norway after 1945' in Jon Elster (ed), *Retribution and Reparation in the Transition to Democracy* (Cambridge University Press, 2006).

Daly E, 'Truth Skepticism: An Inquiry into the Value of Truth in Times of Transition' (2008) 2 *International Journal of Transitional Justice* 23.

Damşa L, *The Transformation of Property Regimes and Transitional Justice in Central Eastern Europe: In Search of a Theory* (Springer, 2017).

Dancy G, 'Impact Assessment, Not Evaluation: Defining a Limited Role for Positivism in the Study of Transitional Justice' (2010) 4 *International Journal of Transitional Justice* 355.

Dapía SG, '"This Is Not a Universe": An Approach to Borges's "Tlön, Uqbar, Orbis Tertius"' (1997) 26 *Chasqui* 94.

David R, 'Lustration Laws in Action: The Motives and Evaluation of Lustration Policy in the Czech Republic and Poland (1989–2001)' (2003) 28 *Law & Social Inquiry* 387.

David R and Hazard J, *Le Droit Soviétique: Les Données Fondamentales du Droit Soviétique* (Librairie Générale de Droit et de Jurisprudence, 1954).

Davis L, 'The European Union and Transitional Justice' (European Peacebuilding Liaison Office, 2014).

Deák I, 'Political Justice in Austria and Hungary after World War II' in Jon Elster (ed), *Retribution and Reparation in the Transition to Democracy* (Cambridge University Press, 2006).

De Brito AB, 'Truth and Justice in the Consolidation of Democracy in Chile and Uruguay' (1993) 46 *Parliamentary Affairs* 579.

De Brito AB, González Enríquez C and Aguilar Fernández P, 'Bibliographical Survey' in Alexandra Barahona de Brito, Carmen González Enríquez and Paloma Aguilar Fernández (eds), *The Politics of Memory: Transitional Justice in Democratizing Societies* (Oxford University Press, 2001).

'Introduction' in Alexandra Barahona de Brito, Carmen González Enríquez and Paloma Aguilar Fernández (eds), *The Politics of Memory: Transitional Justice in Democratizing Societies* (Oxford University Press, 2001).

The Politics of Memory: Transitional Justice in Democratizing Societies (Oxford University Press, 2001).

DeFalco RC, 'Accounting for Famine at the Extraordinary Chambers in the Courts of Cambodia: The Crimes against Humanity of Extermination, Inhumane Acts and Persecution' (2011) 5 *International Journal of Transitional Justice* 142.

De Gaulle C, 'Letter from de Gaulle to Sartre' in John Duffett (ed), *Against the Crime of Silence: Proceedings of the Russell International War Crimes Tribunal, Stockholm, Copenhagen* (Bertrand Russell Peace Foundation, 1968).

De Greiff P, *The Handbook of Reparations* (Oxford University Press, 2008).

'A Normative Conception of Transitional Justice' (2010) 50 *Politorbis* 17.

'Theorizing Transitional Justice' in Melissa Williams, Rosemary Nagy and Jon Elster (eds), *Transitional Justice* (New York University Press, 2012).

'Transitional Justice Gets its Own Encyclopedia: Vitamins or Steroids for a Developing Field?' (2013) 7 *International Journal of Transitional Justice* 547.

De Greiff P and Mayer-Rieckh A, *Justice as Prevention: Vetting Public Employees in Transitional Societies* (Social Science Research Council, 2007).

De Lange J, 'The Historical Context, Legal Origins and Philosophical Foundation of the South African Truth and Reconciliation Commission' in Charles Villa-Vicencio and Wilhelm Verwoerd (eds), *Looking Back, Reaching Forward: Reflections on the Truth and Reconciliation Commission of South Africa* (University of Cape Town Press, 2000).

Desmarais J, *Femmes Tondues: Coupables, Amoureuses, Victimes* (Les Presses de l'Université Laval, 2010).

Deutscher Bundestag, *Materialien Der Enquete-Kommission 'Aufarbeitung von Geschichte Und Folgen Der SED-Diktatur in Deutschland'* (Suhrkamp, 1995).

Materialien Der Enquete-Kommission 'Uberwindung Der Folgen Der SED-Diktatur Im Prozeß Der Deutschen Einheit' (Suhrkamp, 1999).

Diamandouros PN, 'Regime Change and the Prospects for Democracy in Greece: 1974–1983' in Guillermo O'Donnell, Philippe C Schmitter and Laurence Whitehead (eds), *Transitions from Authoritarian Rule: Southern Europe* (Johns Hopkins University Press, 1986).

Diamond LJ, Linz JJ and Lipset SM, *Politics in Developing Countries: Comparing Experiences with Democracy* (L Rienner Publishers, 1990).

Drumbl MA, '"Germans Are the Lords and Poles Are the Servants": The Trial of Arthur Greiser in Poland, 1946', *The Hidden Histories of War Crimes Trials* (Oxford University Press, 2013).

Dube SI, 'Transitional Justice beyond the Normative: Towards a Literary Theory of Political Transitions' (2011) 5 *International Journal of Transitional Justice* 177.

Dubois J, *The Devil's Chemists* (Beacon Press, 1952).

Du Bois-Pedain A, *Transitional Amnesty in South Africa* (Cambridge University Press, 2007).

Dudai R, 'A Model for Dealing with the Past in the Israeli Palestinian Context' (2007) 1 *International Journal of Transitional Justice* 249.

Dudai R and Cohen H, 'Dealing with the Past When the Conflict Is Still Present: Civil Society Truth-Seeking Initiatives in the Israeli-Palestinian Conflict' in Rosalind Shaw, Lars Waldorf and Pierre Hazan (eds), *Localizing Transitional Justice: Interventions and Priorities after Mass Violence* (Stanford University Press, 2010).

Dugard J, 'Is the Truth and Reconciliation Process Compatible with International Law: An Unanswered Question' (1997) *South African Journal on Human Rights* 258.

Duggan C, '"Show Me Your Impact": Evaluating Transitional Justice in Contested Spaces' (2012) 35 *Evaluation and Program Planning* 199.

Duryea Smith C, 'Introduction' in Neil J Kritz (ed), *Transitional Justice: How Emerging Democracies Reckon with Former Regimes* (United States Institute of Peace Press, 1995).

Du Toit A, 'South African Response' in Alex Boraine, Janet Levy and Ronel Scheffer (eds), *Dealing with the Past: Truth and Reconciliation in South Africa* (IDASA, 1994).

Dworkin R, *Sovereign Virtue: The Theory and Practice of Equality* (Harvard University Press, 2000).

Elander M, 'The Victim's Address: Expressivism and the Victim at the Extraordinary Chambers in the Courts of Cambodia' (2013) 7 *International Journal of Transitional Justice* 95.

El Gantri R, 'Tunisia in Transition: One Year after the Creation of the Truth and Dignity Commission' (ICTJ, 2015) www.ictj.org/sites/default/files/ICTJ-Briefing-Tunisia-TJLaw-2015.pdf accessed 30 July 2018.

Ellis MS, 'Purging the Past: The Current State of Lustration Laws in the Former Communist Bloc' (1996) 59 *Law & Contemporary Problems* 181.

Elster J, 'Coming to Terms with the Past: A Framework for the Study of Justice in the Transition to Democracy' (1998) 39 *European Journal of Sociology/Archives Européennes de Sociologie* 7.

Closing the Books: Transitional Justice in Historical Perspective (Cambridge University Press, 2004).

'Justice, Truth, Peace' in Melissa Williams, Rosemary Nagy and Jon Elster (eds), *Transitional Justice* (New York University Press, 2012).

Elster J, Preuss U and Offe C, *Institutional Design in Post-Communist Societies: Rebuilding the Ship at Sea* (Cambridge University Press, 1998).

Engstrom P, 'Transitional Justice and Ongoing Conflict' in Chandra Lekha Sriram and others (eds), *Transitional Justice and Peacebuilding on the Ground: Victims and Ex-Combatants* (Routledge, 2013).

Encarnación OG, *Democracy without Justice in Spain: The Politics of Forgetting* (University of Pennsylvania Press, 2014).

Ensalaco M, 'Truth Commissions for Chile and El Salvador: A Report and Assessment' (1994) 16 *Human Rights Quarterly* 656.

Espíndola Mata J, *Transitional Justice after German Reunification: Exposing Unofficial Collaborators* (Cambridge University Press, 2015).

Ethier D, *Democratic Transition and Consolidation in Southern Europe, Latin America and Southeast Asia* (Macmillan, 1990).

Evans S, 'Good Behaviour Paroles de Kock' *Mail & Guardian* (30 January 2015) http://mg.co.za/article/2015–01-30-good-behaviour-pardons-de-kock, accessed 30 July 2018.

Falk R, 'War, War Crimes, Power, and Justice: Toward a Jurisprudence of Conscience' (2013) 21 *Transnational Law & Contemporary Problems* 667.

Fanon F, *The Wretched of the Earth* (Grove Press; Distributed by Publishers Group West, 2004).

Fay D and James D, 'Giving Land Back or Righting Wrongs? Comparative Issues in the Study of Land Restitution' in Cherryl Walker and others (eds), *Land, Memory, Reconstruction, and Justice: Perspectives on Land Claims in South Africa* (Ohio University Press, 2010).

Feitlowitz M, *A Lexicon of Terror: Argentina and the Legacies of Torture* (Oxford University Press, 1998).

Fernandez L, 'Post-TRC Prosecutions in South Africa' in Gerhard Werle (ed), *Justice in Transition: Prosecution and Amnesty in Germany and South Africa* (BWV, 2006).

Fichter M, 'Non-State Organizations and the Problems of Redemocratization' in John Herz (ed), *From Dictatorship to Democracy: Coping with the Legacies of Authoritarianism and Totalitarianism* (Greenwood, 1982).

Firchow P, 'Must Our Communities Bleed to Receive Social Services? Development Projects and Collective Reparations Schemes in Colombia' (2013) 8 *Journal of Peacebuilding & Development* 50.

Fiss O, 'The Death of a Public Intellectual' (1995) 104 *The Yale Law Journal* 1187.

Fleischer W, 'U.S. Is "Guilty" Says "Tribunal"' *The Washington Post* (10 May 1967).

Fletcher L, 'Editorial Note' (2015) 9 *International Journal of Transitional Justice* 1.

Fletcher L, Weinstein HM and Rowen J, 'Context, Timing and the Dynamics of Transitional Justice: A Historical Perspective' (2009) 31 *Human Rights Quarterly* 163.

Fogelson S, 'The Nuremberg Legacy: An Unfulfilled Promise' (1990) 63 *Southern California Law Review* 833.

Forsythe DP, 'Forum: Transitional Justice: The Quest for Theory to Inform Policy' (2011) 13 *International Studies Review* 554.

Foucault M, *Folie et Déraison: Histoire de la Folie à L'Âge Classique* (Plon, 1961).

Naissance de la Clinique: Une Archéologie du Regard Médical (Presses universitaires de France, 1963).

L'Archéologie du Savoir (Gallimard, 1969).

Surveiller et Punir: Naissance de la Prison (Gallimard, 1975).

Histoire de la Sexualité (Gallimard, 1976).

'Nietzsche, Genealogy, History' in Bouchard, DF (ed), *Language, Counter-Memory, Practice: Selected Essays and Interviews* (Cornell University Press, 1977).

'Nietzsche, La Généalogie, l'Histoire' in Daniel Defert and François Ewald (eds), *Dits et Écrits, 1954–1988 (Vol. I)* (Gallimard, 2001).

Franck TM, *The Power of Legitimacy among Nations* (Oxford University Press, 1990).

Franzki H and Olarte MC, 'Understanding the Political Economy of Transitional Justice: A Critical Theory Perspective' in Susanne Buckley-Zistel and others (eds), *Transitional Justice Theories* (Routledge, 2014).

Freeman M, 'Transitional Justice: Fundamental Goals and Unavoidable Complications' (2000) 28 *Manitoba Law Journal* 113.

Necessary Evils: Amnesties and the Search for Justice (Cambridge University Press, 2009).

Frente Sandinista de Liberación Nacional, 'Entrevista de Sepla Con Gladys Zalaquet, Representante del FSLN', *Nicaragua, Elementos Históricos, Estratégicos y Tácticos de la Revolución* (Seminario Permanente sobre Latino América, 1979).

Friedheim D, 'Accelerating Collapse: The East German Road' in Yossi Shain and Juan José Linz (eds), *Between States: Interim Governments and Democratic Transitions* (Cambridge University Press, 1995).

Friedman J, 'Law and Politics in the Subsequent Nuremberg Trials, 1946–1949' in Patricia Heberer and Jürgen Matthäus (eds), *Atrocities on Trial: Historical Perspectives on the Politics of Prosecuting War Crimes* (University of Nebraska Press, 2008).

Friedman M, *Capitalism and Freedom* (University of Chicago Press, 1963).

Fullard M and Rousseau N, 'Truth Telling, Identities, and Power in South Africa and Guatemala' in Paige Arthur (ed), *Identities in Transition: Challenges for Transitional Justice in Divided Societies* (Cambridge University Press, 2011).

Gadamer H-G, *Truth and Method* (William Glen-Doepel tr, Sheed and Ward, 1979).

Gall C, 'In Tunisia, a Mission of Justice and a Moment of Reckoning' *New York Times* (November 2015) www.nytimes.com/2015/11/07/world/africa/in-tunisia-a-mission-of-justice-and-a-moment-of-reckoning.html, accessed 30 July 2018.

Garay Salamanca LJ, *Memoria y Reparación: Elementos para una Justicia Transicional pro Víctima* (Universidad Externado de Colombia, 2012).

García-Godos J, 'Victim Reparations in the Peruvian Truth Commission and the Challenge of Historical Interpretation' (2008) 2 *International Journal of Transitional Justice* 63.

Garnsey E, 'Rewinding and Unwinding: Art and Justice in Times of Political Transition' (2016) 10 *International Journal of Transitional Justice* 471.

Garro AM, 'Nine Years of Transition to Democracy in Argentina: Partial Failure or Qualified Success?' (1993) 31 *Columbia Journal of Transnational Law* 1.

Garro AM and Dahl H, 'Legal Accountability for Human Rights Violations in Argentina: One Step Forward and Two Steps Backward' (1987) 8 *Human Rights Law Journal* 283.

Garton Ash T, *We the People: The Revolution of '89 Witnessed in Warsaw, Budapest, Berlin & Prague* (Granta Books, 1990).

'The Puzzle of Central Europe' (1999) *The New York Review of Books* www.nybooks.com/articles/1999/03/18/the-puzzle-of-central-europe/, accessed 30 July 2018.

'General Wojciech Jaruzelski - Obituary' *The Telegraph* (25 May 2014) www.telegraph.co.uk/news/obituaries/military-obituaries/10855827/General-Wojciech-Jaruzelski-obituary.html, accessed 30 July 2018.

Gibson J, *Overcoming Apartheid: Can Truth Reconcile a Divided Nation?* (Russell Sage Foundation, 2004).

Overcoming Historical Injustices: Land Reconciliation in South Africa (Cambridge University Press, 2009).

Gibson J, Sonis J and Hean S, 'Cambodians' Support for the Rule of Law on the Eve of the Khmer Rouge Trials' (2010) 4 *International Journal of Transitional Justice* 377.

Gillespie CG, 'Models of Democratic Transition in South America: Negotiated Reform Versus Democratic Rupture' in Diane Ethier (ed), *Democratic Transition and Consolidation in Southern Europe, Latin America and Southeast Asia* (Macmillan, 1990).

Ginsburgs G, *Moscow's Road to Nuremberg: The Soviet Background to the Trial* (M Nijhoff, 1996).

Giussani P, *Los Días de Alfonsín* (Legasa, 1986).

Giussani P and Alfonsín R, *¿Por Qué, Doctor Alfonsín?* (Sudamericana/Planeta, 1987).

Gobodo-Madikizela P, *A Human Being Died That Night: A South African Story of Forgiveness* (Houghton Mifflin, 2004).

Gocking R, 'Ghana's Public Tribunals: An Experiment in Revolutionary Justice' (1996) 95 *African Affairs* 197.

Goetz C, 'The Fifth Annual Ernst C. Steifel Symposium: 1945–1995: Critical Perspectives on the Nuremberg Trials and State Accountability, Panel 1' (1995) 12 *New York Law School Journal of Human Rights* 453.

Goodman M, 'After the Wall: The Legal Ramifications of the East German Border Guard Trials in Unified Germany' (1996) 29 *Cornell International Law Journal* 727.

Gosse PH, *Omphalos: An Attempt to Untie the Geological Knot* (John Van Voorst, 1857).

Gottesman E, *Cambodia after the Khmer Rouge: Inside the Politics of Nation Building* (Yale University Press, 2003).

Graham-Yooll A, 'Argentina: The State of Transition 1983–85' (1985) 7 *Third World Quarterly* 573.

Gramer RU, 'From Decartelization to Reconcentration: The Mixed Legacy of American-Led Corporate Reconstruction in Germany' in Detlef Junker (ed), *The United States and Germany in the Era of the Cold War, 1945–1990* (Cambridge University Press, 2004).

Granger Blair W, 'Russell Discusses His Plan for "War-Crime Trial"' *New York Times* (17 November 1966).

Gray J, *Liberalism* (Open University Press, 1995).

Graybill L, *Truth and Reconciliation in South Africa: Miracle or Model?* (Lynne Rienner Publishers, 2002).
Gready P, *The Era of Transitional Justice: The Aftermath of the Truth and Reconciliation Commission in South Africa and Beyond* (Routledge, 2011).
Gready P and Robins S, 'From Transitional to Transformative Justice: A New Agenda for Practice' (2014) 8 *International Journal of Transitional Justice* 339.
Grodsky B, 'Justice without Transition: Truth Commissions in the Context of Repressive Rule' (2008) 9 *Human Rights Review* 281.
'Re-Ordering Justice: Towards a New Methodological Approach to Studying Transitional Justice' (2009) 46 *Journal of Peace Research* 819.
Grosescu R, 'Judging Communist Crimes in Romania: Transnational and Global Influences' (2017) 11 *International Journal of Transitional Justice* 505.
Grunebaum H, *Memorializing the Past: Everyday Life in South Africa after the Truth and Reconciliation Commission* (Transaction Publishers, 2011).
Guest I, *Behind the Disappearances: Argentina's Dirty War against Human Rights and the United Nations* (University of Pennsylvania Press, 1990).
Guilhot N, 'The Transition to the Human World of Democracy: Notes for a History of the Concept of Transition, from Early Marxism to 1989' (2002) 5 *European Journal of Social Theory* 219.
Guillemin J, 'National Security, Weapons of Mass Destruction at the Tokyo War Crimes Trial, 1946 – 1948' in Kamari Maxine Clarke and Mark Goodale (eds), *Mirrors of Justice: Law and Power in the Post-Cold War Era* (Cambridge University Press, 2010).
Hall R, 'Transforming Rural South Africa? Taking Stock of Land Reform' in Ruth Hall and Lungisile Ntsebeza (eds), *The Land Question in South Africa: The Challenge of Transformation and Redistribution* (HSRC Press, 2007).
Hansen TO, 'Transitional Justice: Toward a Differentiated Theory' (2011) 13 *Oregon Review of International Law* 1.
'The Vertical and Horizontal Expansion of Transitional Justice: Explanations and Implications for a Contested Field' in Susanne Buckley-Zistel and others (eds), *Transitional Justice Theories* (Routledge, 2014).
Harbeson J, *Nation-Building in Kenya: The Role of Land Reform* (Northwestern University Press, 1973).
Hargreaves J, *Decolonization in Africa* (Longman, 1988).
Harsch E, *Thomas Sankara: An African Revolutionary* (Ohio University Press, 2014).
Havel V, 'The Power of the Powerless' in John Keane (ed), *The Power of the Powerless: Citizens against the State in Central-Eastern Europe* (Hutchinson, 1985).
Havel V and Michnik A, 'The Period after 1989' (2009) 15 *Common Knowledge* 319.
Hawkins D, 'Human Rights Norms and Networks in Authoritarian Chile' in Sanjeev Khagram, James V Riker and Kathryn Sikkink (eds), *Restructuring World Politics: Transnational Social Movements, Networks, and Norms* (University of Minnesota Press, 2002).
Hayner P, 'Fifteen Truth Commissions – 1974 to 1994: A Comparative Study' (1994) 16 *Human Rights Quarterly* 597.
'Same Species, Different Animal: How South Africa Compares to Truth Commissions Worldwide' in Charles Villa-Vicencio and Wilhelm Verwoerd (eds),

Looking Back, Reaching Forward: Reflections on the Truth and Reconciliation Commission of South Africa (University of Cape Town Press, 2000).
Unspeakable Truths: Confronting State Terror and Atrocity (Routledge, 2001).
'International Center for Transitional Justice (ICTJ)' in David Forsythe (ed), *Encyclopedia of Human Rights* (Oxford University Press, 2009).
Hazan P, *Justice in a Time of War: The True Story behind the International Criminal Tribunal for the Former Yugoslavia* (Texas A & M University Press, 2004).
Hegburg K, 'The Law Is Such as It Is: Reparations, "Historical Reality," and the Legal Order in the Czech Republic' in Alexander Laban Hinton, Thomas La Pointe and Douglas Irvin-Erickson (eds), *Hidden Genocides: Power, Knowledge, Memory* (Rutgers University Press, 2013).
Heller KJ, *The Nuremberg Military Tribunals and the Origins of International Criminal Law* (Oxford University Press, 2011).
Henkin AH, 'Conference Report', *State Crimes: Punishment or Pardon* (The Aspen Institute, 1989).
Henry N, 'Witness to Rape: The Limits and Potential of International War Crimes Trials for Victims of Wartime Sexual Violence' (2008) 3 *International Journal of Transitional Justice* 114.
'From Reconciliation to Transitional Justice: The Contours of Redress Politics in Established Democracies' (2015) 9 *International Journal of Transitional Justice* 199.
Herz JH, 'On Reestablishing Democracy after the Downfall of Authoritarian or Dictatorial Regimes' (1978) 10 *Comparative Politics* 559.
'Denazification and Related Policies' in John H Herz (ed), *From Dictatorship to Democracy: Coping with the Legacies of Authoritarianism and Totalitarianism* (Greenwood, 1982).
From Dictatorship to Democracy: Coping with the Legacies of Authoritarianism and Totalitarianism (Greenwood, 1982).
'Introduction: Method and Boundaries' in John H Herz (ed), *From Dictatorship to Democracy: Coping with the Legacies of Authoritarianism and Totalitarianism* (Greenwood, 1982).
Hintjens H, 'Land Reform, Social Justice, and Reconstruction: Challenges for Post-Genocide Rwanda' in Dick W Simpson and Cassandra Rachel Veney (eds), *African Democracy and Development: Challenges for Post-Conflict African Nations* (Lexington Books, 2013).
Hinton AL, *Transitional Justice: Global Mechanisms and Local Realities after Genocide and Mass Violence* (Rutgers University Press, 2010).
Hirsch F, 'The Soviets at Nuremberg: International Law, Propaganda, and the Making of the Postwar Order' (2008) 113 *American Historical Review* 701.
Hirsch SF, 'The Victim Deserving of Global Justice: Power, Caution, and Recovering Individuals' in Mark Goodale and Kamari Maxine Clarke (eds), *Mirrors of Justice: Law and Power in the Post-Cold War Era* (Cambridge University Press, 2010).
Hobsbawm E, *Age of Extremes: The Short Twentieth Century, 1914–1991* (Abacus, 1995).
Holmes S, 'Introducing the Center' (1992) 1 *East European Constitutional Review* 13.
'The End of Decommunization' (1994) 3 *East European Constitutional Review* 33.
Holmes Armstead J, 'The United States vs William Calley: An Opportunity Missed' (1983) 10 *Southern University Law Review* 205.

Holvoet M and de Hert P, 'International Criminal Law as Global Law: An Assessment of the Hybrid Tribunals' (2012) 17 *Tilburg Law Review* 228.
Frederick Honig, 'The Reparations Agreement between Israel and the Federal Republic of Germany' (1954) 48 *The American Journal of International Law* 564.
Hopgood S, *Keepers of the Flame: Understanding Amnesty International* (Cornell University Press, 2006).
Horne CM, 'The Impact of Lustration on Democratization in Postcommunist Countries' (2014) 8 *International Journal of Transitional Justice* 496.
Hughes ML, 'Restitution and Democracy in Germany after Two World Wars' (1995) 4 *Contemporary European History* 1.
Human Rights Watch, 'Mozambique: New Constitution Protects Basic Rights but Political Prisoners Still Suffer Unfair Trials' (1991) www.hrw.org/reports/pdfs/m/mozambq/mozambiq912.pdf, accessed 30 July 2018.
'Bulgaria: Human Rights Developments' (1992) www.hrw.org/reports/1993/WR93/Hsw-02.htm, accessed 30 July 2018.
'Ghana: Revolutionary Injustice: Abuse of the Legal System under the PNDC Government' (1992) www.hrw.org/reports/pdfs/g/ghana/ghana921.pdf, accessed 30 July 2018.
'Policy Statement on Accountability for Past Abuses' in Neil J Kritz (ed), *Transitional Justice: How Emerging Democracies Reckon with Former Regimes* (United States Institute of Peace Press, 1995).
Huntford R, 'War Victims at Russell Tribunal' *The Observer* (7 May 1967).
Huntington SP, 'Will More Countries Become Democratic?' (1984) 99 *Political Science Quarterly* 193.
The Third Wave: Democratization in the Late Twentieth Century (University of Oklahoma Press, 1991).
Huyse L, 'Justice after Transition: On the Choices Successor Elites Make in Dealing with the Past' (1995) 20 *Law & Social Inquiry* 51.
ICTJ, *Transitional Justice Mechanisms in Solomon Islands* (2010) www.ictj.org/sites/default/files/ICTJ-SolomonIslands-Fact-Sheet-2011-English.pdf, accessed 30 July 2018.
'Addressing the Past, Building the Future: Justice in Times of Transition Conference Report' (ICTJ, 2011).
'ICTJ Welcomes Tunisia's Historic Transitional Justice Law' (17 December 2013) www.ictj.org/news/ictj-welcomes-tunisia's-historic-transitional-justice-law, accessed 30 July 2018.
Tunisia: Draft Law on Reconciliation in Economic and Financial Areas Approved by Cabinet Meeting (2015) www.ictj.org/news/tunisia-draft-law-reconciliation-economic-and-financial-areas-approved-cabinet-meeting, accessed 30 July 2018.
'About Us' (2018) http://ictj.org/about, accessed 30 July 2018.
'Criminal Justice' (2018) www.ictj.org/our-work/transitional-justice-issues/criminal-justice, accessed 30 July 2018.
'David Tolbert' (2018) www.ictj.org/about/david-tolbert, accessed 30 July 2018.
'Juan E. Méndez' (2018) www.ictj.org/about/juan-e-méndez, accessed 30 July 2018.
Ignatieff M, 'Human Rights as Polictics and Idolatry' in Amy Gutmann (ed), *Human Rights as Politics and Idolatry* (Princeton University Press, 2001).

Igreja V, 'Multiple Temporalities in Indigenous Justice and Healing Practices in Mozambique' (2012) 6 *International Journal of Transitional Justice* 404.

'Amnesty Law, Political Struggles for Legitimacy and Violence in Mozambique' (2015) 9 *International Journal of Transitional Justice* 239.

IJTJ, 'Editorial Note' (2007) 1 *International Journal of Transitional Justice* 1.

'Editorial Note' (2014) 8 *International Journal of Transitional Justice* 1.

'*International Journal of Transitional Justice*' (2018) http://ijtj.oxfordjournals.org/, accessed 30 July 2018.

International War Crimes Tribunal, 'Aims and Objectives of the International War Crimes Tribunal' in John Duffett (ed), *Against the Crime of Silence: Proceedings of the Russell International War Crimes Tribunal, Stockholm, Copenhagen* (Bertrand Russell Peace Foundation, 1968).

'Combined Report on the Complicity of Japan in the Vietnam War: Testimony by the Japanese Committee' in John Duffett (ed), *Against the Crime of Silence: Proceedings of the Russell International War Crimes Tribunal, Stockholm, Copenhagen* (Bertrand Russell Peace Foundation, 1968).

'Summary and Verdict of the Second Session' in John Duffett (ed), *Against the Crime of Silence: Proceedings of the Russell International War Crimes Tribunal, Stockholm, Copenhagen* (Bertrand Russell Peace Foundation, 1968).

'Verdict of the Stockholm Session' in John Duffett (ed), *Against the Crime of Silence: Proceedings of the Russell International War Crimes Tribunal, Stockholm, Copenhagen* (Bertrand Russell Peace Foundation, 1968).

Isaacman B and Isaacman A, 'A Socialist Legal System in the Making: Mozambique before and after Independence' in Richard Abel (ed), *The Politics of Informal Justice* (Academic Press, 1982).

Isaacs A, 'At War with the Past? The Politics of Truth Seeking in Guatemala' (2010) 4 *International Journal of Transitional Justice* 251.

Iverson J, 'Transitional Justice, Jus Post Bellum and International Criminal Law: Differentiating the Usages, History and Dynamics' (2013) 7 *International Journal of Transitional Justice* 413.

James CLR, *The Black Jacobins: Toussaint l'Ouverture and the San Domingo Revolution* (Allison and Busby 1989).

James W and Van de Vijver L, 'Introduction' in Wilmot James and Linda Van de Vijver (eds), *After the TRC: Reflections on Truth and Reconciliation in South Africa* (Ohio University Press, 2001).

January S, 'Tribunal Verité: Documenting Transitional Justice in Sierra Leone' (2009) 3 *International Journal of Transitional Justice* 207.

Jeffreys D, *Hell's Cartel: IG Farben and the Making of Hitler's War Machine* (Metropolitan Books, 2008).

Jelin E, 'Public Memorialization in Perspective: Truth, Justice and Memory of Past Repression in the Southern Cone of South America' (2007) 1 *The International Journal of Transitional Justice* 138.

'Silences, Visibility, and Agency: Ethnicity, Class and Gender in Public Memorialization' in Paige Arthur (ed), *Identities in Transition: Challenges for Transitional Justice in Divided Societies* (Cambridge University Press, 2011).

Jeong HW, *Peacebuilding in Postconflict Societies: Strategy and Process* (Lynne Rienner Publishers, 2005).

Jerman W, *Repression in Latin America: A Report on the First Session of the Second Russell Tribunal, Rome, April 1974* (Spokesman Books, 1975).
Jessberger F, 'On the Origins of Individual Criminal Responsibility under International Law for Business Activity: IG Farben on Trial' (2010) 8 *Journal of International Criminal Justice* 783.
Jones B, 'Exploring the Politics of Reconciliation through Education Reform: The Case of Brcko District, Bosnia and Herzegovina' (2012) 6 *International Journal of Transitional Justice* 126.
Jung C, 'Transitional Justice for Indigenous People in a Non-Transitional Society' (ICTJ, 2009) www.ictj.org/sites/default/files/ICTJ-Identities-NonTransitionalSocieties-ResearchBrief-2009-English.pdf, accessed 30 July 2018.
Kaleck W, 'International Criminal Law and Transnational Businesses: Cases from Argentina and Colombia' in Sabine Michalowski (ed), *Corporate Accountability in the Context of Transitional Justice* (Routledge, 2013).
Kaminski MM and Nalepa M, 'Judging Transitional Justice: A New Criterion for Evaluating Truth Revelation Procedures' (2006) 50 *The Journal of Conflict Resolution* 383.
Kampmark B, 'Citizens' War Crimes' Tribunals' (2014) 33 *Social Alternatives* 5.
Kaplan AY, *The Collaborator: The Trial and Execution of Robert Brasillach* (University of Chicago Press, 2000).
Kaufman Z, 'Transitional Justice for Tōjō's Japan: The United States Role in the Establishment of the International Military Tribunal for the Far East and Other Transitional Justice Mechanisms for Japan after World War II' (2013) 27 *Emory International Law Review* 755.
Kayser-Whande U and Schell-Faucon S, 'Transitional Justice and Conflict Transformation in Conversation' (2010) 50 *Politorbis* 97.
Keck ME and Sikkink K, *Activists beyond Borders: Advocacy Networks in International Politics* (Cornell University Press, 1998).
Kelly P, *Liberalism* (Polity, 2005).
Kelsen H, 'Will the Judgment in the Nuremberg Trial Constitute a Precedent in International Law?' (1947) 1 *International Law Quarterly* 153.
Kennedy D, *A World of Struggle: How Power, Law, and Expertise Shape Global Political Economy* (Princeton University Press, 2016).
Kirchheimer O, *Political Justice: The Use of Legal Procedure for Political Ends* (Princeton University Press, 1961).
Kiuranov D, 'Assessment of the Public Debate on the Legal Remedies for the Reinstatement of Former Owners and the Realization of Liability for Damages Inflicted by the Totalitarian Regime' in Neil J Kritz (ed), *Transitional Justice: How Emerging Democracies Reckon with Former Regimes* (United States Institute of Peace Press, 1995).
Klinghoffer AJ and Klinghoffer JA, *International Citizens' Tribunals: Mobilizing Public Opinion to Advance Human Rights* (Palgrave, 2002).
Kochavi AJ, *Prelude to Nuremberg: Allied War Crimes Policy and the Question of Punishment* (University of North Carolina Press, 1998).
Koopman C, 'Foucault's Historiographical Expansion: Adding Genealogy to Archaeology' (2008) 2 *Journal of the Philosophy of History* 338.

Kopelman ES, 'Ideology and International Law: The Dissent of the Indian Justice at the Tokyo War Crimes Trial' (1991) 23 *New York University Journal of International Law and Politics* 373.

Korey W, *The Promises We Keep: Human Rights, the Helsinki Process, and American Foreign Policy* (St Martin's Press, 1993).

Kosar D, 'Lustration and Lapse of Time: "Dealing with the Past" in the Czech Republic' (2008) 4 *European Constitutional Law Review* 460.

Kritz NJ, 'The Dilemmas of Transitional Justice' in Neil J Kritz (ed), *Transitional Justice: How Emerging Democracies Reckon with Former Regimes* (United States Institute of Peace Press, 1995).

Transitional Justice: How Emerging Democracies Reckon with Former Regimes (United States Institute of Peace Press, 1995).

'Where We Are and How We Got Here: An Overview of Developments in the Search for Justice and Reconciliation' in Alice Henkin (ed), *The Legacy of Abuse: Confronting the Past, Facing the Future* (Aspen Institute, 2002).

Krog A, *Country of My Skull* (Random House, 1998).

Krupp T, 'Genealogy as Critique?' (2008) 2 *Journal of the Philosophy of History* 315.

Kurze A, '#WarCrimes #PostConflictJustice #Balkans: Youth, Performance Activism and the Politics of Memory' (2016) 10 *International Journal of Transitional Justice* 451.

Laclau E and Mouffe C, *Hegemony and Socialist Strategy: Towards a Radical Democratic Politics* (Verso, 1985).

Lambourne W, 'Transitional Justice and Peacebuilding after Mass Violence' (2009) 3 *International Journal of Transitional Justice* 28.

'Outreach, Inreach and Civil Society Participation in Transitional Justice' in Nicola Palmer, Philip Clark and Danielle Granville (eds), *Critical Perspectives in Transitional Justice* (Intersentia, 2012).

'Transformative Justice, Reconciliation and Peacebuilding' in Susanne Buckley-Zistel and others (eds), *Transitional Justice Theories* (Routledge, 2014).

Lamont CK and Boujneh H, 'Transitional Justice in Tunisia: Negotiating Justice during Transition' (2013) 49 *Croatian Political Science Review* 32.

Landrum BD, 'The Yamashita War Crimes Trial: Command Responsibility Then and Now' (1995) 149 *Military Law Review* 293.

Laplante LJ, 'The Plural Justice Aims of Reparations' in Susanne Buckley-Zistel and others (eds), *Transitional Justice Theories* (Routledge, 2014).

Laplante LJ and Theidon K, 'Transitional Justice in Times of Conflict: Colombia's Ley de Justicia y Paz' (2006) 28 *Michigan Journal of International Law* 49.

Leckie S, *Housing, Land, and Property restitution Rights of Refugees and Displaced Persons: Laws, Cases, and Materials* (Cambridge University Press, 2007).

Leebaw B, 'Legitimation or Judgment? South Africa's Restorative Approach to Transitional Justice' (2003) 36 *Polity* 23.

'The Politics of Impartial Activism: Humanitarianism and Human Rights' (2007) 5 *Perspectives on Politics* 223.

'The Irreconcilable Goals of Transitional Justice' (2008) 30 *Human Rights Quarterly* 95.

Lessa F, 'Beyond Transitional Justice: Exploring Continuities in Human Rights Abuses in Argentina between 1976 and 2010' (2011) 3 *Journal of Human Rights Practice* 25.

Letki N, 'Lustration and Democratisation in East-Central Europe' (2002) 54 *Europe-Asia Studies* 529.
Le Vine V, *Politics in Francophone Africa* (Lynne Rienner Publishers, 2004).
Levi P, *The Drowned and the Saved* (Abacus, 1989).
Lewis PH, *Guerrillas and Generals: The 'Dirty War' in Argentina* (Praeger, 2002).
Linz JJ, 'Transitions to Democracy' (1990) 13 *The Washington Quarterly* 143.
Linz JJ and Stepan AC, *Problems of Democratic Transition and Consolidation: Southern Europe, South America, and Post-Communist Europe* (Johns Hopkins University Press, 1996).
Lollini A, *Constitutionalism and Transitional Justice in South Africa* (Berghahn Books, 2011).
'London Transitional Justice Network' (2016) www.londontjnetwork.org/, accessed 16 April 2016.
Longman T, 'Justice at the Grassroots? Gacaca Trials in Rwanda' in Naomi Roht-Arriaza and Javier Mariezcurrena (eds), *Transitional Justice in the Twenty-First Century: Beyond Truth versus Justice* (Cambridge University Press, 2006).
Loytomaki S, 'The Law and Collective Memory of Colonialism: France and the Case of "Belated" Transitional Justice' (2013) 7 *International Journal of Transitional Justice* 205.
Luna E, 'Cuban Criminal Justice and the Ideal of Good Governance' (2004) 14 *Transnational Law & Contemporary Problems* 529.
Lundy P and McGovern M, 'Whose Justice? Rethinking Transitional Justice from the Bottom Up' (2008) 35 *Journal of Law and Society* 265.
'A Trojan Horse? Unionism, Trust and Truth-Telling in Northern Ireland' (2008) 2 *International Journal of Transitional Justice* 42.
Lyster R, 'Amnesty: The Burden of Victims' in Charles Villa-Vicencio and Wilhelm Verwoerd (eds), *Looking Back, Reaching Forward: Reflections on the Truth and Reconciliation Commission of South Africa* (University of Cape Town Press, 2000).
Mack KE, *From Apartheid to Democracy: Deliberating Truth and Reconciliation in South Africa* (The Pennsylvania State University Press, 2014).
Macmillan H, 'Address to Members of Both Houses of the Parliament of the Union of South Africa' (Cape Town, 3 February 1960) https://web-archives.univ-pau.fr/english/TD2doc1.pdf, accessed 30 July 2018.
Macridis RC, 'France: From Vichy to the Fourth Republic' in John H Herz (ed), *From Dictatorship to Democracy: Coping with the Legacies of Authoritarianism and Totalitarianism* (Greenwood, 1982).
Madlingozi T, 'On Transitional Justice Entrepreneurs and the Production of Victims' (2010) 2 *Journal of Human Rights Practice* 208.
Madsen G, 'Becoming a State-in-the-World: Lessons Learned from the American Occupation of Germany' (2012) 26 *Studies in American Political Development* 1.
Mahon M, *Foucault's Nietzschean Genealogy: Truth, Power, and the Subject* (State University of New York Press, 1992).
Maier CS, 'The Politics of Productivity: Foundations of American International Economic Policy after World War II' (1977) 31 *International Organization* 607.
Mainwaring S and Viola EJ, 'Transitions to Democracy: Brazil and Argentina in the 1980s' (1985) 38 *Journal of International Affairs* 193.

Malamud Goti J, 'Trying Violators of Human Rights: The Dilemma of Transitional Democratic Governments', State Crimes: Punishment or Pardon: Papers and Report of the Conference, November 4–6, 1988, *Wye Center, Maryland* (The Aspen Institute, 1989).

'Transitional Governments in the Breach: Why Punish State Criminals?' (1990) 12 *Human Rights Quarterly*.

'Game without End: State Terror and the Politics of Justice' (University of Oklahoma Press, 1996).

'Editorial Note: A Turbulent Past and the Problem with Memory' (2010) 4 *International Journal of Transitional Justice* 153.

Malefakis E, 'Spain and Its Francoist Heritage' in John Herz (ed), *From Dictatorship to Democracy: Coping with the Legacies of Authoritarianism and Totalitarianism* (Greenwood, 1982).

Mallinder L, 'Can Amnesties and International Justice Be Reconciled?' (2007) 1 *The International Journal of Transitional Justice* 208.

Amnesty, Human Rights and Political Transitions: Bridging the Peace and Justice Divide (Hart, 2008).

Mallinder L, Wills S and Hansen T, *Economic Liberalism, Democracy, and Transitional Justice: Workshop Report* (Transitional Justice Institute, 2018).

Mamdani M, 'The Truth according to the TRC' in Ifi Amadiume and Abdullahi Ahmed An-Na'im (eds), *The Politics of Memory: Truth, Healing, and Social Justice* (Zed Books, 2000).

'A Diminished Truth' in Wilmot James and Linda Van de Vijver (eds), *After the TRC: Reflections on Truth and Reconciliation in South Africa* (Ohio University Press, 2001).

'Beyond Settler and Native as Political Identities: Overcoming the Political Legacy of Colonialism' (2001) 43 *Comparative Studies in Society and History* 651.

Mani R, *Beyond Retribution: Seeking Justice in the Shadows of War* (Polity, 2002).

Manning P, 'Reconciliation and Perpetrator Memories in Cambodia' (2015) 9 *International Journal of Transitional Justice* 386.

Markarian V, *Left in Transformation: Uruguayan Exiles and the Latin American Human Rights Networks, 1967–1984* (Routledge, 2005).

Marrus M, *Some Measure of Justice: The Holocaust Era Restitution Campaign of the 1990s* (University of Wisconsin Press, 2009).

Martínez Barahona E and Gutiérrez Salazar ML, 'El Salvador: The Difficult Fight against Impunity' in Elin Skaar, Jemima García-Godos and Cath Collins (eds), *Transitional Justice in Latin America: The Uneven Road from Impunity towards Accountability* (Routledge, 2016).

Maser W, *Nuremberg: A Nation on Trial* (Scribner, 1979).

Matondi PB, *Zimbabwe's Fast Track Land Reform* (Zed Books, 2012).

Maxwell K, 'The Emergence of Portuguese Democracy' in John H Herz (ed), *From Dictatorship to Democracy: Coping with the Legacies of Authoritarianism and Totalitarianism* (Greenwood, 1982).

'Regime Overthrow and the Prospects for Democratic Transitions in Portugal' in Guillermo O'Donnell, Philippe C Schmitter and Laurence Whitehead (eds), *Transitions from Authoritarian Rule: Southern Europe* (Johns Hopkins University Press, 1986).

May L, *After War Ends: A Philosophical Perspective* (Cambridge University Press, 2012).

Mayorga RA, 'Democracy Dignified and an End to Impunity: Bolivia's Military Dicatorship on Trial' in A James McAdams (ed), *Transitional Justice and the Rule of Law in New Democracies* (University of Notre Dame Press, 1997).

McAdams AJ, 'The Honecker Trial: The East German Past and the German Future' (1996) 58 *The Review of Politics* 53.

'Communism on Trial: The East German Past and the German Future' in A James McAdams (ed), *Transitional Justice and the Rule of Law in New Democracies* (University of Notre Dame Press, 1997).

Transitional Justice and the Rule of Law in New Democracies (A James McAdams ed, University of Notre Dame Press, 1997).

McAuliffe P, 'Transitional Justice and the Rule of Law: The Perfect Couple or Awkward Bedfellows?' (2010) 2 *Hague Journal on the Rule of Law* 127.

'From Molehills to Mountains (and Myths?): A Critical History of Transitional Justice Advocacy' (2011) 22 *Finnish Yearbook of International Law* 1.

'Hybrid Tribunals at Ten How International Criminal Justice's Golden Child Became an Orphan' (2011) 7 *Journal of International Law & International Relations* 1.

'Transitional Justice's Expanding Empire: Reasserting the Value of the Paradigmatic Transition' (2011) 2 *Journal of Conflictology* 32.

'The Roots of Transitional Accountability: Interrogating the "Justice Cascade"' (2013) 9 *International Journal of Law in Context* 106.

Transitional Justice and Rule of Law Reconstruction: A Contentious Relationship (Routledge, 2013).

McClintock A, *Imperial Leather* (Routledge, 1995).

McDonald J and Zatz M, 'Popular Justice in Revolutionary Nicaragua' (1992) 1 *Social & Legal Studies* 283.

McEvoy K, 'Beyond Legalism: Towards a Thicker Understanding of Transitional Justice' (2007) 34 *Journal of Law and Society* 411.

McEvoy K and McGregor L, 'Transitional Justice from Below: An Agenda for Research, Policy and Praxis' in Kieran McEvoy and Lorna McGregor (eds), *Transitional Justice from Below: Grassroots Activism and the Struggle for Change* (Hart, 2008).

Transitional Justice from Below: Grassroots Activism and the Struggle for Change (Hart, 2008).

McFaul M, 'A Mixed Record: An Uncertain Future' (2001) 12 *Journal of Democracy* 87.

McKinley D, *The ANC and the Liberation Struggle: A Critical Political Biography* (Pluto Press, 1997).

Meertens D and Zambrano M, 'Citizenship Deferred: The Politics of Victimhood, Land Restitution and Gender Justice in the Colombian (Post?) Conflict' (2010) 4 *International Journal of Transitional Justice* 189.

Mehta HC, 'North Vietnam's Informal Diplomacy with Bertrand Russell: Peace Activism and the International War Crimes Tribunal' (2012) 37 *Peace & Change* 64.

Meister R, 'Forgiving and Forgetting: Lincoln and the Politics of National Recovery' in Carla Alison Hesse and Robert Post (eds), *Human Rights in Political Transitions: Gettysburg to Bosnia* (Zone Books, 1999).

Méndez JE, 'In Defense of Transitional Justice' in A James McAdams (ed), *Transitional Justice and the Rule of Law in New Democracies* (University of Notre Dame Press, 1997).

'Latin American Experiences of Accountability' in Ifi Amadiume and Abdullahi Ahmed An-Na'im (eds), *The Politics of Memory: Truth, Healing, and Social Justice* (ZED Books, 2000).

'Editorial Note' (2009) 3 *International Journal of Transitional Justice* 157.

Meneses MP, 'Powers, Rights and Citizenship: The "Return" of the Traditional Authorities in Mozambique' in Tom Bennett and others (eds), *African Perspectives on Tradition and Justice* (Intersentia, 2012).

Meredith M, *Coming to Terms: South Africa's Search for Truth* (Tina Rosenberg ed, Public Affairs, 1999).

Meron T, 'From Nuremberg to The Hague' (1995) 149 *Military Law Review* 107

'The Internationalisation of Criminal Law: Remarks' (1995) 89 *American Society of International Law Proceedings* 297.

'The Greatest Change in International Law', *The Making of International Criminal Justice* (Oxford University Press, 2011).

Metodiev M, 'Bulgaria' in Lavinia Stan (ed), *Transitional Justice in Eastern Europe and the Former Soviet Union: Reckoning with the Communist Past* (Routledge, 2008).

Meyerstein A, 'Transitional Justice and Post-Conflict Israel/Palestine: Assessing the Applicability of the Truth Commission Paradigm' (2006) 38 *Case Western Reserve Journal of International Law* 281.

Mezarobba G, 'Brazil: The Tortuous Path to Truth and Justice', in Elin Skaar, Jemima García-Godos and Cath Collins (eds), *Transitional Justice in Latin America: The Uneven Road from Impunity towards Accountability* (Routledge, 2016).

Michalowski S, *Corporate Accountability in the Context of Transitional Justice* (Routledge, 2013).

Mignone EF, Estlund C and Issacharoff S, 'Dictatorship on Trial: Prosecution of Human Rights Violations in Argentina' (1984) 10 *The Yale Journal of International Law* 118.

Mihai M, *Negative Emotions and Transitional Justice* (Columbia University Press, 2016).

Mihr A, 'Regime Consolidation through Transitional Justice in Europe: The Cases of Germany, Spain and Turkey' (2017) 11 *International Journal of Transitional Justice* 113.

Mill JS, *On Liberty* (Jean Bethke Elshtain, David Bromwich and George Kateb eds, Yale University Press, 2003).

Miller J, 'Settling Accounts with a Secret Police: The German Law on the Stasi Records' (1998) 50 *Europe-Asia Studies* 305.

Miller Z, 'Effects of Invisibility: In Search of the "Economic" in Transitional Justice' (2008) 2 *International Journal of Transitional Justice* 266.

Minear RH, *Victors' Justice: the Tokyo War Crimes Trial* (Princeton University Press, 1971).

Minow M, *Between Vengeance and Forgiveness: Facing History after Genocide and Mass Violence* (Beacon Press, 1998).

Moon C, 'Prelapsarian State: Forgiveness and Reconciliation in Transitional Justice' (2004) 17 *International Journal for the Semiotics of Law* 185.

'Narrating Political Reconciliation: Truth and Reconciliation in South Africa' (2006) 15 *Social & Legal Studies* 257.
'Healing Past Violence: Traumatic Assumptions and Therapeutic Interventions in War and Reconciliation' (2009) 8 *Journal of Human Rights* 71.
'"Who"ll Pay Reparations on My Soul?' Compensation, Social Control and Social Suffering' (2012) 21 *Social & Legal Studies* 187.
Moorehead C, *Bertrand Russell: A Life* (Sinclair-Stevenson, 1992).
Moreno FJ, 'The Cuban Revolution v Batista's Pilots' in Theodore Lewis Becker (ed), *Political Trials* (Bobbs-Merrill, 1971).
Moreno Ocampo L, 'The Nuremberg Parallel in Argentina' (1990) 11 *New York Law School Journal of International and Comparative Law* 357.
Morris V and Scharf MP, *An Insider's Guide to the International Criminal Tribunal for the Former Yugoslavia: A Documentary History and Analysis* (Transnational Publishers, 1995).
Morrison M and Harris S, 'Working with the World Bank Group in Fragile and Conflict-Affected Situations: A Resource Note for United Nations Staff' (2015) http://documents.worldbank.org/curated/en/922311467999664758/pdf/99008-WP-Box393181B-PUBLIC-Working-with-the-WBG-final1.pdf, accessed 30 July 2018.
Moyn S, *The Last Utopia: Human Rights in History* (Belknap, 2010).
'Substance, Scale, and Salience: The Recent Historiography of Human Rights' (2012) 8 *Annual Review of Law and Social Science* 123.
Not Enough: Human Rights in an Unequal World (Harvard University Press, 2018).
Moyo K, 'Mimicry, Transitional Justice and the Land Question in Racially Divided Former Settler Colonies' (2015) 9 *International Journal of Transitional Justice* 70.
Moyo S, 'The Land Question in Southern Africa: A Comparative Review' in Ruth Hall and Lungisile Ntsebeza (eds), *The Land Question in South Africa: The Challenge of Transformation and Redistribution* (HSRC Press, 2007).
Land and Agrarian Reform in Zimbabwe beyond White-Settler Capitalism (CODESRIA, 2013).
Müller AT and Stegmiller I, 'Self-Referrals on Trial: From Panacea to Patient' (2010) 8 *Journal of International Criminal Justice* 1267.
Mutua M, 'The Transformation of Africa: A Critique of Rights in Transitional Justice' in Ruth Margaret Buchanan and Peer Zumbansen (eds), *Law in Transition: Human Rights, Development and Transitional Justice* (Hart, 2014).
Muvingi I, 'Sitting on Powder Kegs: Socioeconomic Rights in Transitional Societies' (2009) 3 *International Journal of Transitional Justice* 163.
Nadery AN, 'Editorial Note: In the Aftermath of International Intervention: A New Era for Transitional Justice?' (2011) 5 *International Journal of Transitional Justice* 171.
Nagy R, 'Transitional Justice as Global Project: Critical Reflections' (2008) 29 *Third World Quarterly* 275.
Nagy R and Williams M, 'Introduction' in Melissa Williams, Rosemary Nagy and Jon Elster (eds), *Transitional Justice* (New York University Press, 2012).
Nalepa M, *Skeletons in the Closet: Transitional Justice in Post-Communist Europe* (Cambridge University Press, 2010).
Nápoli B, Perosino MC and Bosisio W, *La Dictadura del Capital Financiero* (Ediciones Continente, 2015).

Nedelsky N, 'Czechoslovakia and the Czech and Slovak Republics' in Lavinia Stan (ed), *Transitional Justice in Eastern Europe and the Former Soviet Union: Reckoning with the Communist Past* (Routledge, 2008).

Neff M, 'Eastern Europe's Policy of Restitution of Property in the 1990s' (1992) 10 *Dickinson Journal of International Law* 368.

Neilson J, 'The Nuremberg Factor Haunts the Junta' *The Observer* (2 May 1982).

Nesiah V, 'Discussion Lines on Gender and Transitional Justice' (2006) 15 *Columbia Journal of Gender and the Law* 799.

Neumann F, *Behemoth: The Structure and Practice of National Socialism* (V Gollancz, 1942).

Ni Aolain F, 'Advancing Feminist Positioning in the Field of Transitional Justice' (2012) 6 *International Journal of Transitional Justice* 205.

Nie J-B, 'The West's Dismissal of the Khabarovsk Trial as "Communist Propaganda": Ideology, Evidence and International Bioethics' (2004) 1 *Journal of Bioethical Inquiry* 32.

Nielsen C, 'From Nuremberg to The Hague: The Civilizing Mission of International Criminal Law' (2008) 14 *Te Mata Koi: Auckland University Law Review* 81.

Nino C, 'The Human Rights Policy of the Argentine Constitutional Government: A Reply (Mignone, Estlund & Issacharoff, "Dictatorship on Trial: Prosecution of Human Rights Violations in Argentina," 10 Yale J. Int'l L. 118, 1984)' (1985) 11 *The Yale Journal of International Law* 217.

'The Duty to Punish Past Abuses of Human Rights Put into Context: The Case of Argentina' (1991) 100 *The Yale Law Journal* 2619.

Radical Evil on Trial (Yale University Press, 1996).

Norden DL, *Military Rebellion in Argentina: Between Coups and Consolidation* (University of Nebraska Press, 1996).

'Not since Nuremberg' *The Washington Post* (21 August 1994) www.washingtonpost.com/archive/opinions/1994/08/21/not-since-nuremberg/a8f8c897-6634-4f59-92c1-0db63b4b73f7/, accessed 30 July 2018.

Nouwen SMH, *Complementarity in the Line of Fire: The Catalysing Effect of the International Criminal Court in Uganda and Sudan* (Cambridge University Press, 2013).

'"Hybrid Courts": The Hybrid Category of a New Type of International Crimes Courts' (2006) 2 *Utrecht Law Review* 190.

Nouwen SMH and Werner WG, 'Monopolizing Global Justice: International Criminal Law as Challenge to Human Diversity' (2015) 13 *Journal of International Criminal Justice* 157.

Novaro M, *Historia de la Argentina: 1955–2010* (Siglo Veintiuno Editores, 2010).

Novick P, *The Resistance versus Vichy: The Purge of Collaborators in Liberated France* (Constable, 1968).

Nozick R, *Anarchy, State, and Utopia* (Basic Books, 1974).

Ntebeza D, 'The Struggle for Human Rights: From the UN Declaration of Human Rights to the Present' in Charles Villa-Vicencio and Wilhelm Verwoerd (eds), *Looking Back, Reaching Forward: Reflections on the Truth and Reconciliation Commission of South Africa* (University of Cape Town Press, 2000).

Ntsebeza D, 'A Lot More to Live for' in Wilmot James and Linda Van de Vijver (eds), *After the TRC: Reflections on Truth and Reconciliation in South Africa* (Ohio University Press, 2001).

Nuzov I, 'The Dynamics of Collective Memory in the Ukraine Crisis: A Transitional Justice Perspective' (2017) 11 *International Journal of Transitional Justice* 132.

Obarrio J, *The Spirit of the Laws in Mozambique* (University of Chicago Press, 2014).

Obradovic-Wochnik J, 'The "Silent Dilemma" of Transitional Justice: Silencing and Coming to Terms with the Past in Serbia' (2013) 7 *International Journal of Transitional Justice* 328.

O'Connell S, 'Injury, Illumination and Freedom: Thinking about the Afterlives of Apartheid through the Family Albums of District Six, Cape Town' (2015) 9 *International Journal of Transitional Justice* 297.

O'Donnell G, *Schmitter PC and Whitehead L, Transitions from Authoritarian Rule: Southern Europe* (Johns Hopkins University Press, 1986).

Transitions from Authoritarian Rule: Latin America (Johns Hopkins University Press, 1986).

Transitions from Authoritarian Rule: Prospects for Democracy (Johns Hopkins University Press, 1986).

O'Donnell M, 'New Dirty War Judgments in Argentina: National Courts and Domestic Prosecutions of International Human Rights Violations' (2009) 84 *New York University Law Review*.

Ohlin JD, 'On the Very Idea of Transitional Justice' (2007) 8 *The Whitehead Journal of Diplomacy and International Relations* 51.

O'Keefe R, 'State Immunity and Human Rights: Heads and Walls, Hearts and Minds' (2011) 44 *Vanderbilt Journal of Transnational Law* 999.

Olsen TD, Payne LA and Reiter AG, *Transitional Justice in Balance: Comparing Processes, Weighing Efficacy* (United States Institute of Peace, 2010).

'Transitional Justice in the World, 1970–2007: Insights from a New Dataset' (2010) 47 *Journal of Peace Research* 803.

Omar D, 'Building a New Future' in Alex Boraine and Janet Levy (eds), *The Healing of a Nation?* (Justice in Transition 1995).

O'Rawe M, 'Security System Reform and Identity in Divided Societies: Lessons from Northern Ireland' in Paige Arthur (ed), *Identities in Transition: Challenges for Transitional Justice in Divided Societies* (Cambridge University Press, 2011).

Oré Aguilar G and Gómez Isa F, *Rethinking Transitions: Equality and Social Justice in Societies Emerging from Conflict* (Intersentia, 2011).

Orentlicher DF, 'Settling Accounts: The Duty to Prosecute Human Rights Violations of a Prior Regime' (1991) 100 *The Yale Law Journal* 2537.

'The Role of the Prosecutor in the Transition to Democracy in Latin America' in Irwin P Stotzky (ed), *Transition to Democracy in Latin America: The Role of the Judiciary* (Westview Press, 1993).

'From Viability to Impact: Evolving Metrics for Assessing the International Criminal Tribunal for the Former Yugoslavia' (2013) 7 *International Journal of Transitional Justice* 536.

Orr W, 'Reparation Delayed Is Healing Retarded' in Charles Villa-Vicencio and Wilhelm Verwoerd (eds), *Looking Back, Reaching Forward: Reflections on the Truth and Reconciliation Commission of South Africa* (University of Cape Town Press, 2000).

Orvis SW, *The Agrarian Question in Kenya* (University Press of Florida, 1997).

Osiatynski W, 'Poland' in Alex Boraine, Janet Levy and Ronel Scheffer (eds), *Dealing with the Past: Truth and Reconciliation in South Africa* (IDASA, 1994).

Osiel M, 'The Making of Human Rights Policy in Argentina: The Impact of Ideas and Interests on a Legal Conflict' (1986) 18 *Journal of Latin American Studies* 135.

Mass Atrocity, Collective Memory, and the Law (Transaction, 1997).

'Ousted Bulgarian Gets 7-Year Term for Embezzlement' *New York Times* (September 1992) www.nytimes.com/1992/09/05/world/ousted-bulgarian-gets-7-year-term-for-embezzlement.html, accessed 30 July 2018.

Overy R, 'The Nuremberg Trials: International Law in the Making' in Philippe Sands (ed), *From Nuremberg to The Hague: The Future of International Criminal Justice* (Cambridge University Press, 2003).

'Oxford Transitional Justice Research' (2018) www.law.ox.ac.uk/research-subject-groups/oxford-transitional-justice-research, accessed 30 July 2018.

Paris R, *At War's End: Building Peace after Civil Conflict* (Cambridge University Press, 2004).

Pasipanodya T, 'A Deeper Justice: Economic and Social Justice as Transitional Justice in Nepal' (2008) 2 *International Journal of Transitional Justice* 378.

Peerenboom R, 'Human Rights and Rule of Law: What's the Relationship?' (2005) 36 *Georgetown Journal of International Law* 1.

Pendas DO, *The Frankfurt Auschwitz Trial, 1963–1965: Genocide, History, and the Limits of the Law* (Cambridge University Press, 2006).

'Seeking Justice, Finding Law: Nazi Trials in Postwar Europe' (2009) 81 *The Journal of Modern History* 347.

Peskin V and Boduszynski MP, 'The Rise and Fall of the ICC in Libya and the Politics of International Surrogate Enforcership' (2016) 10 *International Journal of Transitional Justice* 272.

Petrova D, 'Bulgaria' in Alex Boraine, Janet Levy and Ronel Scheffer (eds), *Dealing with the Past: Truth and Reconciliation in South Africa* (IDASA, 1994).

Pettai EC and Pettai V, *Transitional and Retrospective Justice in the Baltic States* (Cambridge University Press, 2015).

Pham P and Vinck P, 'Empirical Research and the Development and Assessment of Transitional Justice Mechanisms' (2007) 1 *International Journal of Transitional Justice* 231.

Pigou P, 'False Promises and Wasted Opportunities?: Inside South Africa's Truth and Reconciliation Commission' in Graeme Simpson and Deborah Posel (eds), *Commissioning the Past: Understanding South Africa's Truth and Reconciliation Commission* (Witwatersrand University Press, 2002).

Pion-Berlin D, 'The Fall of Military Rule in Argentina: 1976–1983' (1985) 27 *Journal of Interamerican Studies and World Affairs* 55.

'The National Security Doctrine, Military Threat Perception, and the "Dirty War" in Argentina' (1988) 21 *Comparative Political Studies* 382.

'To Prosecute or to Pardon? Human Rights Decisions in the Latin American Southern Cone' (1994) 16 *Human Rights Quarterly* 105.

Through Corridors of Power: Institutions and Civil-Military Relations in Argentina (Pennsylvania State University Press, 1997).

Podgers J, 'Repeating Nuremberg' (1993) 79 *ABA Journal*
Pogany I, 'The Restitution of Former Jewish-Owned Property and Related Schemes of Compensation in Hungary' (1998) 4 *European Public Law* 211.
Porter E, *Connecting Peace, Justice and Reconciliation* (Lynne Rienner, 2015).
Posel D and Simpson G, 'The Power of Truth: South Africa's Truth and Reconciliation Commission in Context' in Graeme Simpson and Deborah Posel (eds), *Commissioning the Past: Understanding South Africa's Truth and Reconciliation Commission* (Witwatersrand University Press, 2002).
Posner EA and Vermeule A, 'Transitional Justice as Ordinary Justice' (2004) 117 *Harvard Law Review* 761.
Prashad V, *The Darker Nations: A People's History of the Third World* (New Press; Distributed by WW Norton, 2007).
Prévost AM, 'Race and War Crimes: The 1945 War Crimes Trial of General Tomoyuki Yamashita' (1992) 14 *Human Rights Quarterly* 303.
Priemel KC, 'Tales of Totalitarianism: Conflicting Narratives in the Industrialists Cases at Nuremberg' in Kim Christian Priemel and Alexa Stiller (eds), *Reassessing the Nuremberg Military Tribunals: Transitional Justice, Trial Narratives, and Historiography* (Berghahn Books, 2012).
'Consigning Justice to History: Transitional Trials after the Second World War' (2013) 56 *Historical Journal* 553.
Pritchard RJ, 'The International Military Tribunal for the Far East and Its Contemporary Resonances' (1995) 149 *Military Law Review* 25.
Project TJD, *Transitional Justice Database Project* (2018) www.tjdbproject.com/#, accessed 30 July 2018.
Prugh G, *Law at War: Vietnam 1964–1973* (Department of the Army, 1975).
Przeworski A, *Democracy and the Market: Political and Economic Reforms in Eastern Europe and Latin America* (Cambridge University Press, 1991).
Psomiades HJ, 'Greece: From the Colonels' Rule to Democracy' in John H Herz (ed), *From Dictatorship to Democracy: Coping with the Legacy of Authoritarianism and Totalitarianism* (Greenwood, 1982).
Quill A, 'To Prosecute or Not to Prosecute: Problems Encountered in the Prosecution of Former Communist Officials in Germany, Czechoslovakia, and the Czech Republic' (1996) 7 *Indiana International & Comparative Law Review* 165.
Quint PE, *The Imperfect Union: Constitutional Structures of German Unification* (Princeton University Press, 1997).
Raimundo F and Costa Pinto A, 'From Ruptured Transition to Politics of Silence: The Case of Portugal' in Nico Wouters (ed), *Transitional Justice and Memory in Europe (1945–2013)* (Intersentia, 2014).
Ramírez-Barat C and Duthie R, 'Education and Transitional Justice: Opportunities and Challenges for Peacebuilding' (International Center for Transitional Justice, 2015) www.ictj.org/sites/default/files/ICTJ-UNICEF-Report-EducationTJ-2015.pdf, accessed 30 July 2018.
Ratner SR and Abrams JS, *Accountability for Human Rights Atrocities in International Law: Beyond the Nuremberg Legacy* (Clarendon Press, 1997).
Rawls J, *A Theory of Justice* (Belknap Press of Harvard University Press, 1971).
Reinhard W, *A Short History of Colonialism* (Manchester University Press, 2011).

Reiter AG, 'Transitional Justice Bibliography' *Transitional Justice Data Base* (2015) https://sites.google.com/site/transitionaljusticedatabase/transitional-justice-bibliography, accessed 30 July 2018.

'Reluctance to Allow Mock Trial' *The Guardian* (6 October 1966).

Renner J, 'A Discourse Theoretic Approach to Transitional Justice Ideals: Conceptualising "Reconciliation" as an Empty Universal in Times of Political Transition' in Nicola Frances Palmer, Philip Clark and Danielle Granville (eds), *Critical Perspectives in Transitional Justice* (Intersentia, 2012).

Discourse, Normative Change and the Quest for Reconciliation in Global Politics (Manchester University Press, 2013).

'The Local Roots of the Global Politics of Reconciliation: The Articulation of "Reconciliation" as an Empty Universal in the South African Transition to Democracy' (2014) 42 *Millennium – Journal of International Studies* 263.

Richard G, 'Crimes-against-Humanity Trials in France and Their Historical and Legal Context: A Retrospective Look' in Patricia Heberer and Jürgen Matthäus (eds), *Atrocities on Trial: Historical Perspectives on the Politics of Prosecuting War Crimes* (University of Nebraska Press, 2008).

Robben ACGM, 'Testimonies, Truths, and Transitions of Justice in Argentina and Chile' in Alexander Laban Hinton (ed), *Transitional Justice: Global Mechanisms and Local Realities after Genocide and Mass Violence* (Rutgers University Press, 2010).

Robins S, 'Towards Victim-Centred Transitional Justice: Understanding the Needs of Families of the Disappeared in Postconflict Nepal' (2011) 5 *International Journal of Transitional Justice* 75.

'Mapping a Future for Transitional Justice by Learning from Its Past' (2015) 9 *International Journal of Transitional Justice* 181.

Robinson I, 'Truth Commissions and Anti-Corruption: Towards a Complementary Framework?' (2014) 9 *International Journal of Transitional Justice* 33.

Rock D, *Argentina 1516–1982: From Spanish Colonization to the Falklands War* (Tauris, 1986).

Roehrig T, *The Prosecution of Former Military Leaders in Newly Democratic Nations: The Cases of Argentina, Greece and South Korea* (McFarland, 2002).

Roht-Arriaza N, 'State Responsibility to Investigate and Prosecute Grave Human Rights Violations in International Law' (1990) 78 *California Law Review* 451.

'The Role of International Actors in National Accountability Processes' in Alexandra Barahona de Brito, Carmen González Enríquez and Paloma Aguilar Fernández (eds), *The Politics of Memory: Transitional Justice in Democratizing Societies* (Oxford University Press, 2001).

'The New Landscape of Transitional Justice' in Naomi Roht-Arriaza and Javier Mariezcurrena (eds), *Transitional Justice in the Twenty-First Century: Beyond Truth versus Justice* (Cambridge University Press, 2006).

'Reparations and Development' in Ruth Margaret Buchanan and Peer Zumbansen (eds), *Law in Transition: Human Rights, Development and Transitional Justice* (Hart, 2014).

Roht-Arriaza N and Mariezcurrena J, *Transitional Justice in the Twenty-First Century: Beyond Truth versus Justice* (Cambridge University Press, 2006).

Röling B and Cassese A, *The Tokyo Trial and Beyond: Reflections of a Peacemonger* (Polity Press, 1993).

Romano C, Nollkaemper A and Kleffner JK, *Internationalized Criminal Courts and Tribunals: Sierra Leone, East Timor, Kosovo and Cambodia* (Oxford University Press, 2004).

Romeike S, 'Transitional Justice in Germany after 1945 and after 1990' (2016) Occasional Paper No 1 International Nuremberg Principles Academy.

Romijn P and Schumacher E, 'Transitional Justice in the Netherlands after World War II' in Nico Wouters (ed), *Transitional Justice and Memory in Europe (1945–2013)* (Intersentia, 2014).

Roniger L and Sznajder M, *The Legacy of Human-Rights Violations in the Southern Cone: Argentina, Chile, and Uruguay* (Oxford University Press, 1999).

Roper SD and Barria LA, 'Assessing the Record of Justice: A Comparison of Mixed International Tribunals versus Domestic Mechanisms for Human Rights Enforcement' (2005) 4 *Journal of Human Rights* 521.

Rosenberg T, 'Reconciliation & Amnesty: Latin America' in Alex Boraine, Janet Levy and Ronel Scheffer (eds), *Dealing with the Past: Truth and Reconciliation in South Africa* (IDASA, 1994).

'Overcoming the Legacies of Dictatorship' (1995) 74 *Foreign Affairs* 134.

The Haunted Land: Facing Europe's Ghosts after Communism (Vintage, 1995).

Ross FC, 'An Acknowledged Failure: Women, Voice, Violence, and the South African Truth and Reconciliation Commission' in Rosalind Shaw, Lars Waldorf and Pierre Hazan (eds), *Localizing Transitional Justice: Interventions and Priorities after Mass Violence* (Stanford University Press, 2010).

Rothberg M, 'Progress, Progression, Procession: William Kentridge and the Narratology of Transitional Justice' (2012) 20 *Narrative* 1.

Rothschild A, 'Victims versus Veterans: Agency, Resistance and Legacies of Timor-Leste's Truth Commission' (2017) 11 *International Journal of Transitional Justice* 443.

Rousso H, *Vichy: l'Événement, la Mémoire, l'Histoire* (Gallimard, 2001).

'The Purge in France: An Incomplete Story' in Jon Elster (ed), *Retribution and Reparation in the Transition to Democracy* (Cambridge University Press, 2006).

Rubin J, 'Transitional Justice against the State: Lessons from Spanish Civil Society-Led Forensic Exhumations' (2014) 8 *International Journal of Transitional Justice* 99.

Rush PD and Simić O, *The Arts of Transitional Justice: Culture, Activism, and Memory after Atrocity* (Springer, 2014).

Russell B, 'Closing Address to the Stockholm Session' in John Duffett (ed), *Against the Crime of Silence: Proceedings of the Russell International War Crimes Tribunal, Stockholm, Copenhagen* (Bertrand Russell Peace Foundation, 1968).

'Letter from Russell to Johnson, 25 August 1966' in John Duffett (ed), *Against the Crime of Silence: Proceedings of the Russell International War Crimes Tribunal, Stockholm, Copenhagen* (Bertrand Russell Peace Foundation, 1968).

'Message from Bertrand Russell to the Tribunal' in John Duffett (ed), *Against the Crime of Silence: Proceedings of the Russell International War Crimes Tribunal, Stockholm, Copenhagen* (Bertrand Russell Peace Foundation, 1968).

'Opening Statement to the First Tribunal Session' in John Duffett (ed), *Against the Crime of Silence: Proceedings of the Russell International War Crimes Tribunal, Stockholm, Copenhagen* (Bertrand Russell Peace Foundation, 1968).
'Russell "Tribunal" Hears a US Negro' *New York Times* (26 November 1967).
Ryan M, 'Prosecutor of a New Nuremberg' *The Independent* (7 June 1995) www.independent.co.uk/money/spend-save/prosecutor-of-a-new-nuremberg-1585322.html, accessed 30 July 2018.
Ryngaert C and Schrijver N, 'Lessons Learned from the Srebrenica Massacre: From UN Peacekeeping Reform to Legal Responsibility' (2015) 62 *Netherlands International Law Review* 219.
Sabato E, 'Prologue', *Nunca Mas:(Never Again): A Report* (Faber in association with Index on Censorship, 1986).
Sachs A, 'South African Response' in Alex Boraine, Janet Levy and Ronel Scheffer (eds), *Dealing with the Past: Truth and Reconciliation in South Africa* (IDASA, 1994).
Sachs A and Welch GH, *Liberating the Law: Creating Popular Justice in Mozambique* (Zed Books, 1990).
Salas L, 'The Emergence and Decline of the Cuban Popular Tribunals' (1983) 17 *Law & Society Review* 587.
Sandoval C, Filippini L and Vidal R, 'Linking Transitional Justice and Corporate Accountability' in Sabine Michalowski (ed), *Corporate Accountability in the Context of Transitional Justice* (Routledge, 2013).
Sands P, *From Nuremberg to The Hague: The Future of International Criminal Justice* (Cambridge University Press, 2003).
Sankara T, 'The People's Revolutionary Courts: 3 January 1984', *Thomas Sankara speaks: The Burkina Faso Revolution, 1983–87* (Pathfinder Press, 1988).
Sartre JP, 'Jean Paul Sartre's Inaugural Statement to the Tribunal' in John Duffett (ed), *Against the Crime of Silence: Proceedings of the Russell International War Crimes Tribunal, Stockholm, Copenhagen* (Bertrand Russell Peace Foundation, 1968).
'On Genocide' in John Duffett (ed), *Against the Crime of Silence: Proceedings of the Russell International War Crimes Tribunal, Stockholm, Copenhagen* (Bertrand Russell Peace Foundation, 1968).
Schabas WA, 'The Relationship Between Truth Commissions and International Courts: The Case of Sierra Leone' (2003) 25 *Human Rights Quarterly* 1035.
The UN International Criminal Tribunals: The Former Yugoslavia, Rwanda and Sierra Leone (Cambridge University Press, 2006).
'Foreword' in Michael R Marrus, *Some Measure of Justice: The Holocaust Era Restitution Campaign of the 1990s* (University of Wisconsin Press, 2009).
Scharf MP, *Balkan Justice: The Story Behind the First International War Crimes Trial since Nuremberg* (Carolina Academic Press, 1997).
Scheppele KL, 'Democracy by Judiciary: Or, Why Courts Can Be More Democratic than Parliaments' in Adam W Czarnota, Martin Krygier and Wojciech Sadurski (eds), *Rethinking the Rule of Law after Communism* (Central European University Press, 2005).
Schick FB, 'The Nuremberg Trial and the International Law of the Future' (1947) 41 *The American Journal of International Law* 770.

Schmid E, *Taking Economic, Social and Cultural Rights Seriously in International Criminal Law* (Cambridge University Press, 2015).

Schmid E and Nolan A, '"Do No Harm"? Exploring the Scope of Economic and Social Rights in Transitional Justice' (2014) 8 *International Journal of Transitional Justice* 362.

Schotsmans M, '"But We Also Support Monitoring": INGO Monitoring and Donor Support to Gacaca Justice in Rwanda' (2011) 5 *International Journal of Transitional Justice* 390.

Schwarzenberger G, 'The Problem of an International Criminal Law' (1950) 3 *Current Legal Problems* 263.

Schwarzenberg K, 'Czech Republic' in Alex Boraine, Janet Levy and Ronel Scheffer (eds), *Dealing with the Past: Truth and Reconciliation in South Africa* (IDASA, 1994).

Schwerin K, 'German Compensation for Victims of Nazi Persecution' (1972) 67 *Northwestern University Law Review* 489.

Scoones I, *Zimbabwe's Land Reform: Myths & Realities* (Jacana Media, 2010).

Segreto L and Wubs B, 'Resistance of the Defeated: German and Italian Big Business and the American Antitrust Policy, 1945–1957' (2014) 15 *Enterprise & Society* 307.

Seils P, 'Political Pardons Would Damage the Legacy of South Africa's Truth and Reconciliation Commission' *The Huffington Post* (6 March 2015) www.huffingtonpost.com/paul-seils/political-pardons-would-d_b_6810864.html, accessed 30 July 2018.

'Transitional Justice: Time for a Re-Think' *Open Global Rights* (10 April 2018) www.openglobalrights.org/paul-seils/Transitional-justice-time-for-a-re-think/, accessed 31 July 2018.

Semler D, 'From the Center' (1992) 1 *East European Constitutional Review*.

Senier A, 'Traditional Justice as Transitional Justice: A Comparative Case Study of Rwanda and East Timor' (2008) XXIII *PRAXIS The Fletcher Journal of Human Security* 67.

Shain Y, Linz JJ and Berat L, *Between States: Interim Governments and Democratic Transitions* (Cambridge University Press, 1995).

Sharp D, 'Addressing Economic Violence in Times of Transition: Toward Positive-Peace Paradigm for Transitional Justice' (2012) 35 *Fordham International Law Journal* 780.

'Bridging the Gap: The United Nations Peacebuilding Commission and the Challenges of Integrating DDR and Transitional Justice' in Chandra Lekha Sriram and others (eds), *Transitional Justice and Peacebuilding on the Ground: Victims and Ex-Combatants* (Routledge, 2013).

'Interrogating the Peripheries: The Preoccupations of Fourth Generation Transitional Justice' (2013) 26 *Harvard Human Rights Journal* 149.

'Introduction: Addressing Economic Violence in Times of Transition' in Dustin Sharp (ed), *Justice and Economic Violence in Transition* (Springer, 2014).

Justice and Economic Violence in Transition (Springer, 2014).

'Emancipating Transitional Justice from the Bonds of the Paradigmatic Transition' (2015) 9 *International Journal of Transitional Justice* 150.

Sherman EF, 'Betrand Russell and the Peace Movement: Liberal Consistency or Radical Change' in George Nakhnikian (ed), *Bertrand Russell's Philosophy* (Duckworth, 1974).

Shipway M, *Decolonization and Its Impact: A Comparative Approach to the End of the Colonial Empires* (Blackwell Pub, 2008).

Shklar J, *Legalism* (Harvard University Press, 1964).

Shraga D, 'The Second Generation UN-Based Tribunals: A Diversity of Mixed Jurisdictions' in Cesare Romano, André Nollkaemper and Jann Kleffner (eds), *Internationalized Criminal Courts and Tribunals: Sierra Leone, East Timor, Kosovo and Cambodia* (Oxford University Press, 2004).

Sikkink K, 'From Pariah State to Global Protagonist: Argentina and the Struggle for International Human Rights' (2008) 50 *Latin American Politics and Society* 1.

The Justice Cascade: How Human Rights Prosecutions Are Changing World Politics (WW Norton, 2011).

Sikkink K and Smith J, 'Infrastructures for Change: Transnational Organizations, 1953–93' in Sanjeev Khagram, James V Riker and Kathryn Sikkink (eds), *Restructuring World Politics: Transnational Social Movements, Networks, and Norms* (University of Minnesota Press, 2002).

Siklova J, 'Lustration or the Czech Way of Screening' (1996) 5 *East European Constitutional Review* 57.

Simpson G, *Commissioning the Past: Understanding South Africa's Truth and Reconciliation Commission* (Witwatersrand University Press, 2002).

'"Tell No Lies, Claim No Easy Victories": A Brief Evaluation of South Africa's Truth and Reconciliation Commission' in Graeme Simpson and Deborah Posel (eds), *Commissioning the Past: Understanding South Africa's Truth and Reconciliation Commission* (Witwatersrand University Press, 2002).

Simpson J and Bennett J, *The Disappeared: Voices from a Secret War* (Robson, 1985).

Simpson K, 'Voices Silenced, Voices Rediscovered: Victims of Violence and the Reclamation of Language in Transitional Societies' (2007) 3 *International Journal of Law in Context* 89.

Skaar E, García-Godos J and Collins C, 'Conclusions: The Uneven Road towards Accountability in Latin America' in Elin Skaar, Jemima García-Godos and Cath Collins (eds), *Transitional Justice in Latin America: The Uneven Road from Impunity towards Accountability* (Routledge, 2016) 290.

'Introduction: The Accountability Challenge' in Elin Skaar, Jemima García-Godos and Cath Collins (eds), *Transitional Justice in Latin America: The Uneven Road from Impunity towards Accountability* (Routledge, 2016).

Transitional Justice in Latin America: The Uneven Road from Impunity towards Accountability (Routledge, 2016).

Skinner Q, *Visions of Politics* (Cambridge University Press, 2002).

Smidt M, 'Yamashita, Medina, and Beyond: Command Responsibility in Contemporary Military Operations' (2000) 164 *Military Law Review* 155.

Smith A, *An Inquiry into the Nature and Causes of the Wealth of Nations* (Roy Hutcheson Campbell, Andrew Skinner and William Todd eds, Clarendon Press, 1976).

Smith G, 'Popular Participation in the Administration of Justice in the Soviet Union: Comrades' Courts and the Brezhnev Regime' (1973) 49 *Indiana Law Journal* 238.

Snyder SB, *Human Rights Activism and the End of the Cold War: A Transnational History of the Helsinki Network* (Cambridge University Press, 2011) x.

Somé V, *Thomas Sankara, l'Espoir Assassiné* (L'Harmattan, 1990).

Sorokina M, 'People and Procedures: Toward a History of the Investigation of Nazi Crimes in the USSR' (2005) 6 *Kritika: Explorations in Russian and Eurasian History* 797.

Sorrenson MPK, *Land Reform in the Kikuyu Country: A Study in Government Policy*, (Oxford University Press, 1967).

'South Africa Apartheid Assassin De Kock given Parole' *BBC News* (30 January 2015) www.bbc.com/news/world-africa-31054912, accessed 30 July 2018.

Southern D, 'Restitution or Compensation: The Property Question' (1993) 2 *German Politics* 436.

Speck P, 'The Trial of the Argentine Junta: Responsibilities and Realities' (1987) 18 *University of Miami Inter-American Law Review* 491.

Spence J, 'Institutionalizing Neighborhood Courts: Two Chilean Experiences' in Richard Abel (ed), *The Politics of Informal justice* (Academic Press, 1982).

Springhall J, *Decolonization since 1945: The Collapse of European Overseas Empires* (Palgrave, 2001).

Sriram CL, 'Justice as Peace? Liberal Peacebuilding and Strategies of Transitional Justice' (2007) 21 *Global Society* 579.

and others, *Transitional Justice and Peacebuilding on the Ground: Victims and Ex-Combatants* (Routledge, 2013).

Sriram CL and Pillay S, *Peace versus Justice? The Dilemma of Transitional Justice in Africa* (James Currey, 2010).

Stan L, 'Conclusion: Explaining Country Differences' in Lavinia Stan (ed), *Transitional Justice in Eastern Europe and the Former Soviet Union: Reckoning with the Communist Past* (Routledge, 2008).

'Introduction: Post-Communist Transition, Justice, and Transitional Justice' in Lavinia Stan (ed), *Transitional Justice in Eastern Europe and the Former Soviet Union: Reckoning with the Communist Past* (Routledge, 2008).

'Poland' in Lavinia Stan (ed), *Transitional Justice in Eastern Europe and the Former Soviet Union: Reckoning with the Communist Past* (Routledge, 2008).

'Romania' in Lavinia Stan (ed), *Transitional Justice in Eastern Europe and the Former Soviet Union: Reckoning with the Communist Past* (Routledge, 2008).

Transitional Justice in Eastern Europe and the Former Soviet Union: Reckoning with the Communist Past (Routledge, 2008).

Transitional Justice in Post-Communist Romania the Politics of Memory (Cambridge University Press, 2013).

'Tribunal of Opinion' in Lavinia Stan and Nadya Nedelsky (eds), *Encyclopedia of Transitional Justice (Vol. 1)* (Cambridge University Press, 2013).

Stan L and Nedelsky N, *Encyclopedia of Transitional Justice* (Cambridge University Press, 2013).

Stanton K, 'Canada's Truth and Reconciliation Commission: Settling the Past?' (2011) 2 *International Indigenous Policy Journal* 2.

Stedman JC, 'The German Decartelization Program: The Law in Repose' (1950) 17 *The University of Chicago Law Review* 441.

Steinberg R, 'Judicial Independence in States of Emergency: Lessons from Nicaragua's Popular Anti-Somocista Tribunals' (1986) 18 *Columbia Human Rights Law Review* 359.

'Transitional Justice in the Age of the French Revolution' (2013) 7 *International Journal of Transitional Justice* 267.

Stover E, *The Witnesses: War Crimes and the Promise of Justice in The Hague* (University of Pennsylvania Press, 2005).

Subotic J, 'The Transformation of International Transitional Justice Advocacy' (2012) 6 *International Journal of Transitional Justice* 106.

Szoke-Burke S, 'Not Only "Context": Why Transitional Justice Programs Can No Longer Ignore Violations of Economic and Social Rights' (2015) 50 *Texas International Law Journal* 465.

Taylor G, 'The Rise and Fall of Antitrust in Occupied Germany, 1945–48' (1979) 11 *Prologue* 23.

Taylor T, 'The Krupp Trial: Fact v Fiction' (1953) 53 *Columbia Law Review* 197

Nuremberg and Vietnam: An American Tragedy (Bantam Books, 1971).

The Anatomy of the Nuremberg Trials: A Personal Memoir (Knopf, 1992).

Teitel R, 'Paradoxes in the Revolution of the Rule of Law' (1994) 19 *The Yale Journal of International Law* 239.

'Post-Communist Constitutionalism: A Transitional Perspective' (1994) 26 *Columbia Human Rights Law Review* 167.

'Transitional Jurisprudence: The Role of Law in Political Transformation' (1997) 106 *The Yale Law Journal* 2009.

Transitional Justice (Oxford University Press, 2000).

'Transitional Justice Genealogy' (2003) 16 *Harvard Human Rights Journal* 69.

'The Law and Politics of Contemporary Transitional Justice' (2005) 38 *Cornell International Law Journal* 837.

'Editorial Note-Transitional Justice Globalized' (2008) 2 *International Journal of Transitional Justice* 1.

'Global Transitional Justice' (2010) 16 Center for Global Studies, Project on Human Rights, Global Justice & emocracy, Working Paper No 8 www.gmu.edu/centers/globalstudies/publications/hjd/hjd_wp_8.pdf, accessed 26 August 2018.

Globalizing Transitional Justice: Contemporary Essays (Oxford University Press, 2014).

Terán CF, *El Poder, la Propiedad, Nosotros: La Revolución Sandinista y el Problema del Poder en la Transformación Revolucionaria de la Sociedad Nicaragüense* (Editorial Hispamer, 2005).

The Aspen Institute, *State Crimes: Punishment or Pardon: Papers and Report of the Conference, November 4–6, 1988, Wye Center, Maryland* (The Aspen Institute, 1989).

Theidon K, 'Editorial Note' (2009) 3 *International Journal of Transitional Justice* 295.

'The Institute for Justice and Reconciliation' (2018) www.ijr.org.za/about-us/, accessed 30 July 2018.

Thiesenhusen WC, *Searching for Agrarian Reform in Latin America* (Unwin Hyman, 1989).

Thomas DC, *The Helsinki Effect: International Norms, Human Rights, and the Demise of Communism* (Princeton University Press, 2001).

Thoms ONT, Ron J and Paris R, 'State-Level Effects of Transitional Justice: What Do We Know?' (2010) 4 *International Journal of Transitional Justice* 329.

Thomson P, 'Field' in Michael Grenfell (ed), *Pierre Bourdieu Key Concepts* (Acumen, 2008).

Thomson S and Nagy R, 'Law, Power and Justice: What Legalism Fails to Address in the Functioning of Rwanda's Gacaca Courts' (2011) 5 *International Journal of Transitional Justice* 11.

Tiba FK, 'The Mengistu Genocide Trial in Ethiopia' (2007) 5 *Journal of International Criminal Justice* 513.

'Mass Trials and Modes of Criminal Responsibility for International Crimes: The Case of Ethiopia' in Kevin Jon Heller and Gerry J Simpson (eds), *The Hidden Histories of War Crimes Trials* (Oxford University Press, 2013).

Timm A, *Jewish Claims against East Germany: Moral Obligations and Pragmatic Policy* (Central European University Press, 1997).

Totani Y, *The Tokyo War Crimes Trial: The Pursuit of Justice in the Wake of World War II* (Harvard University Asia Center; Distributed by Harvard University Press, 2008).

Traĭnin AN, *Hitlerite Responsibility under Criminal Law* (Andrey Yanuaryevich Vyshinsky ed, Hutchinson & Co, 1945).

Transitional Justice Institute, 'About' (2018) www.ulster.ac.uk/research-and-innovation/research-institutes/transitional-justice-institute/about, accessed 30 July 2018.

'Transitional Justice Network New York Law School' (2018) www.nyls.edu/global_law_justice_and_policy/transitional-justice-network/, accessed 30 July 2018.

'Transitional Justice Review' (2018) http://ir.lib.uwo.ca/tjreview/, accessed 30 July 2018.

Tribunal Civico Humberto Delgado, 'Julgar a PIDE, Condenar O Fascismo: Decisão Final' (1978) https://ephemerajpp.com/2017/04/04/tribunal-civico-humberto-delgado/, accessed 30 July 2018.

Trindade JC and Pedroso J, 'The Judicial System: Structure, Legal Education and Legal Training' in Boaventura De Sousa Santos, João Carlos Trindade and Maria Paula Meneses (eds), *Law and Justice in a Multicultural Society: The Case of Mozambique* (Council for the Development of Social Science Research in Africa, 2006).

Tronvoll K, Schaefer C and Aneme GA, *The Ethiopian Red Terror Trials: Transitional Justice Challenged* (James Currey, 2009).

Trueheart C, 'New Kind of Justice: The International Criminal Tribunal for the Former Yugoslavia Is the World's First War-Crimes Tribunal since Nuremberg' (2000) 285 *The Atlantic*.

Turner C, 'Deconstructing Transitional Justice' (2013) 24 *Law and Critique* 193.

Tutu D, *No Future without Forgiveness* (Doubleday, 2000).

Tweedy Jr J, 'The Argentine "Dirty Wars" Trials: The First Latin American Nuremberg?' (1987) 44 *Guild Practitioner* 15.

Ubink J and Rea A, 'Community Justice or Ethnojustice? Engaging with Customary Mechanisms to Reintegrate Ex-Combatants in Somalia' (2017) 11 *International Journal of Transitional Justice* 276.

Uitz R, 'Constitutional Courts and the Past in Democratic Transition' in Adam W Czarnota, Martin Krygier and Wojciech Sadurski (eds), *Rethinking the Rule of Law After Communism* (Central European University Press, 2005).

UN, *Growth in United Nations Membership, 1945–Present* (2018) www.un.org/en/sections/member-states/growth-united-nations-membership-1945-present/index.html, accessed 30 July 2018.

UNDP, *Supporting Transitional Justice* (2018) www.undp.org/content/undp/en/home/ourwork/democratic-governance-and-peacebuilding/rule-of-law–justice-and-security/transitional-justice/, accessed 30 July 2018.

USIP 'Truth Commission Digital Collection' (2011) www.usip.org/publications/2011/03/truth-commission-digital-collection, accessed 14 May 2018.

Van den Wyngaert C, 'Victims before International Criminal Courts: Some Views and Concerns of an ICC Trial Judge' (2011) 44 *Case Western Reserve Journal of International Law* 475.

Van der Merwe H, 'National Narrative Versus Local Truths: The Truth and Reconciliation Commission's Engagement with Duduza' in Graeme Simpson and Deborah Posel (eds), *Commissioning the Past: Understanding South Africa's Truth and Reconciliation Commission* (Witwatersrand University Press, 2002).

Van Eck J, 'Reconciliation in Africa?' in Wilmot James and Linda Van de Vijver (eds), *After the TRC: Reflections on Truth and Reconciliation in South Africa* (Ohio University Press, 2001).

Van Zyl Slabbert F, 'Truth without Reconciliation' in Wilmot James and Linda Van de Vijver (eds), *After the TRC: Reflections on Truth and Reconciliation in South Africa* (Ohio University Press, 2001).

Varga C, *Transition to Rule of Law: On the Democratic Transformation in Hungary* (Project on Comparative Legal Cultures of the Faculty of Law of Loránd Eötvös University: Institute for Legal Studies of the Hungarian Academy of Sciences, 1995).

Vázquez I, *Historia de las Madres de Plaza de Mayo: Luchar Siempre, las Marchas de la Resistencia, 1981–2006* (Ediciones Madres de Plaza de Mayo, 2007).

Vegh Weis V, *Marxism and Criminology: A History of Criminal Selectivity* (Brill, 2017).

Venema D, 'Transitions as States of Exception: Towards a More General Theory of Transitional Justice' in Nicola Frances Palmer, Philip Clark and Danielle Granville (eds), *Critical Perspectives in Transitional Justice* (Intersentia, 2012).

Verbitsky H, *La Posguerra Sucia: Un Análisis de la Transición* (Editorial Legasa, 1985).

Civilians and Military Men: Secret Report of the Transition (1987).

Vermeule A, 'Reparations as Rough Justice' in Melissa Williams, Rosemary Nagy and Jon Elster (eds), *Transitional Justice* (New York University Press, 2012).

Verwoerd W, *Equity, Mercy, Forgiveness: Interpreting Amnesty within the South African Truth and Reconciliation Commission* (Peeters, 2007).

Vilas CM, *The Sandinista Revolution: National Liberation and Social Transformation in Central America* (Monthly Review Press, 1986).

Villa-Vicencio C, 'Restorative Justice: Dealing with the Past Differently' in Charles Villa-Vicencio and Wilhelm Verwoerd (eds), *Looking Back, Reaching Forward: Reflections on the Truth and Reconciliation Commission of South Africa* (University of Cape Town Press, 2000).

Walk with Us and Listen: Political Reconciliation in Africa (Georgetown University Press, 2009).

Villa-Vicencio C and Verwoerd W, *Looking Back, Reaching Forward: Reflections on the Truth and Reconciliation Commission of South Africa* (University of Cape Town Press, 2000).

Vinjamuri L and Snyder J, 'Advocacy and Scholarship in the Study of International War Crime Tribunals and Transitional Justice' (2004) 7 *Annual Review of Political Science* 345.

Virgili F, *Shorn Women: Gender and Punishment in Liberation France* (Berg, 2002).

Visker R, *Michel Foucault: Genealogy as Critique* (Verso, 1995).

Von Hayek F, *The Road to Serfdom* (G Routledge & Sons, 1944).

Waldorf L, 'Anticipating the Past: Transitional Justice and Socio-Economic Wrongs' (2012) 21 *Social & Legal Studies* 171.

Waldron J, *Liberal Rights: Collected Papers, 1981–1991* (Cambridge University Press, 1993).

'Liberal Rights: Two Sides of the Coin', *Liberal Rights: Collected Papers, 1981–1991* (Cambridge University Press, 1993).

'Theoretical Foundations of Liberalism', *Liberal Rights: Collected Papers, 1981–1991* (Cambridge University Press, 1993).

Walker C, 'Land, Memory, Reconstruction, and Justice: Perspectives on Land Claims in South Africa' (Ohio University Press, 2010).

Wall S, 'Introduction' in Steven Wall (ed), *The Cambridge Companion to Liberalism* (Cambridge University Press, 2015).

Wechsler H, 'The Issues of the Nuremberg Trial' (1947) 62 *Political Science Quarterly* 11.

Weinke A, 'West Germany: A Case of Transitional Justice Avant la Lettre?' in Nico Wouters (ed), *Transitional Justice and Memory in Europe (1945–2013)* (Intersentia, 2014).

Weinstein HM, 'Editorial Note: The Myth of Closure, the Illusion of Reconciliation: Final Thoughts on Five Years as Co-Editor-in-Chief' (2011) 5 *International Journal of Transitional Justice* 1.

Weinstein HM and Fletcher LE, 'Violence and Social Repair: Rethinking the Contribution of Justice to Reconciliation' (2002) 24 *Human Rights Quarterly* 573.

Weinstein HM and Stover E, 'Introduction: Conflict, Justice and Reclamation' in Eric Stover and Harvey M Weinstein (eds), *My Neighbor, My Enemy: Justice and Community in the Aftermath of Mass Atrocity* (Cambridge University Press, 2004).

Welsh HA, 'When Discourse Trumps Policy: Transitional Justice in Unified Germany' (2006) 15 *German Politics* 137.

'Dealing with the Communist Past: Central and East European Experiences after 1990' (1996) 48 *Europe-Asia Studies* 413.

Westad OA, *The Global Cold War: Third World Interventions and the Making of Our Times* (Cambridge University Press, 2005).

Wheelock J, *La Reforma Agraria Sandinista: 10 Años de Revolución en el Campo* (Editorial Vanguardia, 1990).

Whiting A, 'The ICTY as a Laboratory of International Criminal Procedure' in Bert Swart, Alexander Zahar and Göran Sluiter (eds), *The Legacy of the International Criminal Tribunal for the Former Yugoslavia* (Oxford University Press, 2011).

Wierzynska A, 'Consolidating Democracy through Transitional Justice: Rwanda's Gacaca Courts' (2004) 79 *New York University Law Review* 1934.

Wilke C, 'Remembering Complexity? Memorials for Nazi Victims in Berlin' (2013) 7 *International Journal of Transitional Justice* 136.

'Law on a Slanted Globe: Traveling Models of Criminal Responsibility for State Violence' (2015) 24 *Social & Legal Studies* 555.

Williams S, *Hybrid and Internationalised Criminal Tribunals: Selected Jurisdictional Issues* (Hart, 2012).

Williams T and Buckley-Zistel S (eds), *Perpetrators and Perpetration of Mass Violence: Action, Motivations and Dynamics* (Routledge, 2018).

Wilson H, 'Harold Wilson to Bertrand Russell, 14 March, 1967' in John Duffett (ed), *Against the Crime of Silence: Proceedings of the Russell International War Crimes Tribunal, Stockholm, Copenhagen* (Bertrand Russell Peace Foundation, 1968).

Wilson R, *The Politics of Truth and Reconciliation in South Africa: Legitimizing the Post-Apartheid State* (Cambridge University Press, 2001).

Winter S, 'Towards a Unified Theory of Transitional Justice' (2013) 7 *International Journal of Transitional Justice* 224.

Wittmann R, *Beyond Justice the Auschwitz Trial* (Harvard University Press, 2005).

Wouters N, 'The Use of History in the Field of Transitional Justice: A Critical Introduction' in Nico Wouters (ed), *Transitional Justice and Memory in Europe (1945–2013)* (Intersentia, 2014).

Yofre JB, *Fuimos Todos: Cronología de un Fracaso, 1976–1983* (3rd edn, Sudamericana, 2007).

Yusuf H, 'Colonialism and the Dilemmas of Transitional Justice in Nigeria' (2018) 12 *International Journal of Transitional Justice* 257.

Zalaquett J, 'Confronting Human Rights Violations Committed by Former Governments: Principles Applicable and Political Constraints', *State Crimes: Punishment or Pardon: Papers and Report of the Conference, November 4–6, 1988, Wye Center, Maryland* (The Aspen Institute, 1989).

'Balancing Ethical Imperatives and Political Constraints: The Dilemma of New Democracies Confronting Past Human Rights Violations' (1991) 43 *Hastings Law Journal* 1.

'Why Deal with the Past?' in Alex Boraine, Janet Levy and Ronel Scheffer (eds), *Dealing with the Past: Truth and Reconciliation in South Africa* (IDASA, 1994).

Zunino M, 'Releasing Transitional Justice from the Technical Asylum: Judicial Reform in Guatemala Seen through Techne and Phronesis' (2011) 5 *International Journal of Transitional Justice* 99.

'Review of Evelyn Schmid's Taking Economic, Social and Cultural Rights Seriously in International Criminal Law' (2015) 74 *Cambridge Law Journal* 624.

'Subversive Justice: The Russell Vietnam War Crimes Tribunal and Transitional Justice' (2016) 10 *International Journal of Transitional Justice* 211.

Zuppi A, 'Slave Labor in Nuremberg's IG Farben Case: The Lonely Voice of Paul M. Hebert' (2005) 66 *Louisiana Law Review*.

Index